DIMITRI JELEZKY

FASHIONDESIGN

DIGITAL DRAWING WITH ADOBE ILLUSTRATOR

Techniques & Tips

Dimitri Jelezky, Hamburg 2021

CONTENT

1. INTRODUCTION

Adobe Illustrator is a vector-based drawing program. You can use Adobe Illustrator to create computer graphics without any loss in quality - in contrast to pixel-based image processing programs. It runs on the computer operating systems Apple Mac OS as wellas Microsoft Windows and it applies for years as a standard application in the field of vector graphics. The use of different program functions opens a whole range of design possibilities, a fast and high quality implementation of your projects (i.e. fashion illustrations, technical drawings etc.).

Since Adobe Illustrator is a digital program, the use of a computer should be familiar to you. This book offers you a brief introduction to the structure of the program (tools, control elements and program functions). Then, different projects that were specifically designed for fashion design, follow. Most of the projects are precisely described step-by-step. This is why the book is constructive at one hand, and from the other hand you can also immediately start with a project because we all want hit the target fast! Nevertheless, before you begin with a project, I recommend you to initially study some preceding introduction chapters.

Even if many of the program functions are described in this book, it does not replace an introduction to all of the features of Adobe Illustrator. However, it offers you the possibility to develop your ideas as a fashion designer in a short time!

Working with digital drawing programs requires much patience at first, because each work step must be made consciously, in contrast to the manual drawing, where most of the work steps are taken predominantly unconsciously. At the same time, every step in Adobe Illustrator can be undone without big effort, which is of course a great relief. This is why many illustrators - regardless of their style - are working exclusively with digital drawing programs. Adobe Illustrator allows you to create certain vector aesthetics and also there is the possibility to simulate manual techniques. Digital drawing however does not replace manual drawing, but does complement it in a useful manner.

Good analog drawing skills for working with Adobe Illustrator are of great advantage but not absolutely necessary, because a drawing in Adobe Illustrator is much more „constructed" (with the Pen tool) as „freely" drawn (hand drawn with brush or pencil). Therefore, good feeling of form, line, color and structure should be trained and are an advantage, of course. But whether you can draw great manually or not is not so important in the working process with Adobe Illustrator.

Drawing with Adobe Illustrator is used in the fashion industry to create technical drawings as well as fashion illustrations. The exercises introduced in this book offer methods that are applied in fashion design. In some cases alternative procedures for achieving certain same results, are presented.

If you start with a drawing (i.e. a technical drawing), I recommend you to first create a manual sketch, then to scan it and place it on a separate layer in Adobe Illustrator. Because to immediately create a clean digital drawing without a template, is sometimes difficult, even for artists that are already familiar with the program.

This book is based on the Illustrator version CC. Still, most projects from this book can be realized in older versions. The same is expected in relation to future versions. In recent years certain procedures have been simplified but mainly new tools and functions have been added. For a fast workflow it is recommended to always use the short key commands, which are described in this book, because this approach will accelerate the work process enormously.

This book is intended as a long-term support for fashion designers. Many important techniques for beginners and for advanced fashion designers are compiled in this book but there are, of course, much more techniques that can be used. These techniques will be presented in the following books of the author.

1.1 TECHNICAL DRAWING

A technical drawing in fashion design is a document that, in graphical and written form, contains the most important information for the production of a certain garment.

Mostly a technical drawing is created "flat", without a figure ("figurine"), in b/w (see various display types on pages 137-138). The information transmitted in a technical drawing for the production of the respective product has the highest priority. Therefore, in a technical drawing, the following aspects of a garment should always be pointed out:

- The silhouette of the garment (the outer contour therefore is often drawn a bit richer in order to show the overall appearance).
- The Inner elements: darts, seams, pockets, quilting, zippers, patterns, processing instructions.
- detail view: in some cases, an additional „detail view" or „closeup" should be created to exactly describe certain elements of the garment.

1.2 FASHION ILLUSTRATION

Fashion Illustration is used for both, for technical (technical drawing), as well as for artistic presentations of clothing.

Fashion designers however, regardless of their professional level, should always be able to illustrate their own ideas in principle basically on paper. Because still, handwritten fashion illustration is the easiest, quickest and most expressive visualization of an idea and vision. It allows you to precisely communicate your ideas to all people directly involved in the development process of your collection.

With a fashion illustration you can apply different artistic design techniques, i.e. drawing, painting, collage etc. In the last few years, computers are more and more used to create a fashion illustration. And even in a digital, computer created illustration, with support of graphic software and various input devices, the appearance of traditional techniques, such as watercolor, pencil techniques etc. can be imitated.

FASHION DESIGNER´S SKETCHBOOK - women figures
Part 1 Women Figures
Pages: ca. 108 pages, ISBN: 978-3945549414
Price: 24,90 EUR

2. REQUIREMENTS FOR WORKING WITH THIS BOOK

2.1 PRIME STEPS

-Always activate following settings: **View > Rulers >Show Rulers**, **View > Guides > Lock Guides**, **View > Guides > Show Guides**, **View > Smart Guides**, **View > Snap to Point**.

All menu commands, keyboard shortcuts are marked fat, highlighted in red, or illustrated.

Example: Menu command **Object >Arrange >Send to Back** (In this order click with the left mouse button).

Example: Keybord shortcuts command + C, then command + V
(Hold down first command key and then in addition hold down C key, only then release both keys.
The first part of the keyboard shortcut refers to the Mac OS X operating system, the second part to the PC with the Windows operating system. Example: command + C / Ctrl + C

Graphical representation of keyboard shortcuts:

 < Mac OS X operating system

 < PC with Windows operating system

2.2 SYMBOLS OVERVIEW

These symbols are used to provide a better understanding of the individual steps in this book.

The order of the individual steps occur in this book are graphically represented by the following symbol: 

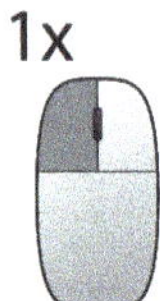

1x

Single-click (left mouse button)

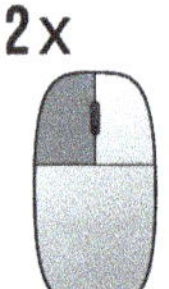

2x

double-click (left mouse button)

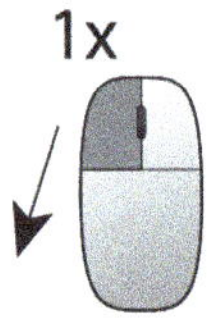

1x

Single-click (hold down the left mouse button) And drag the mouse cursor in the particular direction, then release the mouse button.

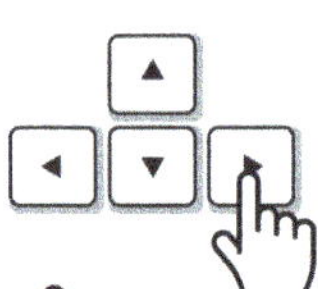

Hand:
Click a particular key or option with the left mouse button.

Click a particular key or option with the left mouse button. The numbers indicate the order of the individual steps.

Deselection: Click on V key (Selection Tool) and click on a empty drawing area to deselect the object or alternatively, activate command + shift + A / Ctrl + shift + A.

Drawing in **90° angle (right angle)**
To activate the right angle hold down **Shift** key when you use for example the Pen Tool.

Meaning: Selection Tool (see Tools panel).
Symbol till Illustrator version CC 2015 >
Symbol from Illustrator version CC 2021>
With the selection tool you can select an object or line or place a guide from the rulers.

Meaning: Direct Selection Tool (see Tools panel).
With Direct Selection Tool you can select parts of an object, paths or individual anchor points.
Symbol till Illustrator version CC 2015 >
Symbol from Illustrator version CC 2021 >

Meaning: Activate the Pen Tool (see Tools panel) and create the first anchor point.

Meaning: Pencil tool in the activated condition (hold down the left mouse button)

Meaning: The path is closed by the Pencil tool (a small circle icon is displayed).

Meaning: Continue to draw on a previously deactivated path (a small line appears).

Meaning: Add Anchor Point Tool (see Tools panel)

Meaning: Delete Anchor Point Tool (see Tools panel)

Meaning: Anchor Point Tool (see Tools panel)

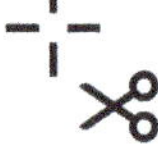

Meaning: Reflect Tool (O) (activated condition), by clicking on the alt/option key the axis of the reflection is set.

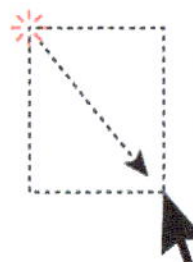

Meaning: Scissors Tool (activated condition), by left-clicking on a line, the line will be disconnected at this point.

With Selection Tool create a selection (hold down the left mouse button and drag), then release the mouse button.

With Direct Selection Tool create a selection (hold down the left mouse button and drag), then release the mouse button.

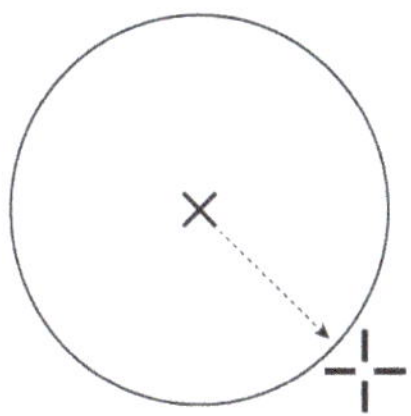
With the Ellipse tool create a circle from the center:
Click alt/option + shift keys, hold down both keys and drag the cursor, (do not release the left mouse button). When the shape is finished, release first the mouse button and then the keyboard keys.

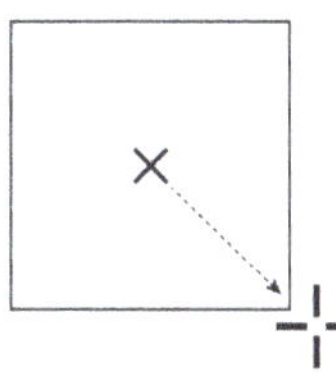
With the Rectangle tool create a rectangle from the center:
Click alt/option + shift keys, hold down both keys and drag the cursor, (do not release the left mouse button). When the shape is finished, release first the mouse button and then the keyboard keys.

While holding down the alt/option key the shape is created proportional from the center.
This also applies to other tools such as rounded rectangle tool, Polygon tool, Star tool.

Selection Tool in copy mode (Drag&Drop)

Meaning: Activate the selection tool, place over an object, in addition hold down alt/option key (do not release) and drag the cursor in any direction.
Then release first the mouse button and then the keyboard keys.

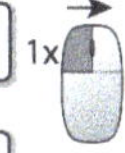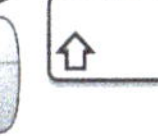

With this combination of keyboard shortcuts an object or line will be copied (drag&drop method), if you activate in addition the Shift key, the copy will be aligned on the same line as the original object (horizontal or vertical).

Note the order of the illustrations.
First press and hold down the alt/option key, then press and hold down the left mouse button, then drag the mouse in a specific direction and only then in addition press and hold down the Shift key.
Then release first the mouse button and only then the keyboard keys.

 Tip

 Warning

 Error

 Identical steps

Digital drawing with Adobe Illustrator

3. IMPORTANT KEYBOARD SHORTCUTS (OVERVIEW)

Mac: command key / PC: Ctrl key

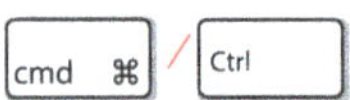

In combination with other keyboard keys, tools and functions are activated.

Shift-key

- When working with the **Pen Tool** (P) the lines are often drawn in 45° or 90° angle. This key is often used to create a right angle (vertical or horizontal).
-When working with the **Pen tool** (P) if you hold down the **Shift** key a straight line can be produced.
-For geometric shapes: tools like **Ellipse tool** (L) and **Rectangle Tool** (M) if you hold down in addition the **Shift** key, circles and squares can be produced.

Mac: option+command+J / PC: alt+Ctrl+J

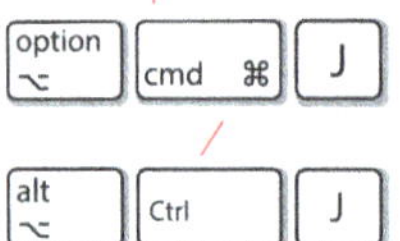

-This keyboard shortcut calculates the average for two points. In the dialog box set "Axis" to "Both". This keyboard shortcut is used to place two points exactly on top of each other (for example if the reflection of an object-half was not entirely correct). This will lead later to the clean join of two anchor points. It is a particularly important keyboard short-cut and is almost always used in combination with Mac: command+J / PC: Ctrl+J (join).

Mac: command+J / PC: Ctrl+J

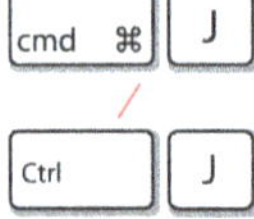

To join end points of two lines together, this keyboard shortcut is used: command+J / PC: Ctrl+J. This keyboard shortcut is often used to join two silhouette halves of a technical drawing to an object together.

Mac: command+A / PC: Ctrl+A

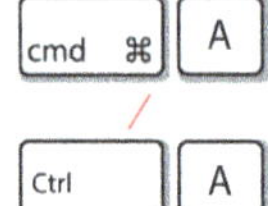

This keyboard shortcut is used to select all drawn objects in the document.

Backspace-key

Deletes a previously selected objects

Mac: command+2 / PC: Ctrl+2

This keyboard shortcut is used to lock selected objects. If you have some disturbing objects when you are working, select these objects with the **Selection tool** (V) and activate the keyboard shortcut Mac: command+2 / PC: Ctrl+2.

Mac: option+command+2 / PC: alt+Ctrl+2

This keyboard shortcut is used to unlock the objects. Though all objects in the document will be unlock.
Important: If the document contains several layers and one layer is locked (see page 21), then the locked layer will not be unlocked by this keyboard shortcut.
You should then open the Layers panel (Window > Layers) and unlock this specific layer.

Mac: command+Z / PC: Ctrl+Z

This keyboard shortcut is used to undo individual work steps.
Depending on the available memory you can create an unlimited number of Undo operations, by repeatedly activating this keyboard shortcut.
The corresponding menu command is **Edit > Undo**.
The command **Edit > Redo** allows you to restore opera-tions.

Space key

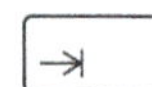

This key corresponds to the **Hand-Tool (H)**. As long as the space key is pressed, each activated tool is replaced by the hand tool. This allows you during the working process to move the working area.

Tab key

Display or hide the control panels and tools panel.

Mac: command+Y / PC: Ctrl+Y

To display the entire image material in form of paths, select **View > Outline**. To display everything again in the Preview mode, select: **View > Preview**.
During working process certain lines/objects that are in the background can be hidden by fill or stroke color of an object in the foreground. To show this hidden objects, lines or anchor points, activate the keyboard shortcut:
Mac: command+Y / PC: Ctrl+Y

 In this case the artwork is displayed without fill or stroke attributes. This will speeds up the time it takes to redraw the screen when working with complex artwork.

The linked files in the outline mode are displayed by default as outlined boxes with an X inside.

Accidentally you can select in the outline mode some linked files (with Direct Selection Tool or Group Selection Tool), to avoid the selection of this files, you should lock this files after selecting it with: Mac: command+2 / PC: Ctrl+2

Mac: Shift+command+S / PC: Shift+Ctrl+S

This keyboard shortcut is used to save a new document. In the options panel choose "Adobe Illustrator ai" (is set by default), then "Save", „Version" > "Illustrator 2021" or higher, then confirm with "OK".

 If you want to open the document in a previous Illustrator version, then you should change the „Version" to the particular version (e.g. CS5). otherwise can happen that errors occurs when you open the file in an earlier version of Adobe Illustrator (e.g. pattern brushes are not accepted, settings for objects will be lost, etc.).

This issue does not occur if a document from a previous version of Illustrator e.g. CS5 is opened in a newer version of Illustrator e.g. CC.

Mac: command+S / PC: Ctrl+S

This keyboard shortcut is used to save individual steps during the work. Better use this keyboard shortcut after each work step.

Mac: command+C / PC: Ctrl+C

This keyboard shortcut is used to copy object to the clipboard.

Mac: command+F / PC: Ctrl+F

This keyboard shortcut is used to place the copied object on the same position as the original object.
The corresponding menu command is
Edit > Paste in Front.

 For all exercises in this book to „copy" and „paste" objects this two keyboard shortcuts were used.

COPY-> Mac: command+C / PC: Ctrl+C
PASTE IN FRONT-> Mac: command+F / PC: Ctrl+F

Mac: command+G / PC: Ctrl+G

This keyboard shortcut is used to group different objects so that they are treated as a single unit.
(e.g. a button consists of multiple elements that should be copied, moved, etc.).
In such a case it makes sense to group all elements of the button, so that it is easier to work with it).
The corresponding menu command is **Object > Group.**

Mac: Shift+command+G / PC: Shift+Ctrl+G

This keyboard shortcut is used to ungroup the objects.
The corresponding menu command is **Object > Ungroup.**

Mac: command+7 / PC: Ctrl+7

This keyboard shortcut is used to mask objects.
A clipping mask is an object whose shape masks other artwork so that only areas that lie within the shape are visible. The corresponding object is clipped to the shape of the mask. The clipping mask itself and the objects that are masked are called a ***clipping set***.
You can make a clipping set from a selection of two or more objects. The corresponding menu command is **Object > Clipping Mask > Make.**
Object-level clipping sets are combined as a group in the Layers panel.
If you create clipping sets, the object on top of the layer clips all of the objects below it.
Therefor it is always important to place the object that should be defined as the „clipping mask" on the top of the layer.
Therefor you should select the „clipping mask" object with **Selection Tool (V)** and activate the command **Object > Arrange > Bring to Front**. Then select all objects that you want to mask (inclusive the „clipping mask" object) and activate the command **Object > Clipping Mask > Make.** All operations that you perform on an object-level clipping set, such as transformations and alignment, are based on the clipping mask's boundary, not the unmasked boundary. Once you have created an object-level clipping mask, you can only select the clipped content by using the Layers panel, the Direct Selection Tool, or by isolating the clipping set.

Mac: option+command+7 / PC: alt+Ctrl+7

This keyboard shortcut is used to release a clipping mask.
The released „clipping mask" object appears without Stroke and Fill colour.
It will be visible only if you activate the outline preview (**command > Y** key / PC: **Ctrl > Y**).

Mac: command+R / PC: Ctrl+R

Show and hide rulers.

Mac: command+, / PC: Ctrl+,

Show and hide guides.

Mac: command+option+Shift+2
PC: Ctrl+alt+Shift+2

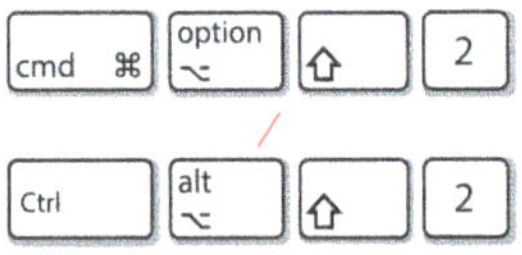

| cmd ⌘ | option ⌥ | ⇧ | 2 |

/

| Ctrl | alt ⌥ | ⇧ | 2 |

To lock not selected image material.

Mac: command+0 / PC: Ctrl+0

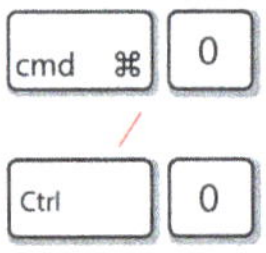

| cmd ⌘ | 0 |

/

| Ctrl | 0 |

To show the activated artboard in the window.

Mac: command+1 / PC: Ctrl+1

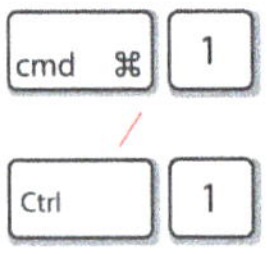

| cmd ⌘ | 1 |

/

| Ctrl | 1 |

Adjust the original size of the artboard.

Mac: X key / PC: X key

| X |

To switch between the contour and fill.

Mac: ⌇ + drag (hold down the left mouse button) /
PC: ⌇ + drag (hold down the left mouse button)

| > < |

Transform pattern regardless of the object, if the selection,
scale, mirrors or rotate- tool
is used.

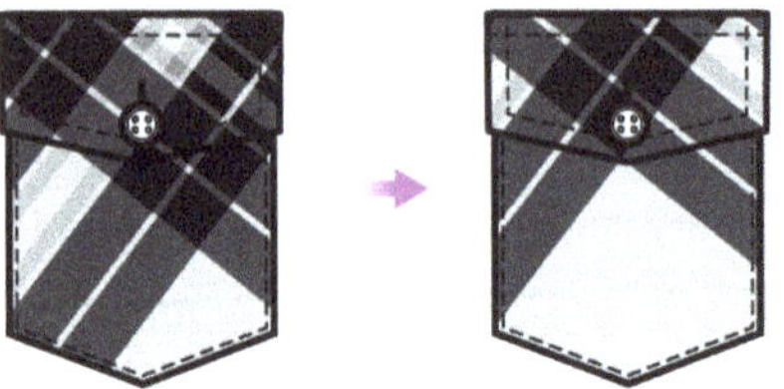

Displace pattern (only on Mac):
Step 1. Select the object with the **Selection tool** (V).
Step 2. Hold down the ⌇ key and drag with the mouse
inside the selected object (the object must be filled with a
pattern).
Rotate pattern:
Step 1. Select the object with the **Selection tool** (V).
Step 2. Activate the **Rotate-Tool** (R)
Step 3. Hold down the ⌇ key and drag with the mouse
inside the selected object (the object must be filled with a
pattern).
The steps are identical, this time activate the **Scale-Tool** (S).

Mac: command+Shift+A Taste / PC: Ctrl+Shift+A Taste

To deactivate the selection.

| cmd ⌘ | ⇧ | A |

/

| Ctrl | ⇧ | A |

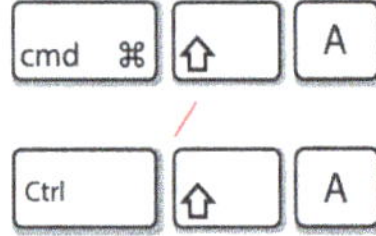

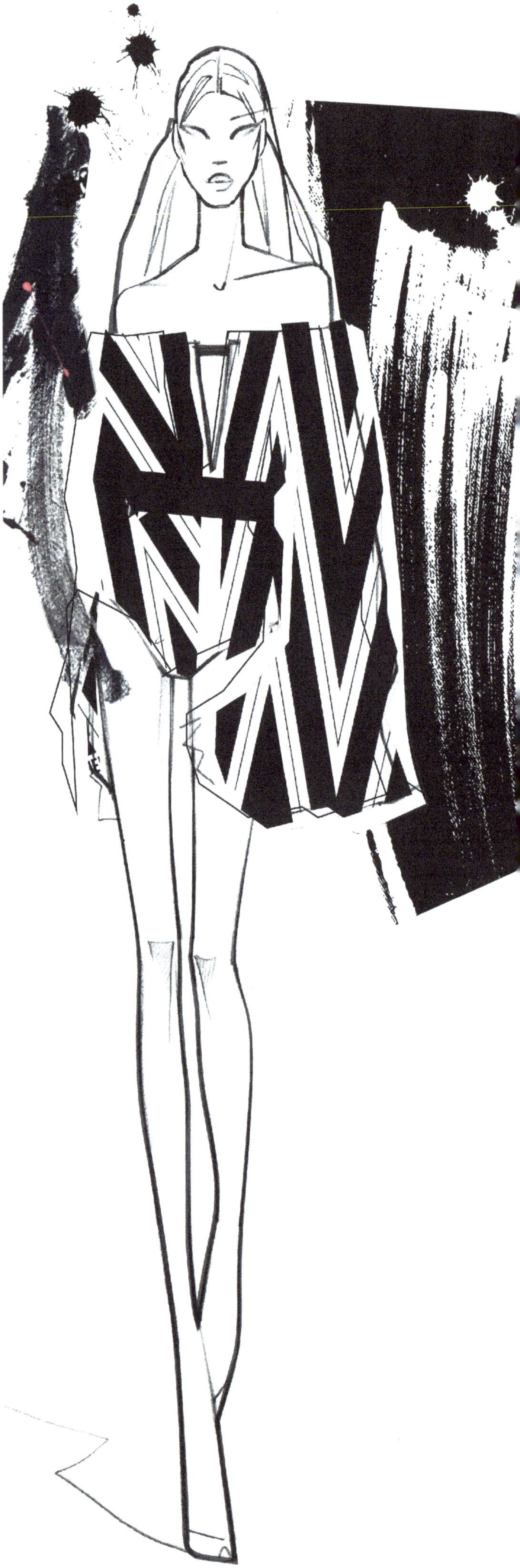

4. OVERVIEW (ADOBE ILLUSTRATOR)

4.1 WORKSPACE

Using various elements, such as bars, panels, and windows you create and manipulate your files and documents.
Any arrangement of these elements is called a workspace. You can also adapt the application to the way you work by creating one of your own or by selecting from several preset workspaces . Different workspace layout varies you can find in the menu:
Window>Workspace

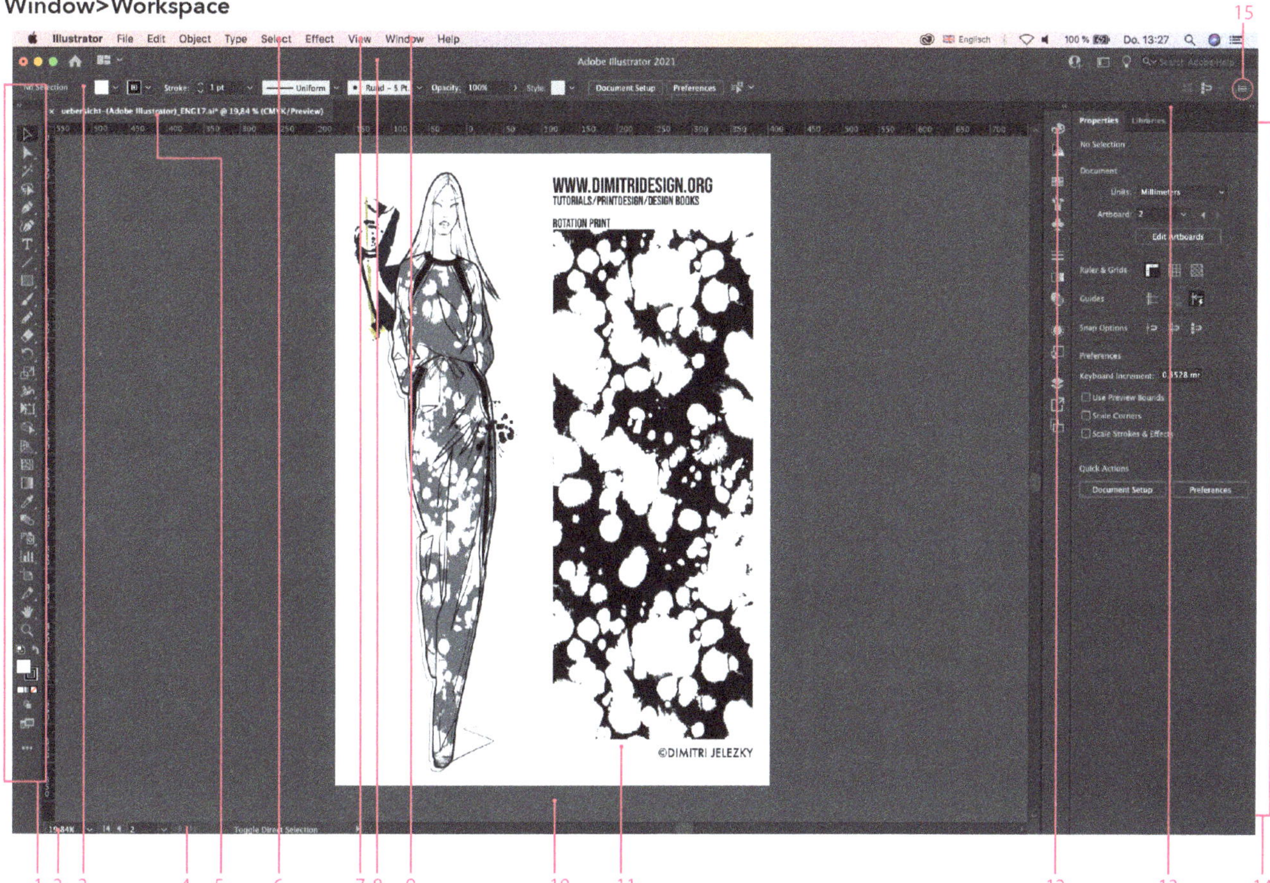

1. Tools panel
2. Current zoom factor
3. Control panel
4. Status bar
5. Tabbed Document windows
6. Menu panel
7. Menu **View:** Activate here View > Rules >Show Rules, View > Guides > Lock Guides, View > Guides > Show Guides, View > Smart Guides, View > Snap to Point.
8. Application bar
9. Menu **Window:** Here you can activate different panels and select different workspaces.

You can also create your own workspace:
Window > Workspace > New Workspace...

10. Work space
11. Artboard
12. Panels are minimized to symbols. Clicking on an icon will open the particular panel.
13. Panel title bar
14. Panel groups in vertical dock
15. This button ⊟ opens further options for the particular panel.

To show or hide panels, Tools panel and Control panel, click the tab key ⇥

4.2 HAND TOOL, ZOOM TOOL

With the **Hand Tool** (H) you can move the Illustrator artboard within the illustration window.

With the **Zoom Tool** (Z) you can increases and decreases the view magnification in the illustration window.

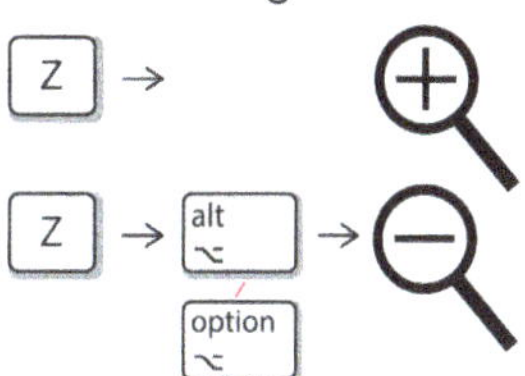

command + 1 / Ctrl + 1 Actual Size
command + 0 / Ctrl + 0 Fit Artboard in Window

4.3 TOOLS
OVERVIEW OF IMPORTANT TOOLS

The Tool panel appears by default at the left side of the screen **(Window > Workspace > Essentials)**. You can use tools in the Tools panel to create, select, and manipulate objects in Illustrator. Some tools have options that appear when you double-click a tool. You can use this tools to select, type, draw, edit, and move images.
Some tools are hidden, you can expand this tools by clicking on a small **triangle** at the lower-right corner to show them (by clicking hold down the left mouse button for 1-2 seconds).

In the Tool panel you can switch between "Draw Normal", "Draw Behind" or "Draw Inside".

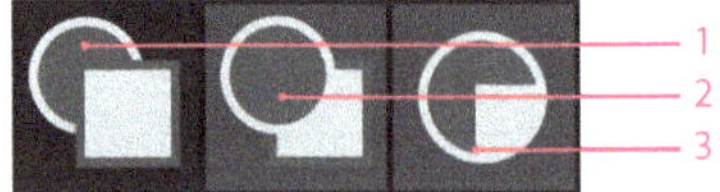

1. „Draw Normal" (by default)
2. „Draw Behind"
3. „Draw Inside"

All exercises in this book are done in "Draw Normal" mode.

1. **Selection Tool** (V)
2. **Direct Selection Tool** (A)
3. **Magic Wand Tool** (Y)
4. **Lasso Tool** (Q)
5. **Pen Tool** (P)
6. **Type Tool** (T)
7. **Line Segment Tool** (/)
8. **Rectangle Tool** (M)
9. **Pencil Tool** (N)
10. **Rotate Tool** (R)
11. **Scale Tool** (S)
12. **Gradient Tool** (G)
13. **Eyedropper Tool** (I)
14. **Blend Tool** (W)
15. **Artboard Tool** (Shift + Q)
16. **Hand Tool** (H)
17. **Zoom Tool** (Z)
18. **Add Anchor Point Tool** (+)
19. **Delete Anchor Point Tool** (-)
20. **Anchor Point Tool** (Shift + C)

 In order to change the screen mode, click the **F** key.
Or click on the symbol „Change Screen Mode". You can switch between:
- *Normal Screen Mode*
- *Full Screen Mode with Menu Bar*
- *Full Screen Mode*

4.4 HIDDEN TOOLS

21. **Group Selection Tool**
22. **Scissors Tool** (C)
23. **Rounded Rectangle Tool**
24. **Ellipse Tool** (L)
25. **Polygon Tool**
26. **Star Tool**
27. **Rotate Tool** (R)
28. **Reflect Tool** (O)
29. **Shear Tool**
30. **Warp Tool** (Shift + R)
31. **Twirl Tool**
32. **Pucker Tool**
33. **Bloat Tool**
34. **Scallop Tool**
35. **Crystallize Tool**
36. **Wrinkle Tool**
37. **Live Paint Bucket Tool** (K)
38. **Eyedropper Tool** (I)
39. **Mesure Tool**

You can also define your own shortcuts.

To do this, select **Edit > Keyboard Shortcuts...** By working with keyboard shortcuts the work process is greatly accelerated. You have the option to define keyboard shortcuts for panels and for tools.

I recommend to set for the following menu commands keybord shortcuts:

File > Export > Export As...
Object > Expand...
Object > Path > Offset Path...

5. BASICS
(WORKING WITH ADOBE ILLUSTRATOR)

5.1 CREATING A NEW DOCUMENT

To create a new document, select **File > New**. The following window appears.
After creating the document, you can change these settings by selecting File > Document Setup > Edit Artboards and setting new preferences.

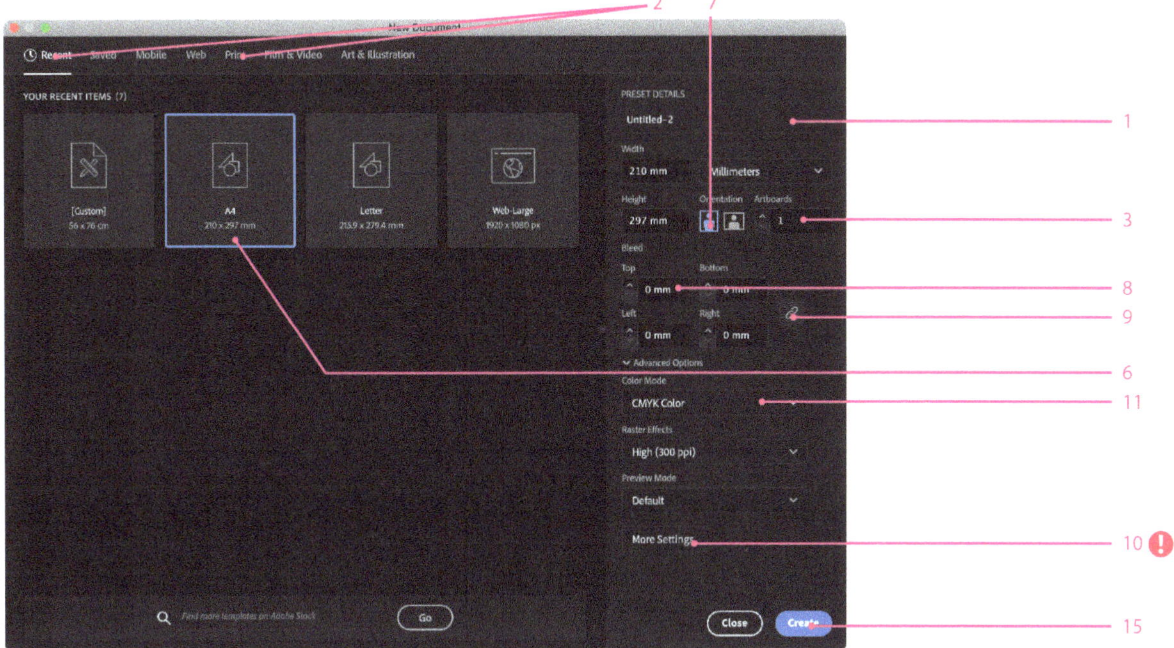

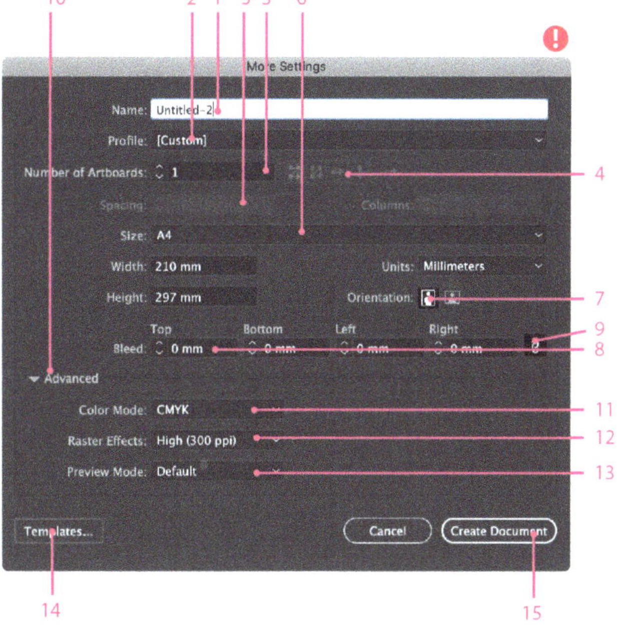

1. Type a name for the document.
2. Set the Print profile.
3. For example, set for the document artboards to 1 or 2 (for example A4 page) and the order in which you want it to appear on the screen.
4. This option is activated only at two or more artboards.
Grid by row: Multiple artboards are arranged in the specified number of rows.
Grid by column: Multiple artboards are arranged in the specified number of columns. **Arrange by row:** Artboards are arranged in a straight row. **Arrange by column:** Artboards are arranged in a straight column. **Change from right to left in layout:** Multiple artboards are arranged in the specified row or column format, it is displayed from right to left.
5. This option is only activated with two or more artboards. Set the default spacing between artboards. This setting affects both horizontal and vertical spacing.
6. Set default size, units of measure for all artboards. You can subsequently adjust the artboards by moving and scaling as desired while you are working.
7. Specify the orientation of the document.
8. Specify the bleed location for each side of the artboard. When the lock symbol (9) is activated, the same values are automatically entered.
10. Click "More Settings" to open another window.
11. Color Mode: sets the color mode of the new document. When you change the color mode, the elements: swatches, brushes, symbols, graphic styles of the selected new document profile are set to a new color mode.

12. Raster effects: sets the resolution for raster effects in the document. For the profile "Print", this option is set to "High" by default.
13. Preview Mode: sets the default preview mode for the document ("Default" is optimal).
"Default" displays artwork created in the document in vector mode in color. Smoothing of curves is retained when zooming.
14. Templates allow you to create new documents with specific preferences and design elements. For example, when you design a collection, you can create a template with the desired artboard format, display settings (such as guides), and print options.

15. Use "Create" to confirm the settings.

5.2 IMPORTANT PRESETTINGS

To make changes to preferences for more convenient work with Illustrator, select (mac) **Illustrator > Preferences > General** or (windows) **Edit > Preferences > General**

Keyboard Increment: 1 pt

Set keyboard steps here: 1pt is optimal.
Note: While holding down the **Shift** key, the distance from the starting position of the object increases tenfold.

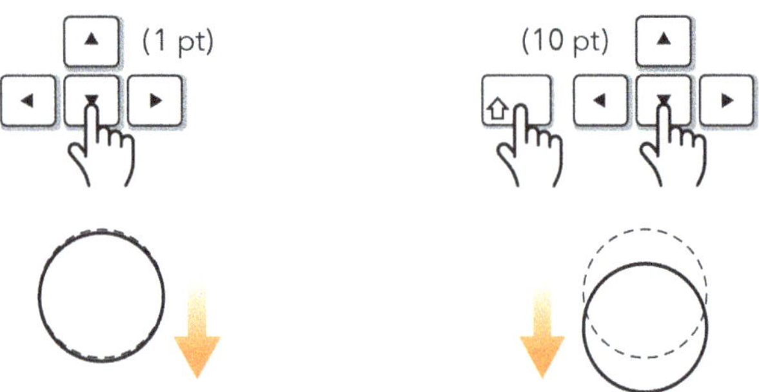

During drawing, objects are moved, among other things to gain access to fragments of an object and thereby ensure a clean selection with the direct selection tool (for example, to merge 2 endpoints to connect two paths).

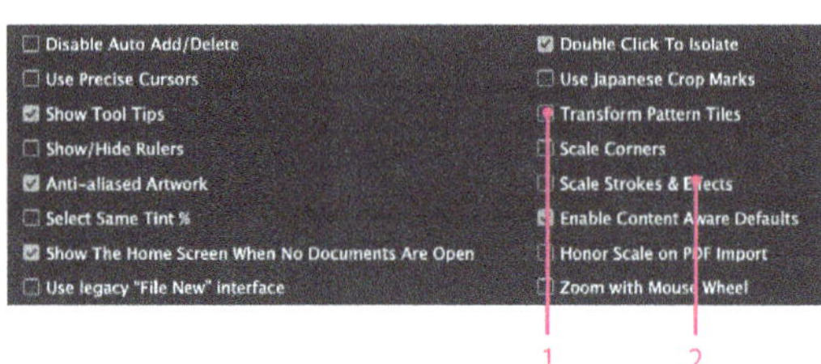

1. „Transform Pattern Tiles"
Enable "Transform Pattern Tiles" so that during the transformation of objects the patterns are also enlarged, decreased, rotated, and distorted.

2. **"Scale Stroke and Effects"**
Enable "Scale Strokes and Effects" to increase or decrease the strokes and effects while transforming objects.
This setting makes sense if, in retrospect, you have to reduce or enlarge the technical drawing (see example).

The stroke weight will be changed

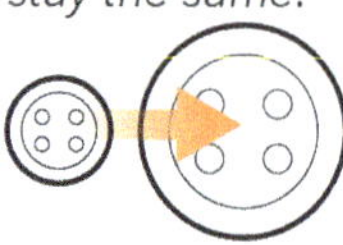

The stroke weights will stay the same.

„Scale Strokes and Effects" is **activated**.

„Scale Strokes and Effects" is **deactivated**.

5.3 SELECTION & ANCHOR DISPLAY

1. Select **Illustrator > Preferences > Selection and Anchor Display** (Mac OS) or **Edit > Preferences > Selection and Anchor Display** (Windows).
2. In the "Selection" panel, set the following settings:
Tolerance: Accuracy with which a point is clicked.
Factory setting 3px is optimal.
Snap to Point: Accuracy with which an auxiliary line is magnetically attracted to a point. Factory setting 2px is optimal.
You can adjust the appearance of the anchor points and handles according to your personal needs.

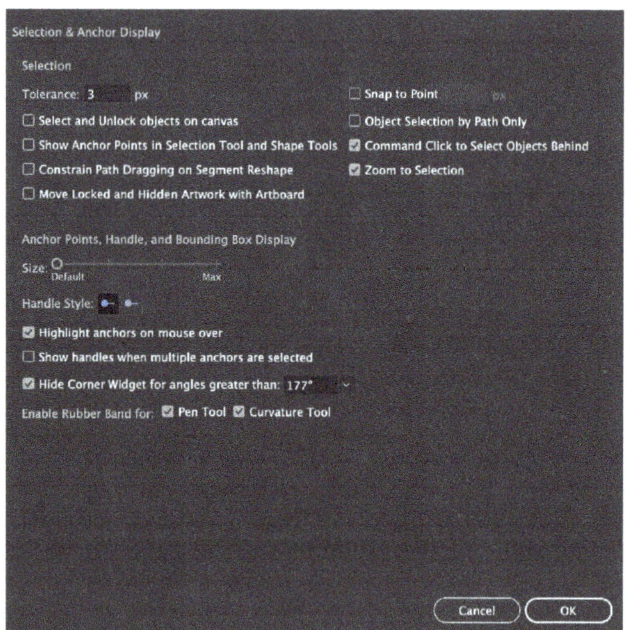

Rubber Band:
The first segment does not become visible until you click a second anchor point. It is also possible to preview path segments by selecting "Rubber Band".

5.4 ADJUSTING UNITS

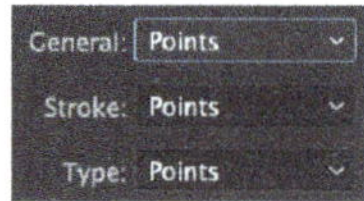

For fashion drawings in "General" it makes sense to set millimeters. For stroke and type, it makes sense to set points.

5.5 SET GUIDES AND GRID

Guides are used to align text and graphic objects.
You can create straight vertical or horizontal lines (ruler guides) and vector objects (guideline objects) converted to guides. Grids and guides are not printed.

You can choose between two helper lines - points and lines. You can also change the color of guides: Mac: **Illustrator > Preferences > Guides and Grid** / PC: **Edit > Preferences > Guides and Grid**.

While working, the guides must always be locked to ensure a faultless workflow.
Therefore, always check if the guides are locked.
View > Guides > Lock Guides must be enabled. Keyboard shortcut command "Lock/Unlock Guides": Mac alt/option + cmd + , / PC alt/option + Ctrl + ,
If guides are not locked, objects and guides are also selected (for example, if selection or direct selection tools are used). This causes problems creating allover prints or pattern brushes.
If guides do not appear, select **View > Guides > Show Guides**.
Show/Hide Guides shortcut:
Mac cmd + , / PC Ctrl + , [cmd ⌘] [,] / [Ctrl] [,]
To place guides on the artboard, you must first activate the rulers. Select **View > Rulers > Show Rulers**.
Show/hide ruler shortcut command:
cmd + R / PC: Ctrl + R

Place guides:
1. Place the pointer on the vertical ruler (create vertical guide), or on the horizontal ruler (create horizontal guide).
2. Drag the guide to the desired location.
You can also convert vector objects to guides if you select the object using the **Selection tool** (V) then right-click the stroke or fill color (if any) and enable Make Guides. Alternatively, select **View > Guides > Make Guides**.
3. If you want the guides to remain confined to a artboard and not extend across the entire work surface, select the **Artboard Tool** (Shift+O) and then drag the guides onto the artboard.

Delete, move, or convert guides:
1. If guides are locked, disable **View > Guides > Lock Guides**.
2. Click the guideline (or drag a selection rectangle around the guideline), then the guideline should take a different color, and then delete the guideline by pressing the **Backspace** key or by selecting **Edit > Cut or Edit > Clear**.
Delete all guides by selecting **View > Guides > Clear Guides**.
Select **View > Guides > Release Guides** to convert the helper object back to a normal graphic object.

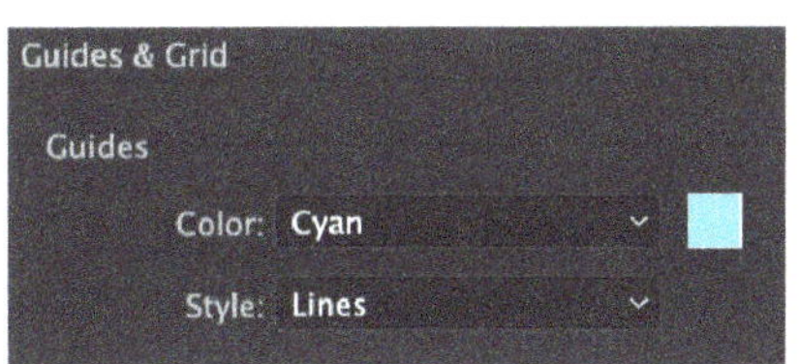

5.6 ALIGN OBJECTS ON ANCHOR POINTS AND GUIDES

1. Select **View > Snap to Point**.
2. Select the object you want to move or drag a guide and place the pointer exactly where you want to align it on an anchor point and guide.
When you enable **Snap to Point** the alignment is based on the position of the mouse pointer, not the edges of the dragged object.
3. Drag the object/guideline to the desired location.
If the pointer is 2 pixels or less apart from the anchor point or the guideline, it aligns with the point. When alignment occurs, the pointer is changed from a completed arrow to an arrow outline.

5.7 SMART GUIDES

Smart guides are temporary guides that appear when you create and edit objects or edit artboards. They automatically align with other objects when editing, aligning, and transforming objects or artboards and they also display X and Y position or delta values.

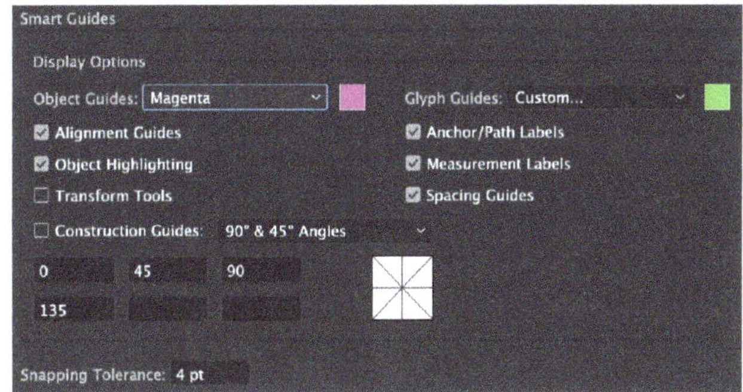

To enable Smart Guides, select **View > Smart Guides**.

Shortcut Mac cmd + U / PC Ctrl + U

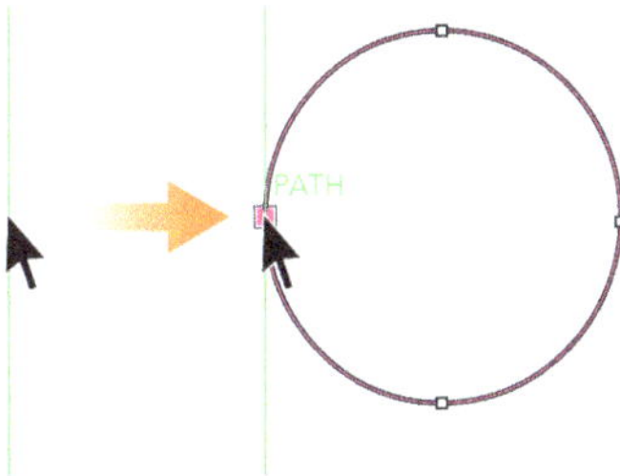

In this example, the guideline automatically aligned at an anchor point (magnetically coupled).

5.8 DOCUMENT SAVE AS

The document is always saved as .ai file (Adobe Illustrator format) to be able to open and edit it again and again. When you send technical drawings or illustrations to your customers (e.g. by email), the documents are in many cases also exported as **.jpg**, **.pdf** or **.tiff** files, because the **.ai** format can be easily opened only with Adobe Illustrator.

Save in adobe illustrator format (Ai):
1. Select **File > Save As...** or **File > Save as Copy...**
2. Type a file name and select a location for the file.
3. Select Illustrator **(.ai)** file format and confirm with **OK** (Mac) or **Save** (PC).
4. In the Illustrator options dialog box, specify the options you want and confirm with OK (by default you don´t have to make any changes).

❗ 1. Use the **Version** option to set the illustrator version with which you want the file to be compatible. If the document is opened in an older version, you should set the version in which the file is to be opened later (e.g. CS5) when saving the file in a newer version (e.g. CC), because older formats do not support all functions of the current version of Illustrator. So if you open a file that was saved with/for Illustrator CC (newer version) in an older version of Illustrator (e.g. CS5), certain types of data are changed (e.g. pattern brushes are converted and can no longer be used correctly, etc.).

2. **Create a PDF-compatible file** saves a PDF version of the document in Illustrator. Select this option if you want the Illustrator file to be compatible with other Adobe applications.

3. **Include linked files embeds files** associated with the artwork.

4. **Embed ICC profiles** creates a document with color management.

5. **Use compression** compresses PDF data in the Illustrator file.

6. **Save each artboard in a separate file** each artboard is saved in a separate file. At the same time, a separate master file is created that contains all the drawing surfaces.

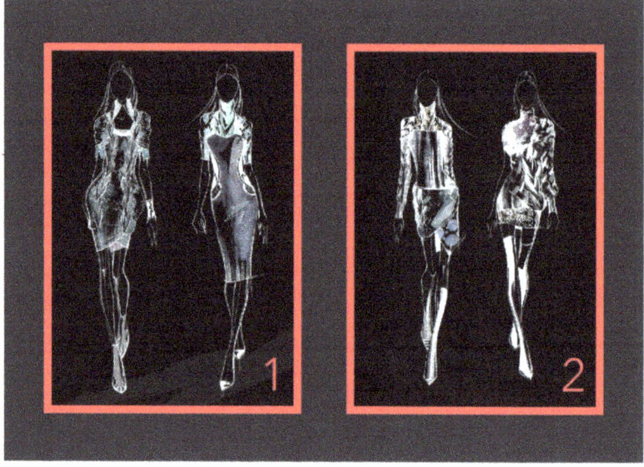

5.9 FILE EXPORT

Save in .jpg or .pdf format:

1. Select **File > Export > Export As...**
2. Type a file name and select a location for the file.
3. Select **.jpg** as the file format and click **Use Artboards.**
4. If **All** is enabled, all the artboards of the document are exported. If **Range** is enabled, you can specify which range is exported. (see example below).

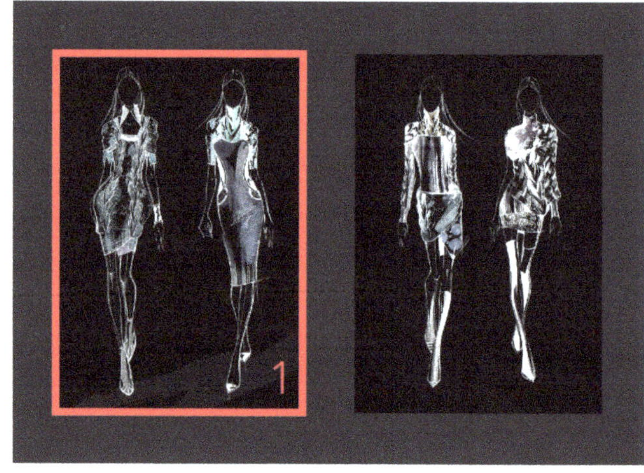

If **All** is enabled, all artboards are exported.

If **range** is enabled, you can specify which range is exported. (e.g. 1). Then only this range is exported.

5. Select **Export**

6. Use the **Color Model** option (see 5.10) to set the color space (set the print to CMYK, for Web, for example, if you send the exported file by email, set the RGB best).

7. The **Quality** option sets the quality of the .jpg file. I recommend adjusting the quality to 8-10.

8. Leave "Baseline" (Standard) for **compression method.**

9. The **Resolution** option sets the "pixels per inch." This is also about quality. For professional printing set 300 ppi or higher, for a "proof" 150 ppi would be sufficient, for example, if you work with a conventional printer.

5.10 DIFFERENCE BETWEEN RGB AND CMYK COLOR

Primary colors are RGB colors in additive color mixing, which is used, among other things, in computer monitors. For printing, you should save the document in the CMYK color space. Cyan, Magenta, Yellow and Black are the primary colors of the subtractive color mixture.

RGB color space includes a larger number of representable colors than the CMYK color space.

It is also possible to change the color mode later **File > Document Color Mode >** enable **CMYK** or **RGB**.
Note: After conversion to CMYK, bright colors are lost. In the fashion industry, "Textil Pantone" colors are often used to coordinate precisely the colors with the supplier.

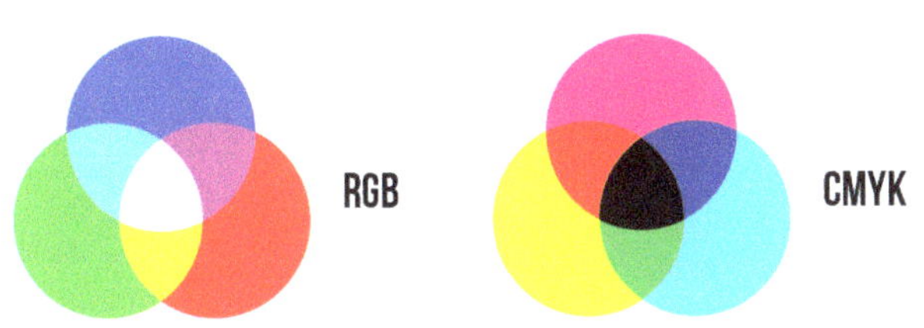

Interesting thematically compiled color swatch libraries are located under **Windows > Swatch Libraries...**

5.11 ADDING ARTBOARDS

To add more artboards, select (**Shift + O**).

1. In the control panel, activate the icon „New artboard".
2. Place the artboard anywhere.

5.12 VECTOR AND PIXEL-ORIENTED GRAPHICS

Adobe illustrator is a vector-oriented graphics programme. Adobe Photoshop is a pixel-oriented graphics programme

With vector graphics the description of a straight line exists of a starting point and a terminator point, if necessary a fill colour and line weight.

Pixel graphics exist of many small rectangles.

Pixel-oriented: have a defined size in pixel, every pixel is square and has only one colour. While increasing these pixels become visible and the picture becomes blurred.

Vector-oriented: Lines, fills are defined by vectors mathematically, the objects thereby are arbitrarily scaleable without degradation (see picture).

If you find out that during the work with illustrator everything is shown in pixels, then you have activated by mistake the pixel preview:
View> Pixel Preview
Shortcut command: Mac: alt/option + cmd + Y /
PC: alt/option + Ctrl + Y

5.13 GRID AND TRANSPARENCY GRID

Grid:

1. Select **View > Show Grid.**
2. Select **View > Snap to Grid.**

Transparency grid:

1. Select **View > Show Transparency Grid.**

Grids and transparency grids are used when drawing rectangular shapes such as bags (accessories).

I personally work only with **Smart Guides (View > Smart Guides)** and (**View > Snap to Point)**. I find grids and transparency grids disturbing when working with illustrations.

5.14 OTHER IMPORTANT SETTINGS

Please make sure that the following options are **always** displayed so that the work with Illustrator is not restricted.

View > Show Artboards
(Mac shortcut: Shift + cmd + H / PC: Shift + Ctrl + H).

View > Show Bounding Box
(shortcut Mac: Shift + cmd + B / PC: Shift + Ctrl + B).

View > Show Edges
(Mac shortcut: cmd + H / PC: Ctrl + H)

View > Show Corner Widget

Under Mac: **Illustrator > Preferences > User Interface** / PC: **Edit > Preferences > User Interface** you can adjust the brightness of your user interface.

5.15 WORKING WITH RULERS

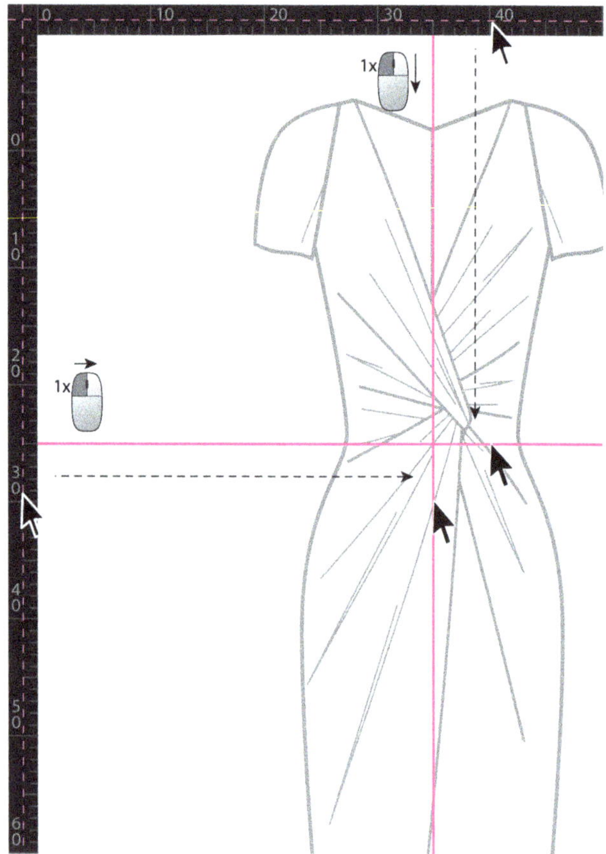

To place objects exact in the work surface and to do measurements, you can use for it rulers. Activate **View > Rulers > Show Rulers** (shortcut command Mac: cmd + R / PC: Ctrl + R). The place in the upper left corner of the sign window on which "0" stand is called ruler zero.

In Adobe Illustrator there are separate rulers for documents and artboards.

„Global Rulers": **View > Rulers > Show Rulers**

are window rulers that appear on the top and left sides of the drawing window. The default ruler zero is located at the top left of the drawing window.

„Artboard Rulers": **View > Rulers > Change to Artboard Rulers** appears on the top and left sides of the active artboard. The standard artboard ruler zero point is located at the top left of the artboard.

The difference between the artboard rulers and the global rulers is that the origin point depends on the active artboard when the artboard rulers are selected. It is also possible to specify different origin points for artboard rulers.

5.16 CONTROL PANEL

Different panels can be found under **Window**.

In the panels, you can set and change different settings for objects and for different Illustrator functions.

e.g.:

- In the **stroke** panel, among other things, you can set the stroke weight for a path or "Dashed Line" for a quilting seam.

- In the swatch panel, among other things, you can set the stroke color of an object (for example, fill a dress with a color, pattern, or gradient).

- In the **Layers** panel, you can change the arrangement of objects within the document, lock them, and so on.

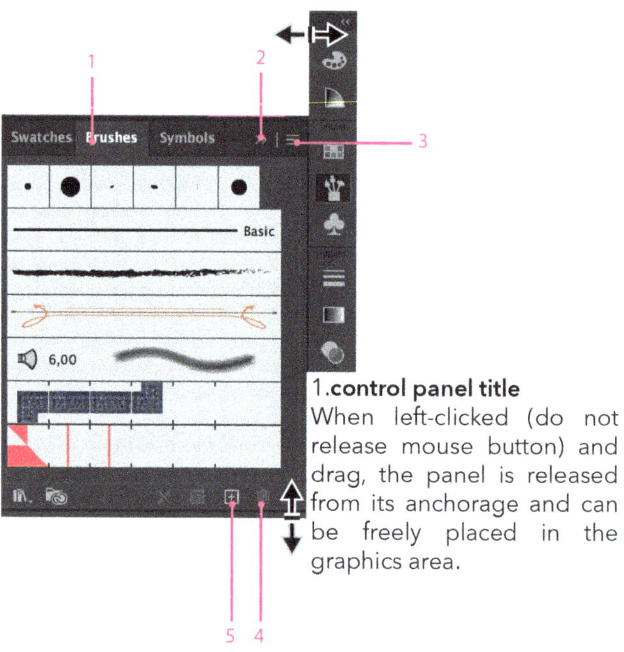

1.control panel title

When left-clicked (do not release mouse button) and drag, the panel is released from its anchorage and can be freely placed in the graphics area.

2.Extend control panel

By clicking on the double arrow, the control panel group is reduced or enlarged.

3. Here you can show **more options** for the respective control panel. 

4. Control panel specific **delete** command (for example, in the brush panel, this will delete a specific brush rapport).

5. Panel specific command **new** (for example, a new color is created in the Swatches panel).

You can adjust the window size by dragging the mouse pointer to the right or left bottom to resize the window.

5.17 MENU COMMANDS

Menu commands are used to activate various program functions, instructions (e.g. Object > Path > Offset Path), open panels, change workspace. Many shortcuts in this book refer to program functions that can be found under menu commands.

If the menu command bar is not visible, press the F key (this will change the screen mode).

5.18 FILL AND STROKE COLOR

In fashion design, mostly technical drawings and fashion illustrations are created with Adobe Illustrator. An object can be assigned a stroke without **fill** color (for example, a black/white technical drawing) or a pattern with a **fill** color but without **stroke** color (for examplea rapport for a check pattern). However, an object can also be assigned both **stroke** and **fill** color (for example, a colored technical drawing/illustration).

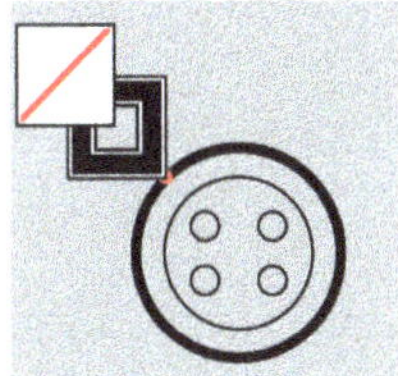
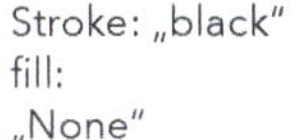

Stroke: „black"
fill:
„None"

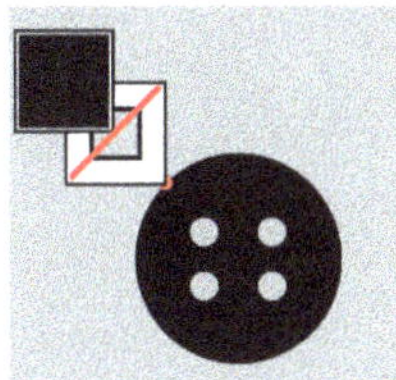

Stroke: „None"
fill:
„black"

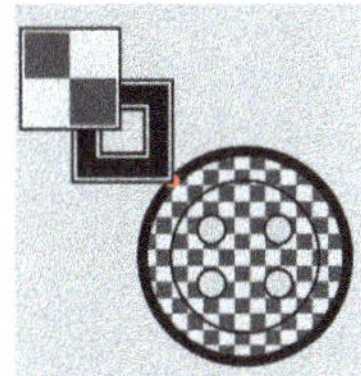
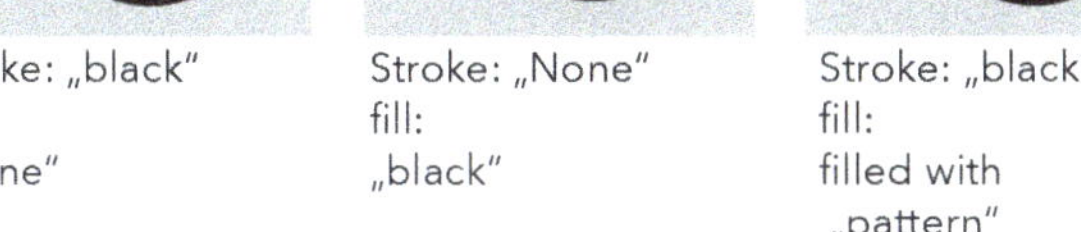

Stroke: „black"
fill:
filled with
„pattern"

A fill in an object can be either a color, a pattern, or a gradient. The visible outline of an object is a stroke. However, stroke can also be the edge of an live painting group or a path.

Different weights, colors, and patterns can be assigned to a stroke. You can also apply different pattern brushes (e.g. overlock seam, blind stitch, etc.)

fills (color, pattern, gradient) can be applied to both open and closed objects, as well as to closed objects of live painting groups.

Fill is activated

Stroke is activated

Option 1:

To set a fill or stroke color
Double-click in the **tools panel** either on a fill or stroke.

Option 2:

To set colors or patterns for a fill or stroke, select **Window > Swatches**.

Always make sure that the fill or stroke is enabled (placed in the foreground) when changing a color while working. Because if you plan to change stroke color, but the "fill" is in the foreground, then the fill color and not the stroke color, is changed. **The** X **button places fill or stroke in the foreground.**

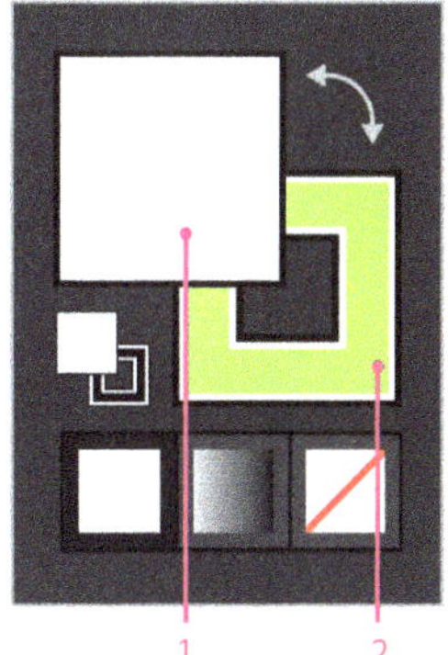
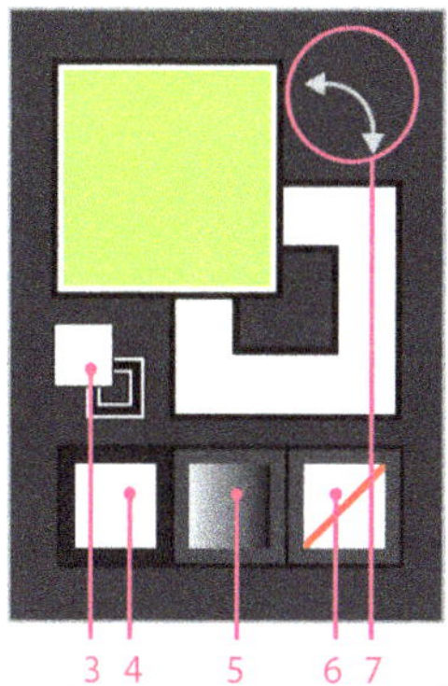

1. A *Single click* (left mouse button) bring the fill to the foreground, then open **Window > Swatches** and select a color/pattern. With a *double click* the **Color Picker** is opened, here you can mix colors individually.

2. A *single click* (left mouse button) brings the stroke to the foreground, then opens **Window > Swatches** and selects a color/pattern. With a *double click* **Color Picker** is opened, here you can mix colors individually.

Under **Window > Swatch Libraries >...** you can find many interesting color libraries (compiled by topic). The selected color from one of these swatches is automatically copied to the swatch panel of the document.

3. The default fill and stroke (S/W) setting is enabled (D).

4. Activates the most recently selected fill color on an object with a gradient fill or an object with no fill color or stroke color (,) .

5. Activates the B&W gradient (.) .

6. Deselects the fill color or stroke color of the selected object (#) .

7. Fill and stroke color are exchanged (Shift + X).

5.19 DIFFERENT FILL AND STROKE COLORATION SETTINGS

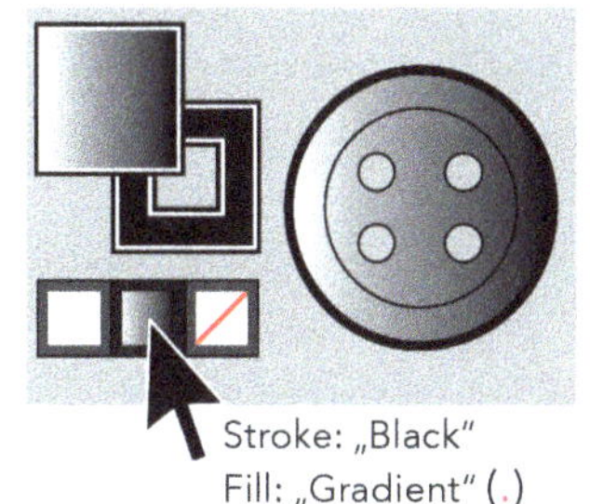

Stroke: „Black"
Fill: „Gradient" (.)

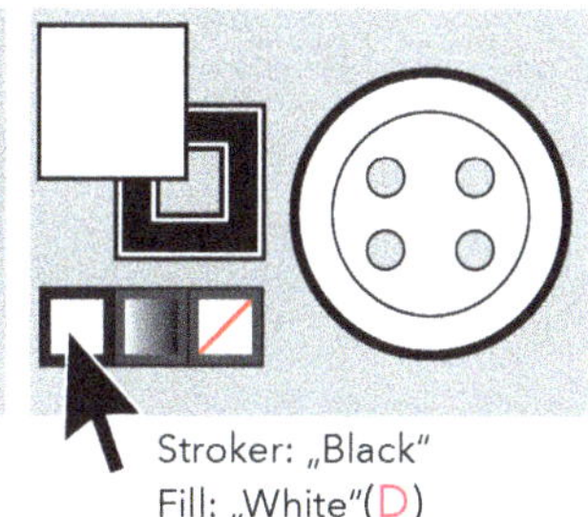

Stroker: „Black"
Fill: „White"(D)

Stroke: „None" (#)
Fill: „None" (#)

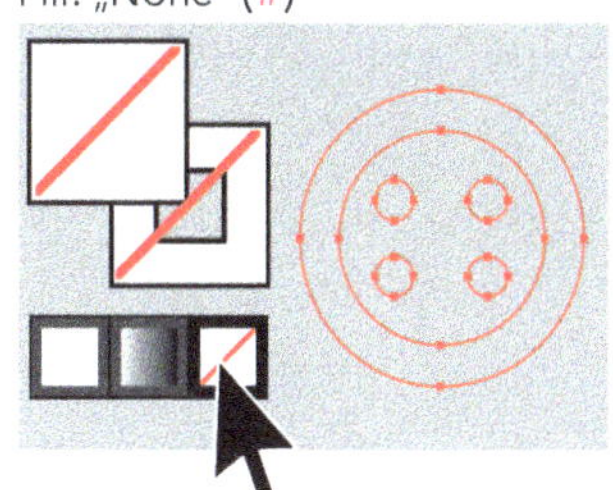

Stroke: filled with a Pattern"
Fill: „White"

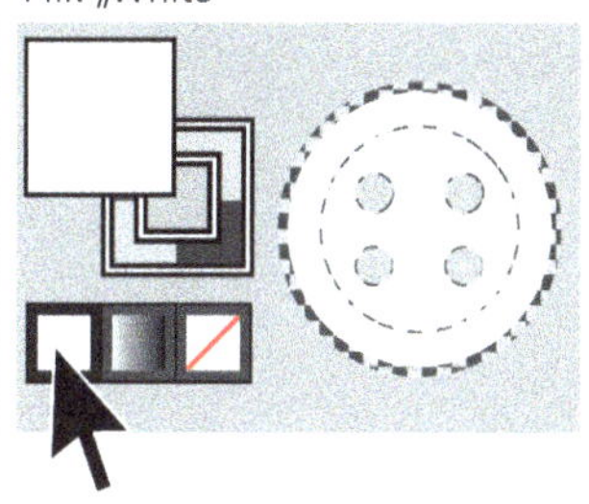

5.20 COLOR PICKER

To select a color, double-click the fill or stroke to select a color using the Color Picker.

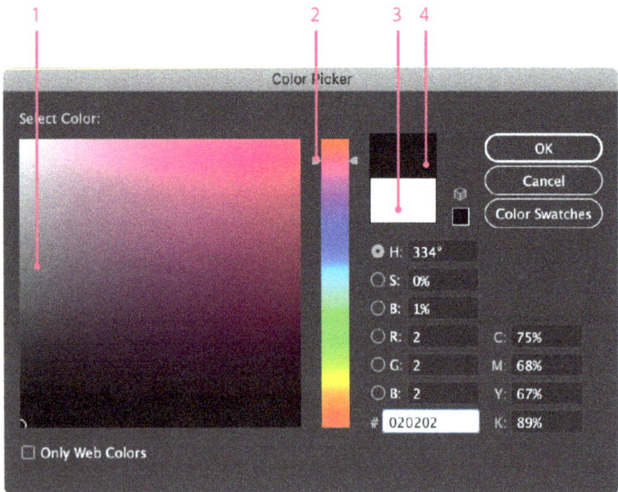

- You can mix colors or enter them numerically in the color picker.

Mix colors:
1. Click in the color spectrum (1) and use the mouse pointer to drag within the color spectrum.
2. Drag along the color slider at the triangles (2).
4. Then confirm with "OK."

Note: (3) is the original color and
(4) the new color (preview).

5.21 SWATCHES

Swatches include colors, gradients, and patterns. The swatches stored in Illustrator file appear in the Swatches panel. Color fields can be stored individually or arranged in groups (4) (**important for summerizing the season collection colors**).
An interesting way that is often used at work is to import color field libraries from other Illustrator documents:

1. **Window > Swatches** (opens swatches).
2. Click on the icon ▤
3. **Open Swatch Library > Other Library...**
4. Select an Illustrator (.ai) document with a swatch library and confirm with "Open."

This allows you to import colors/patterns/gradients from other documents.

This is especially important when designing a fashion collection, because a collection contains a certain number of colors and patterns. Therefore, you only need to create your swatches once, and then you can import this library into a new document again and again from an Illustrator document.

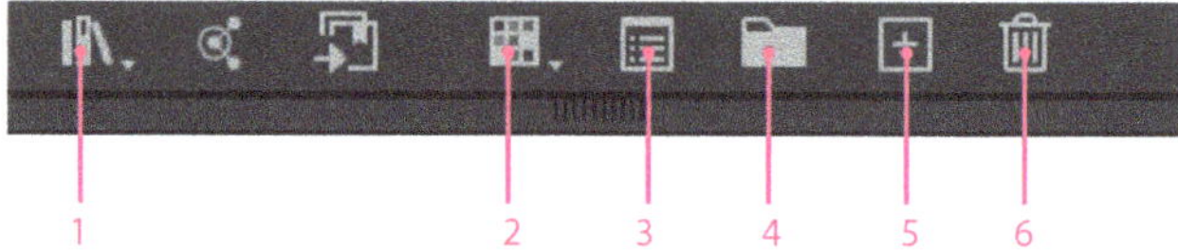

1. "Swatch Libraries menu" menu: Here are different swatch libraries arranged by topics.
2. Show Swatch Kinds menu: Here you can define which swatch types are displayed. For example, when you click Show Pattern Swatches, only patterns that are in your document are displayed.
3. For a selected color, you can click Swatch Options, which displays the swatch name, color style, and color mode.
4. New Color Group: A new color group is created. You can click a specific swatch (left-click) and drag into the new swatch. You can also select and drag multiple swatches with **Shift** key.
5. Create a new swatch.
6. Delete swatch.

5.22 COLOR
Window > Color (F6)
You can also enable "fill" and "stroke" and assign colors here.

5.23 GRADIENT

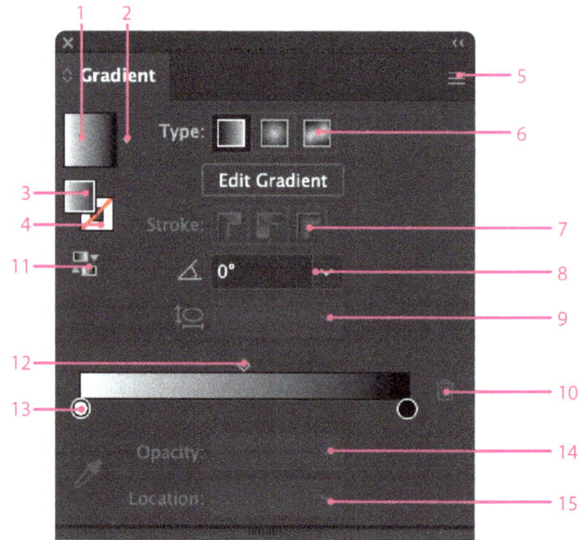

Gradient is a gradual adjustment from at least two colours. Gradient fills are stored as swatches and can be opened from the swatch window.
In a fashion illustration or technical drawings gradients are used in different ways, e.g. for metal elements like chains, push buttons etc. You can apply a gradient to a technical drawing to let it look more three-dimensional.
Open **Window > Gradient**

1. **Gradient** box: Selected gradient.
2. Menu **Gradient**: More gradients.
3. Apply Gradient to "**Fill**".
4. Apply Gradient to "**Stroke**"
5. **Panel Menu** (show options)
6. **Type of gradient** (linear or radial)
7. **Stroke gradient type** (see "chain" example)
8. **Angle** (set angle for gradient)
9. **Aspect Ratio**
10. **Delete stop**
11. **Reverse Gradient** (reverse gradient for stroke or fill)
12. **Midpoint** (determines the transition density of colors)
13. **Gradient slider** (gradient consists of at least 2 swatches, more can be added). By double-clicking a color slider, the swatches are opened, here you can change the color. When you move the pointer to the gradient slider, you can create additional color sliders:
14. **Opacity** (Transparency of the gradient is set)
15. **Position**

Example "Chain"

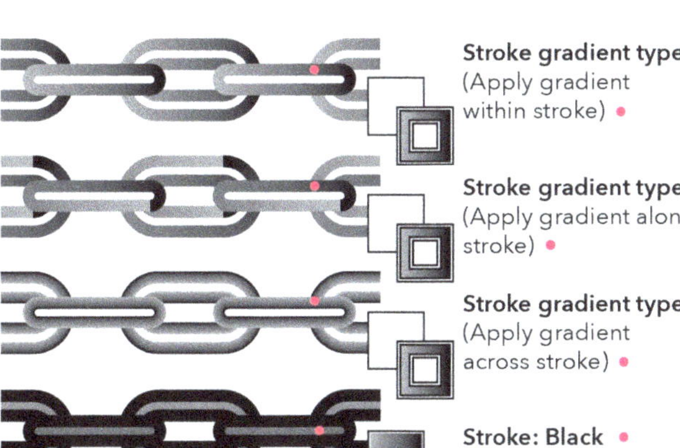

5.24 GRADIENT TOOL

Activate the **Gradient Tool** (G) in the Tools panel

Gradients can be added or edited using the Gradient tool. When you click in an object with a fill color using the Gradient tool, the object is filled with a gradient. The Gradient Optimizer lets you specify the angle, position, extent of a linear gradient, or focus, origin, and extent of a circular gradient for an object.

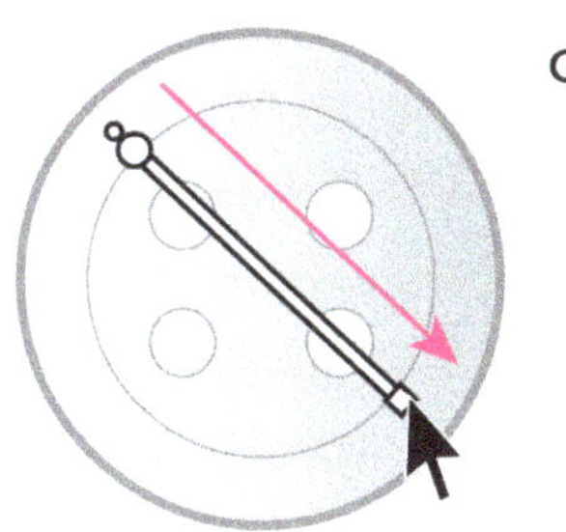

Gradient Tool

Gradient Optimizer

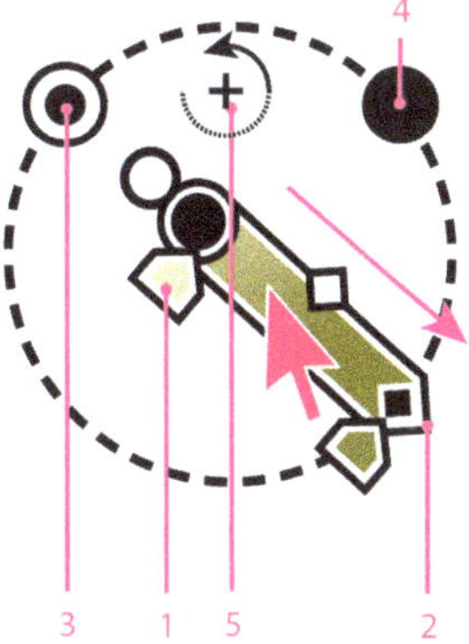

Appears when the mouse pointer is moved over the gradient tool (gradient must already exist).

1. Colour regulator
2. Gradient direction
3. Expansion
4. Aspect ratio (only for type: "Radial Gradient")
5. Drag and rotate the „spin icon" to reposition the angle.

5.25 LAYERS

To keep track of all objects in the document, "Layers" panel is used. For example, each document can contain hundreds of objects such as paths, shapes, anchor points, etc., and each object automatically creates a new "Sublevel" in the "Layer" panel.
Since the selection of certain artwork becomes more difficult, for example when several copies lie on top of each other or smaller elements are hidden by larger ones, it is recommended to work with several layers. This allows you to control the order of the image material much more easily and change the stacking order of the objects.
You can also move objects between layers later. Use the Layers panel to select, hide, lock, and modify the objects.

Open **Windows > Layers**

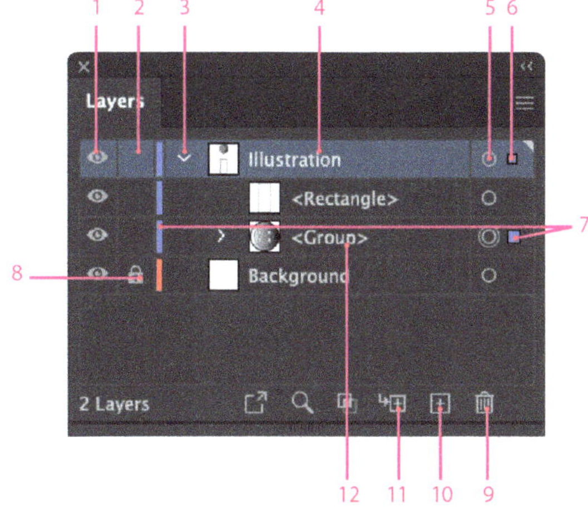

1. **Visibility column**: Indicates whether items in the layers are visible or hidden.
2. **Edit column**: Indicates whether elements are locked (lock icon is displayed) or unlocked.
3. Fold up (sublayers become visible) or close.
4. Layer name or sublevel name

5. **Target column**: Objects were selected as the target for applying effects and editing attributes in the Appearance panel > ◎ or were not selected > ○
6. **Selection column:** Indicates whether an object is selected or not. When selected, the layer color is displayed.
7.**Layer color:** Each layer automatically gets its own color. Double-click the swatch to change the color.
8. Layer is locked.
9. Delete layer or sublayer.
10. Create a new layer.
11. Create a new sublayer (only if a layer is enabled).
12. A sublayer is displayed as "<group>," several elements are grouped.

All layers or sublayers can be moved freely by clicking and dragging with the mouse.

Layers order in an illustration

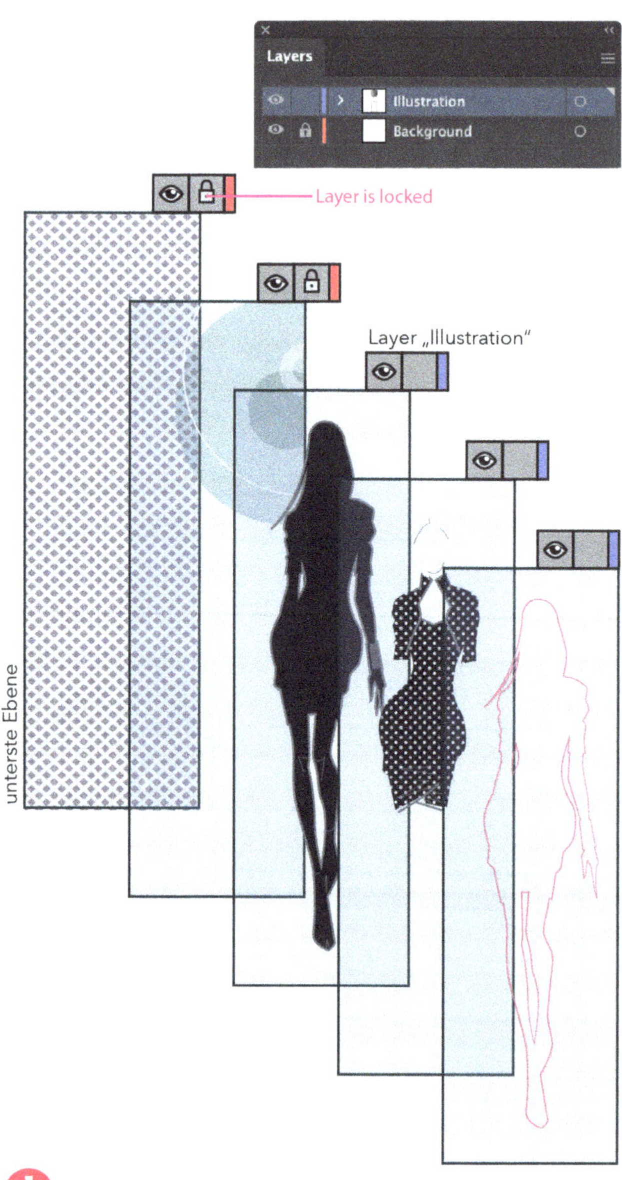

If you try to work on a layer and the following icon appears ✎⊘ , then this layer is locked. You must unlock the layer (click the lock icon) before you can continue working.

5.26 VECTOR GRAPHICS

Lines and curves in Illustrator are vector objects defined by mathematical calculations. A vector graphic is resolution independent, so you can move, resize, enlarge, copy, and change all objects as desired and the quality of the graphic is not changed. The quality of the graphic remains unchanged also when the document is saved as a PDF file.

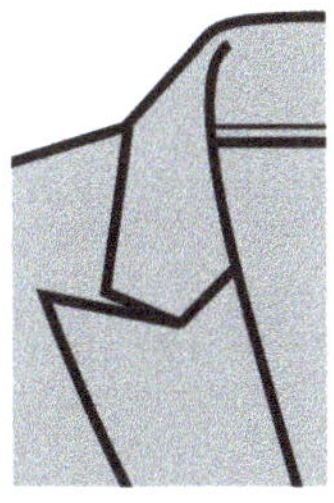

original size 100%   Increased by 500%

5.27 PATHS

Lines are predominantly created in Illustrator using the **Pen Tool** (P) . Lines are called paths and have curved or straight segments. Segments consist of points, which are called anchor points.

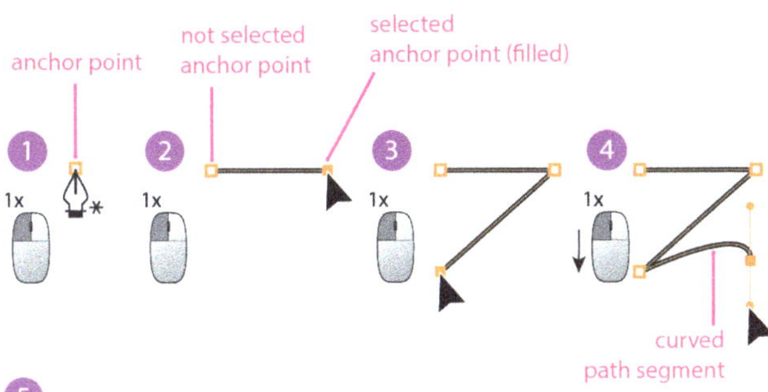

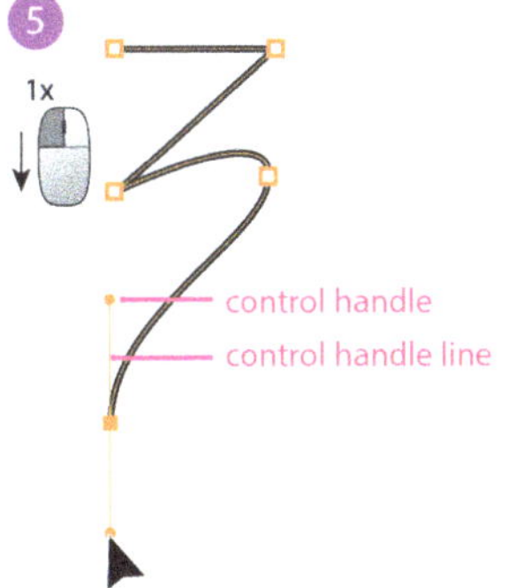

Select the **Pen tool** (P).

Step 1. Place the **Pen Tool** (P) anywhere in the artboard where you want the line to begin, and left-click (do not drag!) to define the first anchor point. The path does not become visible until you create a second anchor point by clicking.
Step 2. Click again where you want the line to end.
Shift key will limit the angle of the path to 45 °.
Step 3. Set an anchor point by another click.

Step 4. Position the tool where you want the curve to begin, hold down the left mouse button, and drag the pointer (release only when you are satisfied with the curve). **Shift** key constrains the angle of the path to 45 °.

The pointer of the **Pen Tool** becomes an arrowhead.

You can also adjust the control handle line from both sides by dragging the control handle.

Step 5. Position the tool where you want the curve to continue and hold down the left mouse button. Hold down **Shift** key to limit the angle of the path to 45 °.

Paths can be open or closed (see example).

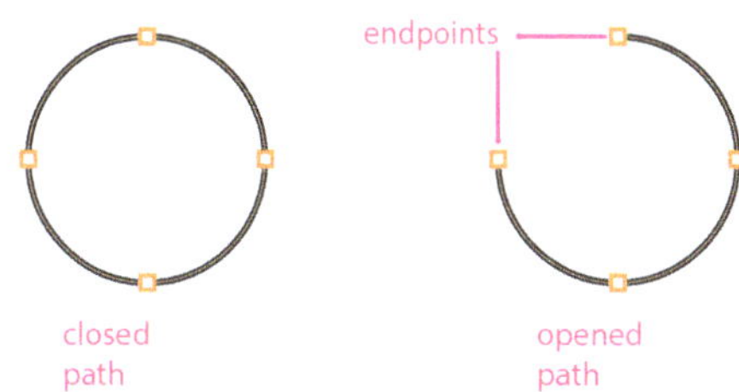

When you drag, rotate, or drag the path segment with the **Direct Selection Tool** (A) at the control handle of the control handle line, the shape of the path is changed. The shape and size of the curve segments determines the angle and length of a direction line.

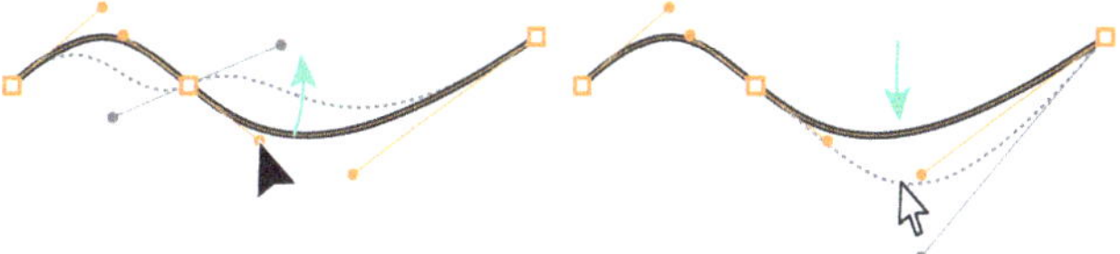

Paths have two types of anchor points: **smooth points** and **corner points** (see example below). At a smooth point, path segments are connected to a continuous curve, and at a corner point, the direction of a path is changed. A smooth point connects only curve segments. A corner point connects both straight segments and curve segments, or both in combination. A smooth point always has two direction lines, they are moved together as a straight unit.

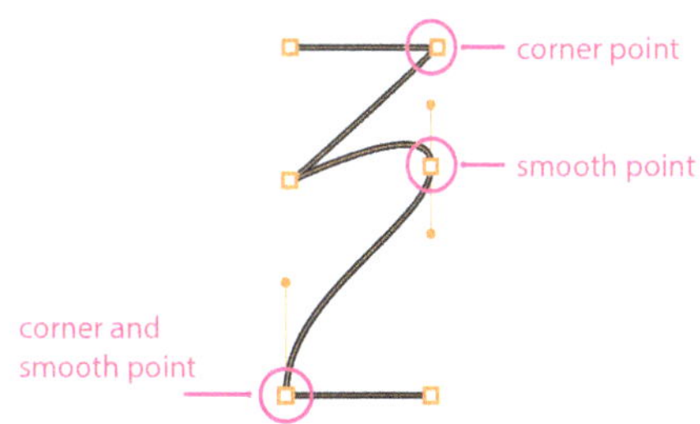

Use the **Anchor Point Tool** (Shift + C) to create a smooth point (curve) from a corner point or vice versa. If there are errors while drawing with the **Pen Tool** (P), you can correct them at any time with the **Direct Selection Tool** (A) and in some difficult cases with the **Anchor Point Tool** (Shift + C).

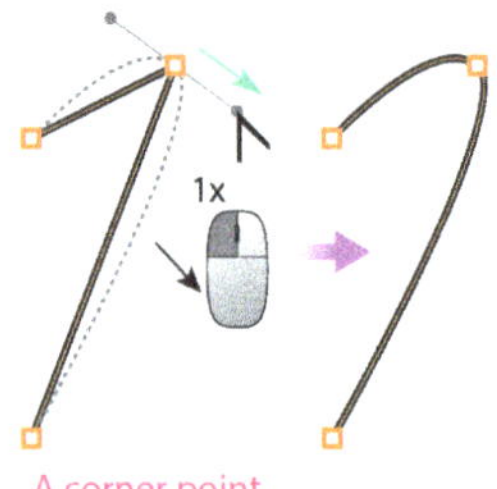
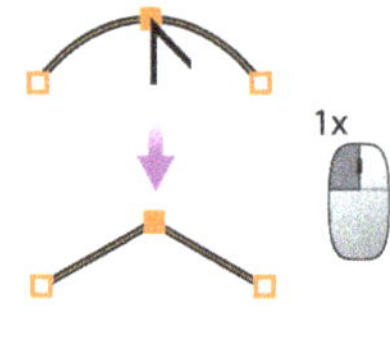
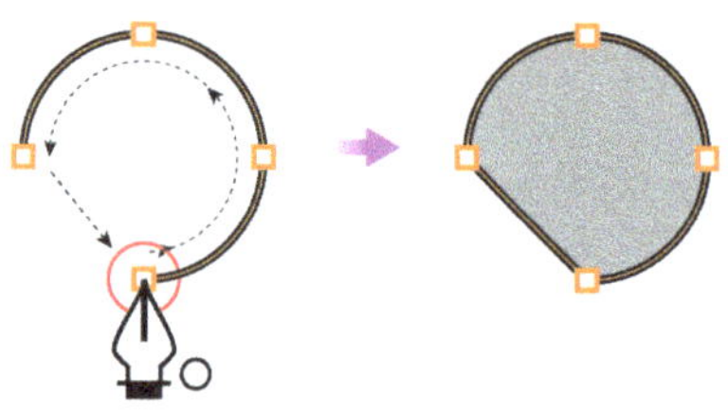

A corner point
becomes a smooth point

A smooth point
becomes a corner point

The line of a path is called a **Stroke**. Paths can contain patterns, colors, or gradients on their interior, this area is called a **Fill**. A stroke can be applied to a path, the stroke can have a width, color, or pattern.

Add Anchor Point Tool (+)

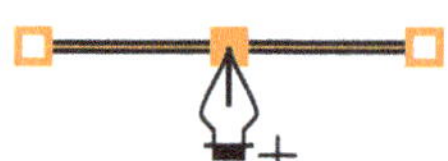

Using **Add Anchor Point Tool** (+), you can add new anchor points on a path.

Note: Pen Tool (P) is automatically replaced by **Anchor Point Adding Tool** when you move the pointer over a path.

Delete Anchor Point Tool (-)

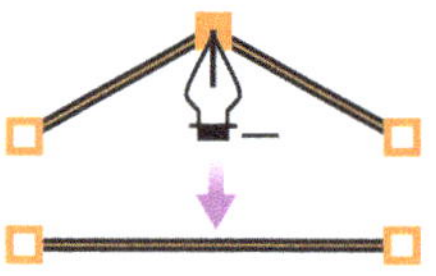

Use the **Anchor Point Delete Tool** (-) to delete anchor points on a path.

Note: Pen tool (P) is automatically replaced by **Anchor Point Delete Tool** when you place the mouse pointer over an anchor point. However, it **does not** work at a start or end point of the path!

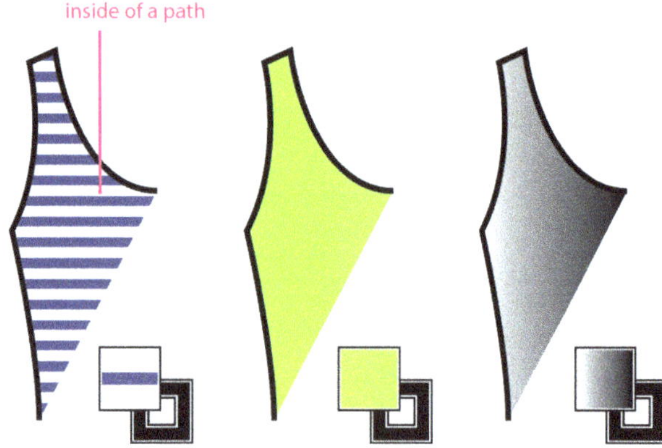

inside of a path

When you click an anchor point with the **Direct Selection Tool** (A), the control handle line appear on all connected curve segments.

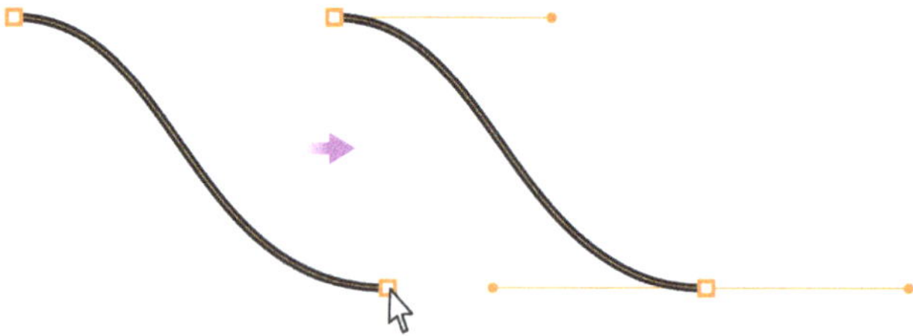

If you place the **Pen Tool** (P) over a start or end point of a previously *unselected* path (do not click), the tool appears with a slash, which means that the path can be drawn further from that anchor point.

When the existing path is connected to a current path at the start or end point, the **Pen Tool** (P) appears with a rectangle.

5.28 CONTROL PANEL OPTIONS

Select **Window > Control** (Default is always enabled).

When anchor points are selected using the **Direct Selection Tool** (A), the control panel appears at the top. Here you can set different settings for anchor points, this panel fulfills a quick access to functions e.g. from the pen tool group.

PATH B   PATH A

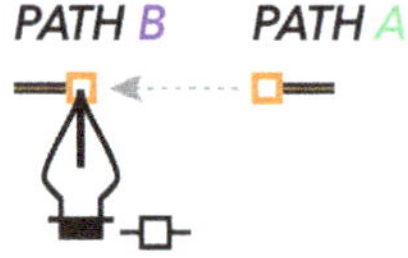

When the **Pen Tool** (P) is moved to the starting point when drawing a path, a small circle symbol appears, which means that the shape can be closed with a click (left click).

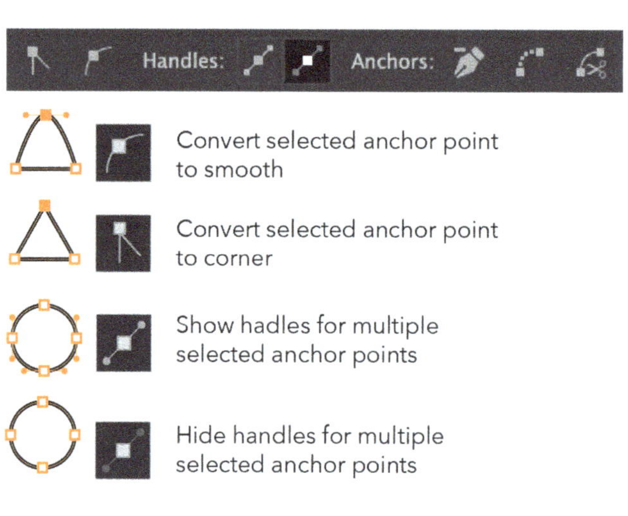

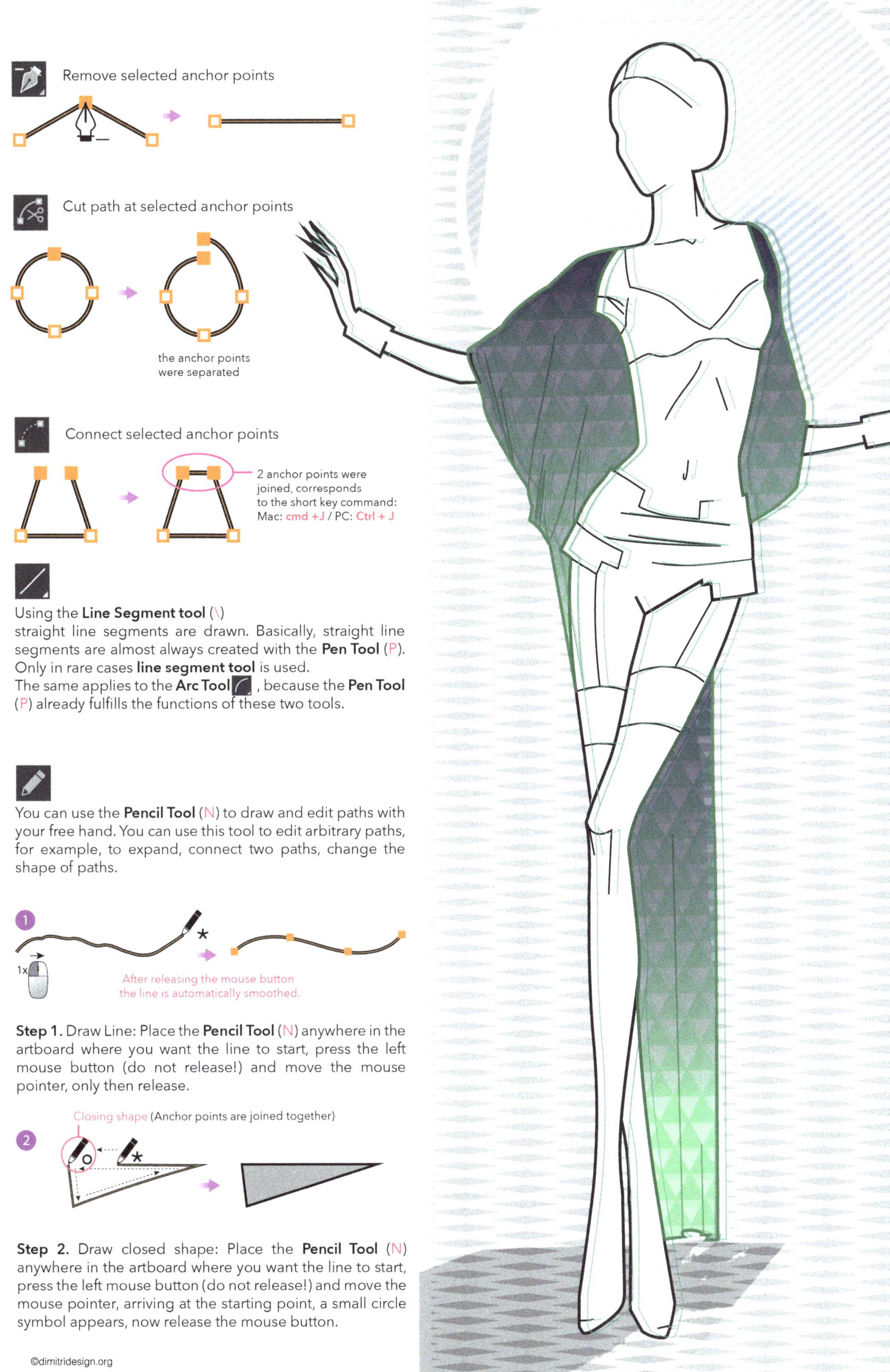

Remove selected anchor points

Cut path at selected anchor points

the anchor points
were separated

Connect selected anchor points

2 anchor points were
joined, corresponds
to the short key command:
Mac: cmd +J / PC: Ctrl + J

Using the **Line Segment tool** (\)
straight line segments are drawn. Basically, straight line
segments are almost always created with the **Pen Tool** (P).
Only in rare cases **line segment tool** is used.
The same applies to the **Arc Tool** , because the **Pen Tool**
(P) already fulfills the functions of these two tools.

You can use the **Pencil Tool** (N) to draw and edit paths with
your free hand. You can use this tool to edit arbitrary paths,
for example, to expand, connect two paths, change the
shape of paths.

1x

After releasing the mouse button
the line is automatically smoothed.

Step 1. Draw Line: Place the **Pencil Tool** (N) anywhere in the
artboard where you want the line to start, press the left
mouse button (do not release!) and move the mouse
pointer, only then release.

Closing shape (Anchor points are joined together)

Step 2. Draw closed shape: Place the **Pencil Tool** (N)
anywhere in the artboard where you want the line to start,
press the left mouse button (do not release!) and move the
mouse pointer, arriving at the starting point, a small circle
symbol appears, now release the mouse button.

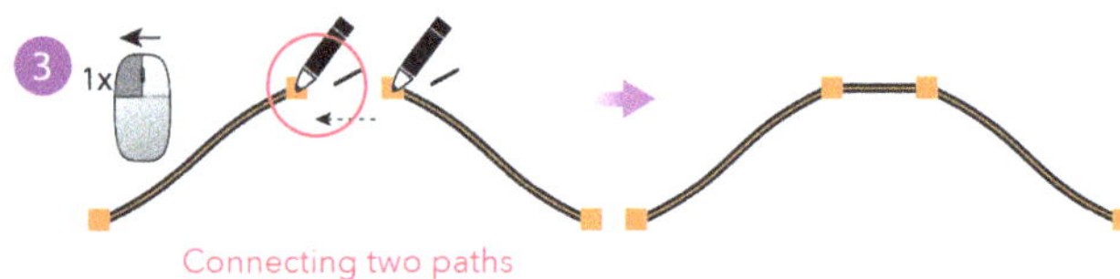

Step 3. Connecting two paths: To connect two paths, use the **Selection Tool** (V) to select both paths (see working with the selection tool). Place the pointer of the pencil tool on the start or end point (press left mouse button, do not release) and drag to the other path (start or end point), then release.

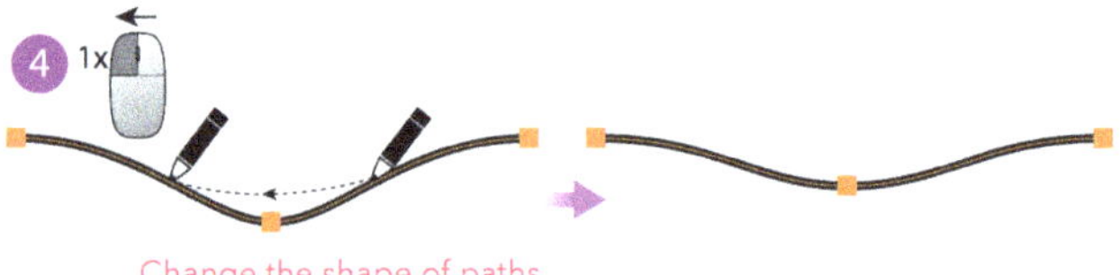

Step 4. Changing the shape of paths: To change the shape of a path, first select the path using the **Selection Tool** (V) Place the pointer of the pencil tool on the path (X symbol on the tool should disappear, then they are close enough to the path). Then press the left mouse button (do not release) and drag to the desired place, then release the mouse button.

You can use the options for the pencil tool to set different settings for the pencil tool.

Double-click the pencil tool to set the following options:

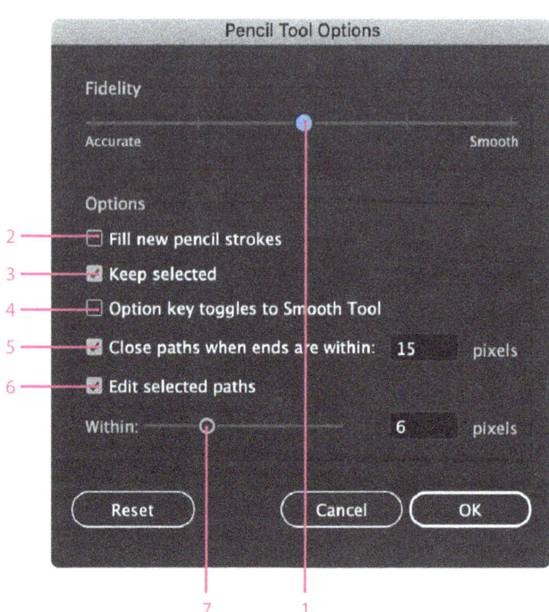

1.Fidelity: The higher the value, the smoother and less complex the path is.
2.Fill new pencil strokes: Applies a filling to a pencil stroke.
3.Keep selected: After drawing, the path remains selected.
4.Option key toggles to Smooth Tool: When the Shift button is activated, it is switched to smooth tool.
5.Close paths when ends are within: Determines whether you can change a selected path or not.

6/7.Edit selected paths: Determines how close the mouse (pixel spacing) must be to a path in order to edit a path using the Pencil tool.

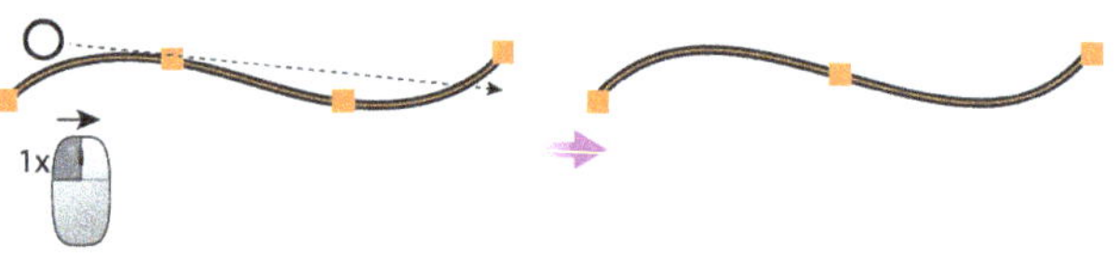

With the **smooth tool** you can smooth paths.

First, select the path with **Selection Tool** (V). Then drag the tool along the entire path segment.

Double-click the **Smooth Tool** to change the degree of smoothing.

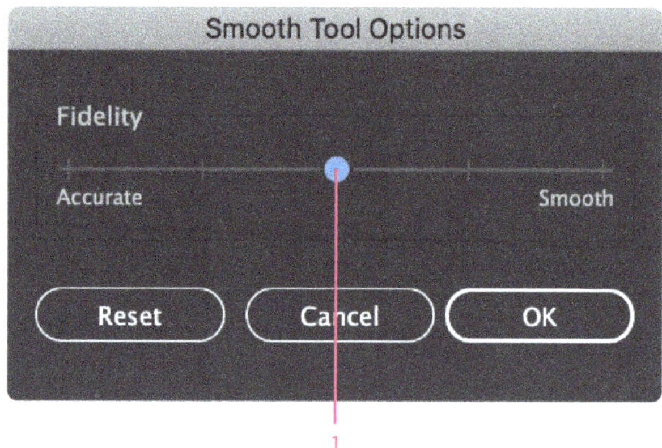

1.Fidelity: The higher the value, the smoother and less complex is the path.

Use the **Scissors Tool** (C) to split paths.

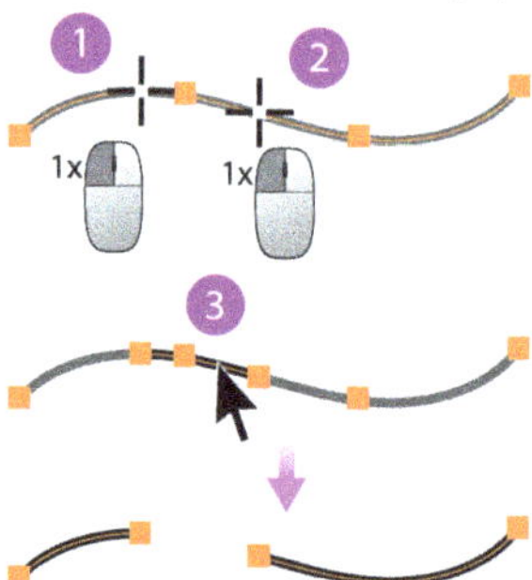

Step 1 and 2. To split a path, click in two places on the path.

Step 3. Use the **Selection Tool** (V) or **Direct Selection Tool** (A) to click the segment between the two new anchor points.

Step 4. Press the Backstep button to delete the selected segment.   ←

The **Scissors Tool** (C) is better suited for separating paths and deleting segments than the **Eraser Tool** (Shift+E), because eraser tool change the shape of the path so that precise separation is not possible. Eraser Tool is used to delete fills inside an objects.

5.29 STROKE SETTINGS

In the stroke panel you can adjust the strock weight, for technical drawings different stroke weights are used to make a technical fashion drawing look more aesthetic (see examples on pages 137 -138).

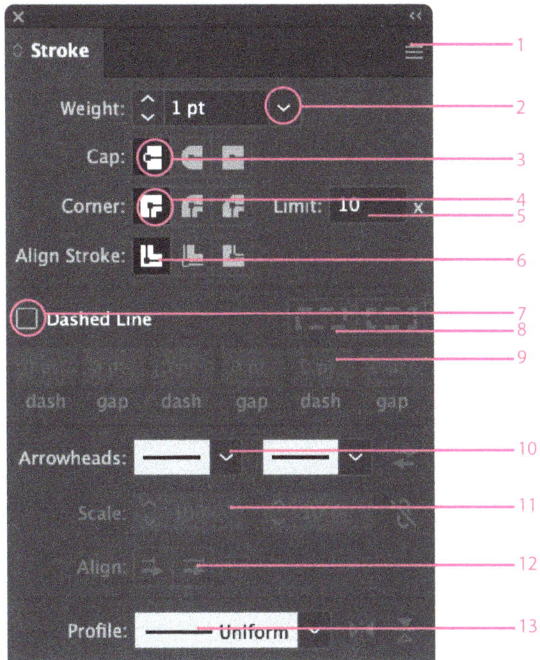

Step 1. Select an object using the selection tool **Selection Tool** (V) (see page 32 for selection techniques).

Step 2. Open the stroke panel:
Window > Stroke

1. Show options
2. Stroke weight corresponds to the thickness of the stroke (see example)

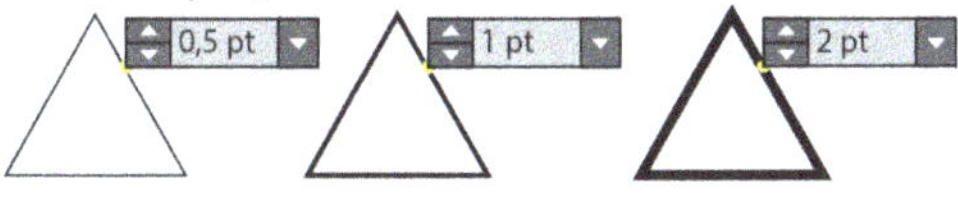

3. "Cap" determines how you want the path to look at the start or end point. You have three options: "Butt Cap" "Round Cap" "Projecting Cap".

When the dashed line (point 9) are activated, the set "Cap" is automatically applied to the line. If "Cap" is set to "Round Cap" and the distance between stroke and gap is too small, there is a risk that after exporting the drawing (e.g. jpg format) "dashed line" will no longer be clearly distinguishable from a normal line. Which can lead to misunderstanding, because "dashed line" is used in the technical fashion drawing, among other things, to represent a simple quilting seam. Therefore, better is to set the "Cap" to "Butt Cap".

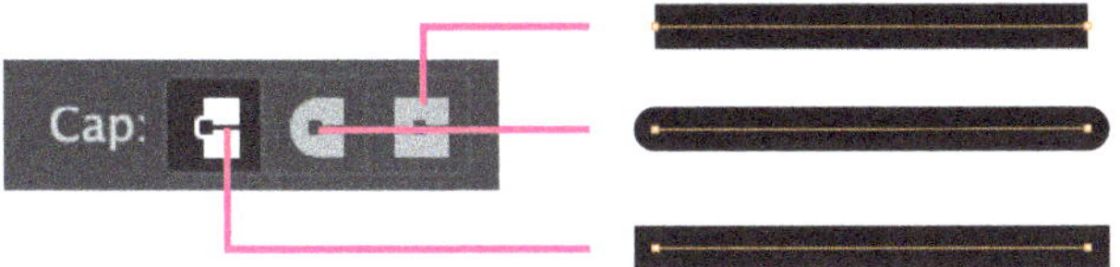

4. Corner determines how corners of a previously selected path should look. You have three options: "Miter Join" "Rounded Join" "Bevel Join".

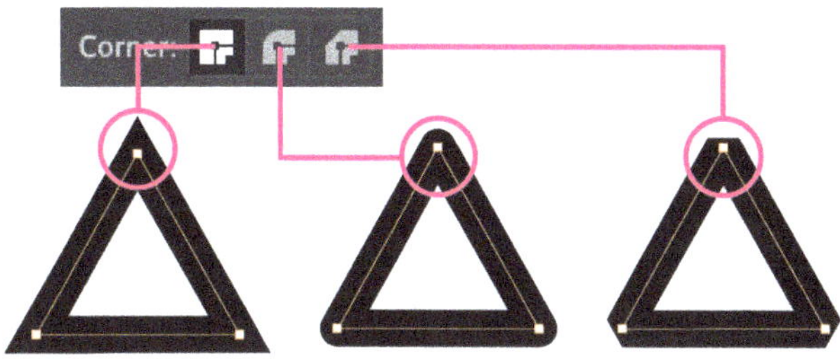

5.The miter limit determines (between 1 and 500) when the program switches from a pointed to a flattened corner. The standard miter limit is 10.

6. With „align stroke" you can align the stroke along the path (possible only for closed objects). You have again three options: „Align Stroke to Center", „Align Stroke to Inside", „Align Stroke to Outside".

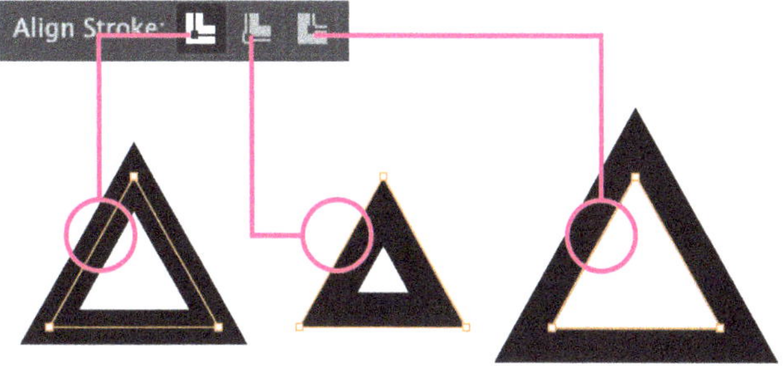

7. Dashed line setting is predominantly used to represent a simple quilting seam in technical fashion drawings.

8. The setting „Preserves exact dash and gap lengths" and „Aligns dashes to corners and path ends, adjusting lengths to fit"

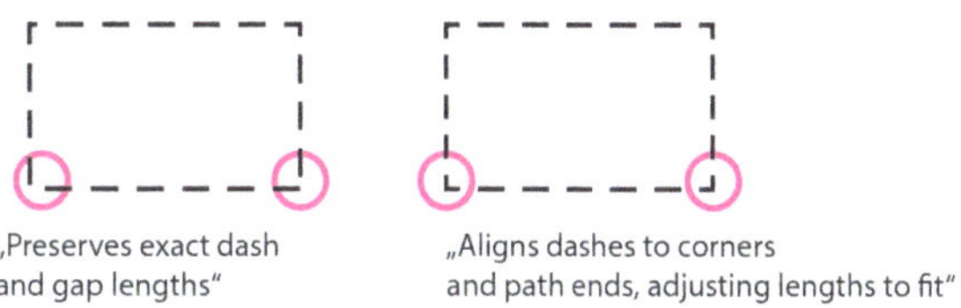

„Preserves exact dash and gap lengths"

„Aligns dashes to corners and path ends, adjusting lengths to fit"

Both settings are used for technical fashion drawings.

9. Entering the line length and gap length in the corresponding fields defines a line pattern (e.g. quilting seam).

Depending on the size of the drawing, use the following settings:
- dash: **5**/gap: **3,5**, dash: **3**/gap: **2**, dash: **2**/gap: **1,5**.

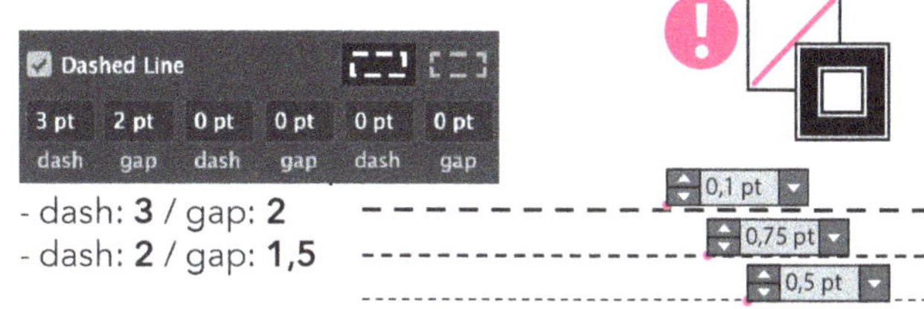

- dash: **3** / gap: **2**
- dash: **2** / gap: **1,5**

10. „Arrowheads" can be used for dimensioning of technical drawings (see example on page 138).

11. You can scale the beginning and end of the arrowheads independently.

12. You can place arrowhead at the end of the path.

13. With the "Profile" setting, you can set different stroke profiles for the stroke, for example, to make a line look graphically more interesting.

6. SHAPE TOOLS

With the shape tools you can create for example angular and rounded pockets, buttons, various accessories.

These tools are summarized in the tools panel. The following tools are available for selection:

- **Rectangle Tool** (M)

- **Rounded Reactangle Tool**

- **Ellipse Tool** (L)

- **Polygon Tool**

- **Star Tool**

- **Flare Tool**

The tools are grouped together, click the group with the left mouse button and hold down the button for about 1 second, then the group opens and you have access to other tools (or click the right mouse button). It applies to all tools with a small triangle at the bottom right.

6.1 RECTANGLE TOOL

The **Rectangle Tool** (M) draws squares and rectangles.

Select the Rectangle tool and set the stroke color to "black" and fill color to "without."

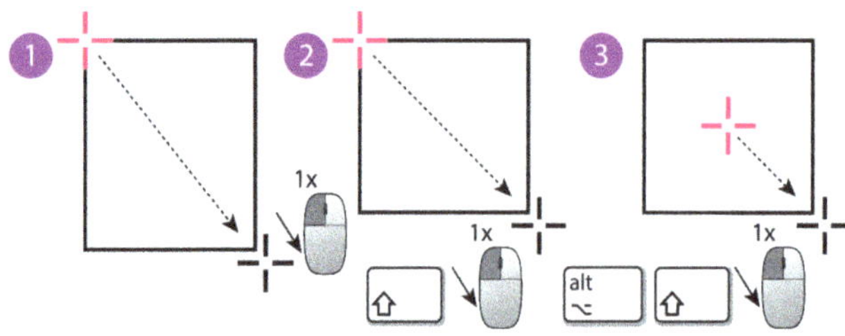

Step 1. To draw a rectangle, drag the mouse pointer (displayed as a cross) in the diagonal direction while holding down the left mouse button until the rectangle assumes the desired shape and size.

Step 2. To draw a square, hold down the **Shift** key and pull the cursor by holding down the left mouse button in diagonal direction, until the square assumes the desired size.

Step 3. To draw a square from the center, hold down the **alt/option** + **Shift key** and drag the mouse pointer in the diagonal direction while holding down the left mouse button until the square assumes the desired size.

To create a rectangle by entering values, click anywhere in the document, set the width and height in the options window, then click OK.
Starting with **Illustrator CC**, you can create a rounded rectangle or circle from a rectangle.

Step 1. Draw a rectangle. **Step 2.** Activate the **Selection Tool** (V). **Step 3.** While holding down the left mouse button, drag one of the four small circular symbols ⊙ until the desired shape is reached.

6.2 ROUNDED RECTANGLE TOOL

The **Rounded Rectangle Tool** is used to draw rounded pocket forms, belt buckles etc.
Select rounded reactangle tool and put the stroke colour to "Black" and fill colour to "without".

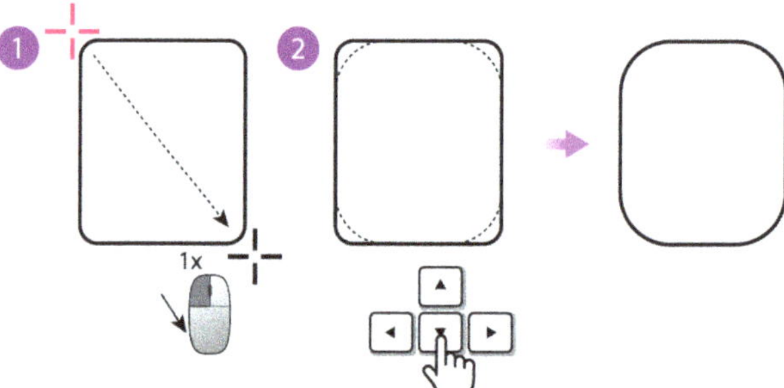

Step 1. To draw a rounded rectangle, drag the mouse pointer in the diagonal direction while holding down the left mouse button until the rectangle assumes the desired shape and size.
Step 2. Do not release the left mouse button and click the keyboard arrow keys (▲ increases the round, ▼ decreases the round).
When the **Shift** key is additionally pressed, an isosceles square is drawn and by holding down the **alt/option** key the square is drawn from the center. With **alt/option** + **Shift** key, an isosceles square is drawn from the center.

You can also round each corner individually.

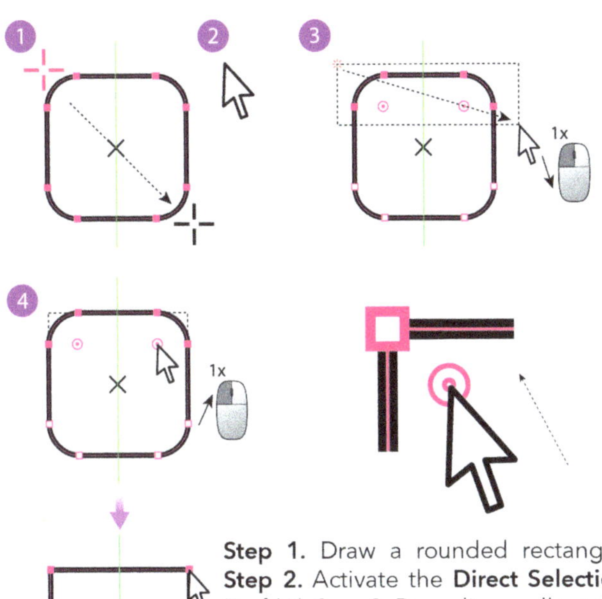

Step 1. Draw a rounded rectangle. **Step 2.** Activate the **Direct Selection Tool** (A). **Step 3.** Drag diagonally at the top four anchor points to create a selection. **Step 4.** While holding down the left mouse button, drag one of the two small circular symbols ⊙ until the desired shape is reached.

To create a rounded rectangle by entering values, use the **rounded rectangle tool** and click anywhere in the document, set the width, height, and corner radius in the options window, then confirm with OK.

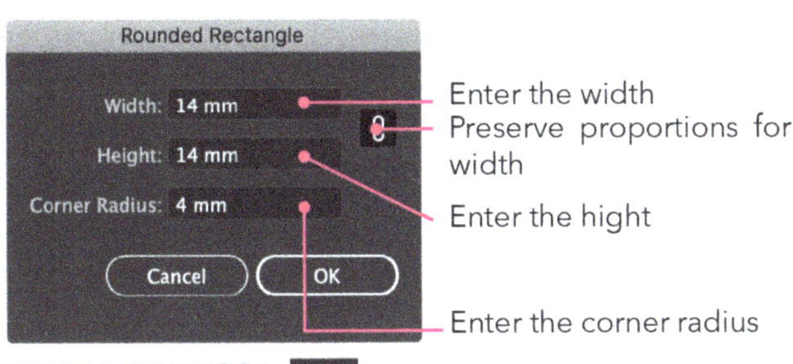

6.3 ELLIPSE TOOL

The **Ellipse Tool** (L) creates circles and ellipses. The ellipse tool is used to draw buttons, various metal elements, etc.

Select the ellipse tool and set the stroke color to "black" and "fill" color to without.

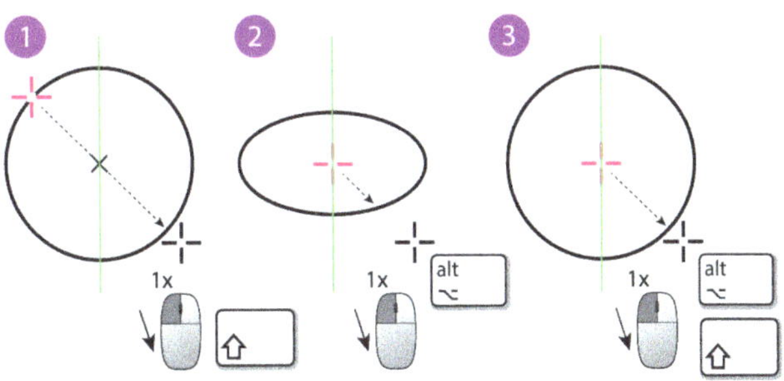

Step 1. To draw an ellipse, hold down the left mouse button and drag the pointer in the diagonal direction until the ellipse becomes the desired shape and size. To draw a circle, hold down the **Shift** button and drag the pointer in the diagonal direction while holding down the left mouse button.
Step 2. When the **alt/option** key is activated, the ellipse is pulled from the center.
Step 3. To draw an ellipse proportionally from the center, hold down the **alt/option** + **Shift** button and drag the mouse pointer in the diagonal direction while holding down the left mouse button until the ellipse assumes the desired size.

6.4 POLYGON TOOL 

Select the **Polygon Tool** and set the stroke color to "black" and fill color to "without."

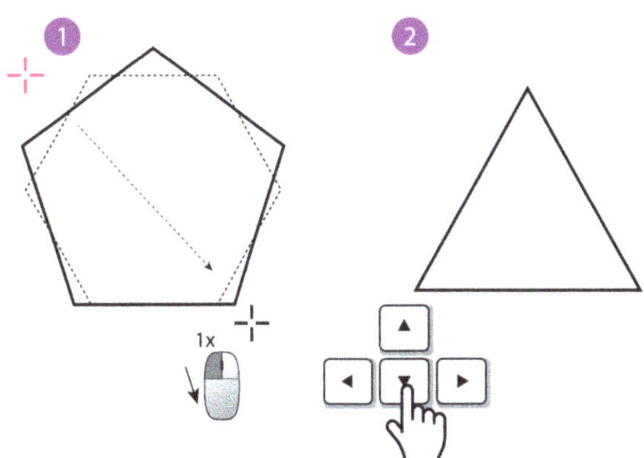

Step 1. While holding down the left mouse button, drag the pointer clockwise or counterclockwise until the polygon assumes the desired shape and size.
Step 2. *Do not* release the left mouse button and click the keyboard arrow keys (▲ increase the number of sides, ▼ decrease the number of sides).
When the **Shift** button is additionally pressed, the object is aligned at a 90 ° angle and by holding down the **alt/option** key the object is drawn from the center.

You can also create a polygon by entering values. Click anywhere in the document, select the radius and number of sides for the polygon, and click OK.

6.5 STAR TOOL

Select the **Star tool** and set the stroke color to "black" and fill color to "without."

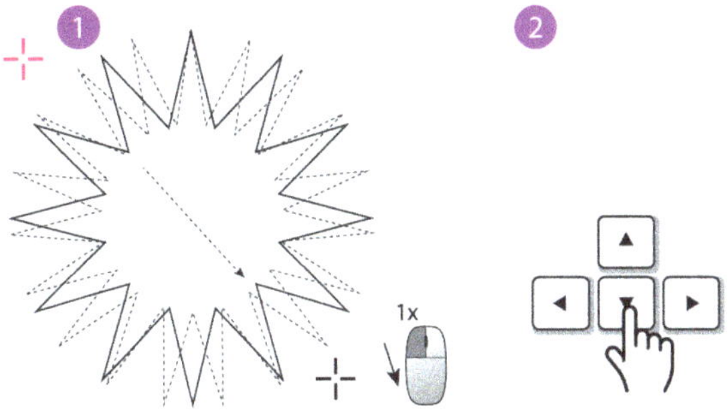

Step 1. While holding down the left mouse button, drag the pointer clockwise or counterclockwise until the star assumes the desired shape and size.

Step 2. *Do not* release the left mouse button and click the keyboard arrow keys (⬆ increase the number of points of the star, decrease the number of points of the star ⬇). When the **Shift** button is additionally pressed, the object is aligned at a 90 ° angle.

You can also create a star by entering values. Click anywhere in the document, **Radius 1** enters the distance between the center and the inner points of the star, and **Radius 2** enters the distance between the center and the outer points of the star. Under "Points" you can enter the desired number of points. Confirm your entries with "OK."

There are three important settings in the dialog box. **Width and height**: Tool size is set, **Angle**: Tool angle is set, **Intensity**: Tool intensity is set (see example ②, here the setting was set between 10% -15% to keep precise control over the tool).

Apply: Place the tool over an selected object and hold down the left mouse button and move the mouse pointer.

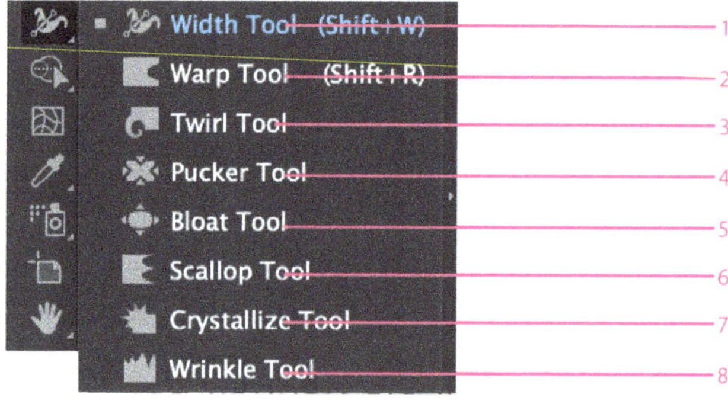

ⓘ

With the Rectangle, Rounded Rectangle, Ellipse, Polygon, Star Tool, Line Segment, Arc, Spiral Tool, you can achieve interesting effects by holding down the following keyboard keys on Mac [><] when drawing these shapes: (Due to the different keyboard assignments, this option is mostly available on the Mac OS system).

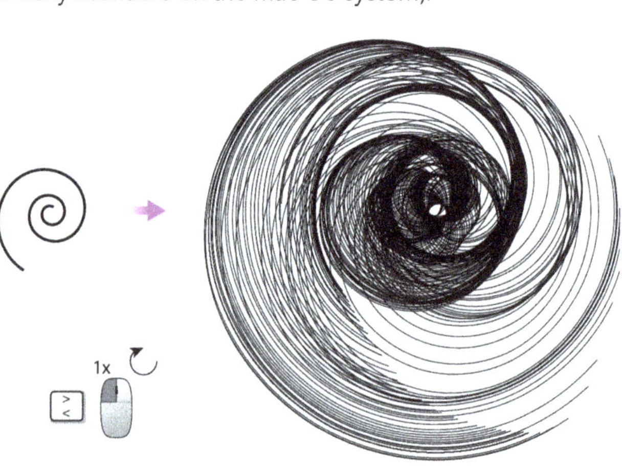

6.6 FLARE TOOL

The **Flare Tool** is hardly used in technical fashion drawing, but in fashion illustrations you can use it to better highlight the plasticity of a figurine or spatiality.

Select the **flare tool** and drag the pointer in the diagonal direction while holding down the left mouse button. By double-clicking on the tool in the toolbar, the dialog box opens, where you can make further settings.

6.7 DEFORMATION TOOLS

With the deformation tools, you can deform strokes and fills in different ways to create, for example, fur optics, pleated optics, etc. (see examples). By double-clicking on one of these tools in the toolbar, the dialog box is opened, where you can make further settings.

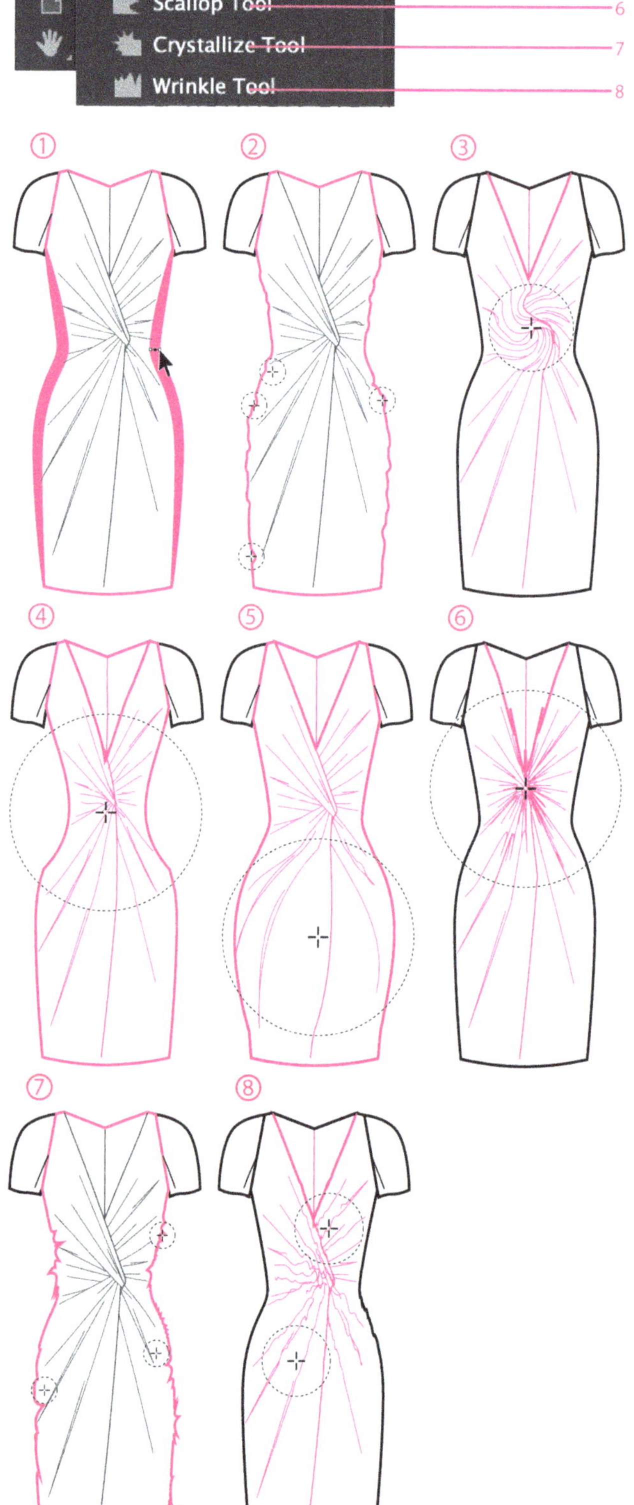

7. SELECTION TOOLS

To modify an object (shape, stroke, color, anchor point etc.) in Adobe Illustrator, it must be selected first.

Various selection techniques are available for this purpose.

Under menu View, the following options must always be activated: **View > Show Edges** and **View > Show Bounding Box**.

Selection Tools

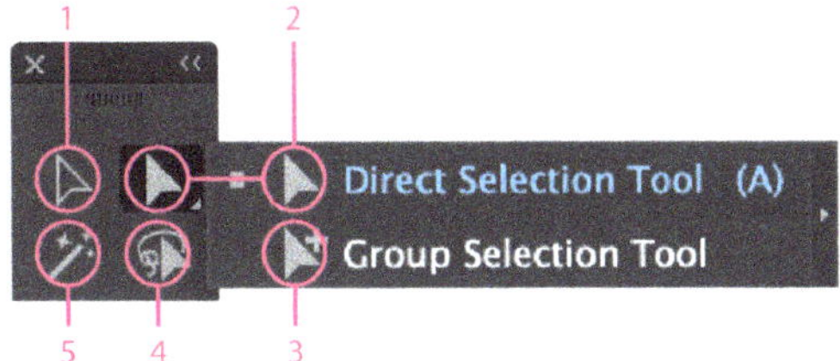

There are five selection tools available:

1. Selection Tool (V)

2. Direct Selection Tool (A)

3. Group Selection Tool

4. Lasso Tool (Q) 

5. Magic Wand Tool (Y)

Predominantly is used the
selection tool  and the direct selection tool 

1. Selection Tool (V)
The Selection tool allows you to select only the entire object or group of objects. All anchor points of the object are selected.
Selection tool is mostly used to transform, move, and delete entire objects.

2. Direct Selection Tool (A)
You can use the direct selection tool to precisely select individual anchor points of an object or group of objects. Thus, individual anchor points of the object can be selected.
Direct selection tool is mostly used to make corrections to objects (paths), delete individual anchor points, or copy fragments of a path.

3. Group Selection Tool
Use the group selection tool to select individual objects in an object group. All anchor points of an object are always selected.

4. Lasso Tool (Q)
The lasso tool allows you to precisely select individual anchor points of an object or group of objects. Lasso tool performs the same functions as the direct selection tool. This tool is mostly used for very complicated objects if it is to difficult to make a selection with a rectangle (direct selection tool).

6. Magic Wand Tool (Y)

With the magic wand tools you can select objects with similar surface colour, stroke colour, stroke weight. Double-click the tool to set the tolerance for selection in the options window.

7.1 SELECTION TECHNIQUES

Select entire objects using the **Selection Tool** (V).

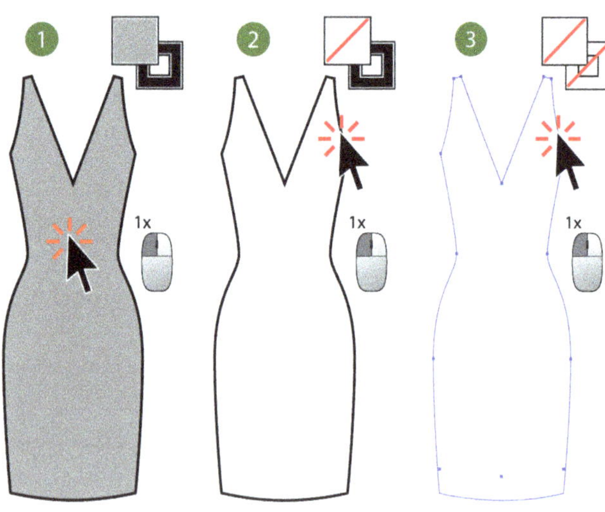

Step 1. To select the entire object, left-click the fill color of the object (press and release the left mouse button).

Step 2. To select the entire object, left-click the stroke color of the object (press and release the left mouse button).

Step 3. To select the entire object, click on the path of the object if there is no stroke or fill color, activate the outline view: **View > Outline** (cmd + Y / Ctrl + Y)

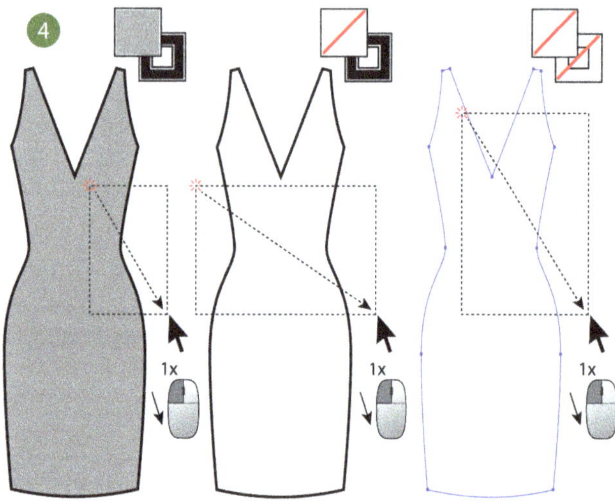

Step 4. Use the selection tool to drag a selection rectangle around the object while holding down the left mouse button. The selection rectangle can only touch the object in one place, so it does not have to be dragged over the entire object. (Press, drag, and release the mouse button).

Select individual anchor points using the **Direct Selection Tool** (A).

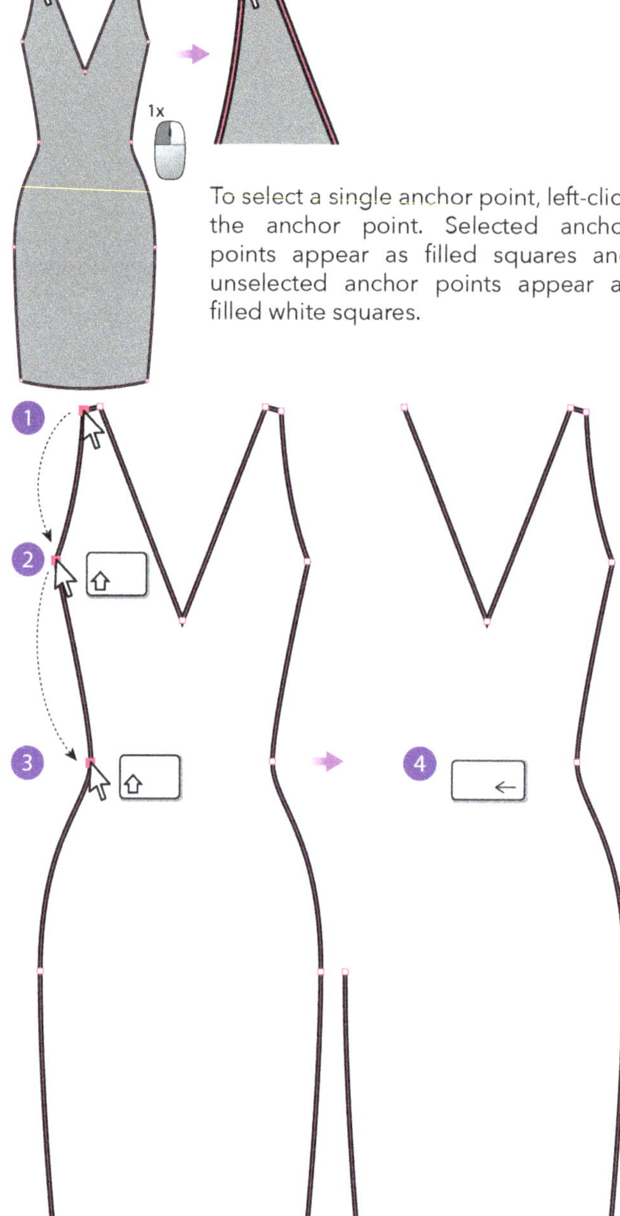

To select a single anchor point, left-click the anchor point. Selected anchor points appear as filled squares and unselected anchor points appear as filled white squares.

Step 1. To select the first anchor point, left-click an anchor point.
Step 2. Activate **Shift** key (do not release) and select another anchor point.
Step 3. Do not release **Shift** key and select another anchor point.
Step 4. Click the **Backspace** key (or **delete** button) to delete selected anchor points (the path created by connecting anchor points is deleted).

Select individual anchor points using the **Lasso Tool** (Q)

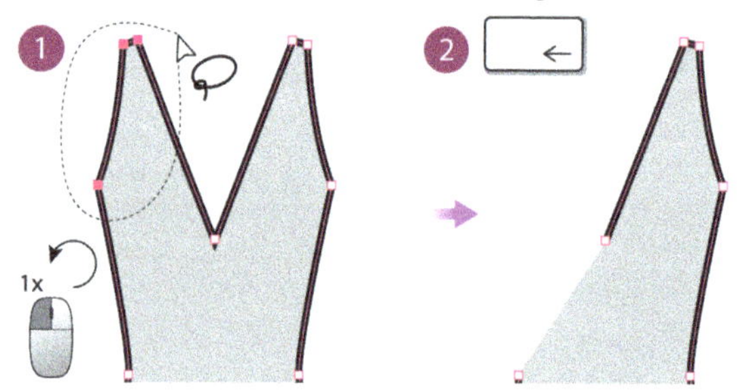

Step 1. To select a single or multiple anchor points, hold down the left mouse button and move around the anchor points you want to select.
Step 2. Click the **Backstep** key to delete selected anchor points (the path created by the anchor point connection is deleted).

Step 1. To select a single or multiple anchor points, hold down the left mouse button and move the pointer around the anchor points you want to select.
Step 2. Activate **Shift** key (do not release) and select another anchor point.
Step 3. Activate **backstep** key to delete selected anchor points (the path created by connected anchor points is deleted).

If the **Shift** key is not pressed, the previous selection is disabled.

Use the **Magic Wand tool** (Y) to select similar objects.

Use the Magic Wand tool to click an object if there are objects with similar fill color in the document, then they will be selected.
To select the objects with the same stroke color, stroke width, opacity, or blending method, double-click the magic wand tool (options window opens).

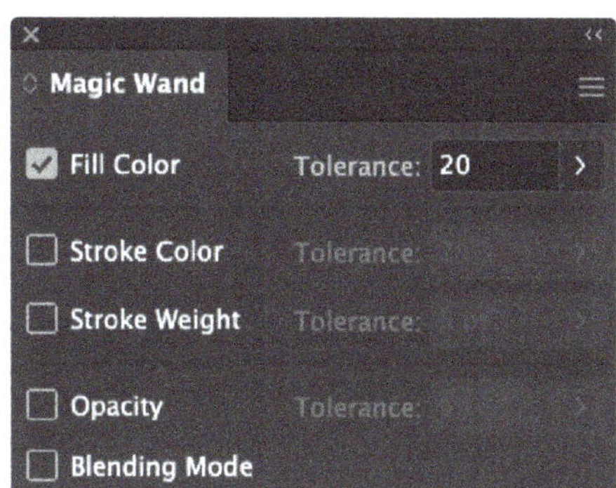

The higher the tolerance value, the more objects with a similar, for example, fill color are selected.

Select objects in the Layers panel.

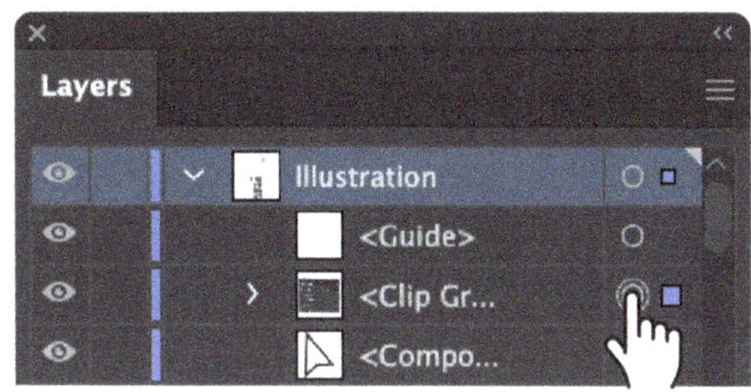

Open Layers panel: **Window > Layers**
Clicking the circle next to the layer or sublayer name, than all objects on that layer or sublayer will be selected.

If you additionally hold down the **Shift** key and click more circles when selecting in the layers panel, you can add more layers and sublayers to the existing selection.

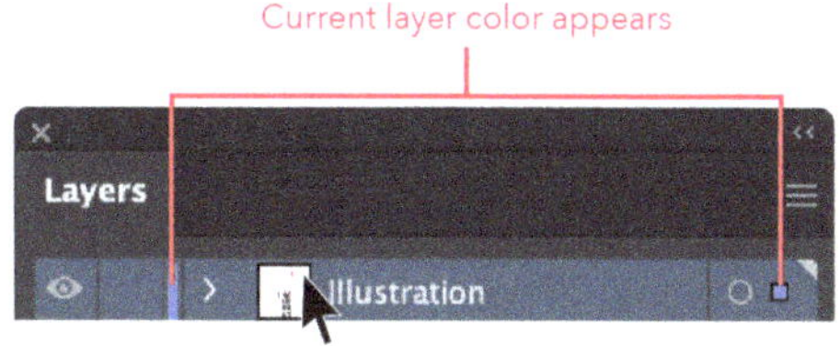

Double-click the layer preview to change the selection color of this layer.

Other selection techniques.

Select > Same... and **Select > Object...**
Here, various possibilities are offered to select objects, e.g. by brush strokes, clipping masks etc.
These choices are very precise (there is no tolerance setting as with the magic wand tool).

When selecting objects that have different fill or stroke colors, a question mark appears to highlight the inconsistency of colors (see example).

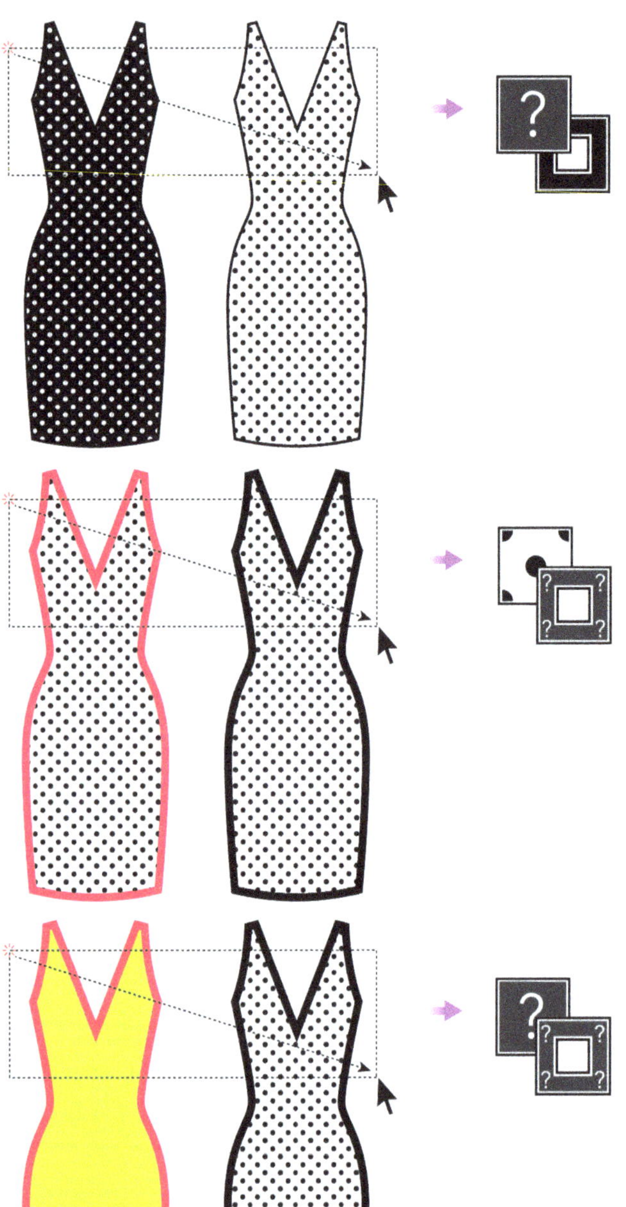

Move objects and individual anchor points.

Use the **Selection Tool** (V) to move entire objects: Hold down the left mouse button and drag the object in any direction.

Alternatively, you can use the arrow keys
(but the object must be selected first with the selection tool).

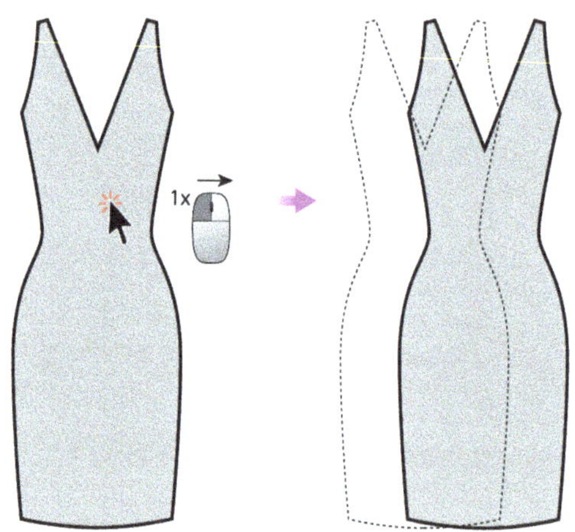

Use the **Direct Selection tool** (A) to move individual anchor points: Place the tool over an anchor point, click on the point, do not release the left mouse button, and drag.

Alternatively, you can use the arrow keys
(the anchor points must be selected first using the direct selection tool).

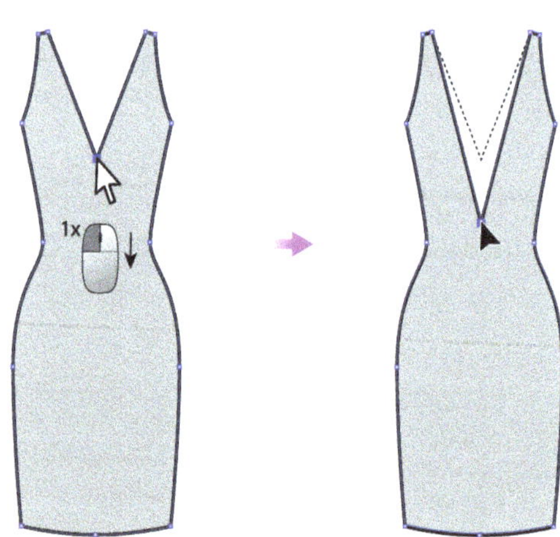

7.2 COPY OBJECTS

Adobe Illustrator has a variety of ways to duplicate objects (copy and paste).

Option 1:

Mostly, the "create a copy on the same place" command is used. In this case, the duplicate is created above the original object.

The object must be selected first.
Then activate the following shortcut command:
command + C / Ctrl + C (**Edit > Copy**)

Deselect

Option 1:
To deselect, use the **Selection tool** (V) or **Direct Selection tool** (A) (left mouse button) and click in the blank drawing area.

Option 2:
Select the following shortcut key command:
Mac: command + Shift + A key / PC: Ctrl + Shift + A key

Option 3:
Select > Deselect.

 Before you start drawing a new object (path), it is always better to deselect the previous object!

Than **Edit > Paste in Front**: cmd + F / Ctrl + F

The duplicate is placed on the original object, which does not clearly indicate whether a duplicate is present.

However, it is visible in the **Layers panel** because a new sublayer is created for each duplicate.

two duplicates lie
above one another

Option 2:

You can also insert the duplicate behind the original object.
Edit > Copy: cmd + C / Ctrl + C
Edit > Paste in Back: cmd + B / Ctrl + B

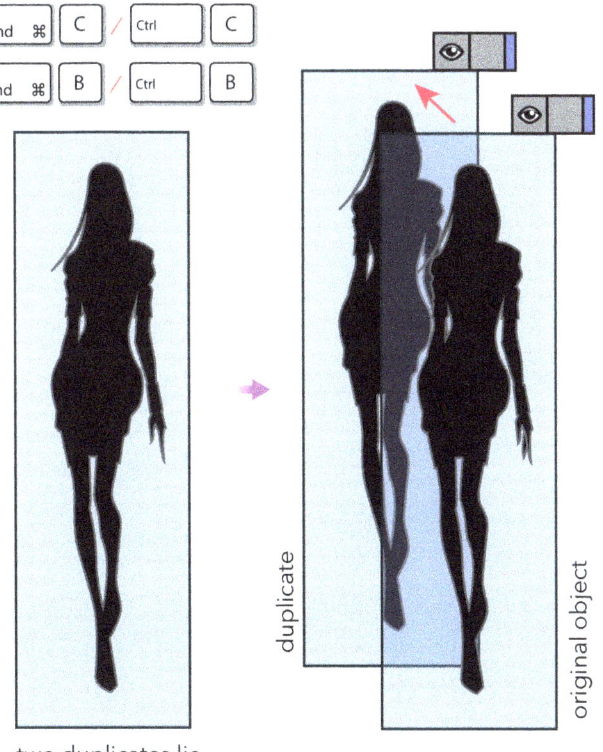

two duplicates lie
above one another

Option 3:

You can paste the duplicate in an offset location (but it is rarely used because this copy method is inaccurate).
Edit > Copy: cmd + C / Ctrl + C
Edit > Paste: cmd + V / Ctrl + V

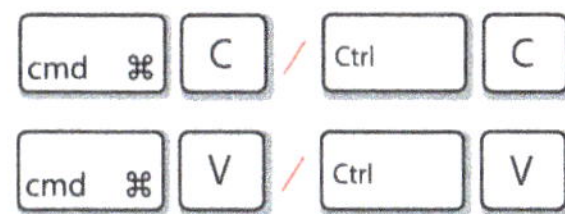

Option 4:

You can insert the duplicate at the original location. This copying method is identical to "Paste in Front".
Edit > Copy: cmd + C / Ctrl + C
Edit > Paste in Place:
Shift + cmd + V / Shift + Ctrl + V

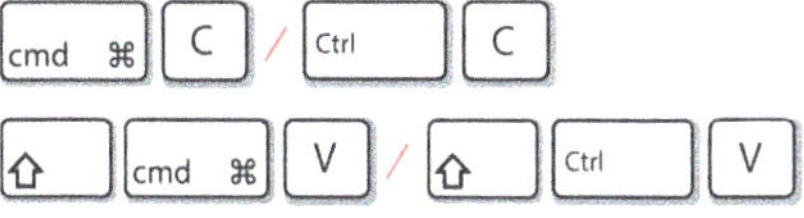

Option 5:

You have the option by dragging with the mouse cursor to create a duplicate (drag&drop method)

To do this, press the **alt/option** key (do not release the mouse button) and drag the object with the **Selection Tool** (V) while holding down the left mouse button. At a possible destination, first release the mouse button and then release the **alt/option** key (see Example A).

If you also hold down the **Shift** key, the duplicate is aligned vertically or horizontally with the original object (see Example B).

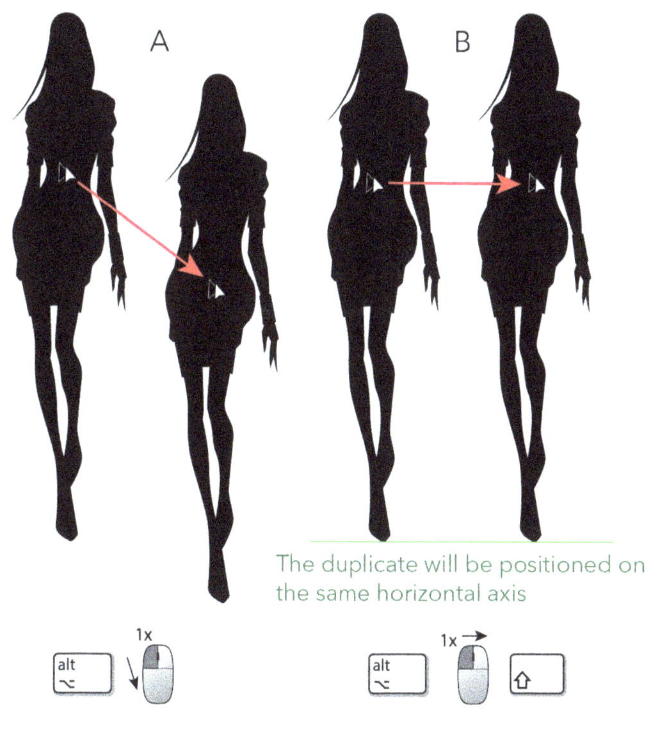

When copying, the selection tool arrow ▲ is replaced by a double arrow ▷▷ .

Option 6:

You can use arrow keys to create a duplicate.

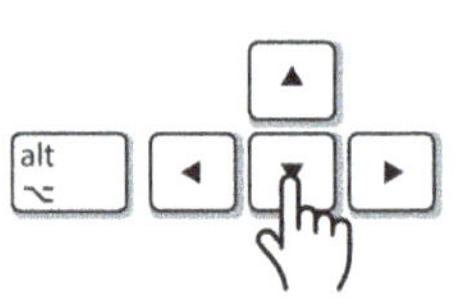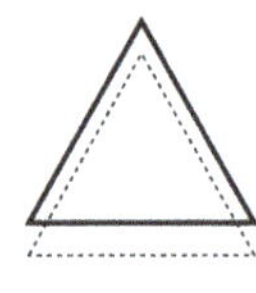

Select an object, press the **alt/option** key (do not release the mouse button), press the arrow key and release, then release the **alt/option** key.

Option 7:

You can create duplicates from the Layers panel.
Open the Layers panel **Window > Layers**
The object should not be selected.

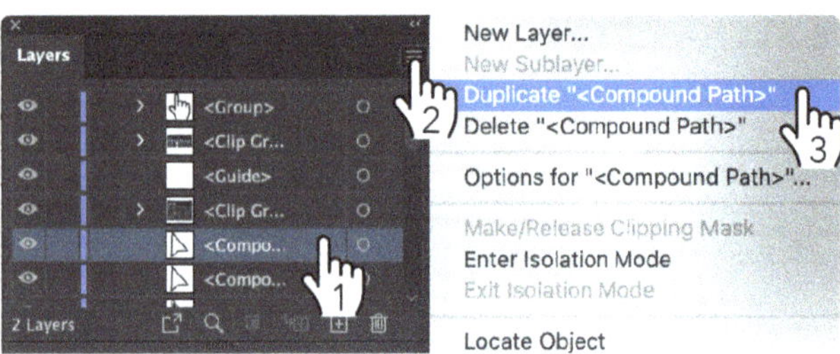

Step 1. Select layer or sublayer.
Step 2. Select layer or sublayer menu.
Step 3. Click on „..." duplicate.

7.3 REFLECTING OBJECTS AND SIMULTANEOUSLY COPY THEM 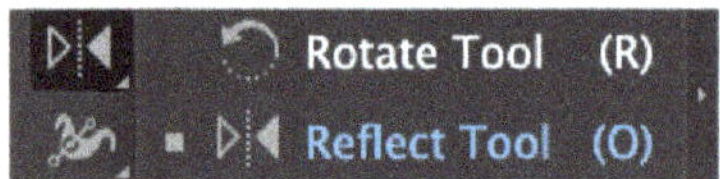

With the **Reflect Tool** (O) reflects objects along a fixed axis. The object is reflected on a specified invisible axis. You also have the option to reflect objects using the "Reflect" menu command **Object > Transform > Reflect**. In a technical fashion drawing, a lot is done with the reflection tool, because in most cases only half of the technical drawing is drawn and then a reflected "copy" of it is created.

Step 1. Use the **Selection Tool** (V) to select one or more objects.

Step 2. Activate the **Reflect Tool** (O) (it is in a common group with the Rotate tool). The cursor is converted into a crosshairs. –¦– Press the **alt/option** key (do not release) and left-click where you want the mirror axis to be (a dialog box opens), then release the **alt/option** key and the mouse button.

Step 3. In the dialog box, select Vertical and click Copy. Always activate the "Preview" to see the result immediately. Note: If you want to reflect the object horizontally, select Horizontal.

Before the object is reflected, it must always be selected with the **Selection Tool** (V)! For example, if you try to reflect immediately after creating the last anchor point, then only this single anchor point is reflected and not the entire object. See further information on "Error Checklist" on page 134.

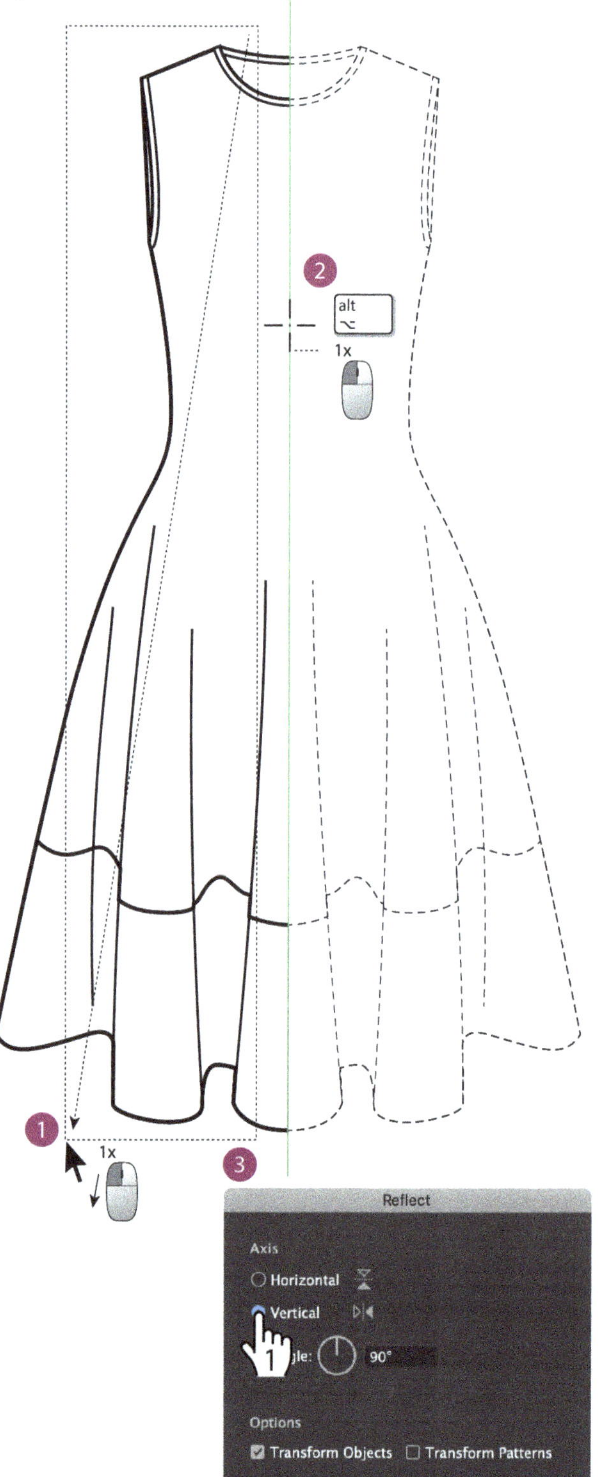

7.4 ROTATE TOOL

With the **Rotate Tool** (R) the objects will be rotated around a fixed point. You can also rotate and copy objects simultaneously.

Step 1. Use the **Selection Tool** (V) to select one or more objects.
Step 2. Activate the **Rotate Tool** (R) (it is in a common group with the Reflect Tool). The cursor is replaced by a crosshairs. —¦— Press the **alt/option** key (do not release) and left-click where you want the axis of rotation to be (a dialog box opens), then release the **alt/option** key and mouse button.
Step 3. In the dialog box, type 30° for the "Angle" option and click "Copy". Always activate the "Preview" to see the result immediately.
Step 4. Now you can generate an other copy with the same settings, activate the following short key command: cmd + D / Ctrl + D or **Object > Transform > Transform Again**.

Further possibilities to work with the rotate tool:

- You can also rotate the object around its center point by dragging the pointer in a circular motion anywhere in the document window.

- If you want to set a new origin for the rotation, click anywhere in the document window once, then move the pointer away from the origin and drag it in a circular motion.

Objects can also be rotated with the bounding box.

1. Use the **Selection tool** (V) to select one or more objects.
2. Place the pointer outside the bounding box near a handle so that the pointer appears as a double arrow ↘, and then move the pointer.

7.5 SCALE TOOL

The **Scale Tool** (S) scales objects by a fixed point. An object is enlarged or reduced horizontally (X-axis) and/or vertically (Y-axis). In fashion drawings, Scale tool is rarely used in its entirety because you can easily scale the objects with the **Selection Tool** (V) That is why I present you at this point three most important methods that you can use in your work.

Option 1: Scale with the **Selection Tool** (V)

Step 1. Use the **Selection Tool** (V) to select one or more objects.
Step 2. Press the **Shift** key (do not release during the operation), place the pointer on a corner (see figure), and drag the mouse while holding down the left mouse button in the diagonal direction. As a result, the proportions of the object are retained. First release the mouse button and then release the Shift key (otherwise the proportions of the object will not remain). If the **alt/option** key is additionally pressed during scaling, the object is scaled from the center.

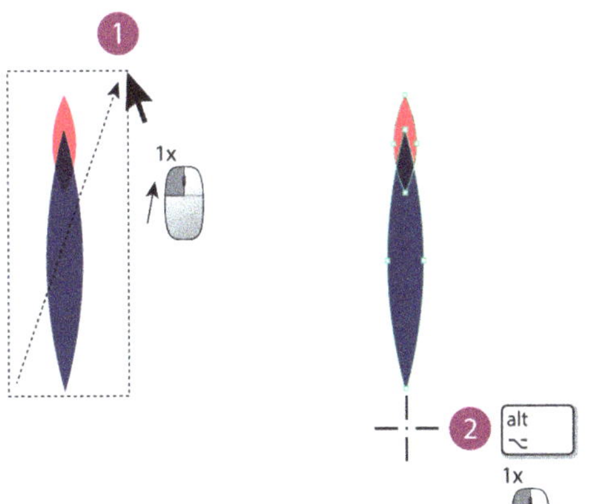

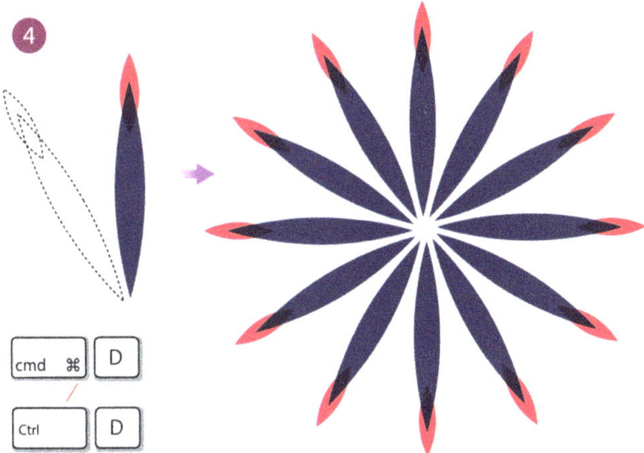

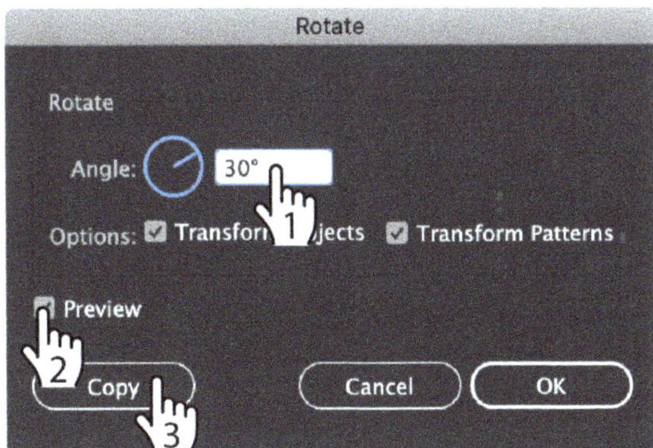

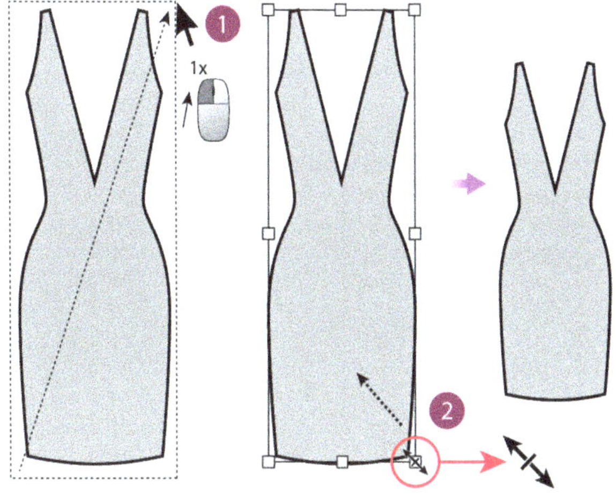

Option 2: Scale using the „Scale" panel.

Step 1. Use the **Selection Tool** (V) to select one or more objects.
Step 2. Double-click the scale tool in the toolbar (a dialog box opens), select the option "Uniform" and enter a percentage value in the box and click "OK" or "Copy" to create a duplicate with the new dimensions.

Source size is 100%, if e.g. 150% is given, the object is increased about 50%.

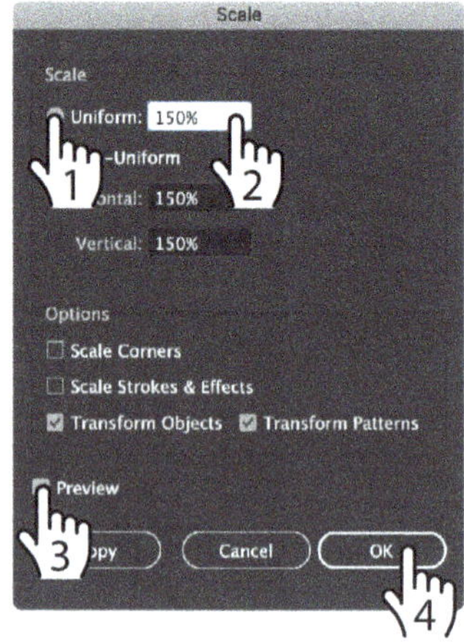

Option 3: Scale using the "Transform" panel. This possibility is very often used in technical fashion drawings (for example, to enter exact height and width for bags, buttons, etc.).

Step 1. Use the **Selection Tool** (V) to select one or more objects. By default it should appears in the control panel (at the top) "Transform" panel, if not, open **Window > Transform**.

Step 2. Adjust Width (1) and Height (2). You can also activate "Constrain Width and Height Proportions" (3) to lock proportions.

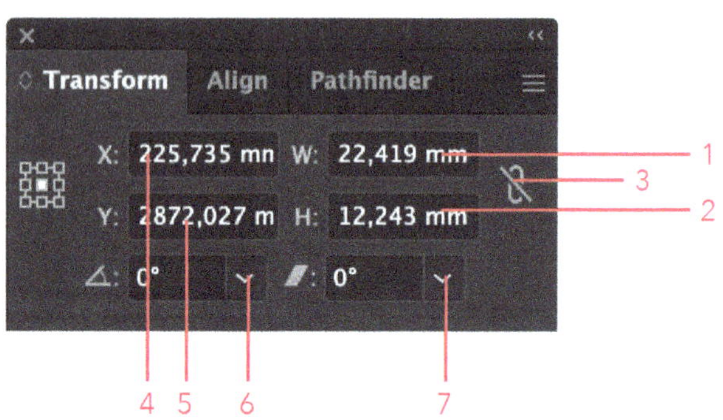

1. Enter "width" (also possible as cm, px input, it is then automatically changed to the default unit). You can change the units in the Units preferences (Illustrator>Preferences or Edit>Preferences).
2. "Height" value.
3. "Constrain Width and Height Proportions".
4. Position of the object in the workspace: Horizontal (X-axis)
5. Position of the object in the workspace: Vertical (Y-axis)
6. "Rotate" see **Rotate Tool** (R)
7. "Shear" see **Shear Tool**

7.6 SHEAR TOOL 

The **Shear Tool** deform objects around a fixed point. An object is deformed along the horizontal or vertical axis or by entering a specific angle relative to a specific axis. In fashion drawings shear tools is used in different ways, e.g. in the creation of patterns, pattern brushes or also accessories (bags, jewelry) which are created in three-quarter (3/4) presentation.

Option 1:

Step 1. Use the **Selection Tool** (V) to select one or more objects.
Step 2. Select the **Shear Tool** (it is in a common group with the Scale tool). While holding down the left mouse button, drag the mouse pointer arbitrarily in the document window until the object has the desired inclination. If you also activate the Shift key, the object retains its original width or height. Release the mouse button first and then the Shift key (otherwise the settings will be lost).

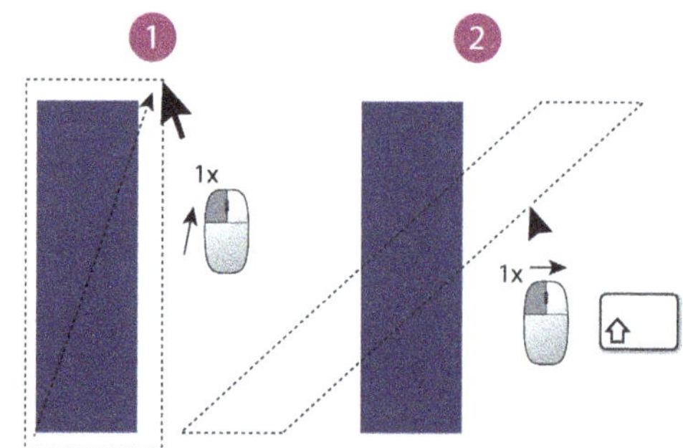

Option 2:

Step 1. Use the **Selection Tool** (V) to select one or more objects.
Step 2. In the toolbar, double-click the Shear Tool (a dialog box opens), select Horizontal or Vertical, and type a percentage in the shear angle box, and click "OK" or "Copy" to create a duplicate.

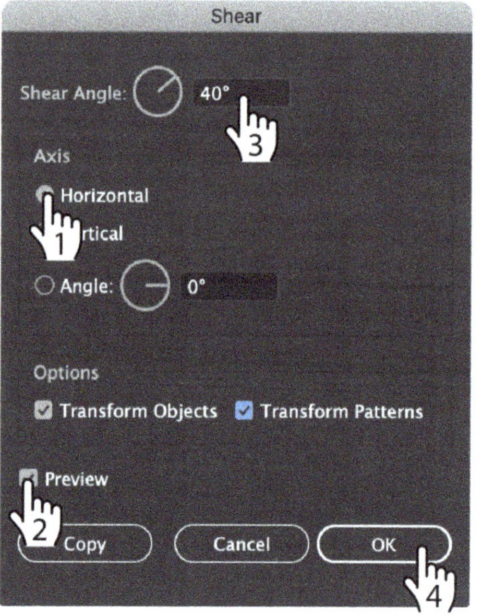

8.1 TUTORIAL: ROUND NECK T-SHIRT

REQUIREMENTS

-Choose in the tools panel the stroke color „black" and the fill color „None".

-Change the stroke weight (**Window > Stroke**) to **1pt** or **2pt**.

-Choose: **View > Rules >Show Rules, View > Guides > Lock Guides, View > Guides > Show Guides, View > Smart Guides, View > Snap to Point** and place a vertical guide.

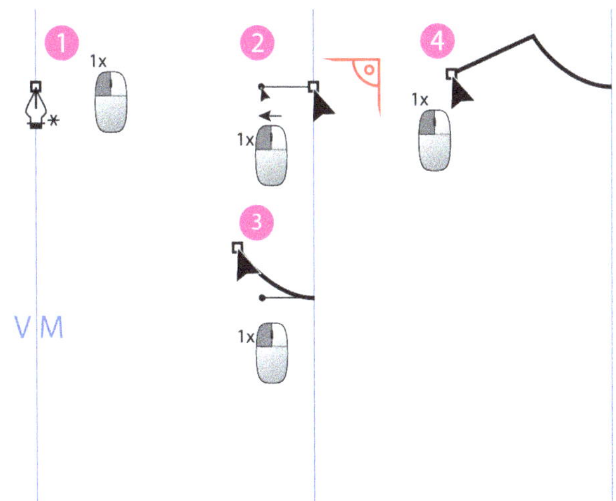

Step 1. Select the **Pen Tool** (P) and position the pen tool on the vertical guide, now hold down the left mouse button (do not release) to create the first anchor-point.
Step 2. Additionally hold down the **Shift** key (90° angle), also do not release, now drag the direction point to the left, then release first the mouse button and then the **Shift** key.
Step 3. Create a further anchor point (press and release the left mouse button, do not drag).
Step 4. Create a further anchor point (press and release the left mouse button, do not drag).
Step 5. Drag the direction point diagonally to the left down, then release the mouse button.

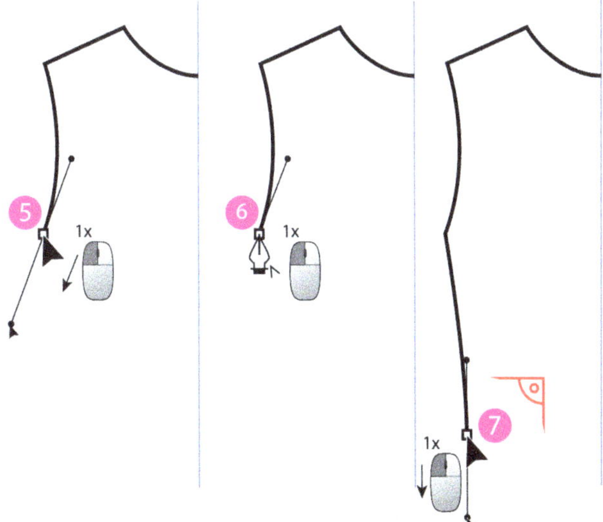

Step 6. Click the last anchor point (press and release the left mouse button) to create a corner. In this case the „pen tool" will be changed to **Anchor Point Tool** (Shift+C).

Step 7. Create a further anchor point (do not release the left mouse button), in addition hold down the **Shift** key (90° angle), also do not release the **Shift** key and drag the direction point down, then release first the mouse button and then the **Shift** key.

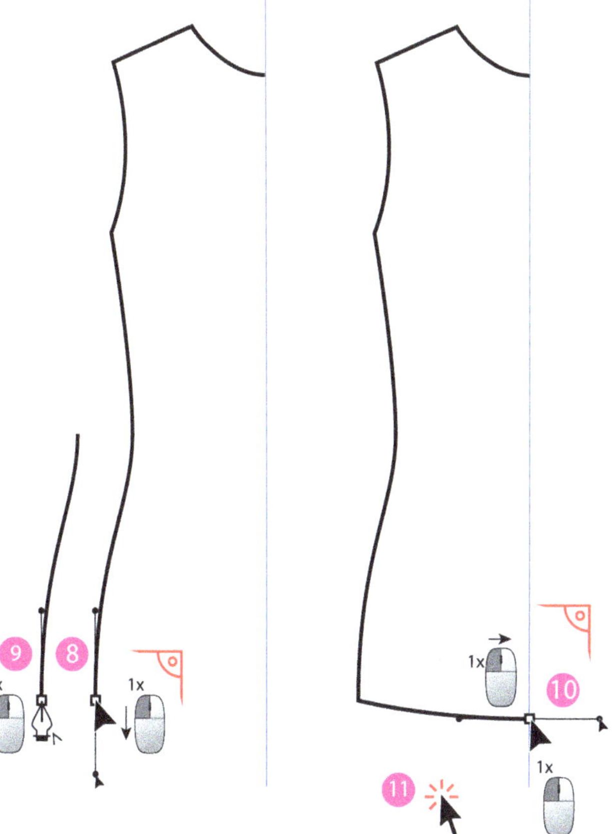

Step 8. Create a further anchor point (do not release the left mouse button), additionally hold down the **Shift** key (90° angle), also do not release the **Shift** key and drag the direction point down, then release first the mouse button and then the **Shift** key.
Step 9. Click the last anchor point (press and release the left mouse button).
Step 10. Create a further anchor point (do not release the mouse button), in addition hold down the **Shift** key (90° angle), also do not release the **Shift** key, now drag the direction point to the right, then release first the mouse button and then the **Shift** key.
Step 11. Click the V button (Selection Tool) and click on the empty drawing area to deselect the object. Alternatively you can activate the shortcut command+Shift+A / Ctrl+Shift+A.
Step 12. Hold down the left mouse button and drag with the **Selection Tool** (V) around the object to select it.
Step 13. Select the **Reflect Tool** (O), position the cursor on the vertical guide, hold down the **alt/option** key (do not release the alt key) and click the left mouse button. The Reflect dialog box appears ,then release the **alt** key.
Step 14. Activate the option „Vertical", then „Preview", check whether everything is OK and click „Copy". A mirrored duplicate is created.

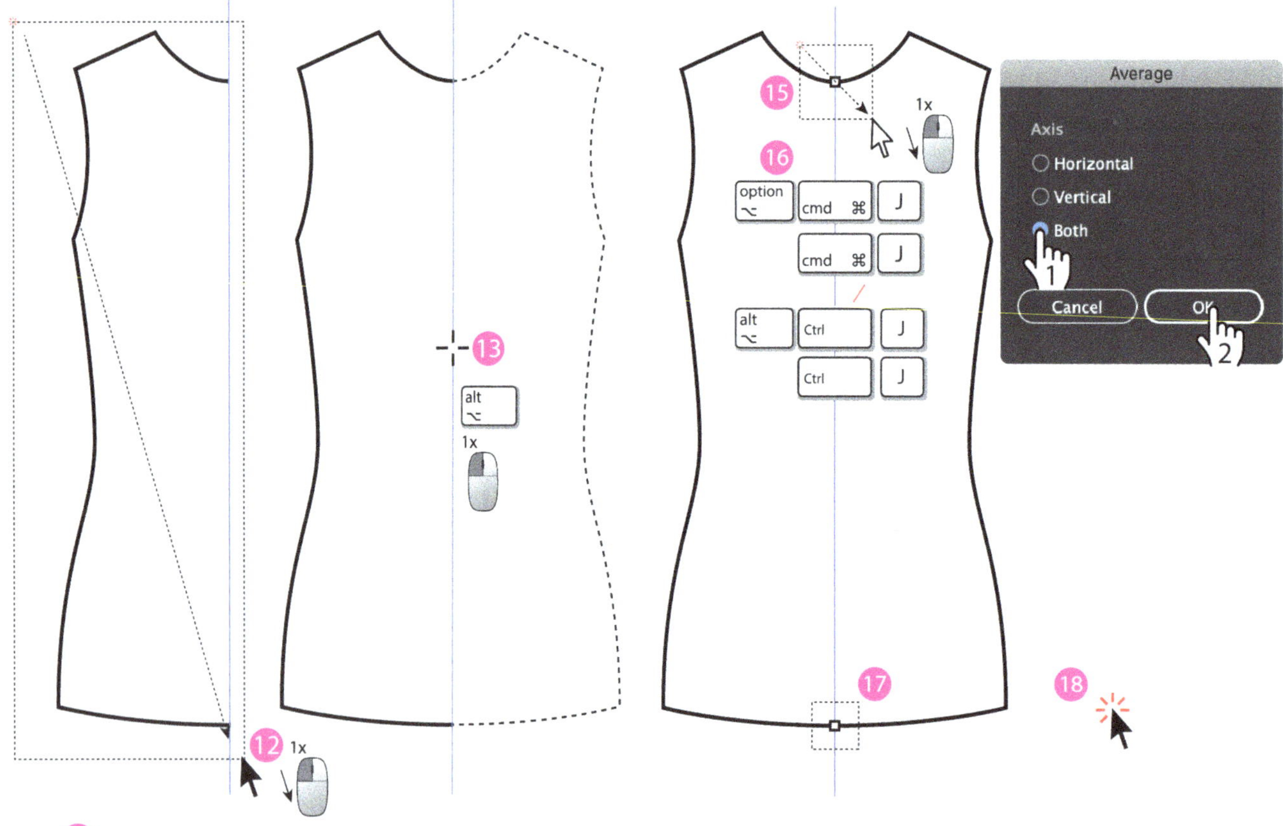

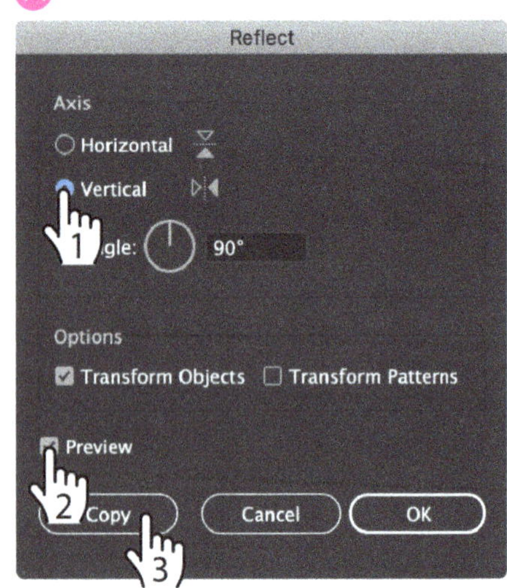

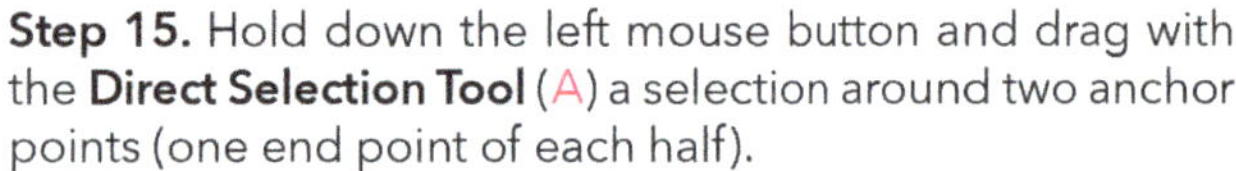

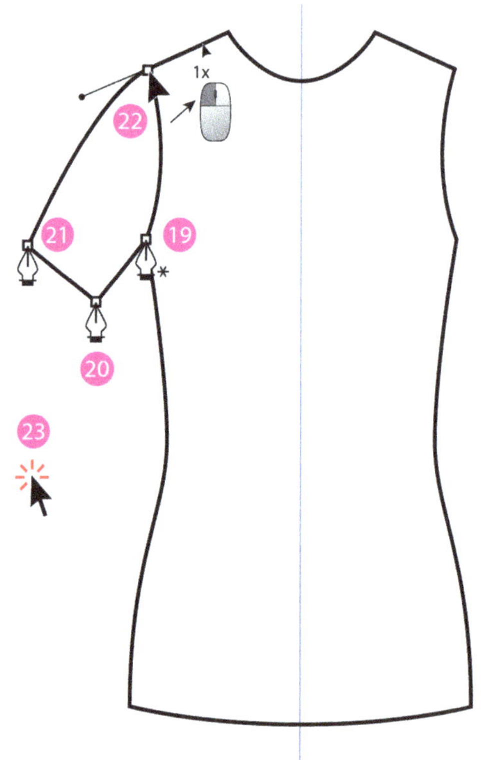

Step 15. Hold down the left mouse button and drag with the **Direct Selection Tool** (A) a selection around two anchor points (one end point of each half).
To join two paths always select two end points. If you choose more than two points the "join" command won´t function (see error-checklist page 134).
Step 16. Activate the shortcut option+command+J /alt+Ctrl+J (Average…). In the dialog box activate „Both", then „OK", then activate the shortcut command+J / Ctrl+J (Join).
Step 17. Repeat the steps 15 and 16.
Step18. Click on V key (Selection Tool) and click on a empty drawing area to deselect the object. Alternatively you can activate the shortcut command+Shift+A / Ctrl+Shift+A.
Step 19. Select the **Pen Tool** (P) and click the left mouse button to start a new path.
Steps 20/21. Create further anchor points (press and release the left mouse button).

Step 22. Create a further anchor point (do not release the left mouse button) and drag the direction point diagonally right, then release the mouse button.
Schritt 23. Click on V key (Selection Tool) and click on an empty drawing area to deselect the object. Alternatively you can activate the shortcut command+Shift+A / Ctrl+Shift+A.

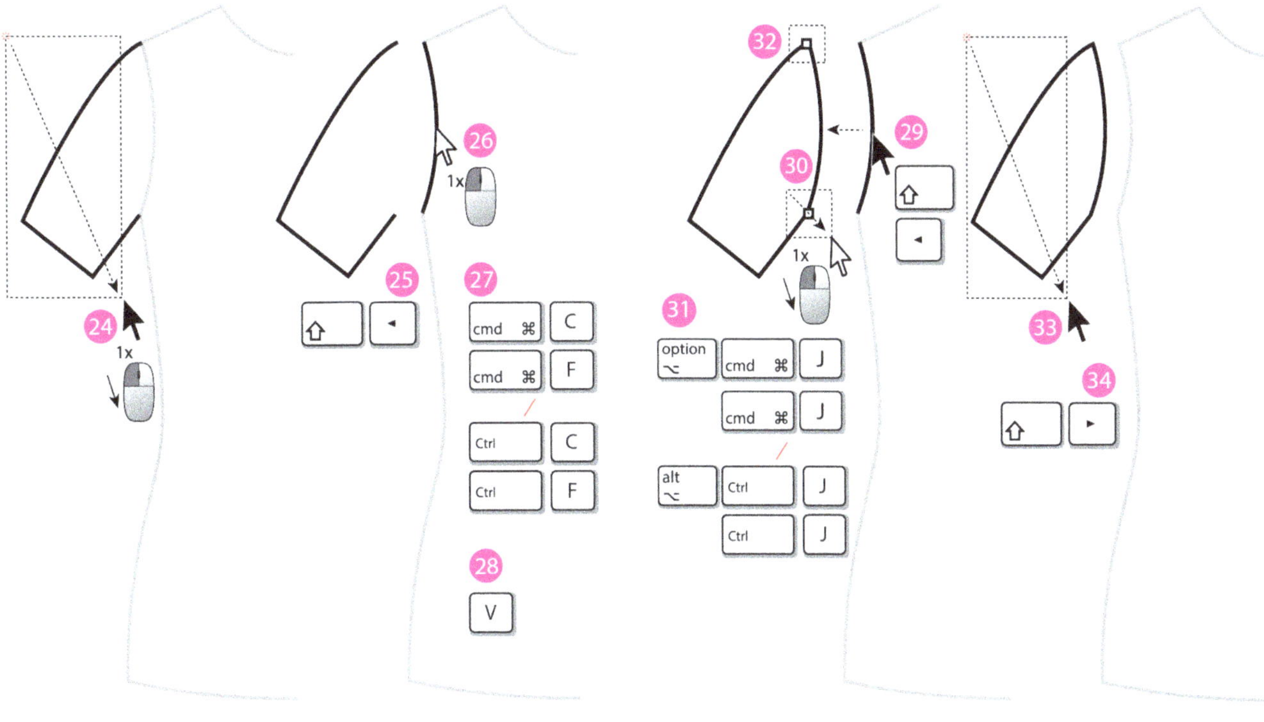

Step 24. Hold down the left mouse button and drag with the **Selection Tool** (V) around the object to select it.

Step 25. Hold down the **Shift** key double click on the left keyboard arrow button. The object is displaced.
Step 26. Click with the **Direct Selection Tool** (A) on the path (only the area between the nearest anchor points is selected).
Step 27. Activate the shortcut command+C / Ctrl+C (Copy) and the shortcut command+F / Ctrl+F (Paste in Front). 
Step 28. Click on V key (Selection Tool).
Step 29. Hold down the **Shift** key double click on the left keyboard arrow button. The line is displaced.
Step 30. Hold down the left mouse button and drag with the **Direct Selection Tool** (A) a selection around two anchor points (one end point of each half).
Step 31. Activate the shortcut option+command+J /alt+Ctrl+J (Average...). In the dialog box activate „Both", then „OK", then activate the shortcut command+J / Ctrl+J (Join).
Step 32. Repeat the steps 30 and 31.
Step 33. Hold down the left mouse button and drag with the **Selection Tool** (V) around the object to select it.
Step 34. Hold down the **Shift** key double click on the right keyboard arrow button. The object is displaced to the original position.
Step 35. Select the **Reflect Tool** (O), position the mouse cursor on the vertical guide, hold down the **alt/option** key (do not release the alt key) and click the left mouse button. The Reflect dialog box appears ,then release the **alt** key. Activate the option „Vertical", then „Preview", check whether everything is OK and click „Copy". A mirrored duplicate is created.

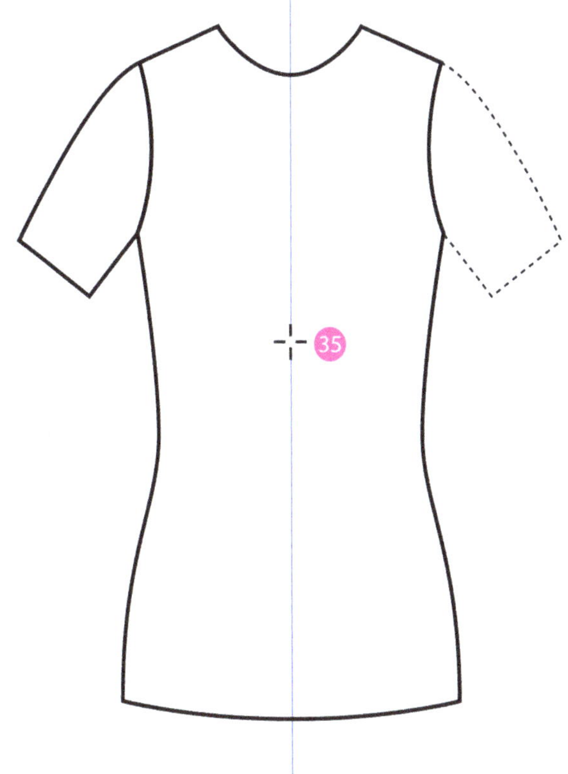

Attention: when you use the shortcut cmd+F / Ctrl+F (Paste in front) release the **F** - key very fast, otherwise several copys of the object will be created and this will be later the reason for several problems (paths won´t be joined correctly etc.)

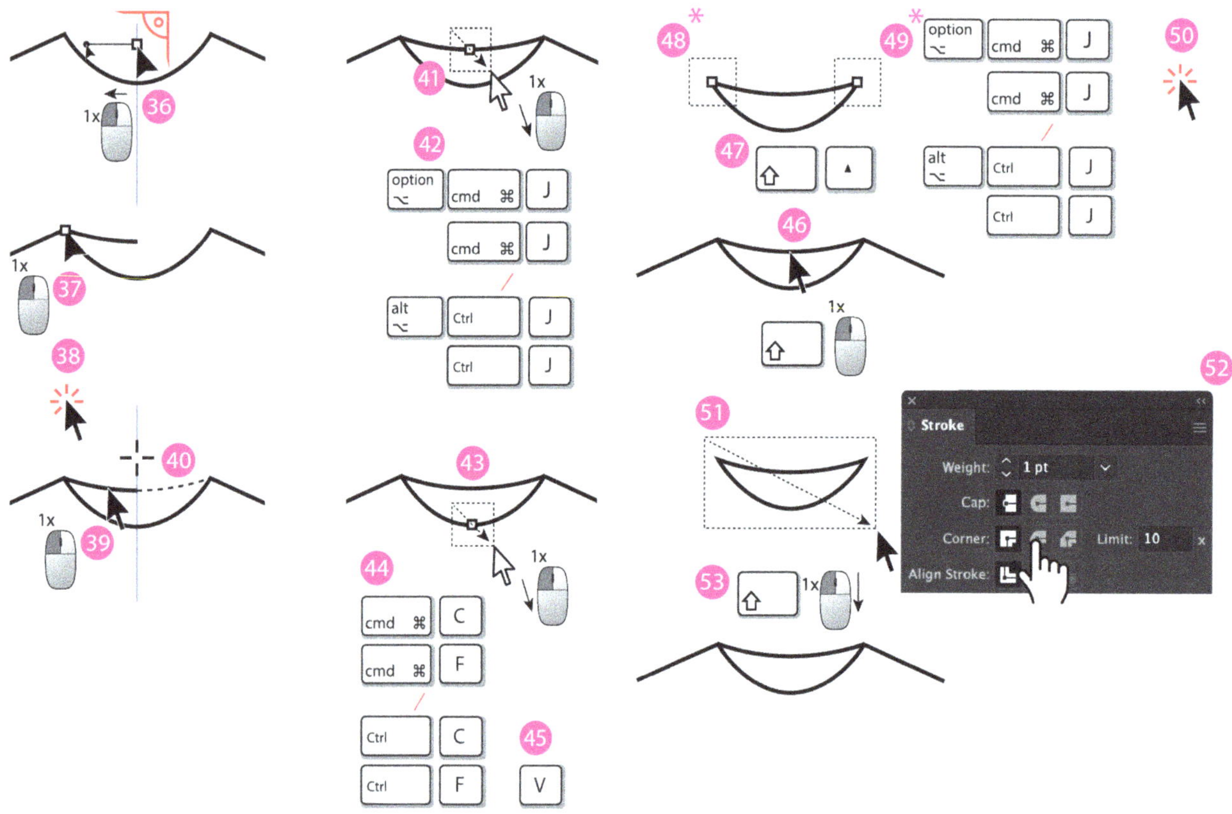

Step 36. Select the **Pen Tool** (P) and position the pen tool on the vertical guide, now hold down the left mouse button (do not release) to create the first anchor-point, in addition hold down the **Shift** key (90° angle), also do not release it, now drag the direction point to the left, then release first the mouse button and then the **Shift** key.

Step 37. Create a further anchor point (press and release the left mouse button, do not drag).

Step 38. Click on V key (Selection Tool) and click on a empty drawing area to deselect the object. Alternatively you can activate the shortcut command+Shift+A / Ctrl+Shift+A.

Step 39. Click with the **Selection Tool** (V) on the path (press and release the left mouse button).

Step 40. Select the **Reflect Tool** (O), position the mouse cursor on the vertical guide, hold down the **alt/option** key (do not release the alt key) and click the left mouse button. The Reflect dialog box appears, then release the **alt** key. Activate the option „Vertical", then „Preview", check whether everything is OK and click „Copy". A mirrored duplicate is created.

Step 41. Hold down the left mouse button and drag with the **Direct Selection Tool** (A) a selection around two anchor points (one end point of each half).

Step 42. Activate the shortcut option+command+J /alt+Ctrl+J (Average...). In the dialog box activate „Both", then „OK", then activate the shortcut command+J / Ctrl+J (Join). Two paths have been joined together.

Step 43. Hold down the left mouse button and drag with the **Direct Selection Tool** (A) a selection. (Only the area between the nearest anchor points is selected).

Step 44. Activate the shortcut command+C / Ctrl+C (Copy) and the shortcut command+F / Ctrl+F (Paste in Front).

Step 45. Click on the V key (Selection Tool).

Step 46. Hold down the **Shift** key (do not release) and click on the path. The **Shift** key in combination with the Selection tool ensures that to the existing selection further object will be added.

Step 47. Hold down the **Shift** key, double click on the up keyboard arrow button. The object is displaced to the top.

Steps 48/49. Repeat the steps 41 and 42.

Step 50. Click on the V key (Selection Tool) and click on an empty drawing area to deselect the object. Alternatively you can activate the shortcut command+Shift+A / Ctrl+Shift+A.

Step 51. Hold down the left mouse button and drag with the **Selection Tool** (V) around the object to select it.

Step 52. Open the „Stroke" panel **Window > Stroke** and set the „Corner" to „Round Join".

Step 53. Hold down the **Shift** key double click on the down arrow key. The object is displaced to the original position.

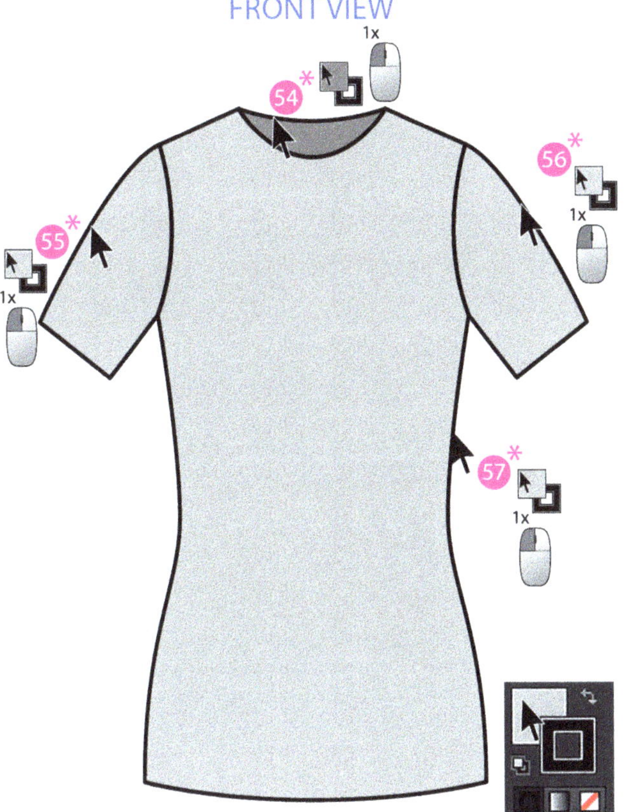

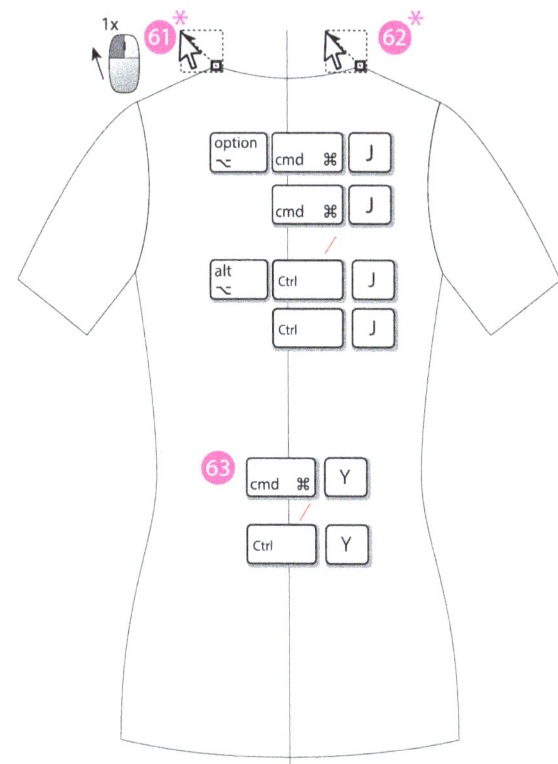

Step 54. Click on the object with the **Selection Tool** (V) and change the fill colour (e.g. #9F9F9F).
Step 55-57. Click on the objects with **Selection Tool** (V) and change the fill colour (e.g. #D3D3D3). The T-Shirt drawing is finished (front view).

Now create a copy of the T-Shirt (select the T-Shirt with the Slection Tool, then copy (cmd+C/ Ctrl+C), paste in front (cmd+F/ Ctrl+F) and move the copy to another location in the document. From **Step 58** you are working with the **Copy** of the T-Shirt to construct the back view.

Step 58. Activate the „Outline" view cmd+Y/ Ctrl+Y (**View > Outline**).
Step 59. Hold down the left mouse button and drag with the **Direct Selection Tool** (A) a selection.
Step 60. Click several times on **Backspace** key or activate the shortcut: cmd + X / Ctrl +X until the selected path and all anchor points are deleted.
Step 61/62. Repeat the steps 41 and 42.
Step 63. Activate the „Preview" view cmd+Y/ Ctrl+Y (**View > Preview**).

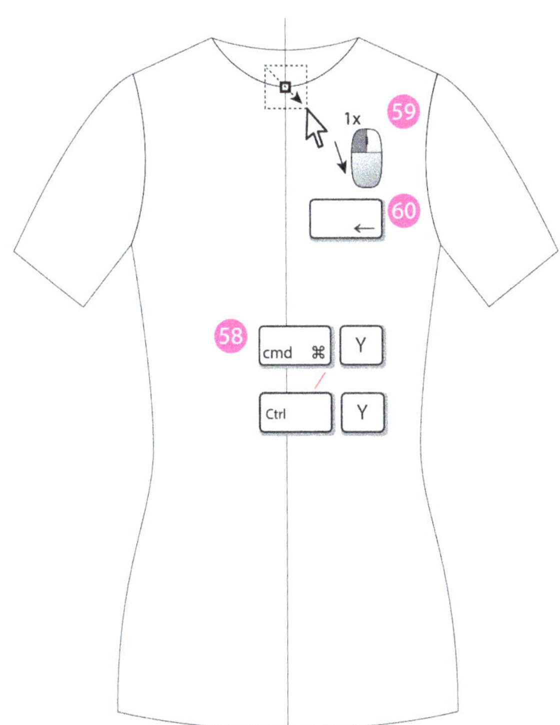

8.2 TUTORIAL: PARALLEL LINES

As a template take the T-Shirt (front view) from the previous exercise. Choose in the tools panel the stroke color „black" and the fill color „None".

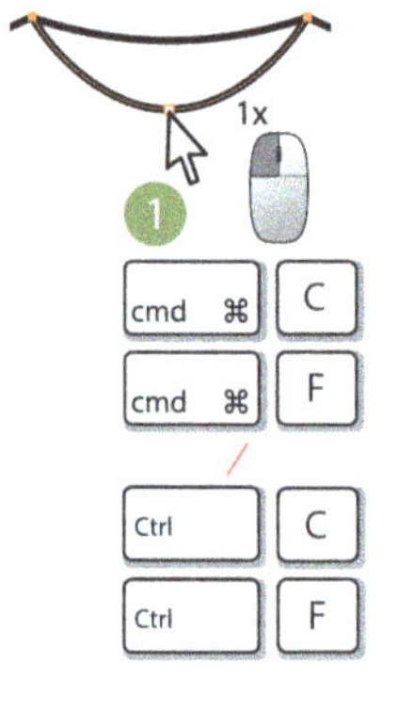

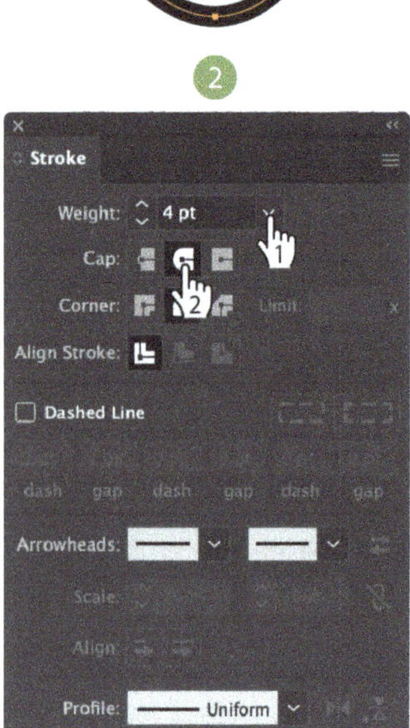

Step 1. Click on the anchor point with the **Direct Selection Tool** (A), then activate the shortcut command+C / Ctrl+C (Copy) and the shortcut command+F / Ctrl+F (Paste in Front).
(Only the area between the nearest anchor points will be selected).
Step 2. Open the „Stroke" panel **Window > Stroke** and change the „Weight" to e.g. 4pt (depending on the size of the drawing) and „Cap" to „Round Cap".

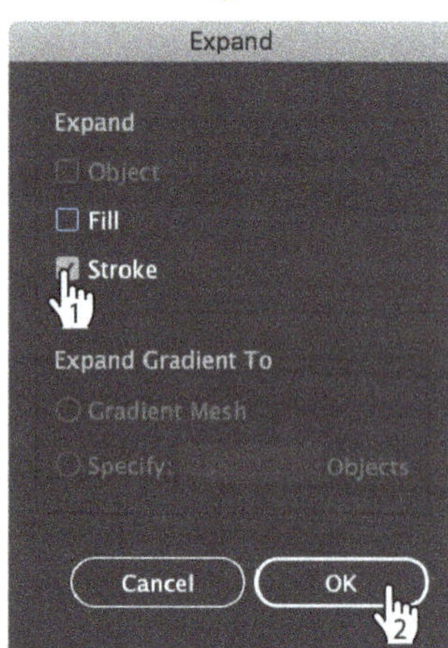

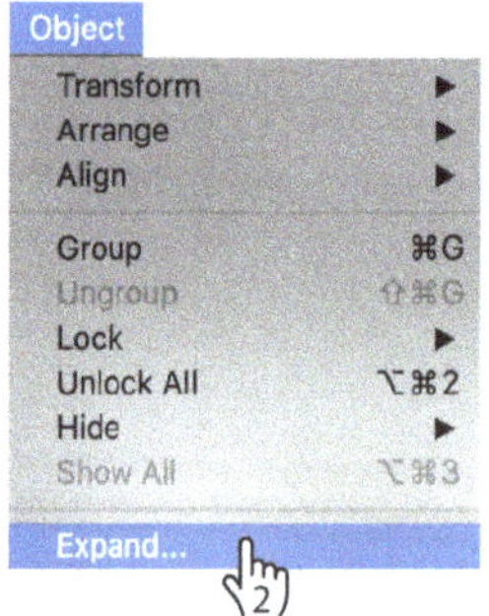

Step 3. Activate the following command: **Object > Expand...** or **Expand Appearance**.
Activate in the dialog box „Fill" and „Stroke", then confirm with „OK".
Through that process the **Stroke** is converted to **Fill**.

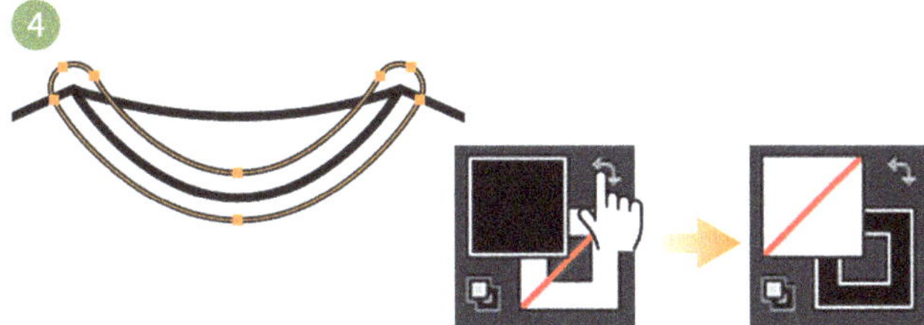

Step 4. Click in the tools panel the arrow "Swap Fill and Stroke".
The „Stroke" becomes „black" and Fill becomes „None".

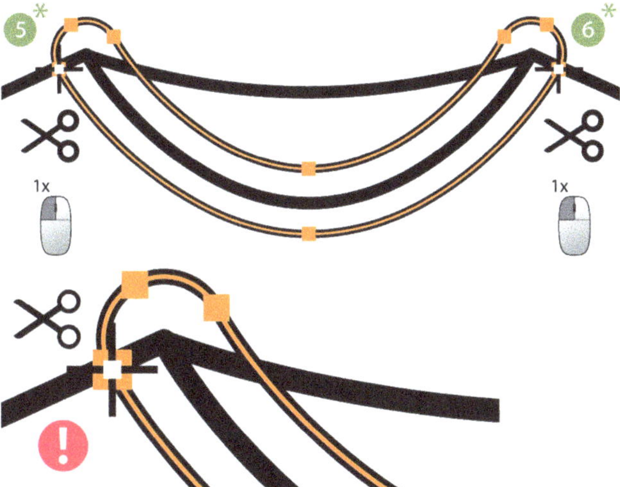

If the mouse cursor is over an anchor point, the rectangle of the anchor point will be enlarged.

Step 5 and 6. Click on the anchor point with the **Scissors Tool** (C) to separate the shape at that point.

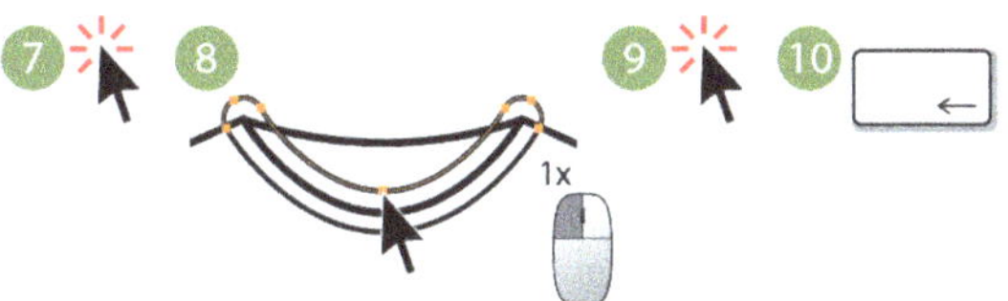

Step 7 Click on the V key (Selection Tool) and click on a empty drawing area to deselect the object. Alternatively you can activate the shortcut command+Shift+A / Ctrl+Shift+A.
Step 8 Click with the **Selection Tool** (V) on the path (above) and activate the command:
Object > Ungroup. (You may need to select this command several times until all objects are ungrouped. It depends on the complexity of the group).
Step 9 Click on the V key (Selection Tool) and click on a empty drawing area to deselect the object. Alternatively you can activate the shortcut command+Shift+A / Ctrl+Shift+A.
Step 10 Click the **Backspace** key to delete the separated path.

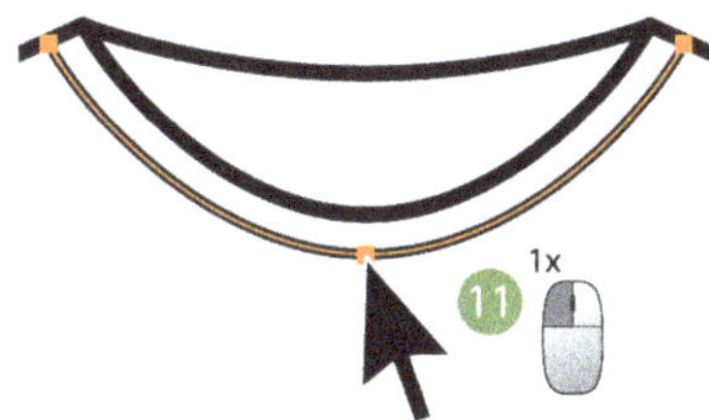

Step 11 Click with the **Selection Tool** (V) on the remaining part of the object.

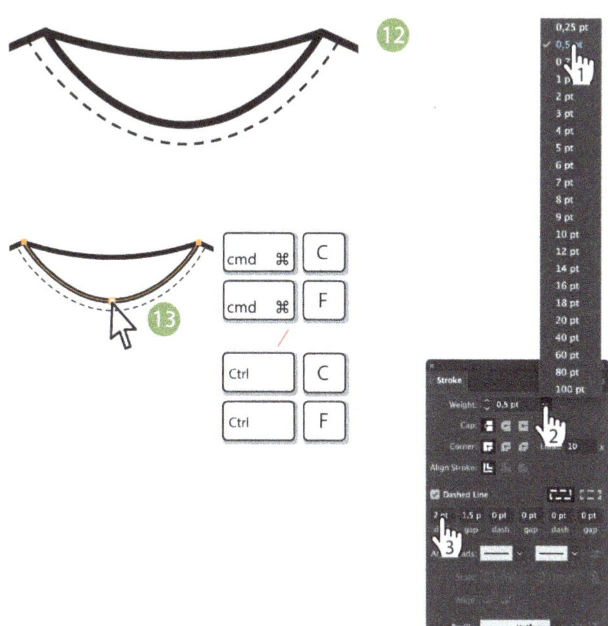

Step 12. Change in the „Stroke" panel **Weight** to 0,5pt or 0,75pt. Ideal for seams and inner elements such as pleats. Activate „Dashed Line", „dash" indicate 2pt and „gap" 1pt. If the option „Dashed Line" is not visible, click on more options ▤ , then Show Options.

Step13. Repeat the **first step**.

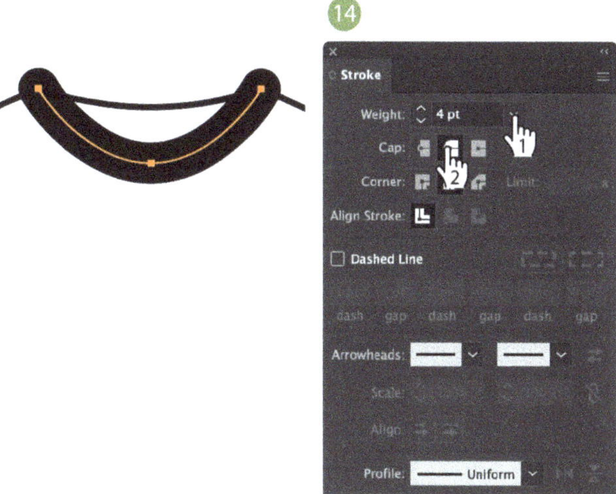

Step 14. Change in the „Stroke" panel **Weight** to 6pt.
The value must be few points higher than in **step 2** so that the new line does not match with the dashed line.

Step15. Activate the following command: **Object > Expand...** or **Expand Appearance**.
Activate in the dialog box „Fill" and „Stroke", then confirm with "OK". Through that process the **Stroke** is converted to **Fill**.(see step 3).
Step 16. Repeat **step 4**.

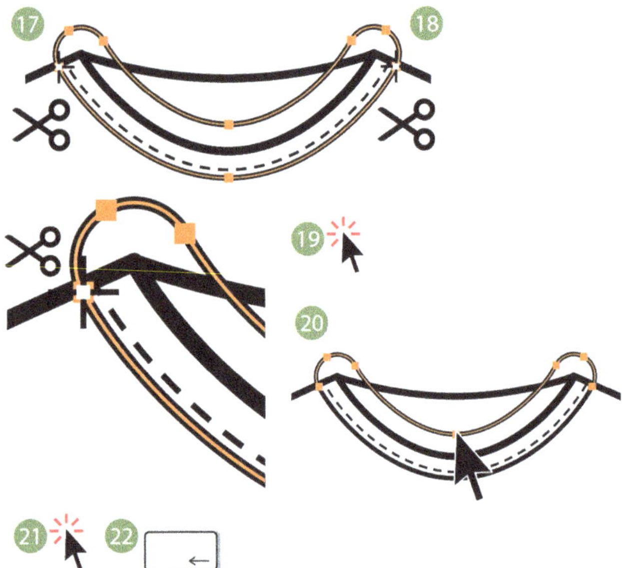

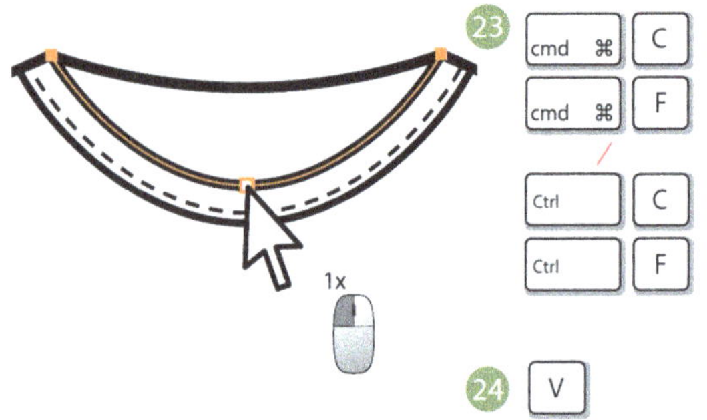

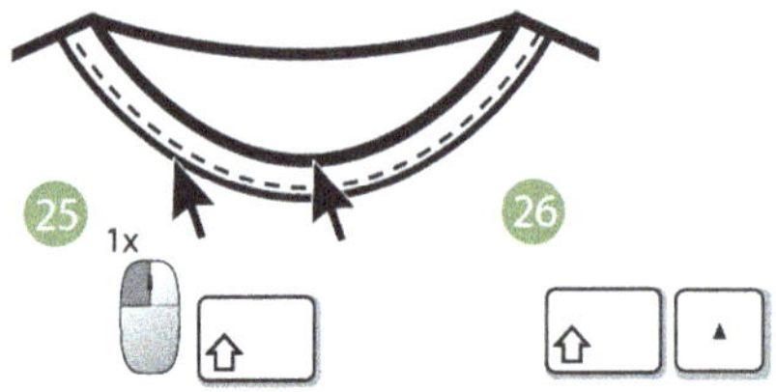

Step 17-22. Repeat the **step 5** to **step 10**.

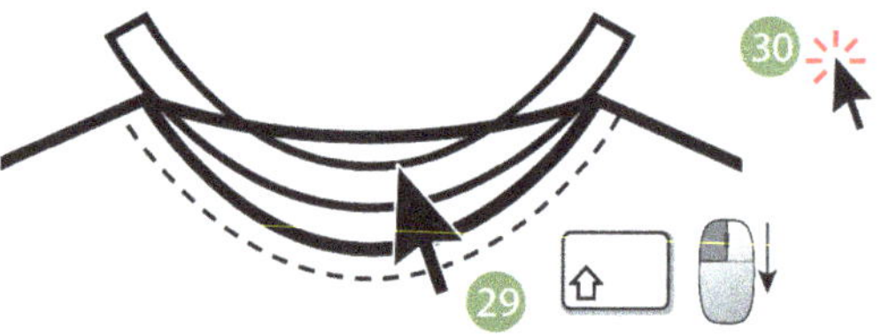

Steps 27 and 28. Hold down the left mouse button and drag with the **Direct Selection Tool** (A) a selection. One end point of each path is selected, then activate the shortcut command+J / Ctrl+J (Join). Two paths have been joined by a stroke together.

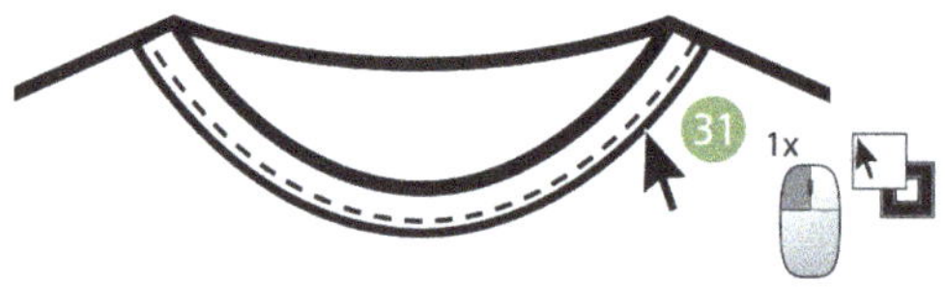

Step 29 Click on the object with the **Selection Tool** (V), then hold down the **Shift** key, double click on the down keyboard arrow key. The object is displaced to the original position.

Step 30 Click on the V key (Selection Tool) and click on a empty drawing area to deselect the object. Alternatively you can activate the shortcut command+Shift+A / Ctrl+Shift+A.

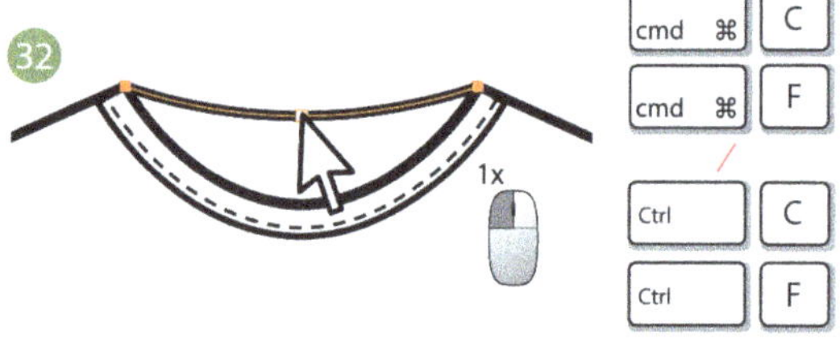

Step 23 Click on the anchor point with the **Direct Selection Tool** (A), then activate the shortcut command+C / Ctrl+C (Copy) and the shortcut command+F / Ctrl+F (Paste in Front).
(Only the area between the nearest anchor points will be selected).

Step 24. Click on the V key (Selection Tool).

Step 31 Click on the objects with the **Selection Tool** (V) and change the fill colour (e.g.#FFFFFF).

Step 25 Click on the line with the **Selection Tool** (V), then press **Shift** key (do not release Shift key) and click the second line (to the existing selection further object are added).

Step 26 Hold down the **Shift** key, double-click on the up arrow key. The both lines are displaced to the top.

Step 32 Click on the anchor point with the **Direct Selection Tool** (A), then activate the shortcut command+C / Ctrl+C (Copy) and the shortcut command+F / Ctrl+F (Paste in Front).
(Only the area between the nearest anchor points will be selected).

Then repeat the **steps 2** to **4**.
Further steps. Repeat the **steps 5** to **step 26**.

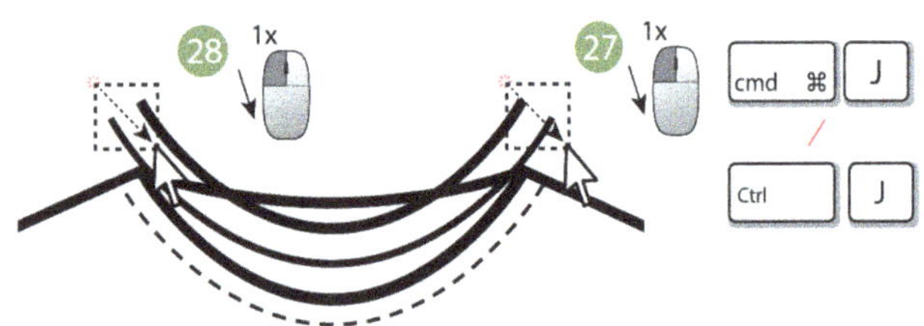

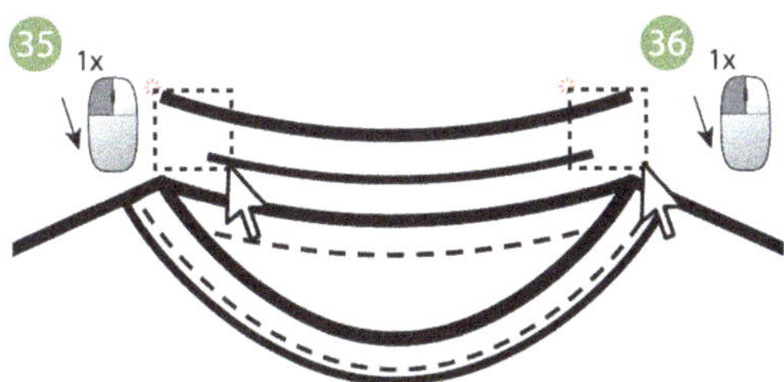

Steps 35 and 36 Hold down the left mouse button and drag with the **Direct Selection Tool** (A) a selection. One end point of each path is selected, then activate the shortcut command+J / Ctrl+J (Join). Two paths have been joined by a stroke together.

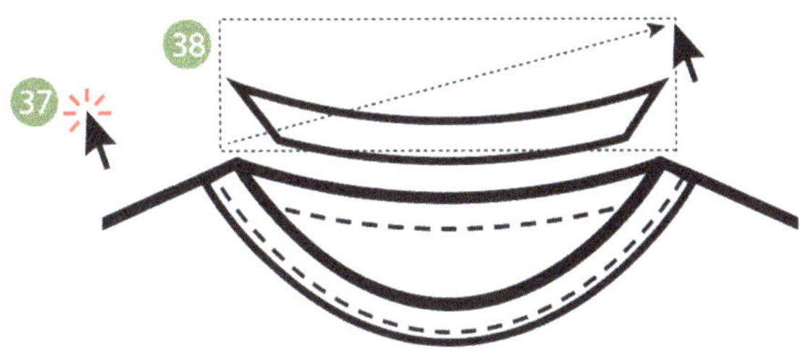

Step 37 Click on the V key (Selection Tool) and click on a empty drawing area to deselect the object. Alternatively you can activate the shortcut command+Shift+A / Ctrl+Shift+A.

Step 38 Hold down the left mouse button and drag with the **Selection Tool** (V) around the object to select it.

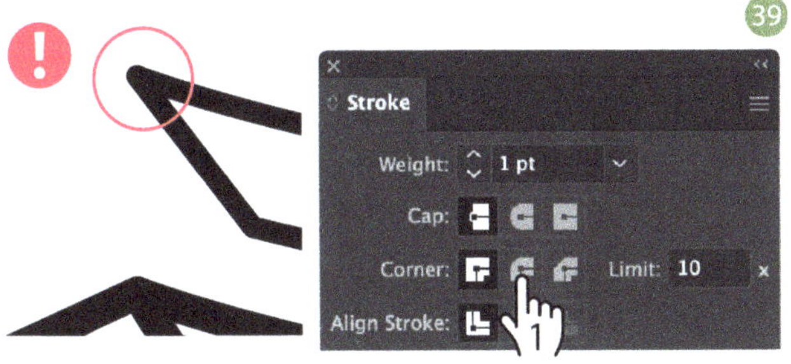

Step 39 Open the „Stroke" panel **Window > Stroke** and set the „Corner" to „Round Join".

Step 40 Click on the object with the **Selection Tool** (V), then hold down the **Shift** key, double click on the down keyboard arrow button. The object is displaced to the original position.

Step 41 Click on the V key (Selection Tool) and click on a empty drawing area to deselect the object. Alternatively you can activate the shortcut command+Shift+A / Ctrl+Shift+A.

Step 42 to 44 Repeat the **steps 1** to **12**.

To copy simple lines (like in the steps 42-44) you can click on the anchor point of the „template" line (step 45) with the **Direct Selection Tool** (A), then activate the shortcut command+C / Ctrl+C (Copy) and the shortcut command+F / Ctrl+F (Paste in Front). And then displace the duplicate with the keyboard arrow key to the new position.

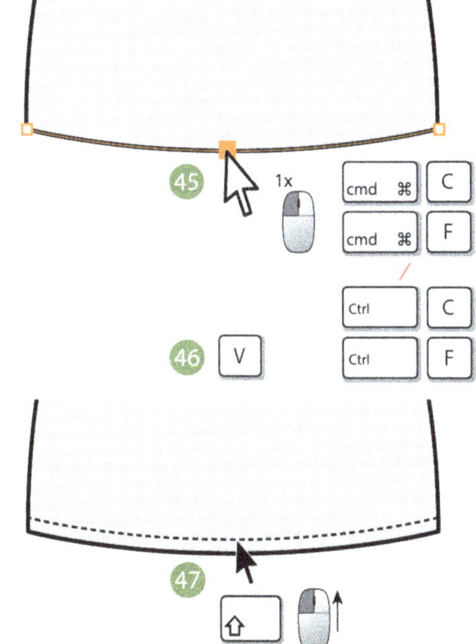

Change in the „Stroke" panel **Weight** to 0,5pt or 0,75pt. Activate „Dashed Line", „dash" indicate 2pt and „gap" 1pt.

8.3 TUTORIAL: MARINE STRIPES PATTERN
REQUIREMENTS

-Choose: **View > Rules >Show Rules, View > Guides > Lock Guides, View > Guides > Show Guides, View > Smart Guides, View > Snap to Point.**

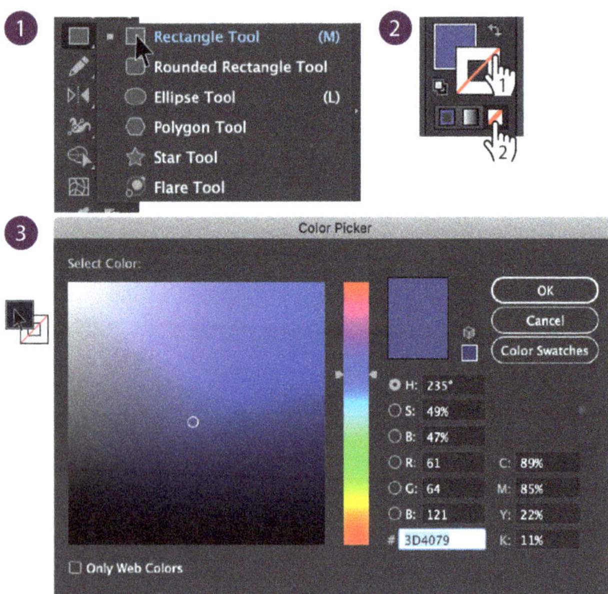

Step 1. Select the **Rectangle Tool** (M).
Step 2. And choose in the tools panel the stroke color „None".
Step 3. Double click with the left mouse button on the „Fill", in the „Color Picker" dialog box set the fill colour „blue" (e.g. #14172A).

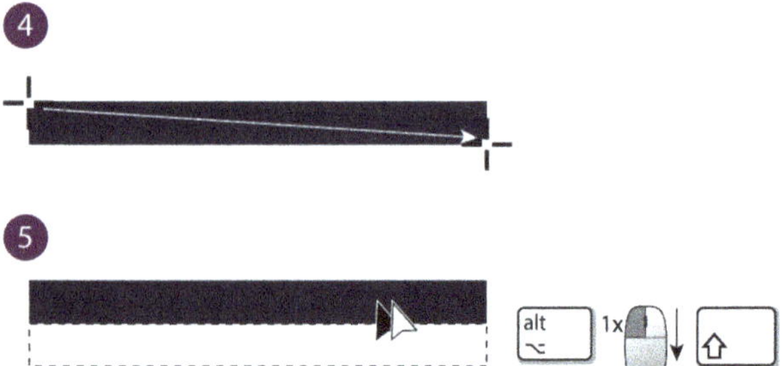

Step 4. Now hold down the left mouse button (do not release) and create with the **Rectangle Tool** (M) an rectangle.
Step 5. Hold down the **alt/option** key (do not release), then hold down the left mouse button and drag the object with the mouse cursor down. In addition hold down the **Shift** key (also do not release). When the position of the duplicate is beneath the original object, release the mouse button (first the mouse button, then **Shift** and **alt** key).

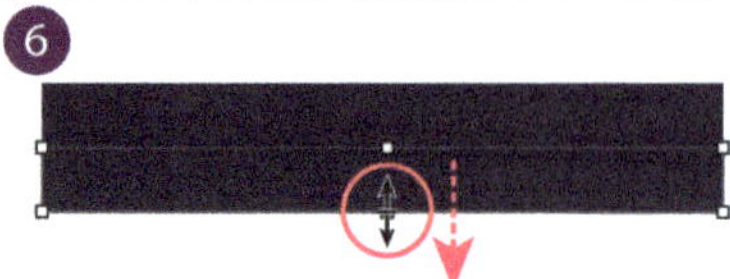

Step 6. Click V key (Selection Tool) and drag on the center square down to transform the new object.
Step 7. Set in the Tools panel the fill colour „white" and Stroke colour „None".

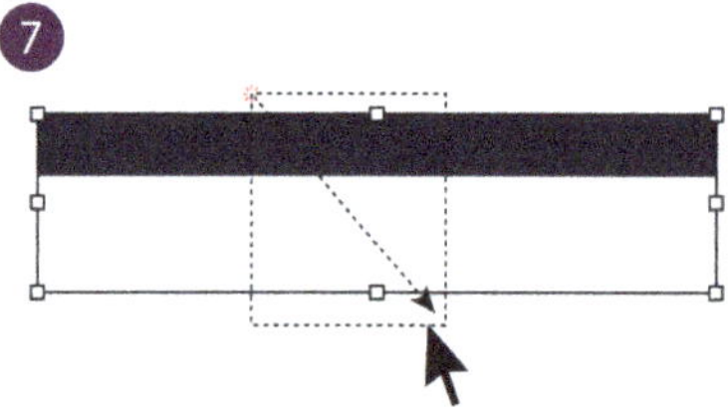

Step 7. Hold down the left mouse button and drag with the **Selection Tool** (V) a selection to select both objects.

To set the pattern you have two options.

Option1:

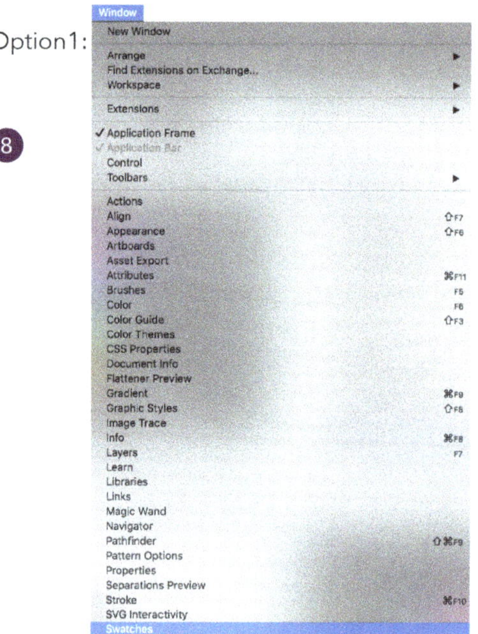

Open the „Swatches": **Window > Stwatches**

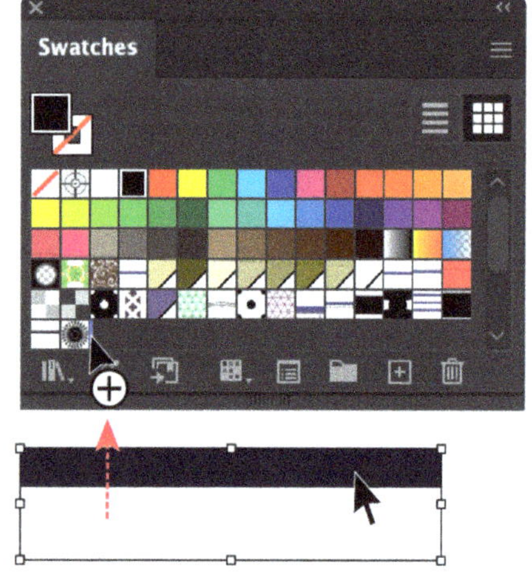

And drag both object to the „Swatches" panel (Drag&Drop method). A plus sign appears next to the arrow, then release the mouse button.
You can see now a small preview of your pattern.

If you click on the ▤ symbol, further options will be opened, you can change here the setting for symbols (e.g. „Large Thumbnail View", then you will have a larger preview of colours and pattern).

Option 2:
Hold down the left mouse button and drag with the **Selection Tool** (V) a selection around both object, then activate the command **Object > Pattern> Make.**

Enter a name for the pattern and click "Done" at the top-left corner.

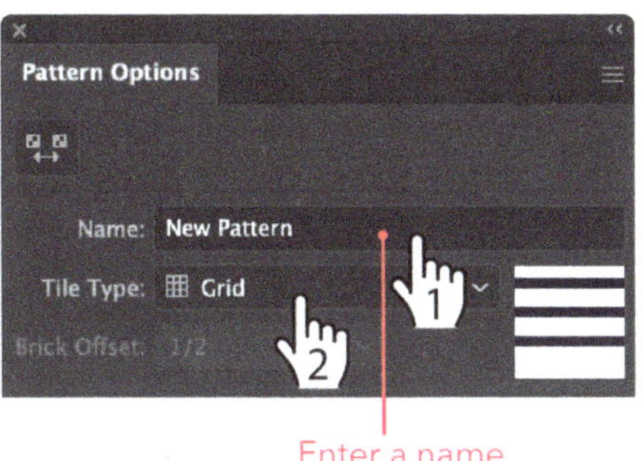

Enter a name

Click „Done".

Steps 9 and 11. Hold down the **Shift** key and click with the **Selection Tool** (V) on the objects (to select several object at the same time), then release the mouse button and click in the swatches panel on the stripes-pattern to activate it.

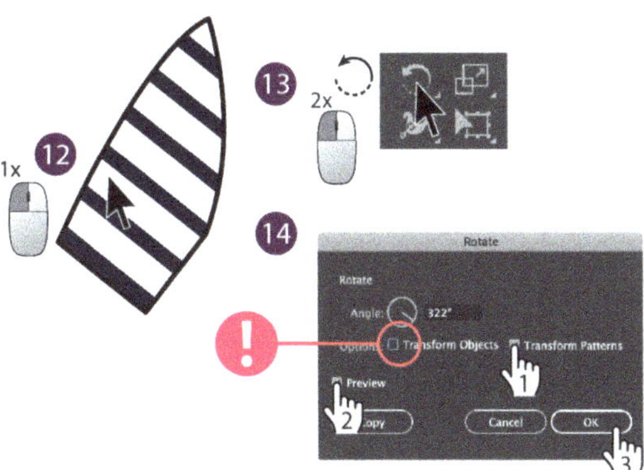

Step 12. Click with the **Selection Tool** (V) the right sleeve.
Step 13. Double click on the **Rotate Tool** (R).
Step 14. In the dialog box deactivate the option „Transform Objects", we want only to rotate the pattern, then activate the „Preview", for „Angle" type e.g. **322°** (it depends of cours on the angle of the object) and confirm with "OK".

Step 15. Repeat the step 14 for the left sleeve, this time type for the angle (minus) **-322°**. Or create with the „Reflect Tool" a copy of the right sleeve for the left side.

Step 16 to 18. Hold down the **Shift** key and click with the **Selection Tool** (V) on the three objects and double click in the Tools panel on the **Scale Tool** (S).

Step 19. In the dialog box deactivate the option „Transform Objects", we want only to reduce the size of the pattern, then on „Uniform" type e.g. **60%** (the size of the pattern will be reduced to 40%) and confirm the settings with "OK".

8.4 TUTORIAL: PATCH POCKET WITH ROUNDED CORNERS

REQUIREMENTS

-Choose in the tools panel the stroke color „black" and the fill color „None".

-Set in the stroke panel (**Window > Stroke**) the stroke weight to **1pt** or **2pt**.

-Choose: **View > Rules >Show Rules, View > Guides > Lock Guides, View > Guides > Show Guides, View > Smart Guides, View > Snap to Point.**

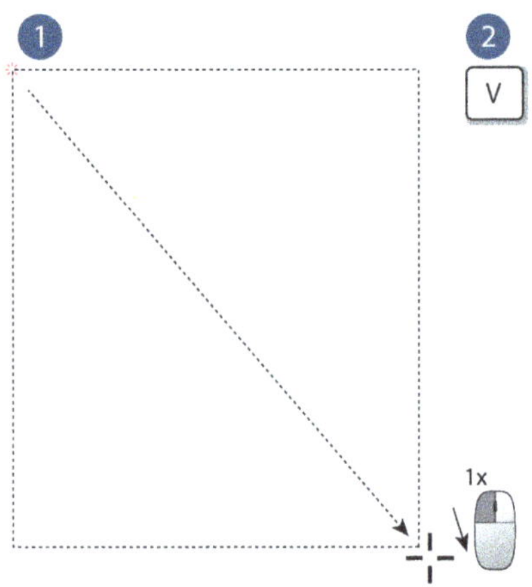

Step 1. Select the **Rectangle Tool** (M) and create an rectangle.
Step 2. Click V key (Selection Tool).
Step 3. Drag a vertical guide. While dragging, place the cursor over the middle square below (object center-point). The guide is magnetically fixed to the point.

Step 4. Hold down the left mouse button and drag with **Direct Selection Tool** (A) a selection around two anchor points. The two anchor points are selected.
Step 5. Hold down the left mouse button and drag the cursor diagonally on the circle-symbol to the center point of the rectangle. The corners of the pocket are rounded.
Step 6. Click V key (Selection Tool).
Step 7. Activate the shortcut command+C / Ctrl+C (Copy) and the shortcut command+F / Ctrl+F (Paste in Front).

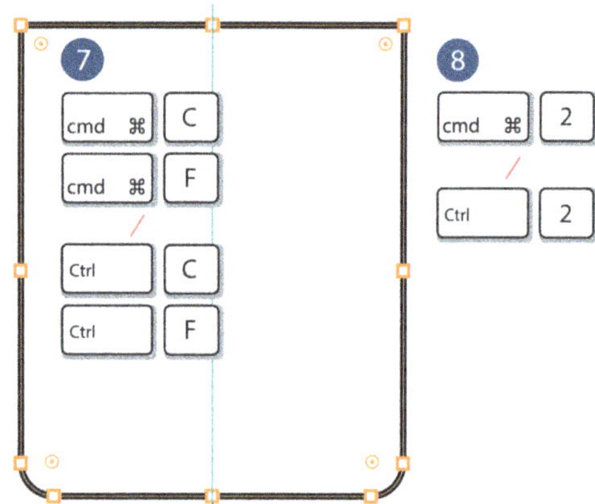

Step 8. Activate the shortcut cmd+2 / Ctrl+2 (or choose **Object>Lock>Selection**) to lock the copy of the object.
Step 9. Drag with the **Direct Selection Tool** (A) a selection around four anchor points. The anchor points are selected.
Step 10. Click several times on the up keyboard arrow key, the line is displaced. Or hold down the left mouse button and drag the line to the top (additionally hold down the **Shift** key „90° angle".

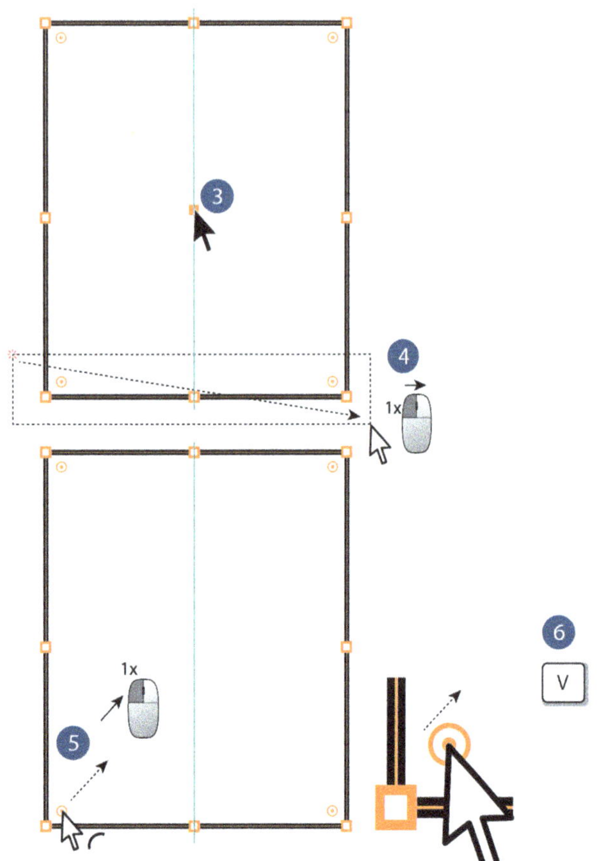

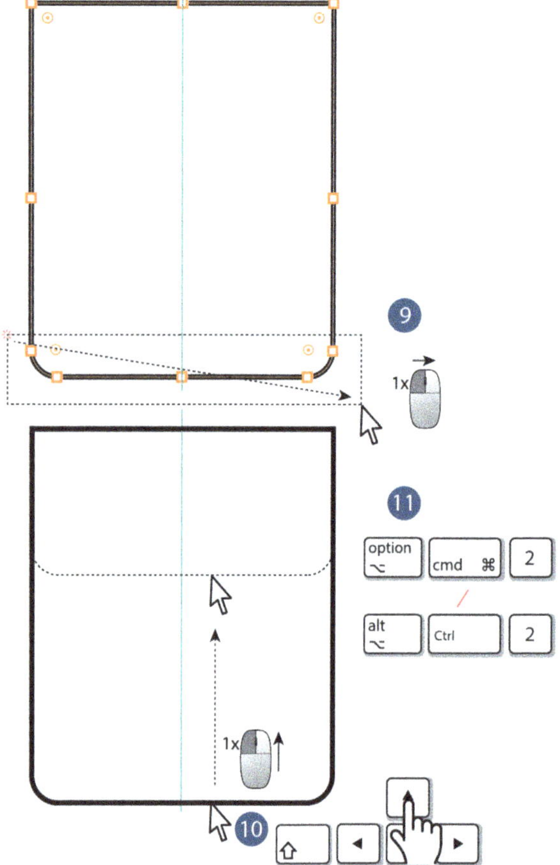

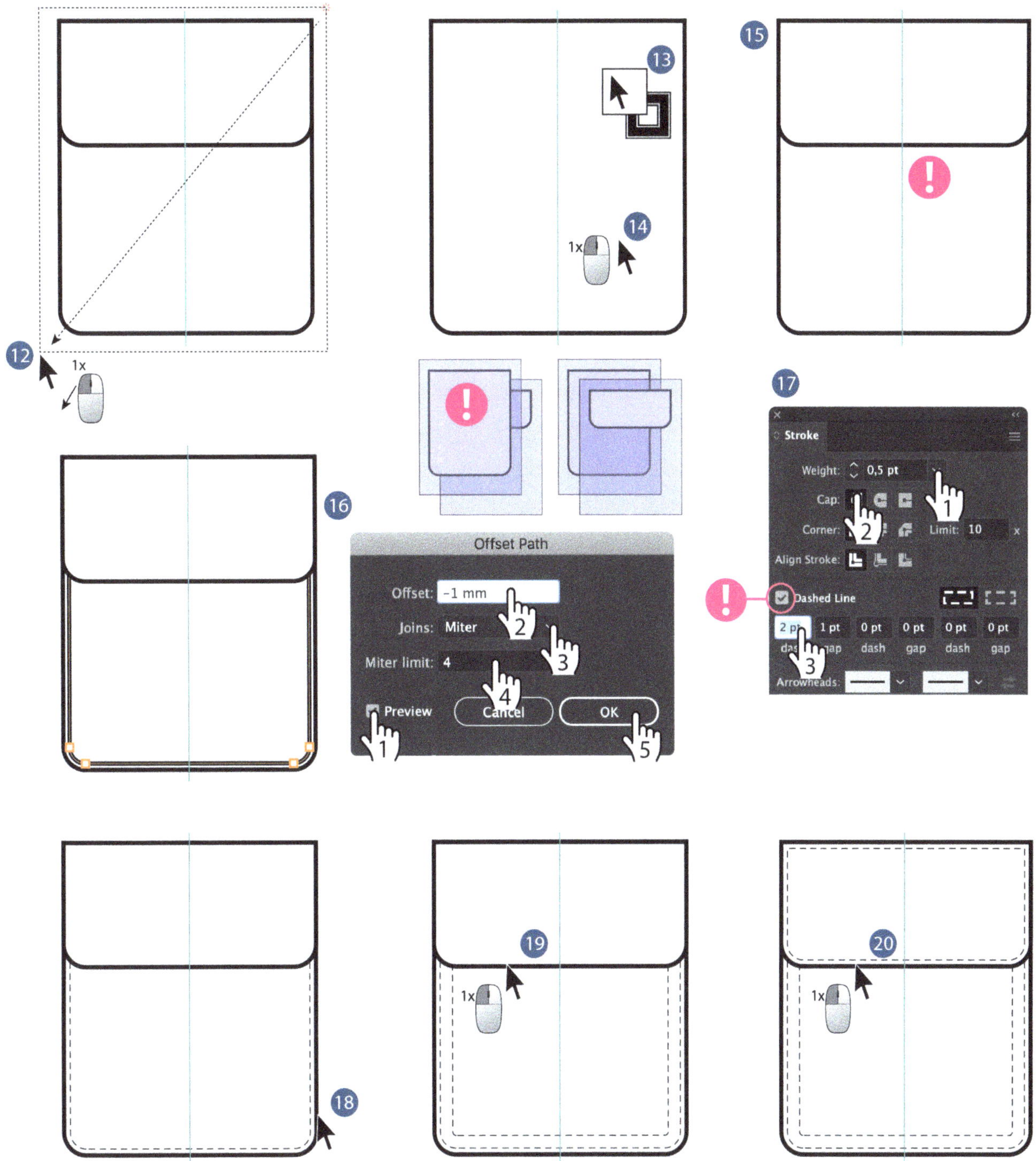

Step 11. Activate the shortcut option+cmd+2 / alt+Ctrl+2 (or choose **Object>Unlock All**) to unlock the object in the document.

Step 12. Hold down the left mouse button and drag with the **Selection Tool** (V) a selection around the objects.

Step 13. Change the fill color to „white".

Step 14. Click with the **Selection Tool** (V) on the object (press and release the left mouse button).

Step 15. Choose **Object>Arrange>Send to Back.** The object is displaced to the back, so that the pocket flap will be revealed.

Step 16. Choose **Object>Path>Offset Path…** and type e.g. -1mm. Minus means that the duplicate will be displaced inwards, by displacing external do not type the „Minus" symbol. „Joins" leave at „Miter" and „Miter limit" leave at 4, then confirm with „Ok".

Step 17. Change in the „Stroke" panel **Weight** to 0,5pt or 0,75pt. Ideal for seams and inner elements such as pleats. Activate „Dashed Line", „dash" indicate 3pt and „gap" 2pt. If the option „Dashed Line" is not visible, click on more options ▤ , then Show Options.

Step 18. Click on the object with **Selection Tool** (V), then activate the command **Object>Path>Offset Path…**, then type e.g. -3mm and confirm with „Ok".

Step 19. Click on the object with **Selection Tool** (V), then activate the command **Object>Path>Offset Path…**, then type e.g. -1mm and confirm with „Ok".

Step 20. Repeat the step 18.

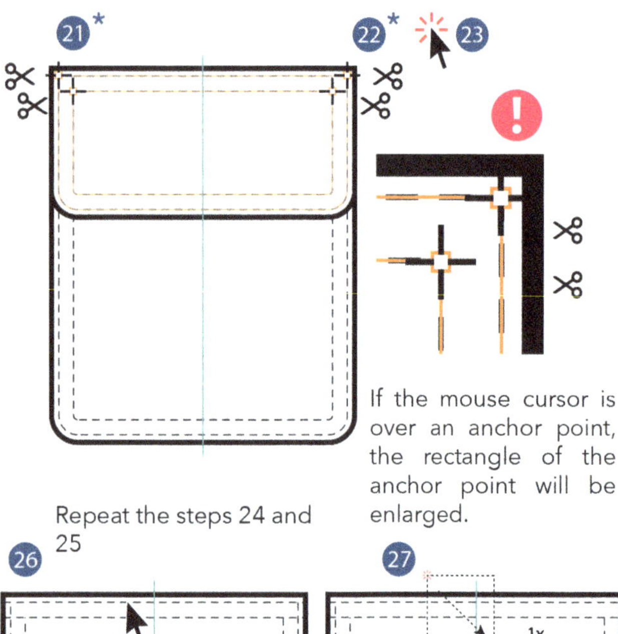

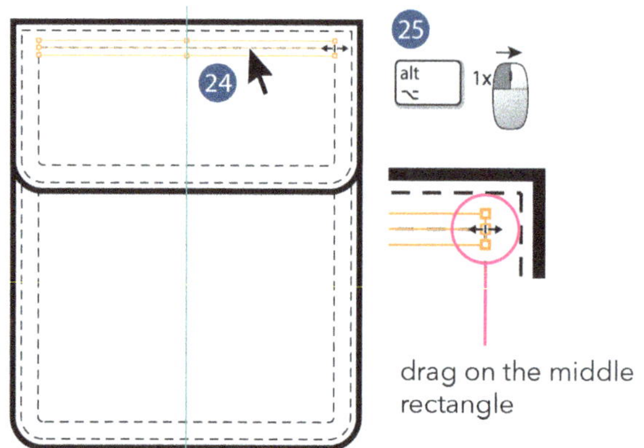

If the mouse cursor is over an anchor point, the rectangle of the anchor point will be enlarged.

Repeat the steps 24 and 25

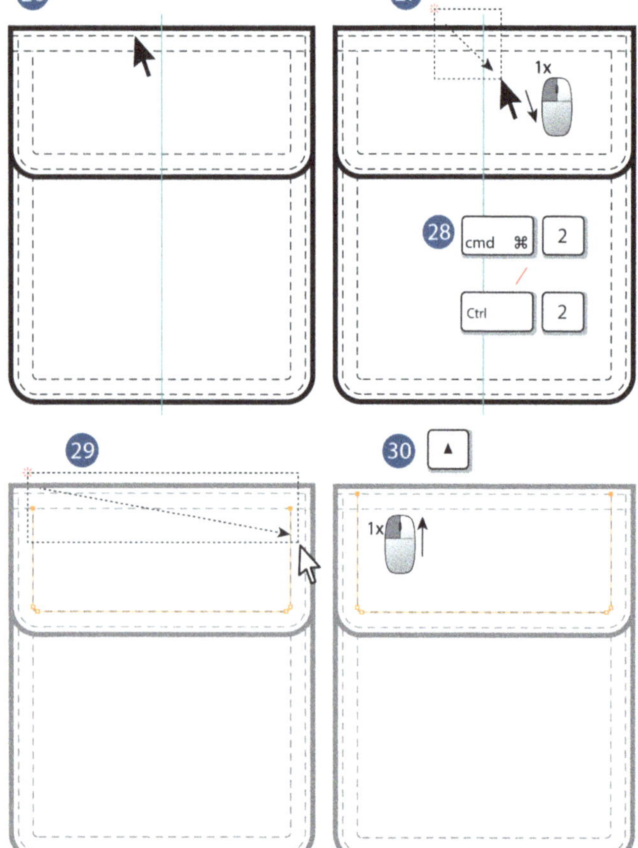

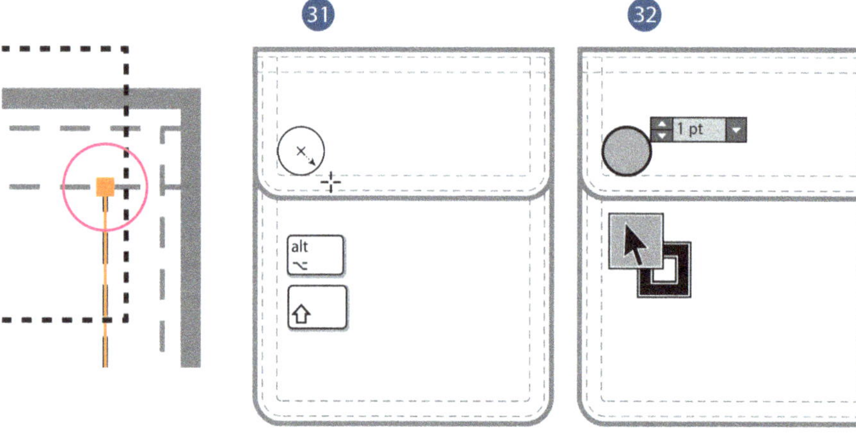

Step 21 and 22. Click on the anchor point with **Scissors Tool** (C) to separate the shape at that points (see figure).

Step 23. Click on V key (Selection Tool) and click on a empty drawing area to deselect the object. Alternatively you can activate the shortcut command+Shift+A / Ctrl+Shift+A.

Step 24. Click on the dashed line with **Selection Tool** (V)

Step 25. Hold down **alt/option** key (so that the line is transformed on both sides) and transform the line (hold down the left mouse button and drag on the central white square).

Step 26. Repeat the steps 24 and 25 for the upper dashed line.

Step 27. Hold down the left mouse button and drag with **Selection Tool** (V) around the objects to select them.

Step 28. Activate the shortcut cmd+2 / Ctrl+2 (or choose **Object>Lock>Selection**) to lock the objects.

Step 29. Hold down the left mouse button and drag with **Direct Selection Tool** (A) a selection around two endpoints of the line.

Step 30. Click several times on the up keyboard arrow key, the path is transformed. Or hold down the left mouse button and drag the line to the top (additionally hold down the **Shift** key „90° angle".

Step 31. Select the **Ellipse Tool** (L), hold down **alt/option** and **Shift** key and drag a circle, then first release the mouse button and then alt/option & Shift.

Step 32. -Change the stroke weight to **1pt** (**Window>Stroke**) and the fill color „grey".

Metal elements for technical fashion drawings can be generally filled grey.

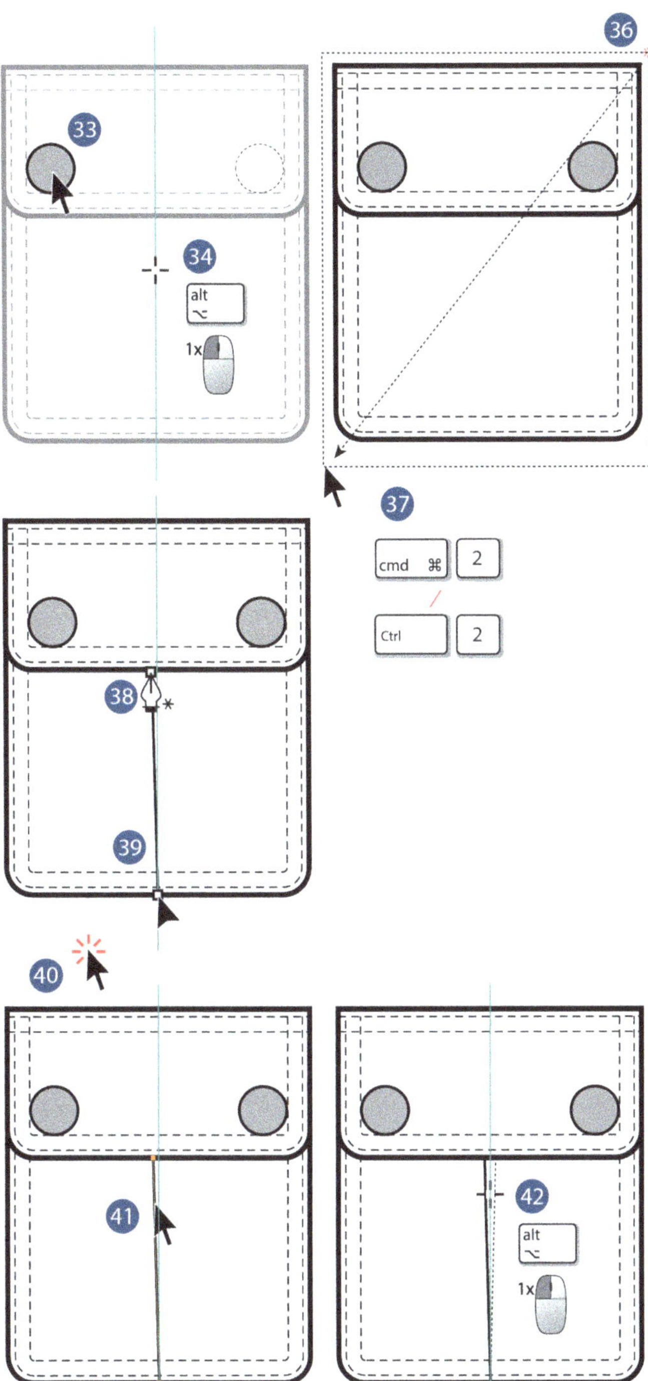

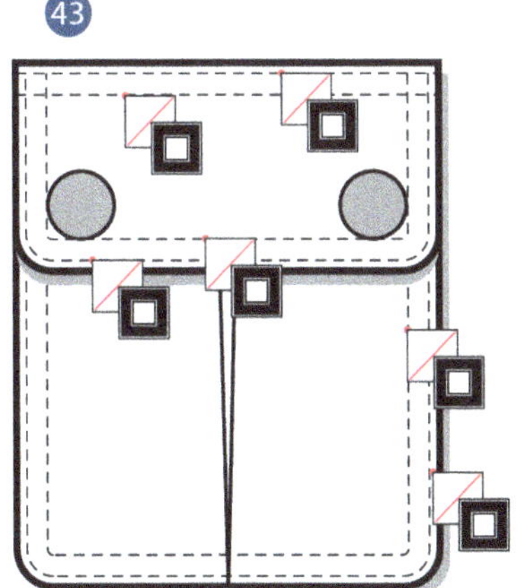

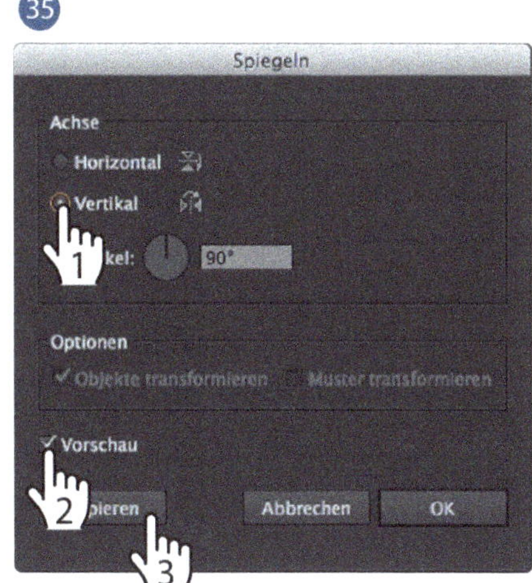

Step 33. Click with **Selection Tool** (V) the metal press button.

Step 34. Select the **Reflect Tool** (O), position the mouse cursor on the vertical guide, hold down the **alt/option** key (do not release the alt key) and click the left mouse button (press and release). The Reflect dialog box appears ,then release the **alt/option** key.

Step 35. In the dialog box activate the option „Vertical", then „Preview", check whether everything is OK and click „Copy". A mirrored duplicate is created.

Step 36. Hold down the left mouse button and drag with **Selection Tool** (V) around the objects to select the pocket.

Step 37. Activate the shortcut cmd+2 / Ctrl+2 (or choose **Object>Lock>Selection**) to lock the objects.

It is important always to lock previously drawn objects/lines in the vicinity of the current work area before you start to create a new object. This will avoid many of problems in advance.

Step 38 and 39. Create with the **Pen Tool** (P) a new straight line (press and release the left mouse button, do not drag).

Step 40 Click the V button (Selection Tool) and click on an empty drawing area to deselect the object. Alternatively you can activate the shortcut command+Shift+A / Ctrl+Shift+A.

Step 41 Click on the object with the **Selection Tool** (V).

Step 42 Select the **Reflect Tool** (O), position the mouse cursor on the vertical guide, hold down the **alt/option** key (do not release the alt key) and click the left mouse button. The Reflect dialog box appears ,then release the **alt/option** key. Activate the option „Vertical", then „Preview", check whether everything is OK and click „Copy". A mirrored duplicate is created.

Step 43. Activate the shortcut option+cmd+2 / alt+Ctrl+2 (or choose **Object>Unlock All**) to unlock the object in the document.

And to complete the project, deactivate on all quilting seams all fill colours.

Then hold down the left mouse button and drag with **Selection Tool** (V) around the pocket and activate the shortcut cmd+G / Ctrl+G (Group).

8.5 TUTORIAL: APPLY EFFECTS (FLOWER)

REQUIREMENTS

-Choose in the tools panel the stroke color „None" and the fill color e.g. „blue".

-Choose: **View > Rules >Show Rules, View > Guides > Lock Guides, View > Guides > Show Guides, View > Smart Guides, View > Snap to Point** and place a vertical guide.

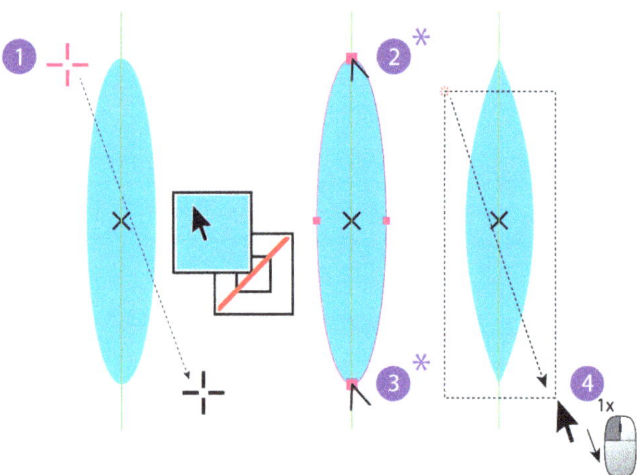

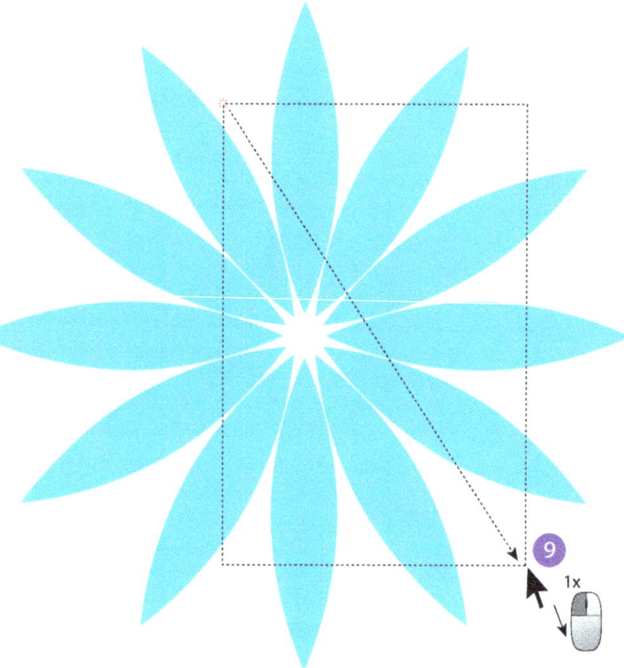

Step 1. Select the **Ellipse Tool** (L) and create an ellipse.
Step 2 and 3. Select the **Anchor Point Tool** (Shift + C) and click the top and lower anchor point. Through that process the smooth points are transfered to corner points.

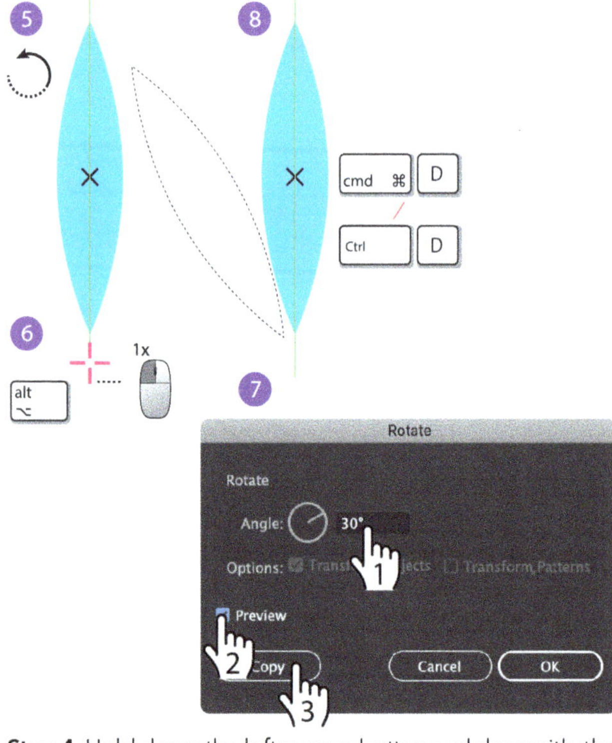

Step 4. Hold down the left mouse button and drag with the **Selection Tool** (V) around the object to select it.
Step 5. Select the **Rotate Tool** (R) (it is located in a joint group with the Reflect Tool). The Cursor will be changed to –¦– crosshair.

Step 6. Hold down **alt/option** key (do not release **alt** key) and click with the left mouse button on a location where the rotation axis should be (a dialog box appears), then release the **alt/option** key and mouse button.

Step 7. Type in the dialog box „Angle" 30° click on „Copy". Always select the "Preview" in order to make the result immediately visible.
Step 8. Now you can create a copy (with the same settings) with the shortcut: cmd + D / Ctrl + D or **Object > Transform > Transform Again**.
Step 9. Hold down the left mouse button and drag with the **Selection Tool** (V) around the objects to select them.
Step 10. Activate the shortcut cmd+G / Ctrl+G to group the objects .
Step 11. Open the panel „Transparency" (**Window>Transparency**) and change the blending mode to „Multiply".

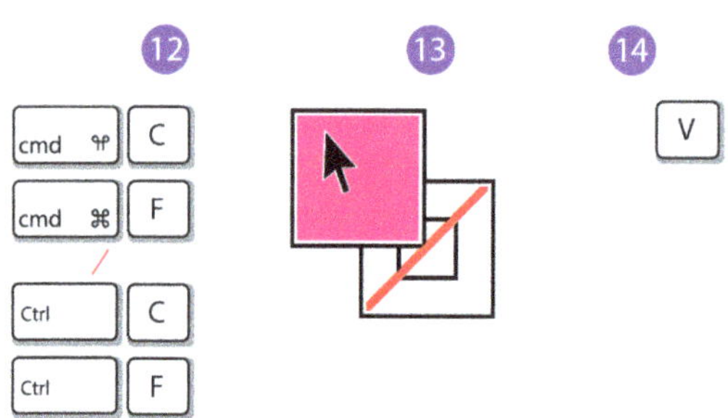

Step 12. Activate the shortcut command+C / Ctrl+C (Copy) and the shortcut command+F / Ctrl+F (Paste in Front). A copy of the selected object is created.

Step 13. Change the fill colour.
Step14 Click V key (press and release).
Step 15 Hold down the **alt/option** and **Schift** key, place the mouse cursor on a corner, then drag the selected objects to the center to transform them. This will reduce the objects evenly. Then first release the mouse button and then the keyboard keys.

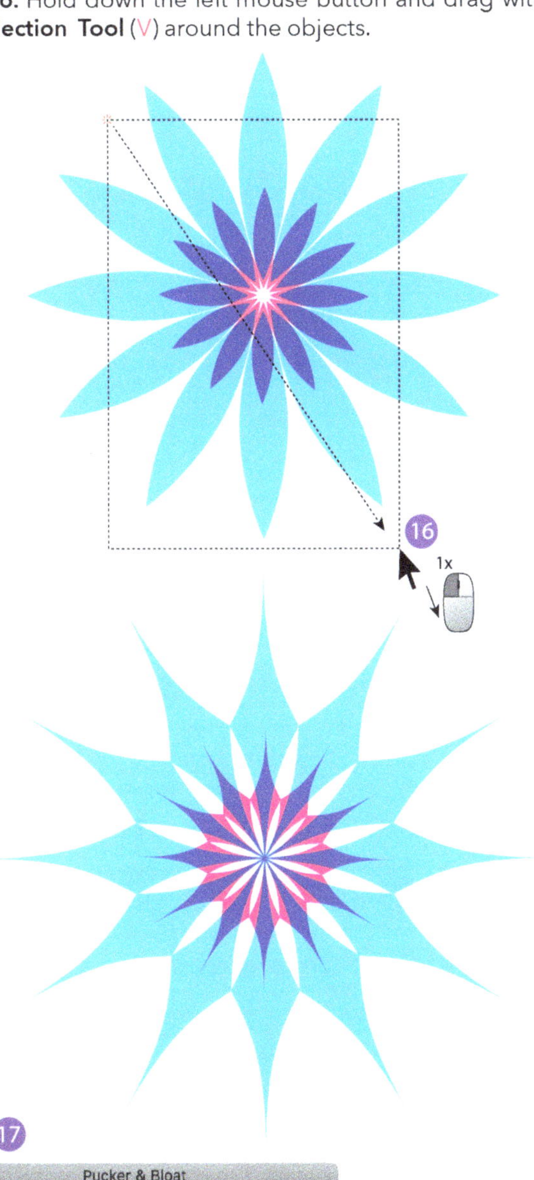

Step 16. Hold down the left mouse button and drag with the **Selection Tool** (V) around the objects.

Step 17. Activate the Effect: **Effect>Distort&Transform>Pucker&Bloat...**
In the dialog box type e.g. -33% and confirm the settings with „OK".
Step 18. Activate the Effect: **Effekt>Distort&Transform>Twist...**
In the dialog box type e.g. 98° or more and confirm the settings with „OK".

Step 19. Choose **Object>Expand...** or **Object>Expand Appearance.**
Through that process the shape of the object will be changed, so that it is possible now to work with anchor points of the object.
(After that process all objects will be grouped).

Step 20. (This step is not necessary) Open the panel „Pathfinder" (**Window>Pathfinder**) and click on „Unite". Through that process all objects are united.
This can produce also interessting effects.

8.6 TUTORIAL: BLAZER

REQUIREMENTS

-Choose in the tools panel the stroke color „black" and the fill color „None".

-Change the stroke weight (**Window > Stroke**) to **1pt** or **2pt**.
-Choose: **View > Rules >Show Rules, View > Guides > Lock Guides, View > Guides > Show Guides, View > Smart Guides, View > Snap to Point** and place a vertical guide.

-Work in this exercise with a figure template that you can download using the following link:
www.dimitridesign.org/templates

Step 1. Select the **Pen Tool** (P) and position it on the vertical guide, now hold down the left mouse button (do not release) to create the first anchor-point.
Step 2. Additionaly hold down the **Shift** key (90° angle), also do not release it, now drag the direction point to the left, then release first the mouse button and then the **Shift** key.
Step 3. Create a further anchor point (drag the direction point to the left down).
Step 4. Create a further anchor point (press and release the left mouse button, do not drag).
Step 5. Create a further anchor point (press and release the left mouse button, do not drag).
Step 6. Create a further anchor point (do not release the left mouse button), in addition hold down the **Shift** key (90° angle), also do not release the **Shift** key and drag the direction point down, then release first the mouse button and then the **Shift** key.
Step 7. Create a further anchor point (drag the direction point diagonally to the left down, then release the mouse button).
Step 8. Click the last anchor point (press and release the left mouse button) to create a corner.
Step 9. Create a further anchor point (drag the direction point to the right down).
Step 10. Create a further anchor point (drag the direction point to the right up).
Step 11. Create a further anchor point (drag the direction point diagonally to the right up).
Step 12. Create a further anchor point (drag the direction point to the left up).
Step 13. Create a further anchor point (drag the direction point diagonally to the left up).
Step 14. Create a further anchor point (drag the direction point diagonally to the right up).

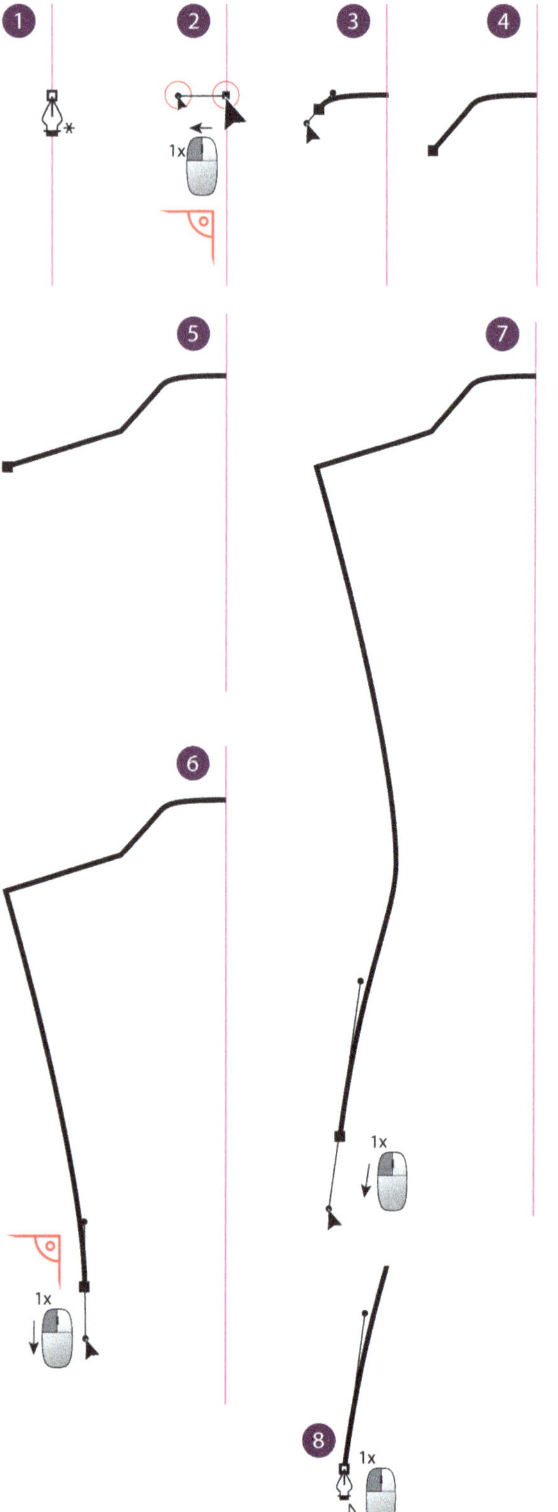

Step 15. Click the V button (Selection Tool) and click on the empty drawing area to deselect the object. Alternatively you can activate the shortcut command+Shift+A / Ctrl+Shift+A.

Step 16. Activate the **Pen Tool** (P) and start a new line.

Step 17. Create a further anchor point (drag the direction point diagonally to the left up).

Step 18. Click the last anchor point (press and release the left mouse button) to create a corner.

Step 19. Create a further anchor point (press and release the left mouse button, do not drag).

Step 20. Create a further anchor point (press and release the left mouse button, do not drag).

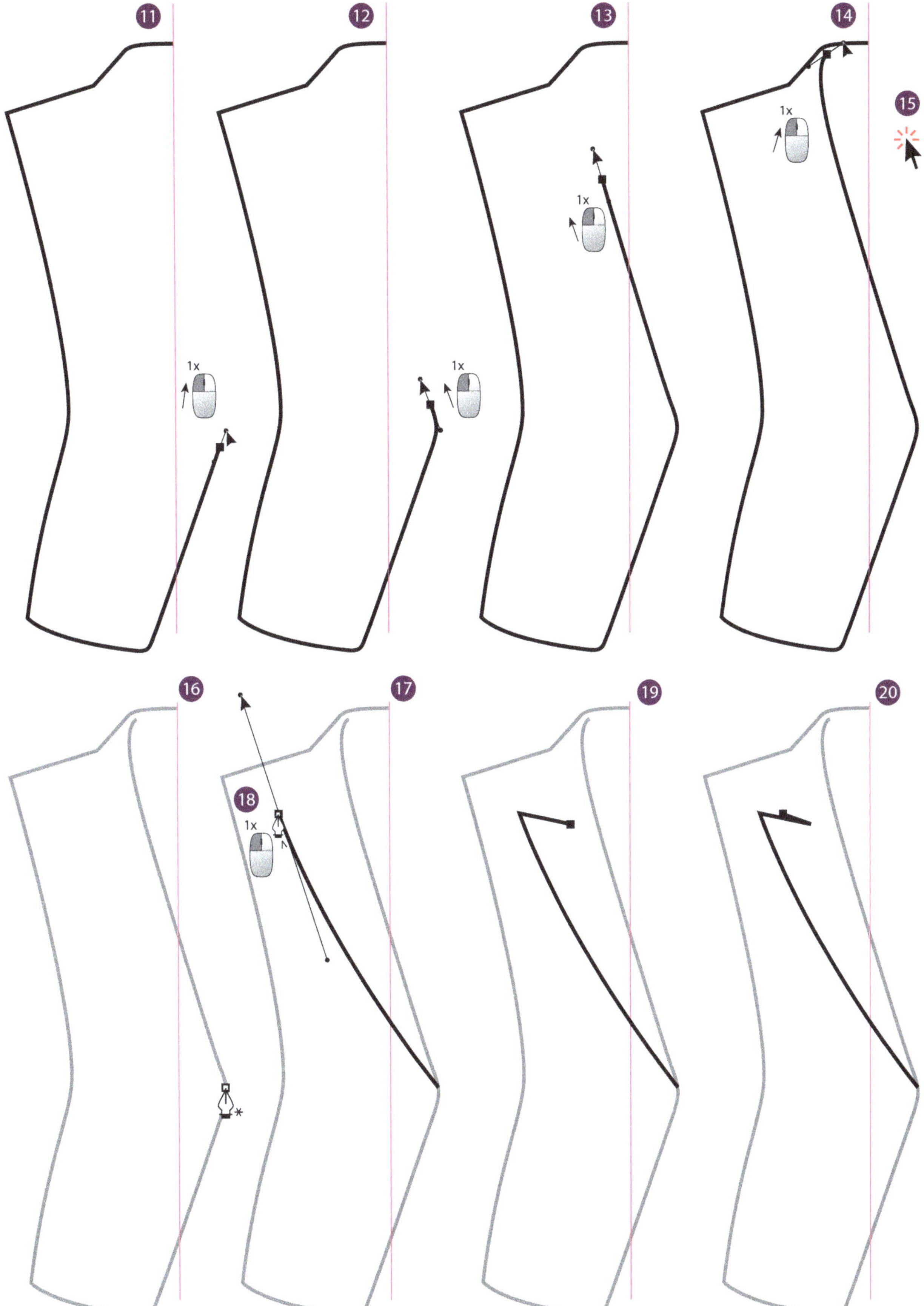

Step 21. Create a further anchor point (press and release the left mouse button, do not drag).
Step 22. Click the V button (Selection Tool) and click on the empty drawing area to deselect the object.
Step 23. Activate the **Pen Tool** (P) and start a new line.
Step 24. Create a further anchor point (press and release the left mouse button, do not drag).

Step 25. Hold down the left mouse button and drag with the **Selection Tool** (V) around the objects to select them.

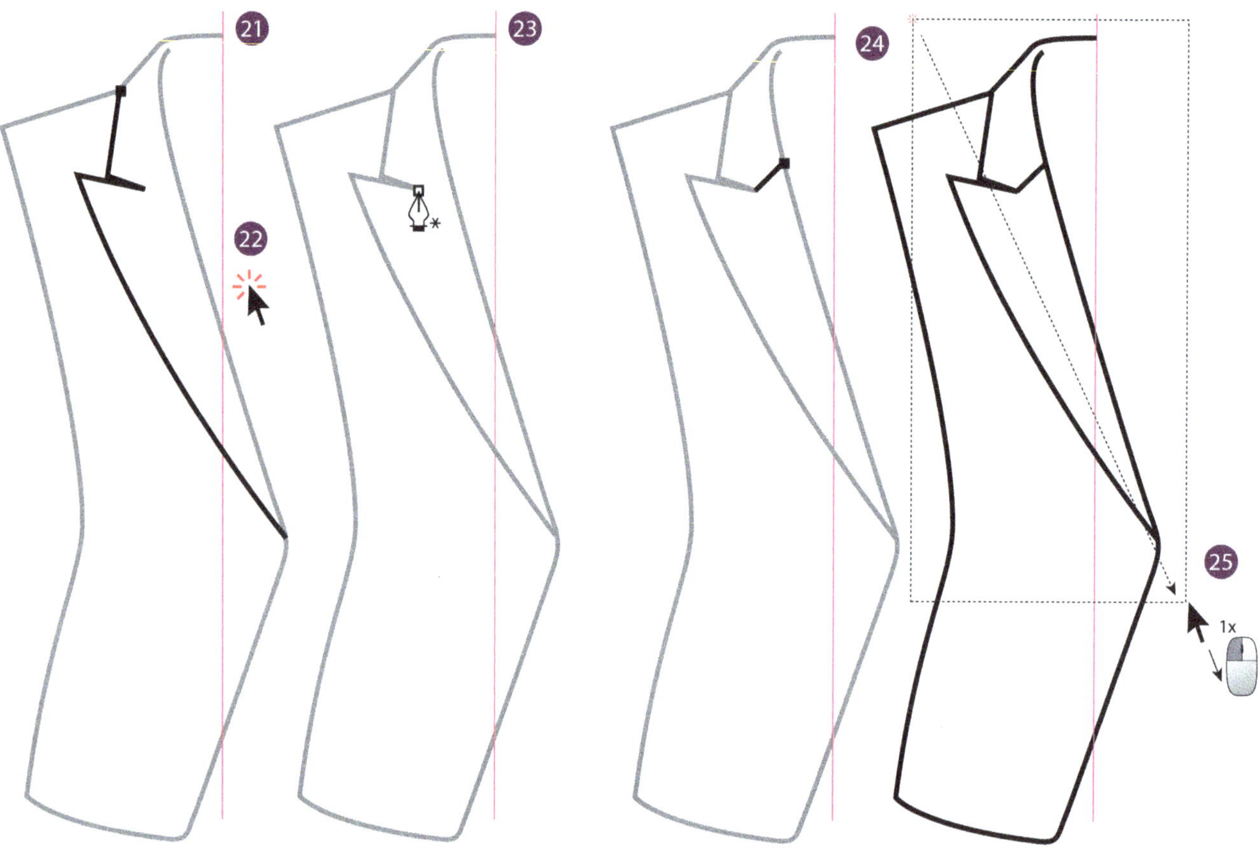

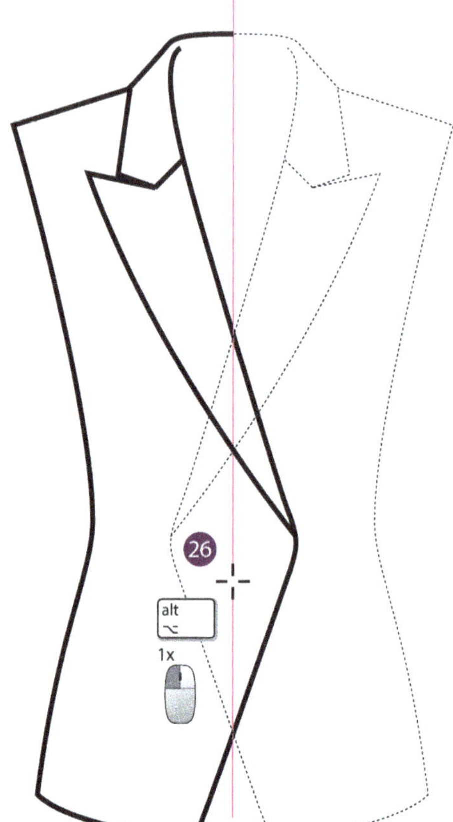

Step 26. Select the **Reflect Tool** (O), position the mouse cursor on the vertical guide, hold down the **alt** key (do not release the alt key) and click the left mouse button. The Reflect dialog box appears ,then release the **alt** key.
Activate the option „Vertical", then „Preview", check whether everything is OK and click „Copy". A mirrored duplicate is created.
Step 27. Hold down the **Shift** key and create with **Pen Tool** (P) a new straight line (press and release the left mouse button, do not drag).
Step 28. Hold down V key (Selection Tool) to select the line. Then hold down **alt** key (do not release), then hold down the left mouse button and drag to the top, in addition activate **Shift** key (also do not release). When the duplicate is located beneath the first object, release the mouse button (first the mouse button, then **Shift** and **alt** key).

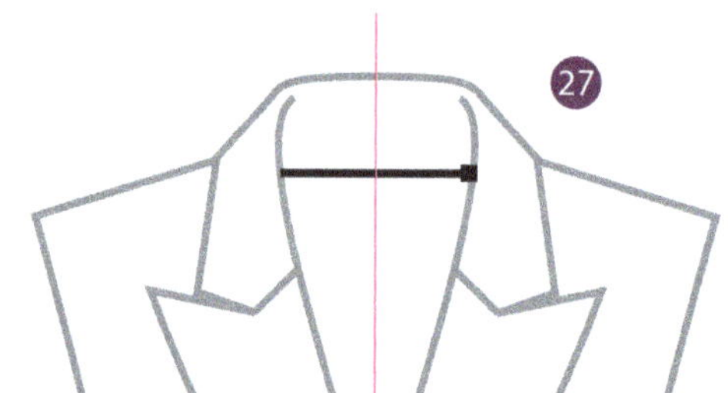

©dimitridesign.org

Step 29. Activate the **Pen Tool** (P) and start a new line.
Step 30. Create a further anchor point.

Step 31. Click the V key (Selection Tool) and click on the empty drawing area to deselect the object.

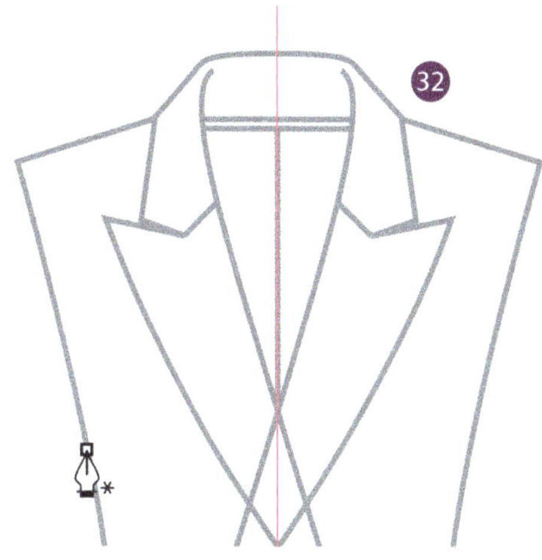

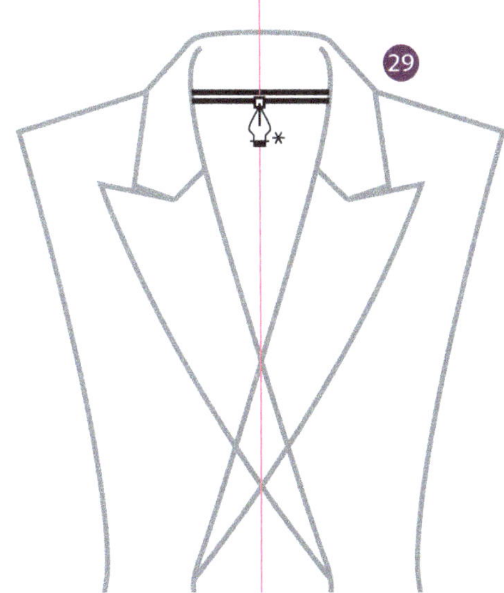

Step 32. Activate the **Pen Tool** (P) and start a new line (press and release the left mouse button, do not drag).
Step 33. Create a further anchor point (do not release the left mouse button), in addition hold down the **Shift** key (90° angle), also do not release it, now drag the direction point down, then release first the mouse button and then the **Shift** key.

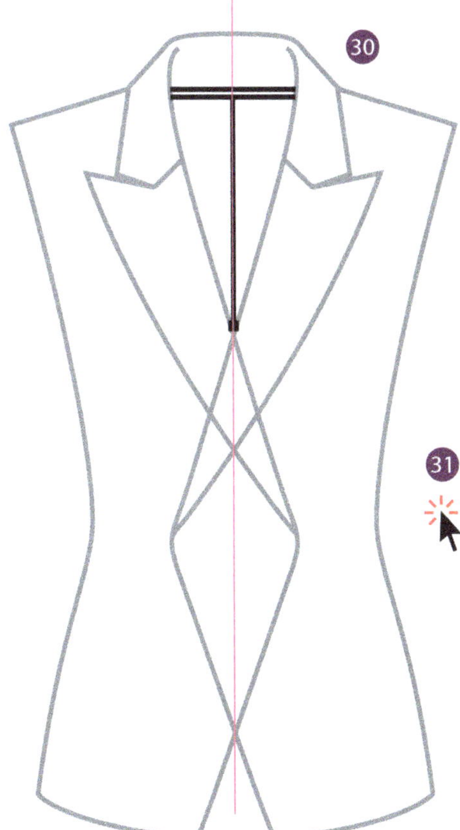

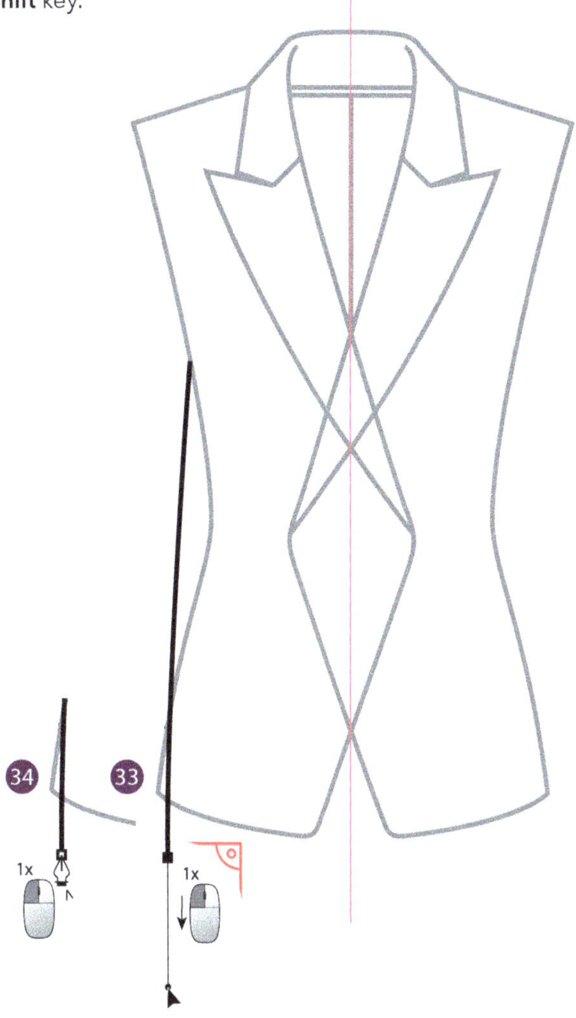

Step 34. Press the last anchor point (press and release the left mouse button) to create a corner.

Step 35. Create a further anchor point (drag the direction point diagonally to the left, then release the mouse button).

Step 36. Press the last anchor point (press and release the left mouse button) to create a corner.

Step 37. Create a further anchor point (drag the direction point to the top, then release the mouse button).

Step 38. Press the last anchor point to turn off for now the direction point and direction line (do not release the mouse button!).

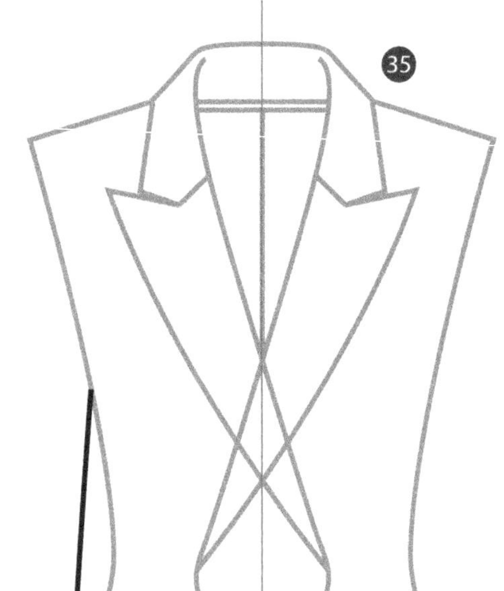

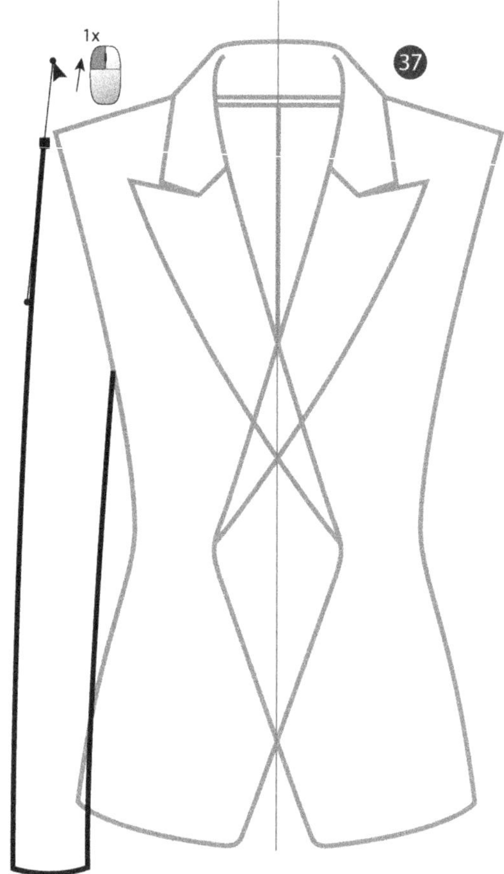

Step 39. Drag a new direction point, this time a little bit shorter (this way you can correct the paths afterwards).

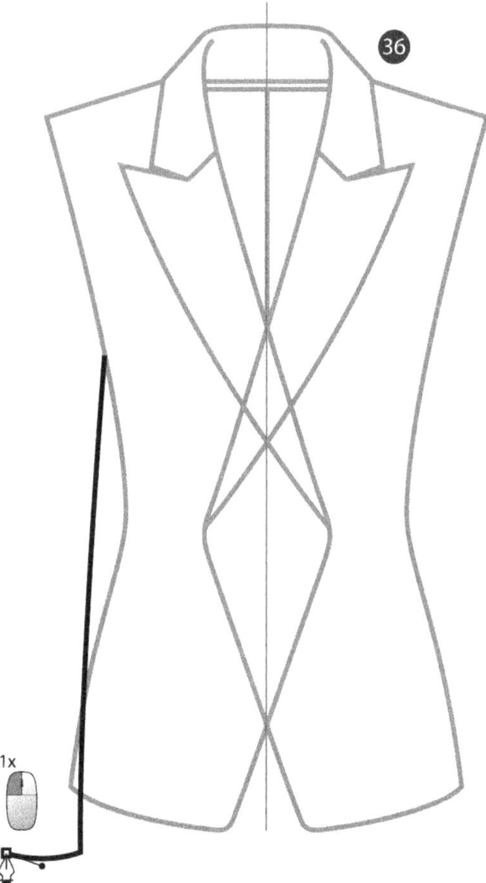

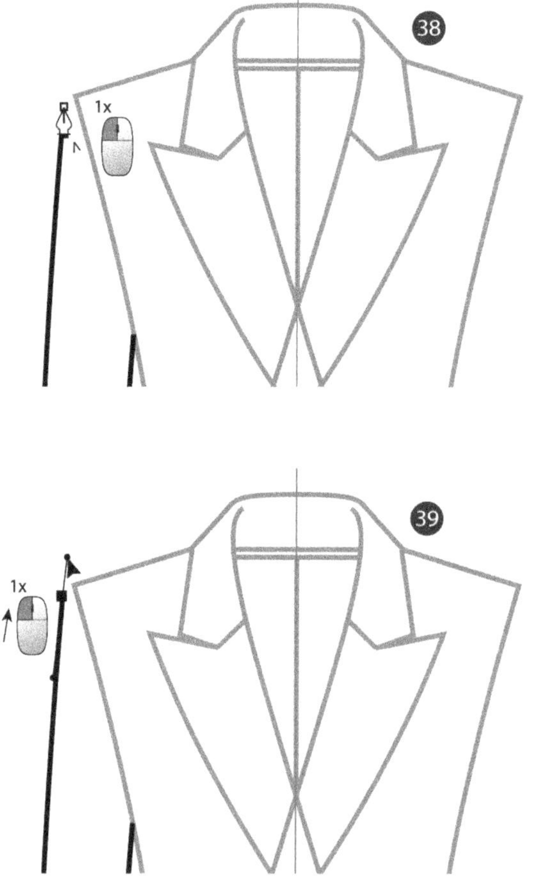

Step 40. Create a further anchor point
Step 41. Hold down the left mouse button and drag with the **Selection Tool** (V) around the object to select it.
Step 42. Activate the shortcut cmd+2 / Ctrl+2 (or choose **Object>Lock>Selection**) to lock the object.

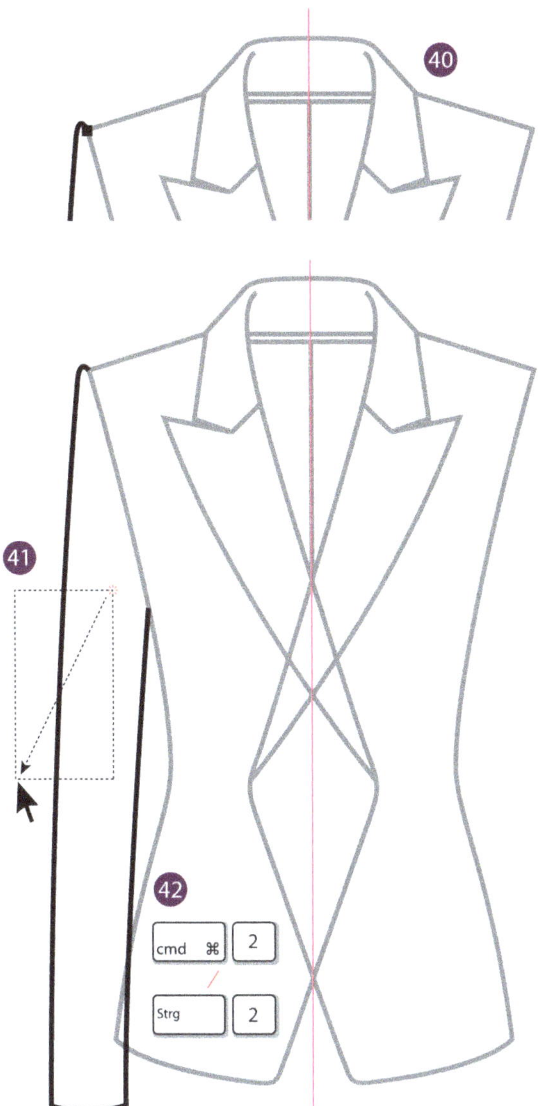

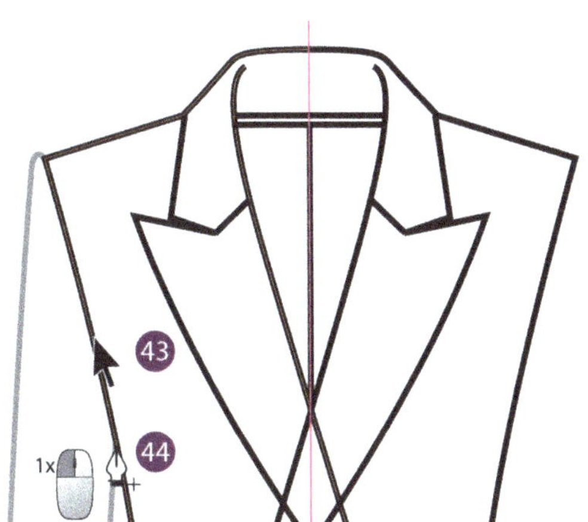

Step 43. Click the path with **Selection Tool** (V).
Step 44. Click with **Pen Tool** (P) on the path to create an additional anchor point (press and release the left mouse button). By clicking a plus sign near pen tool should be visible, that means that the pen tool was changed to „Add anchor point tool".

Step 45. Click with **Direct Selection Tool** (A) on the path (only the area between the nearest anchor points is selected).
Step 46. Activate the shortcut command+C / Ctrl+C (Copy) and the shortcut command+F / Ctrl+F (Paste in Front). Then activate the shortcut alt+cmd2 / alt+Ctrl+2 (or choose **Object>Unlock All**) to unlock again the sleeve.

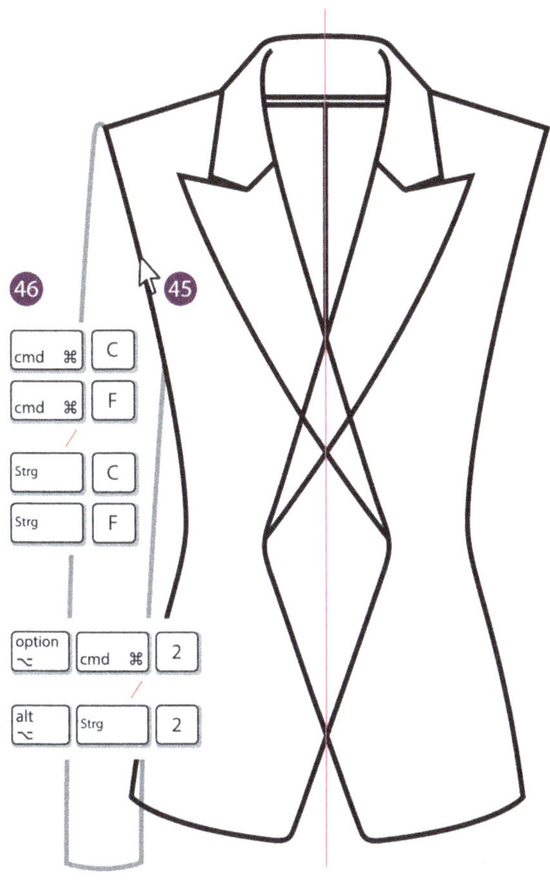

Step 47. Hold down **Shift** key and click with **Selection Tool** (V) on the objects (to select both objects at the same time), And click several times on the left keyboard arrow key to displace the objects.

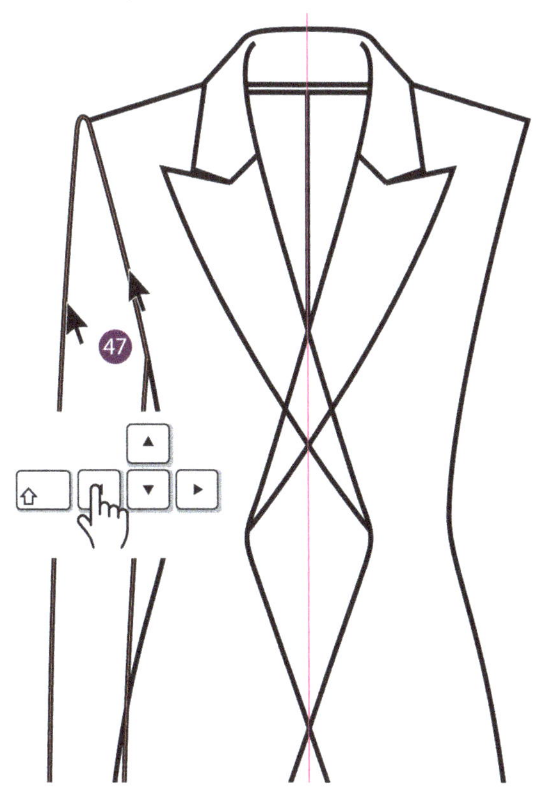

Step 48 and 49. Hold down the left mouse button and drag with the **Direct Selection Tool** (A) a selection around two anchor points (one end point of each half). Activate the shortcut alt+command+J /alt+Ctrl+J (Average...). In the dialog box activate „Both", then „OK", then activate the shortcut command+J / Ctrl+J (Join). Two paths were joined together.

Step 51. Click with the **Selection Tool** (V) the sleeve.
Step 52. Hold down **Shift** key and click several times on the right keyboard arrow key to displace the object to the original position.
Step 53. Click with the **Direct Selection Tool** (A) on the path (only a fragment between the nearest anchor points is selected).
Step 54. Activate the shortcut command+C / Ctrl+C (Copy) and the shortcut command+F / Ctrl+F (Paste in Front).
Step 55. Click the V key (Selection Tool).

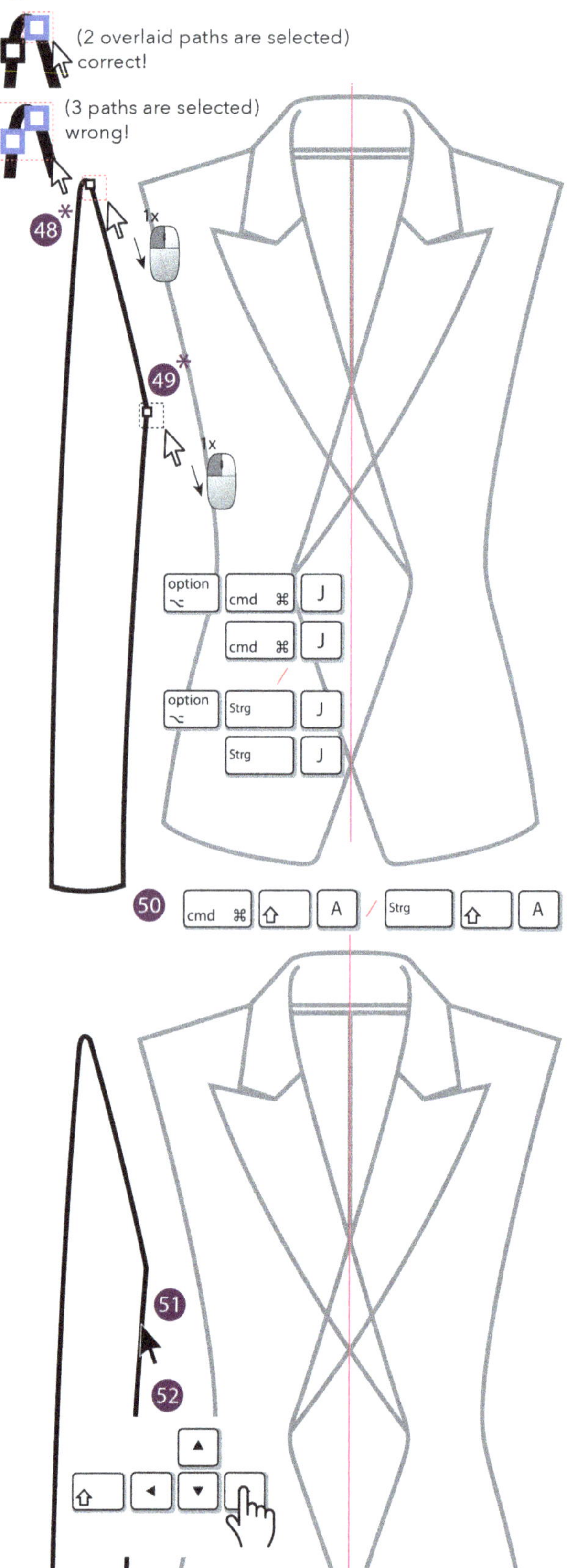

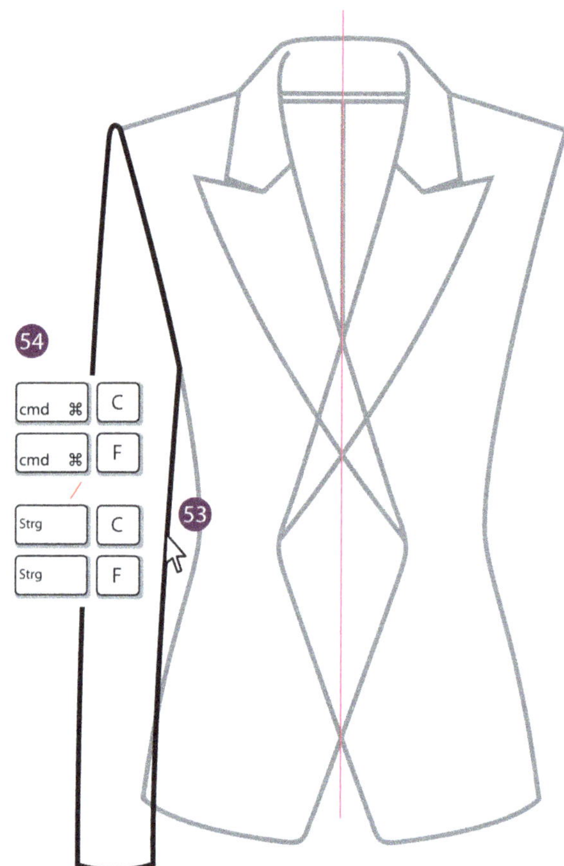

Step 56. And click several times on the left keyboard arrow key to displace the object.

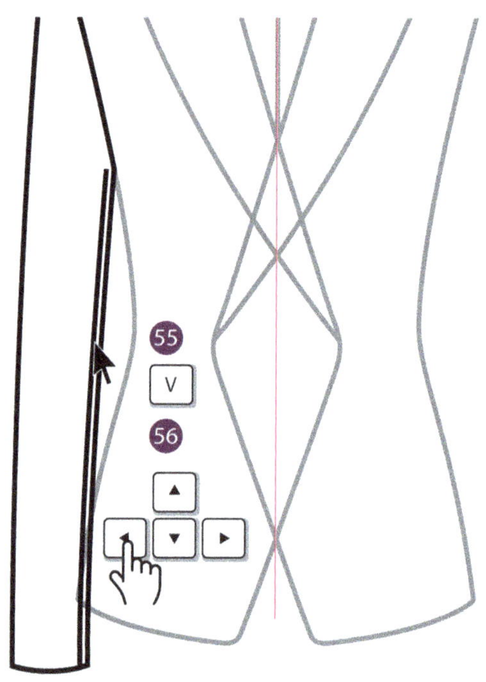

Step 50. Click on V key (Selection Tool) and click on a empty drawing area to deselect the object. Alternatively you can activate the shortcut command+Shift+A / Ctrl+Shift+A.

Step 57. With the **Selection Tool** (V) click on the end point of the line and finish to draw the line by creating a new end point.

Step 58. With the **Ellipse Tool** (L) create an ellipse (press the left mouse button, drag the mouse cursor and release the mouse button).

Step 59. Hold down the left mouse button and drag with the **Selection Tool** (V) around the objects to select them.

Step 61. Create with the **Rectangle Tool** (M) an rectangle (stroke colour „black", fill colour „None").

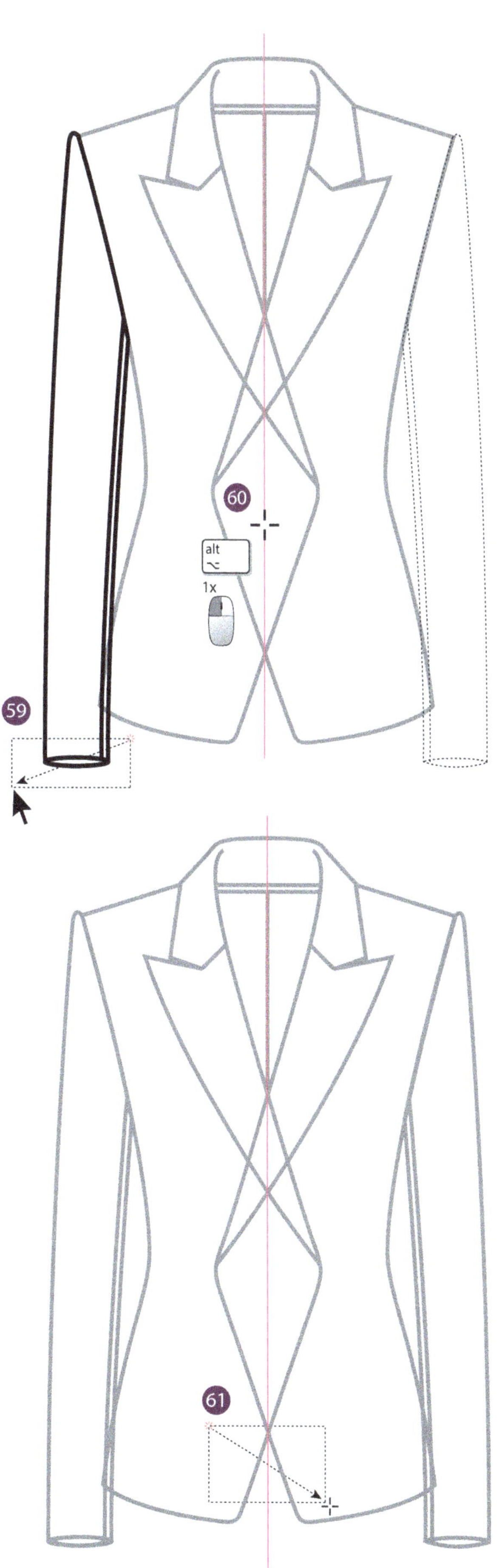

Step 60. Select the **Reflect Tool** (O), position the mouse cursor on the vertical guide, hold down the **alt** key (do not release the alt key) and click the left mouse button. The Reflect dialog box appears ,then release the **alt** key.
Activate the option „Vertical", then „Preview", check whether everything is OK and click „Copy". A mirrored duplicate is created.

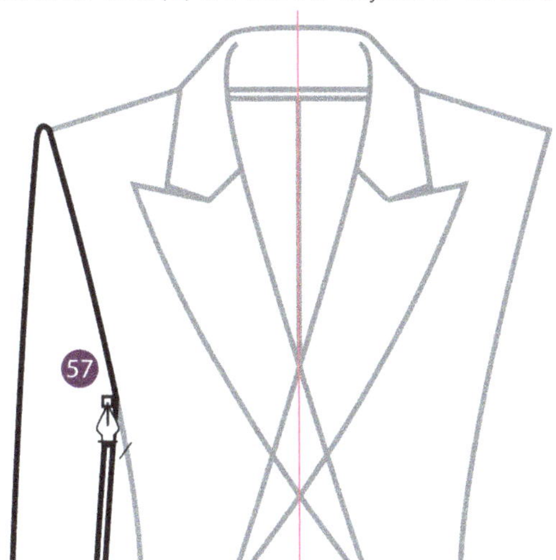

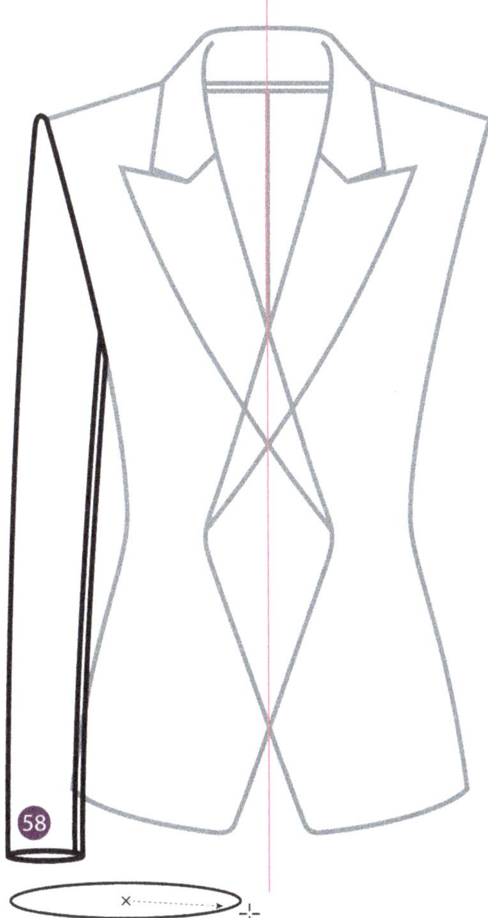

Step 62. Activate the **Pen Tool** (P) and start a new line.
Step 63. Hold down the **Shift** key and create with the **Pen Tool** (P) a new straight line (press and release the left mouse button, do not drag). Click the V key and click on the empty drawing area to deselect the object.
Step 64. Activate the **Pen Tool** (P) and start a new line.
Step 65. Hold down the **Shift** key and create with the **Pen Tool** (P) a new straight line (press and release the left mouse button, do not drag).

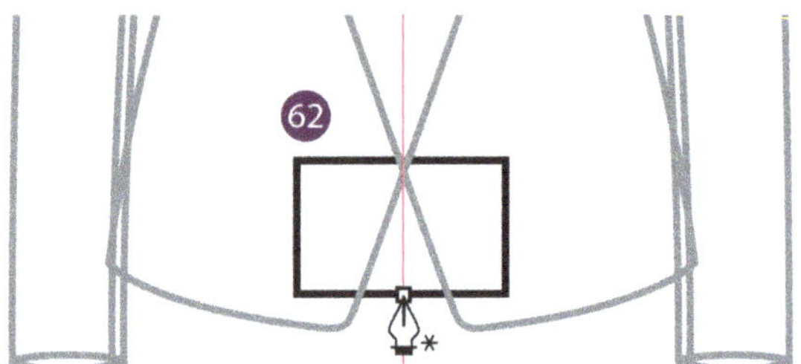

Step 66. Hold down the left mouse button and drag with the **Selection Tool** (V) around the objects to select them.
Step 67. Activate the shortcut cmd+2 / Ctrl+2 (or choose **Object>Lock>Selection**) to lock the objects.

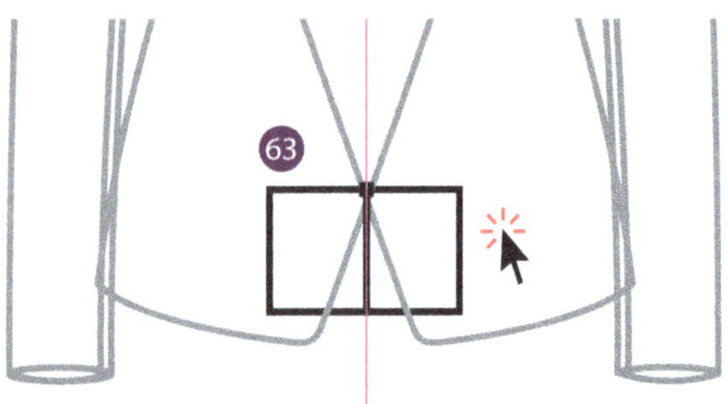

Step 68. Drag with the **Selection Tool** (V) around the objects (marked green) and activate the command **Object>Arrange>Send to Back**.

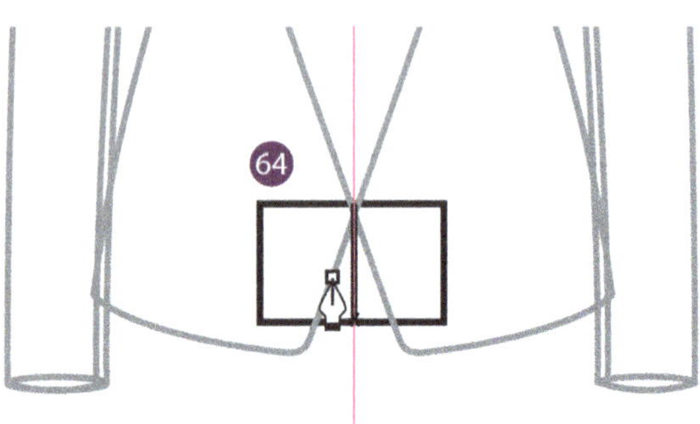

Step 69-71. Click on the path with **Scissors Tool** (C) to separate the lines at this points (see figure).

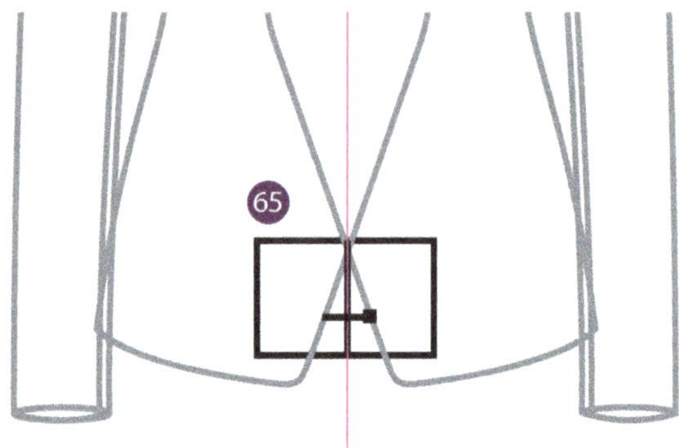

Step 72. Drag with the **Selection Tool** (V) around the separated lines and click several times on **Backspace** key to delete the unnecessary lines.
Step 73. Activate the shortcut alt+cmd+2 / alt+Ctrl+2 (or choose **Object>Unlock All**) to unlock the object in the document.

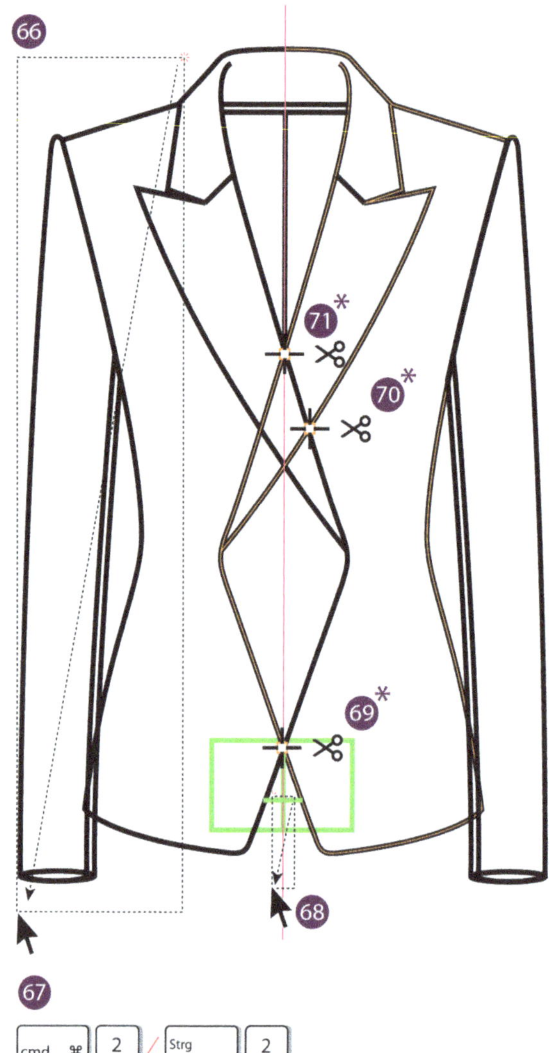

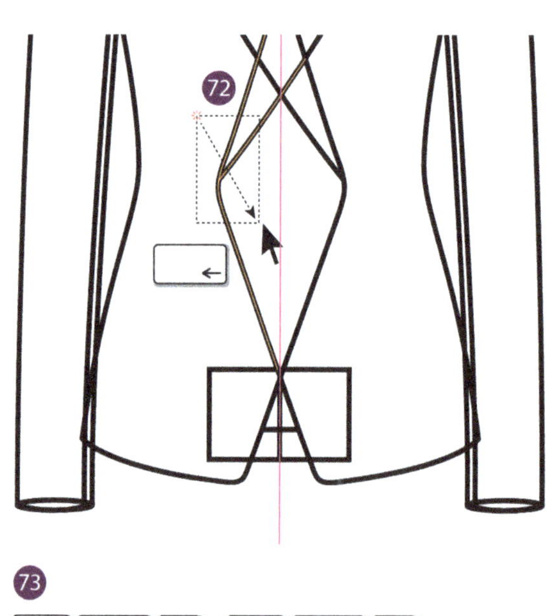

Step 74. Hold down the left mouse button and drag with the **Selection Tool** (V) around the objects.
Step 75. Activate **Live Paint Bucket** (K). Change the fill colour to grey (#BBBDC0).
Step 76. Then click inside the objects with the left mouse button (the stroke is displayed in red). Then activate the command **Expand** in the control panel.
Step 77. Hold down the left mouse button and drag with the **Selection Tool** (V) around the objects.
Step 78. Change the fill colour to grey (#BBBDC0).

Step 79. Hold down the left mouse button and drag with the **Selection Tool** (V) around the objects.
Step 80. Change the fill colour to grey (#BBBDC0).
Step 81. Click with the **Selection Tool** (V) on the object.
Step 82. Change the fill colour to grey (#BBBDC0).

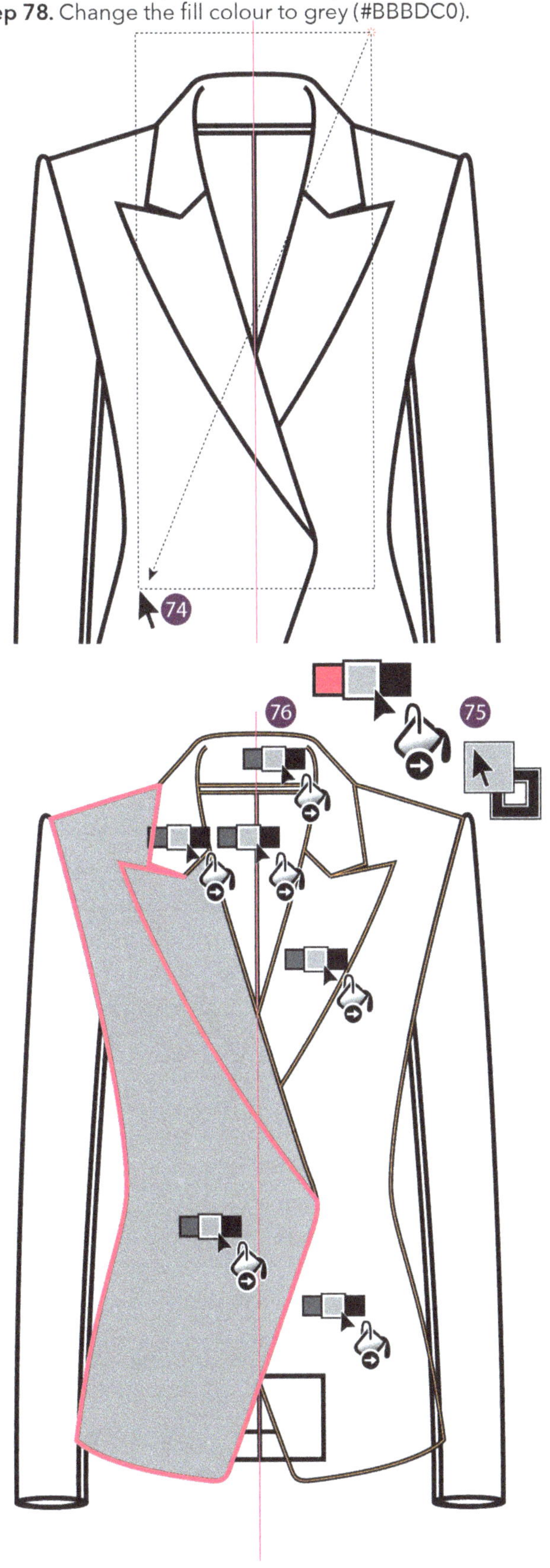

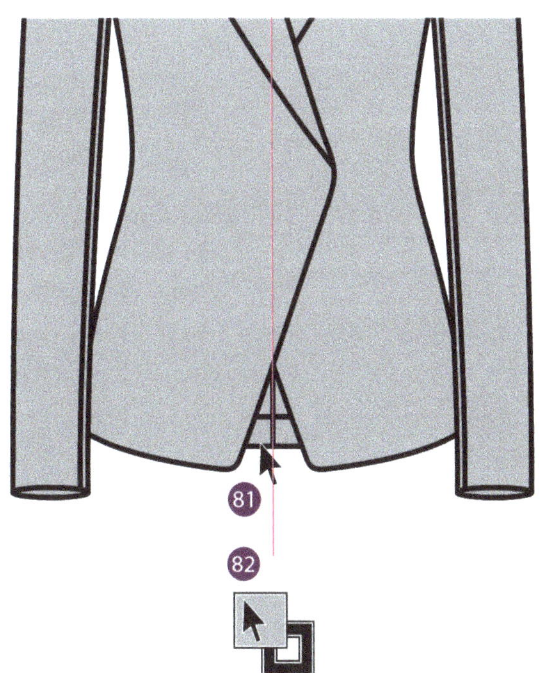

Step 83. Create with the **Rectangle Tool** (M) an rectangle (stroke colour „black", fill colour „None").
Step 84. Hold down the left mouse button and drag with the **Direct Selection Tool** (A) a selection around two anchor points. The two anchor points are selected.

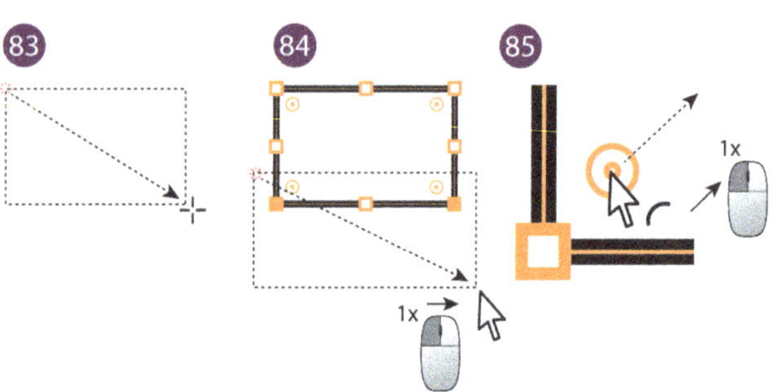

Step 85. Hold down the left mouse button and drag the cursor diagonally on the circle-symbol to the center point of the rectangle. The corners of the pocket are rounded.

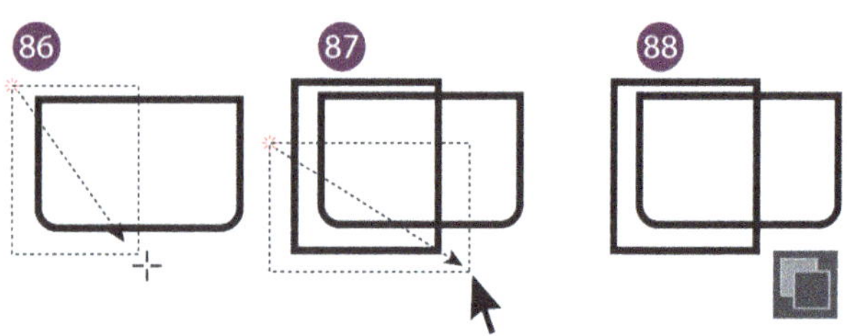

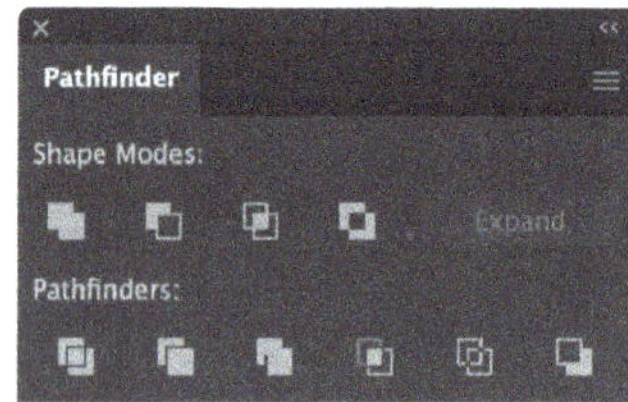

Step 86. Create with the **Rectangle Tool** (M) an rectangle (stroke colour „black", fill colour „None").
Step 87. Hold down the left mouse button and drag with the **Selection Tool** (V) around the objects.
Step 88. Open   „Pathfinder" panel (**Window>Pathfinder**) and click on the button „Minus Front".

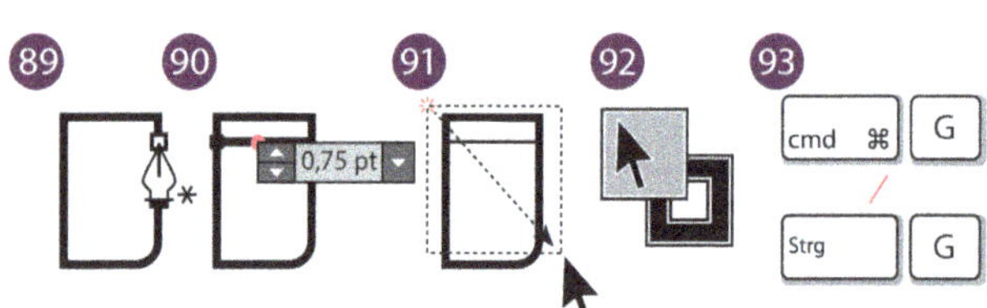

Step 89. Activate the **Pen Tool** (P) and start a new line.
Step 90. Change in the „Stroke" panel **Weight** to 0,5pt or 0,75pt.
Step 91. Hold down the left mouse button and drag with the **Selection Tool** (V) around the objects.
Step 92. Change the fill colour to grey (#BBBDC0).
Step 93. Activate the shortcut cmd+G / Ctrl+G (or choose **Object>Group**) to group both objects.
Step 94. Rotate the object a little bit to the right.
Step 95. And place the object on the blazer

Step 96. Select the **Reflect Tool** (O), position the mouse cursor on the vertical guide, hold down the **alt** key (do not release the alt key) and click the left mouse button. The Reflect dialog box appears ,then release the **alt** key.
Activate the option „Vertical", then „Preview", check whether everything is OK and click „Copy". A mirrored duplicate is created.

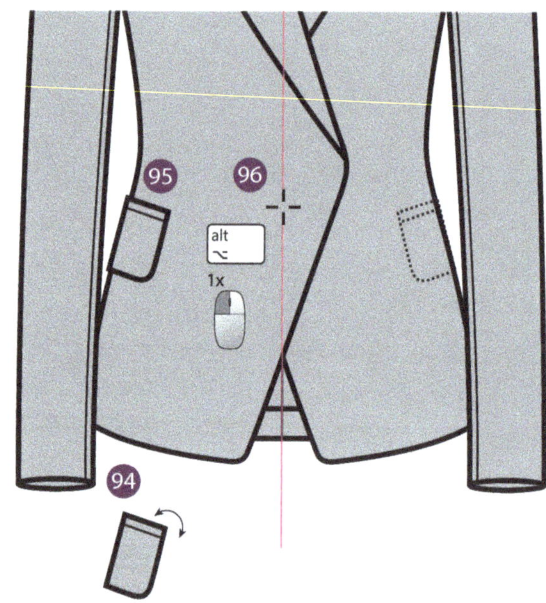

Step 97. Change the fill colour to grey (#838589).
Adjust in the „stroke" panel (**Window>Stroke**) different stroke weights.

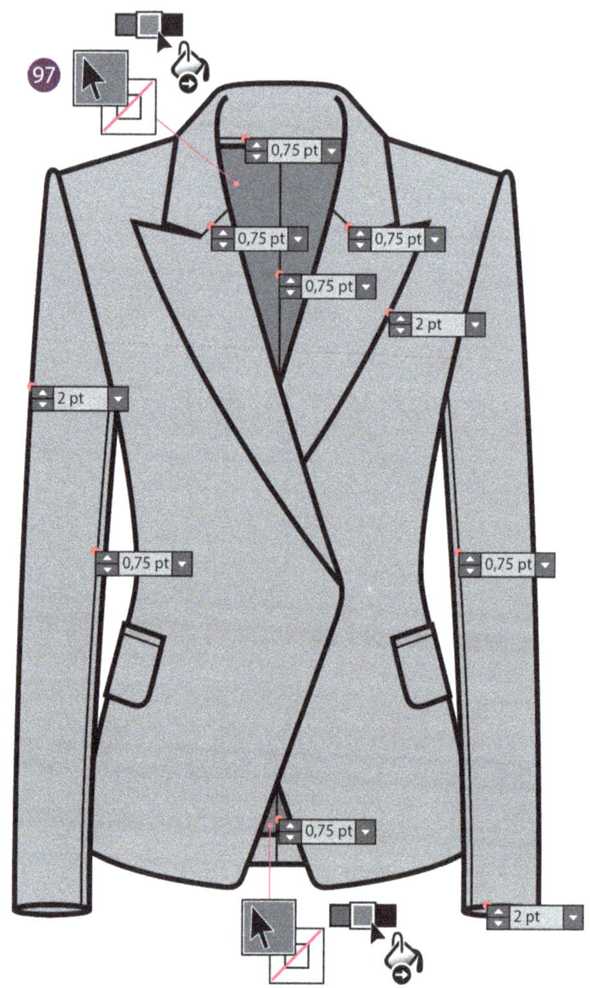

Step 98. Draw a button (see tutorial p.73)
And place two copys of the button on the blazer.
Click on both objects with the **Blend Tool** (W).
Step 99. Double-click in the tools panel on the **Blend Tool** (W) to change further settings in the dialog box.
Change „Spacing" to „Specified Steps", then type „1" and confirm with „OK".

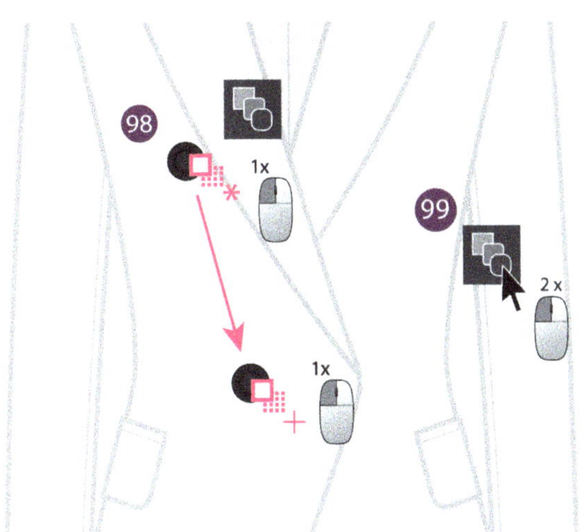

Step 100. Click with the **Selection Tool** (V) on the object group.
Step 101. Select the **Reflect Tool** (O), position the mouse cursor on the vertical guide, hold down the **alt** key (do not release the alt key) and click the left mouse button. The Reflect dialog box appears ,then release the **alt** key.
Activate the option „Vertical", then „Preview" and click „Copy". A mirrored duplicate is created.

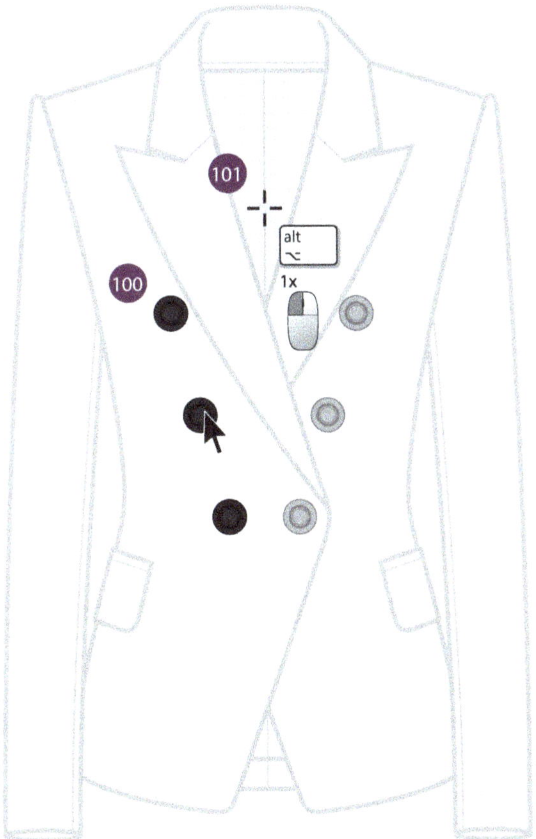

Step 102. Create with the **Pen Tool** (P) a short new line.

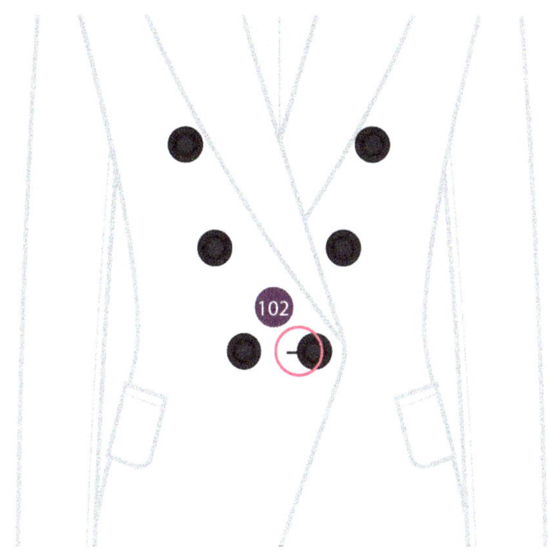

Step 103. Choose in the tools panel the stroke color „None" and the fill color „grey". Draw new objects to apply shades to the blazer.
Step 104 and 105. Open the panel „**Window>Transparency**" and apply different settings (see figure).

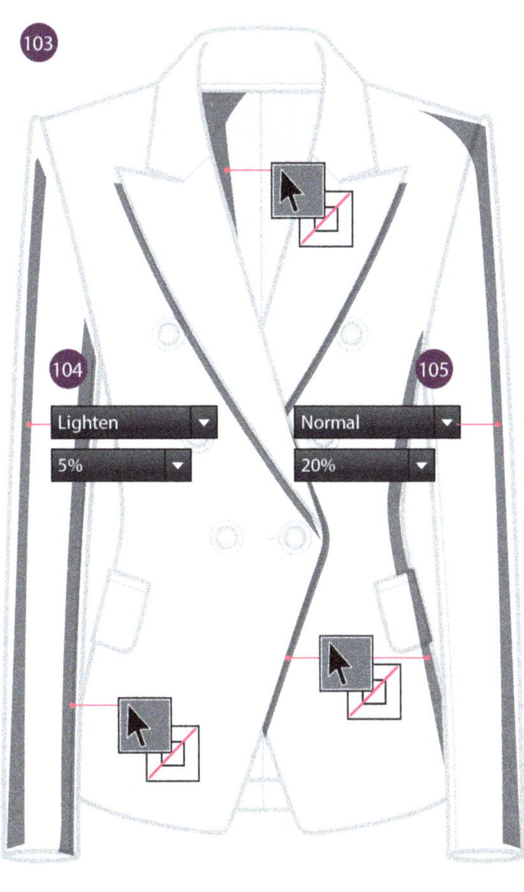

Step 106. Activate the effect: „**Effect>Blur>Gaussian Blur**"
Step 107. Type in the dialog box e.g. 4,1 pixel.

It makes sense to draw „shadow" objects on a new layer to control better the modifications.

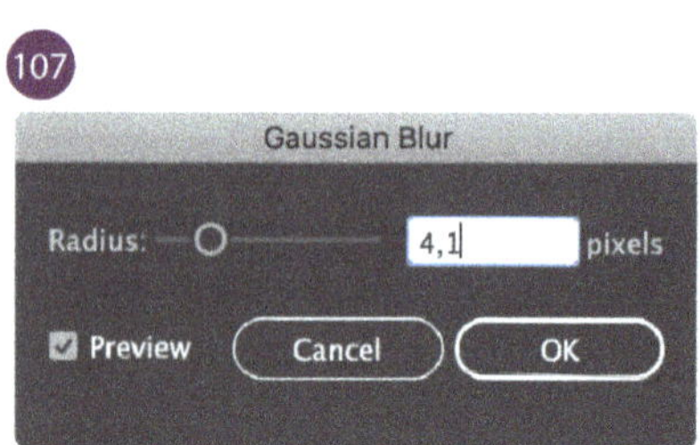

8.7 TUTORIAL: CREATE PATTERN

VERSION CC

First draw an object e.g. „mandala" pattern from tutorial on page 54.

 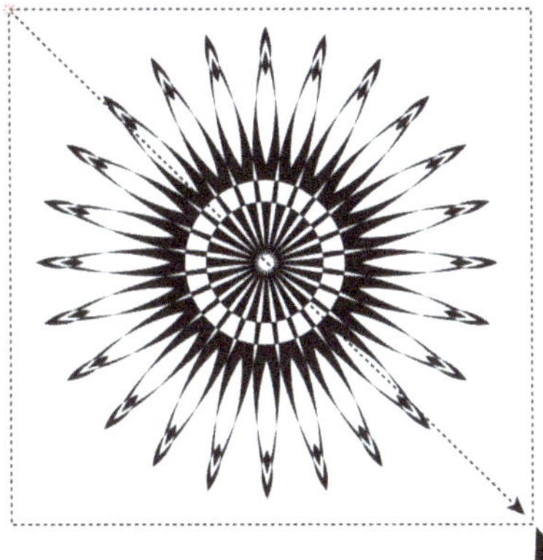

Step 1. Hold down left mouse button and drag with **Selection Tool** (V) around the object to select it.
Step 2. Activate the command:
Object > Pattern > Make
The dialog box „Pattern Options" appears. You can set different options here.
Step 3. Click on „Done" to confirm the settings. The pattern is automatically added to the "Swatches".

To edit later an existing pattern, double-click in the „Swatches" (Window>Swatches) on the particular pattern or activate the command **Object > Pattern > Edit pattern**.

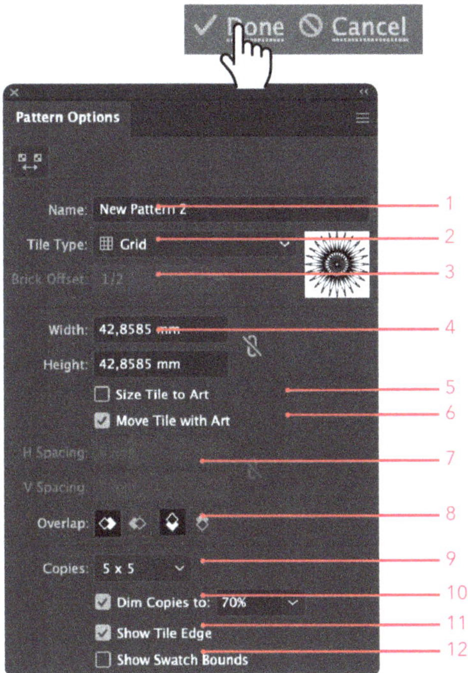

1. Type pattern name.
2. Tile type (rapport) (see examples on the right).
3. Type brick offset, valid only for „Brick by Row" and „Brick by Column" tile types.
4. Specifies the height and width of the tile.
5. With this option, the tile is reduced to the size of the art.
6. Pattern (tile) will be displaced together with the art, Through that process the position of the pattern will not be changed.
7. Adds space between two contiguous tiles.

8. Decide which tiles are in the foreground when adjacent tiles overlap.
9. Determines how many rows and columns with tiles are visible, while the pattern is changed.
10. Determines the opacity of the Tile copies from the preview.
11. Displays a frame around the tile.
12. Shows a section of the pattern to be duplicated in order to create the pattern.

Grid

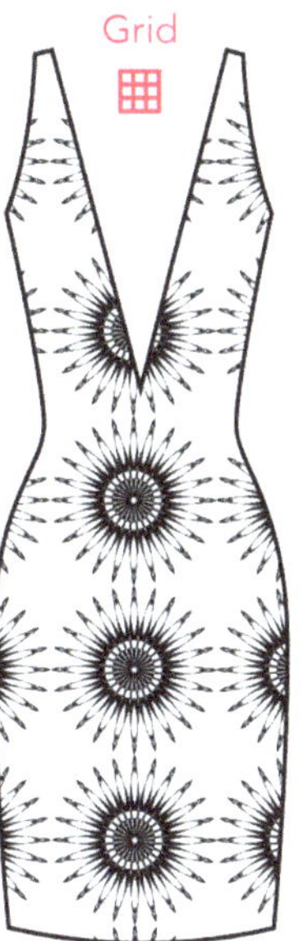

Brick by Row

Brick by Column

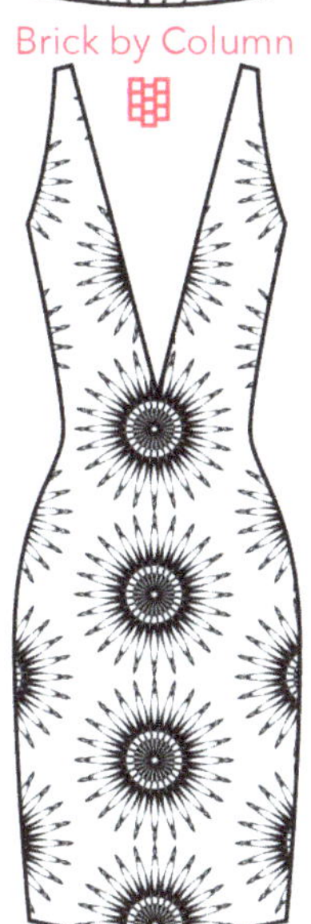

Hex by Column

Hex by Row

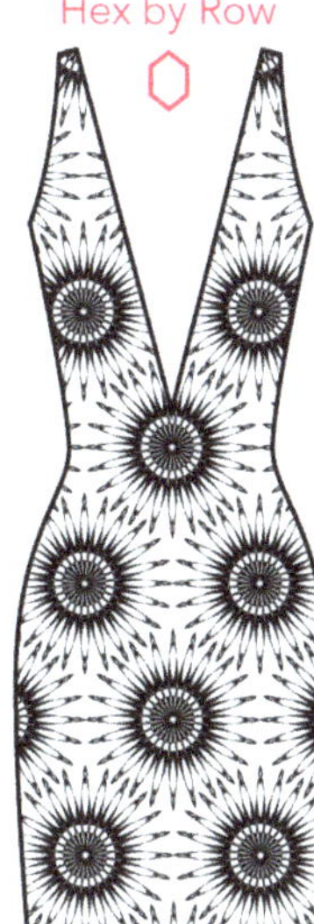

To displace a pattern inside an object, hold down the ⌥ key (only on Mac) and drag with **Selection Tool** (V) inside the selected object (the object must be filled with pattern).
Alternatively hold down ⌥ key and click on the arrow keys to displace the pattern.

You can also double click on the **Selection Tool** (V) and type exact value (you should deactivate in this case in the dialog box the option "Transform objects"). Or activate the command **Object>Transform>...**

8.8 TUTORIAL: PATCH POCKET

REQUIREMENTS

-Choose in the tools panel the stroke color „black" and the fill color „None".

-Set in the stroke panel (**Window > Stroke**) the stroke weight to **1pt** or **2pt**.

-Choose: **View > Rules >Show Rules, View > Guides > Lock Guides, View > Guides > Show Guides, View > Smart Guides, View > Snap to Point.**

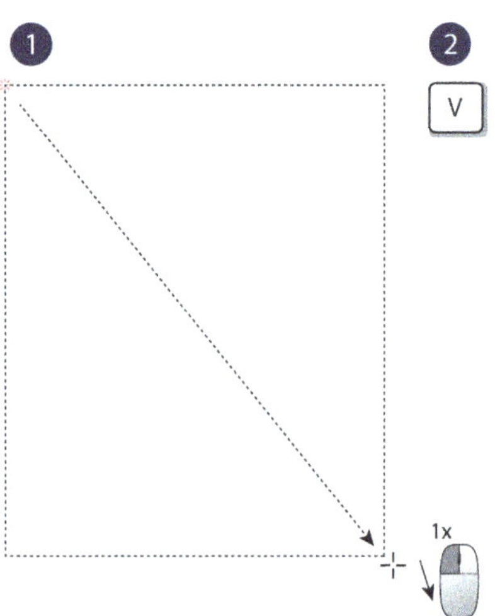

Step 1. Select the **Rectangle Tool** (M) and create an rectangle.
Step 2. Click V key (Selection Tool).
Step 3. Drag a vertical guide. While dragging, place the cursor over the middle square below (object center-point). The guide is magnetically fixed to the point.

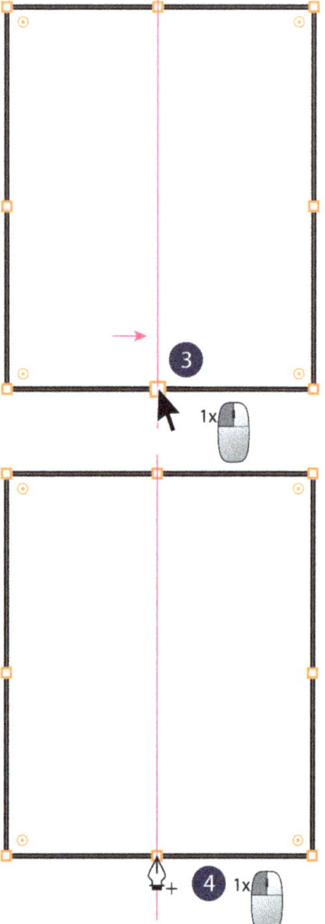

Step 4. Click with the **Pen Tool** (P) on the path to create an additional anchor point (press and release the left mouse button). By clicking a plus sign near pen tool should be visible,   that means that the pen tool was changed to „Add anchor point tool".

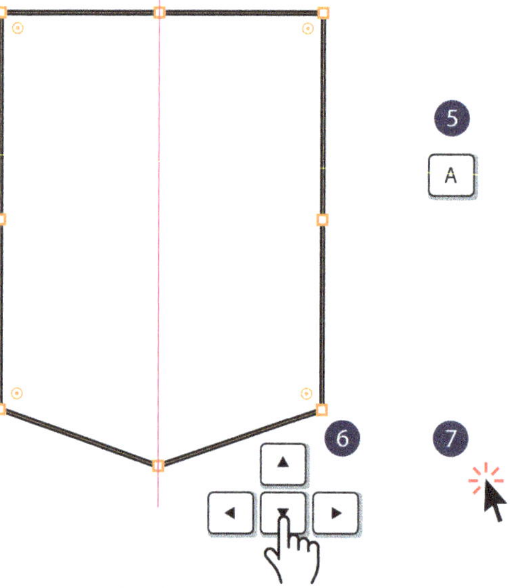

Step 5. Click A key (Direct Selection Tool) (press and release).
Step 6. Click several times on the down keyboard arrow key, the line is displaced.
Step 7. Click on V key (Selection Tool) and click on a empty drawing area to deselect the object. Alternatively, you can activate the shortcut command+Shift+A / Ctrl+Shift+A.

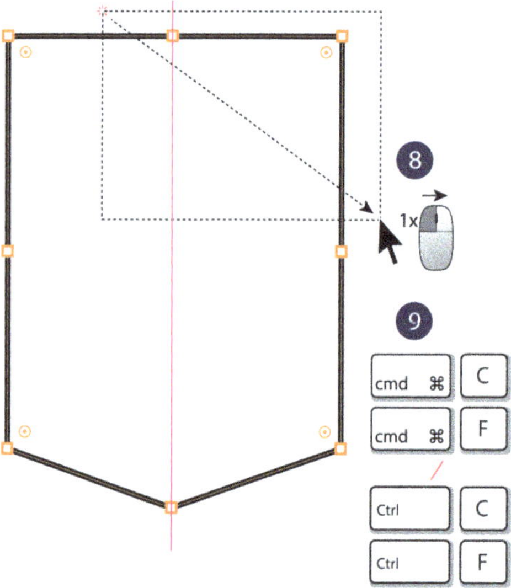

Step 8. Hold down the left mouse button and drag with **Selection Tool** (V) around the object.
Step 9. Activate the shortcut command+C / Ctrl+C (Copy) and the shortcut command+F / Ctrl+F (Paste in Front).
Step 10. Displace the duplicate with the up keyboard arrow key to the top (additionally hold down the **Shift** key).
Step 11. Hold down the left mouse button and drag with **Direct Selection Tool** (A) a selection around two anchor points. The two anchor points are selected.
Step 12. Click several times the down keyboard arrow key, until the line is on the same horizontal level as the line of the pocket base. Alternatively, drag with the mouse cursor, until the lines overlap each other.

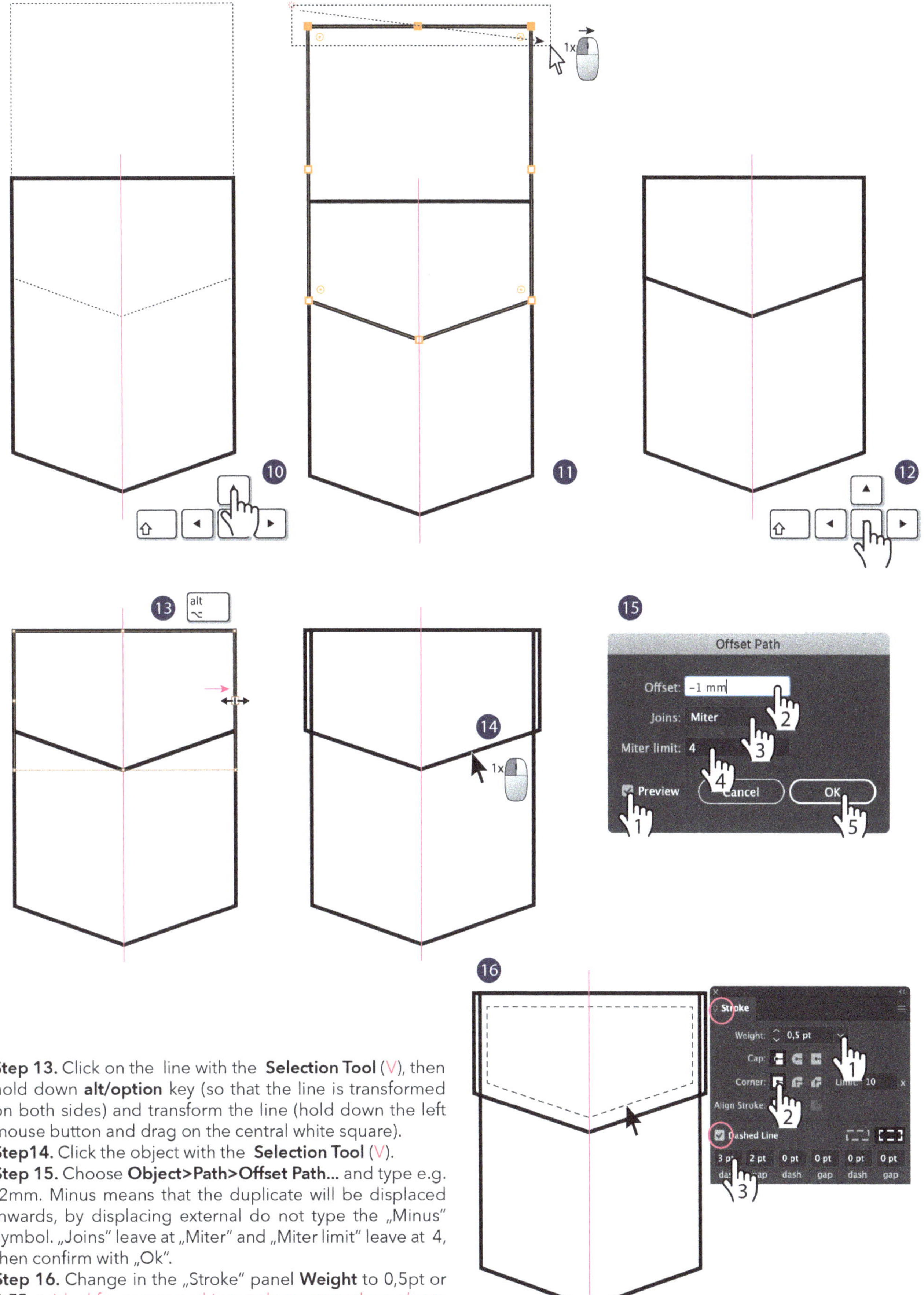

Step 13. Click on the line with the **Selection Tool** (V), then hold down **alt/option** key (so that the line is transformed on both sides) and transform the line (hold down the left mouse button and drag on the central white square).
Step14. Click the object with the **Selection Tool** (V).
Step 15. Choose **Object>Path>Offset Path...** and type e.g. -2mm. Minus means that the duplicate will be displaced inwards, by displacing external do not type the „Minus" symbol. „Joins" leave at „Miter" and „Miter limit" leave at 4, then confirm with „Ok".
Step 16. Change in the „Stroke" panel **Weight** to 0,5pt or 0,75pt. Ideal for seams and inner elements such as pleats. Activate „Dashed Line", „dash" indicate 3pt and „gap" 2pt. If the option „Dashed Line" is not visible, click on more options ▤ , then Show Options.

Step17. Change the fill color to „white".

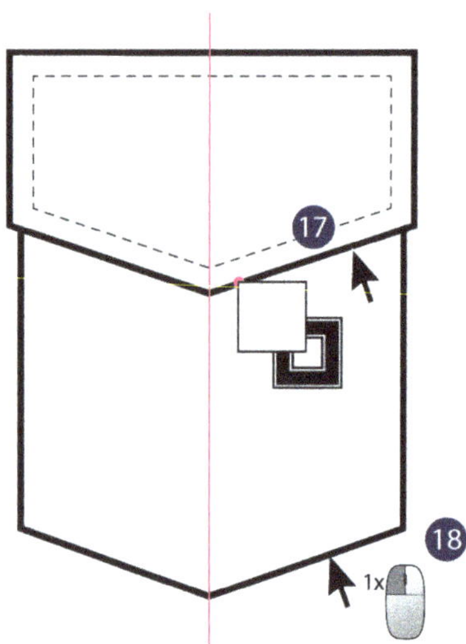

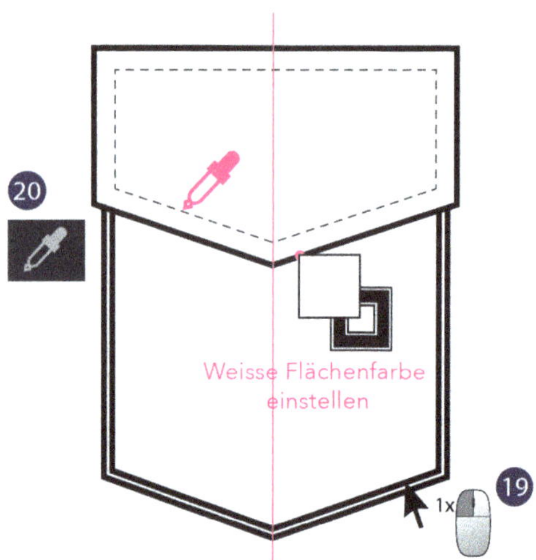

Step 18. Click the object with the **Selection Tool** (V).
Step 19. Choose **Object>Path>Offset Path...** and type e.g. -1mm.
Step 20. Activate **Eyedropper Tool** (I) and click on the dashed line to take over the settings of this line.

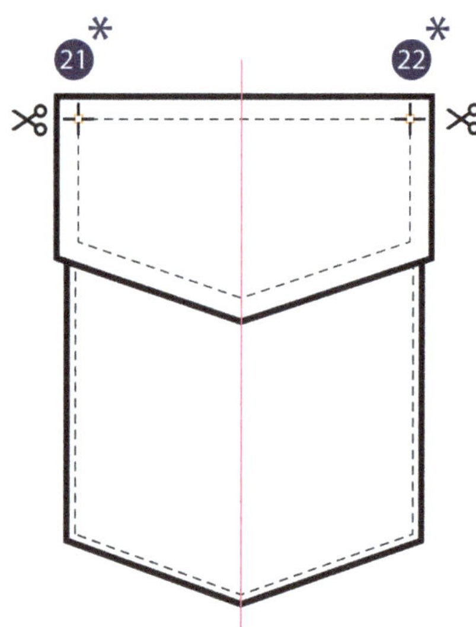

Step 21 and 22. Click on both anchor points with **Scissors Tool** (C) to separate the shape at that points (see figure).

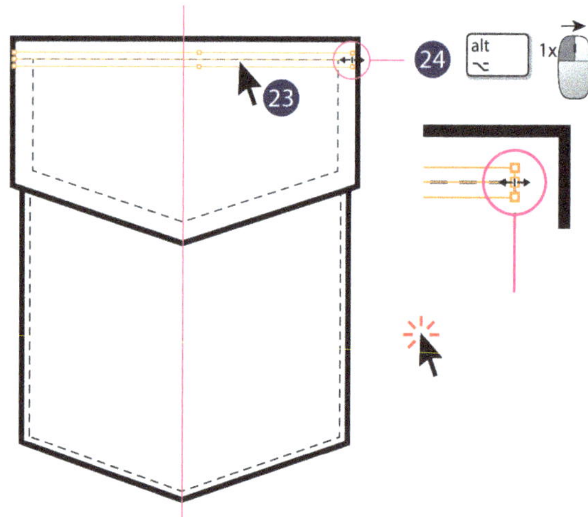

Step 23. Now click the separated line with **Selection Tool** (V).
Step 24. Hold down **alt/option** key (so that the line is transformed on both sides) and transform the line (hold down the left mouse button and drag on the central white square).

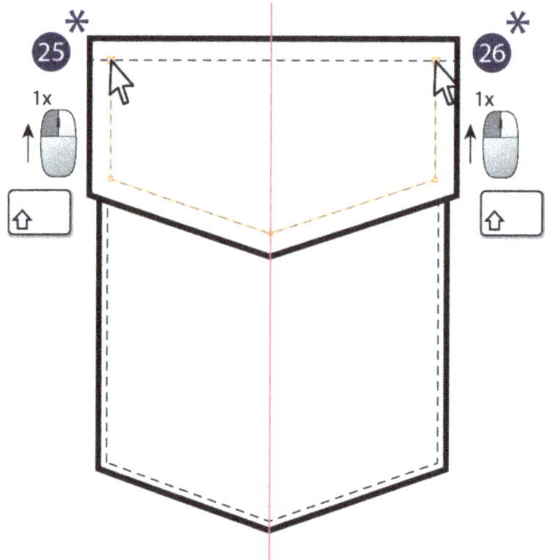

Step 25 and 26. Hold down the **Shift** key (do not release) and click with the **Direct Selection Tool** (A) on both anchor points (see figure), then drag the both anchor points to the top.

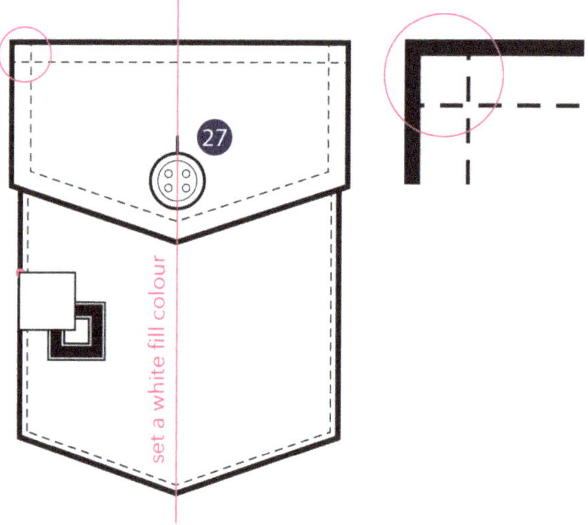

Step 27. Construct a button (see next tutorial).

8.9 TUTORIAL: DRAW A BUTTON

REQUIREMENTS

-Choose in the tools panel the stroke color „black" and the fill color „white".

-Set in the stroke panel (**Window > Stroke**) the stroke weight to **1pt** or **2pt**.

-Choose: **View > Rules >Show Rules, View > Guides > Lock Guides, View > Guides > Show Guides, View > Smart Guides, View > Snap to Point**.

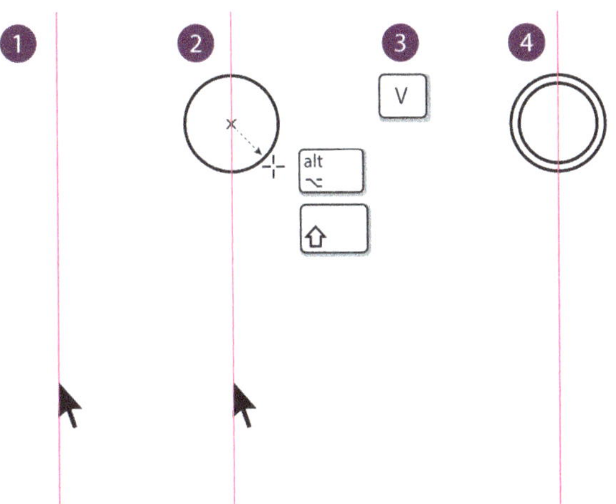

Step 1. Place a vertical guide.
Step 2. Activate **Ellipse Tool** (L), hold down **alt/option** and **Shift** key, then create a circle.
Step 3. Activate V key (Selection Tool).
Step 4. Activate the command **Object>Path>Offset Path...** and type e.g. -2mm.

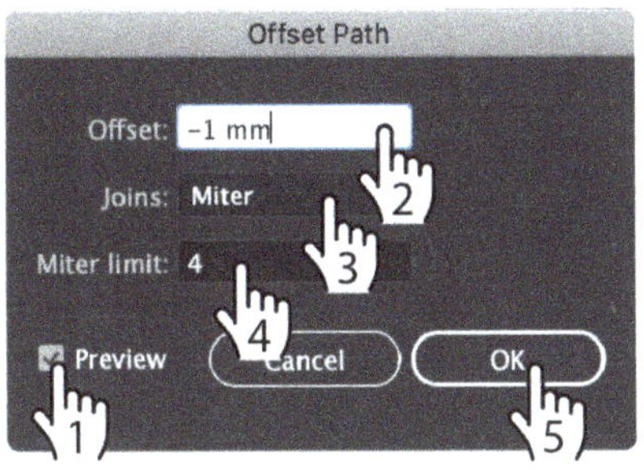

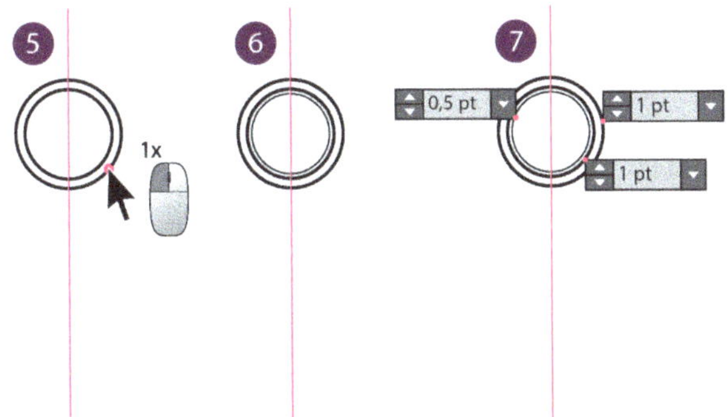

Step 5. Click with the **Selection Tool** (V) the outer circle.
Step 6. Activate again the command **Object>Path>Offset Path...** and type e.g. -2,5mm.
It is important that the value is higher than in the step 4 in order to ensure that the line is visible.
Step 7. Adjust different stroke weights (**Window > Stroke**).

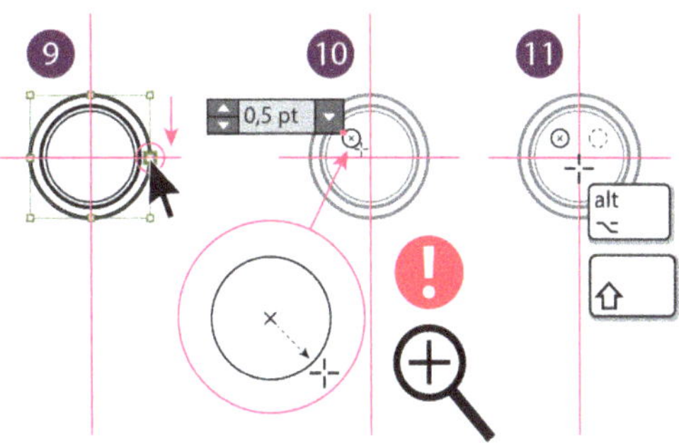

Step 9. Drag a vertical guide. While dragging, place the cursor over the middle white square below. The guide is magnetically fixed to the point.
Step 10. Activate **Ellipse Tool** (L), hold down **alt/option** and **Shift** key, then create a further circle for the buttonhole. (Try to work always with the **Zoom Tool** (Z) when it comes to precise work).
Step 11. Select the **Reflect Tool** (O), position the cursor on the vertical guide, hold down the **alt/option** key (do not release the alt key) and click the left mouse button. The Reflect dialog box appears ,then release the **alt/option** key. Activate the option „Vertical", then „Preview" and click „Copy". A mirrored duplicate is created.

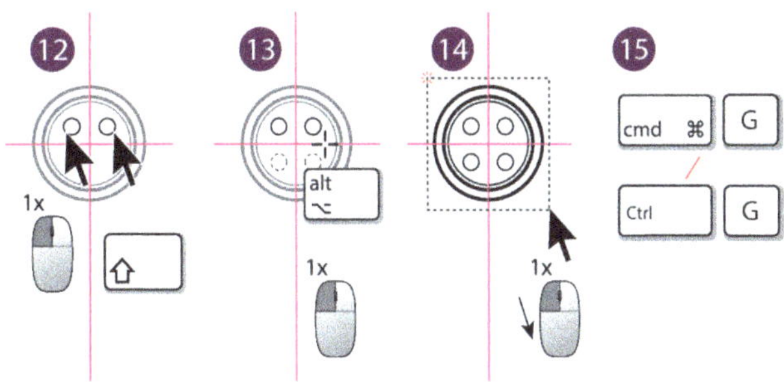

Step 12. Hold down **Shift** key and click with the **Selection Tool** (V) both„buttonholes".
Step 13. Select the **Reflect Tool** (O), position the cursor on the vertical guide, hold down the **alt/option** key (do not release the alt key) and click the left mouse button. The Reflect dialog box appears, then release the **alt/option** key. Activate the option „Horizontal", then „Preview" and click „Copy". A mirrored duplicate is created.
Step 14. Hold down the left mouse button and drag with the **Selection Tool** (V) around the objects to select them.
Step 15. Activate the shortcut cmd+G / Ctrl+G to group the objects.

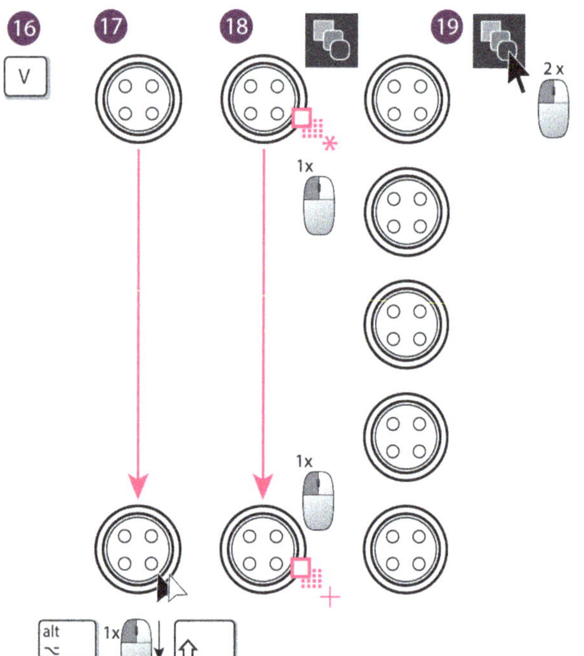

Step 16. Activate V key (Selection Tool).
Step 17. Hold down the **alt/option** key (do not release), then hold down the left mouse button and drag the object with the cursor down. Additionaly hold down **Shift** key (also do not release). When the position of the duplicate is beneath the original object, release the mouse button (first the mouse button, then **Shift** and **alt** key).
Step 18. Activate the **Blend Tool** (W).
Click on the first button to define the „initial object" and click then on the second button.
Step 19. Double-click on the **Blend Tool** (W) in the tools panel.

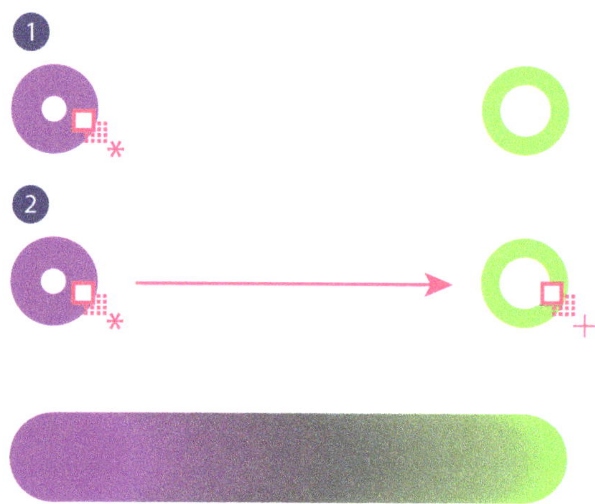

Step 20. Change „Spacing" to „Specified Steps", then type „3" (3 copies will be produced, then change „Orientation" to „Align to Page" and confirm with „OK".

8.10 TUTORIAL: BLEND OBJECTS

You can create blendings with the **Blend Tool** (W) and the command **Object > Blend > Make**. Blendings consist of a series of intermediate objects and colors between at least two objects.
In fashion, blendings are used, for example, to create interesting allover prints.

Blend Tool

First draw two different objects with different colors.

Step 1. Activate the **Blend Tool** (W).
Step 2. Click on the first object and then on the second.

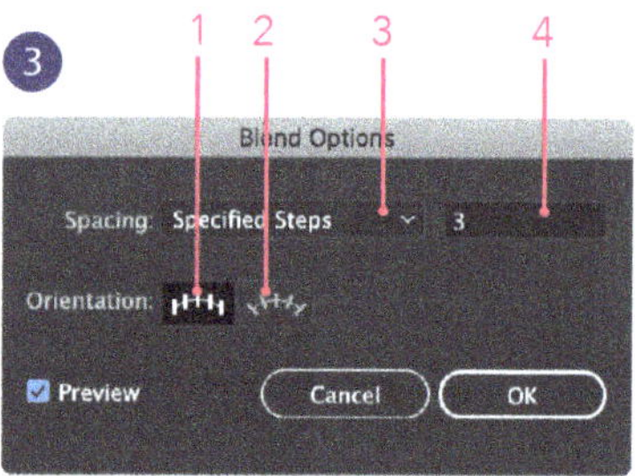

Step 3. To set the numbers of steps or the distance between the steps, double-click on the **Blend Tool** (W).
In the dialog box change „Spacing" to „Specified Steps", then type „3", change „Orientation" to „Align to Page", then confirm with „OK".

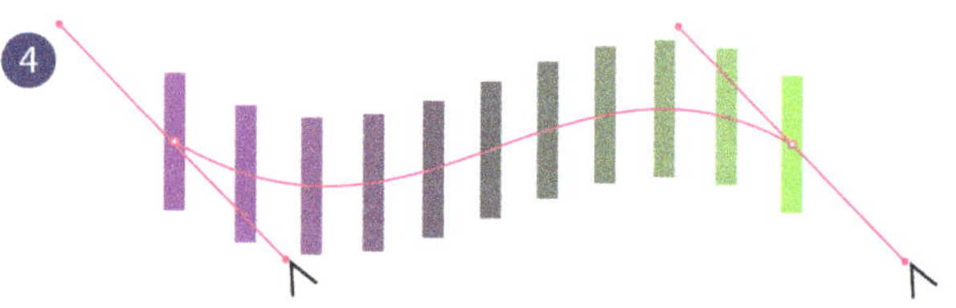

1. Aligns the blending perpendicular to the x-axis of the side.
2. Aligns the blending horizontally to the path.
3. "Specified Steps" determines how many steps are created between the beginning and the end of the blending. Specified Distance determines how far are apart the individual stages of the blending.
4. Specifies how many steps of blending are added.

Step 4. You can change the shape of the axis with **Anchor Point Tool** (Shift+C), while drawing a straight line in a curve.
You can release the blending **Object > Blend > Release** or also show options **Object > Blend > Blend Options**.
You have also the possibilitie to repleace the existing axis by another path, draw an object that will be used as a new axis. Select the axis object and the blended object and choose **Object > Blend > Replace Spine**.

8.11 TUTORIAL: CHECKED PATTERN

REQUIREMENTS

-Choose in the tools panel the stroke color „None" and the fill color „blue".

-Choose: **View > Rules >Show Rules, View > Guides > Lock Guides, View > Guides > Show Guides, View > Smart Guides, View > Snap to Point**.

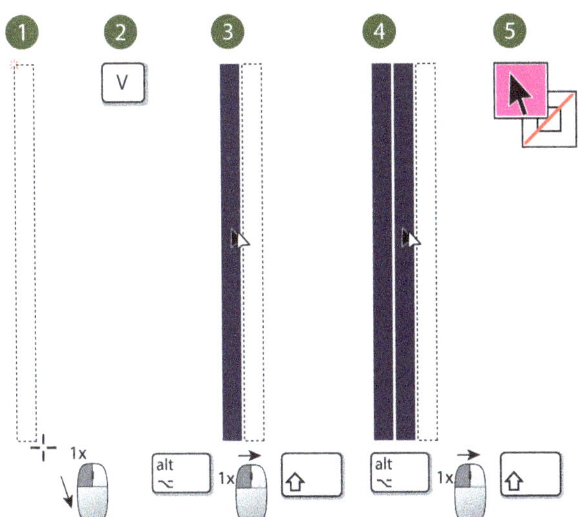

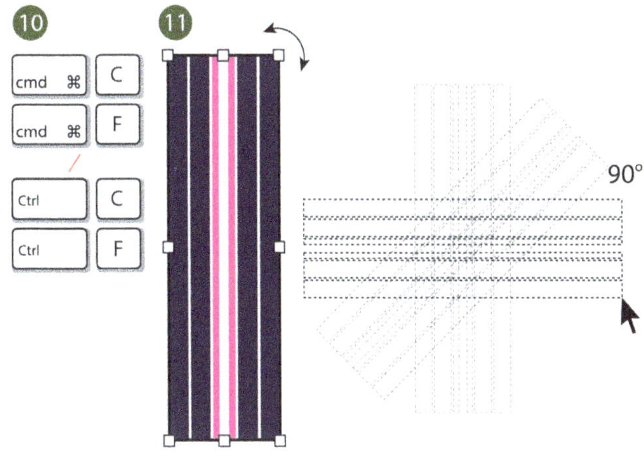

Step 1. Select the **Rectangle Tool** (M) and create an rectangle.
Step 2. Click V key (Selection Tool).
Step 3. Click with the **Selection Tool** (V) on the object, hold down the **alt/option** key (do not release), then hold down the left mouse button and drag the object with the cursor to the right. Additionaly hold down **Shift** key (also do not release). If the duplicate is located on the new position, release the mouse button (first the mouse button, then **Shift** and **alt** key).

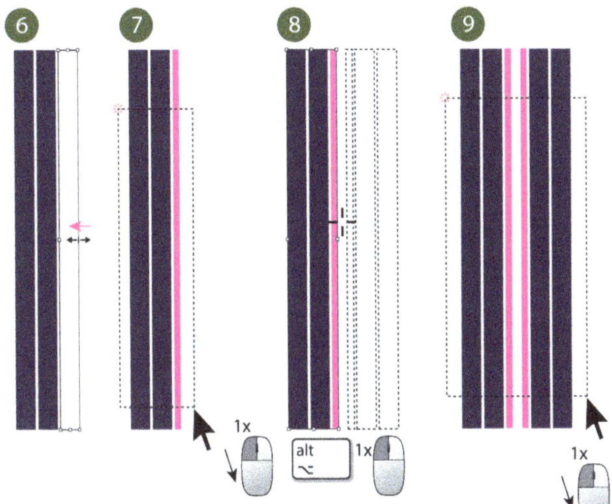

Step 4. Repeat the step 3.
Step 5. Change the fill colour to e.g. „magenta".
Step 6. Transform the last stripe (see figure).
Step 7. Hold down the left mouse button and drag with the **Selection Tool** (V) around the object.
Step 8. Select the **Reflect Tool** (O), position the cursor on the vertical guide, hold down the **alt/option** key (do not release the alt key) and click the left mouse button. The Reflect dialog box appears ,then release the **alt** key. Activate the option „Vertical", then „Preview" and click „Copy". A mirrored duplicate is created.

Step 9. Hold down the left mouse button and drag with the **Selection Tool** (V) around the object.
Step 10. Activate the shortcut command+C / Ctrl+C (Copy) and the shortcut command+F / Ctrl+F (Paste in Front).
Step 11. Hold down **Shift** key and rotate the objects clockwise (90°).
Step 12. Hold down the left mouse button and drag with the **Selection Tool** (V) around the objects.
Step 13. Open the panel „Transparency" (**Window>Transparency**), then change the blending mode to „Multiply" and „Opacity" to 80%.

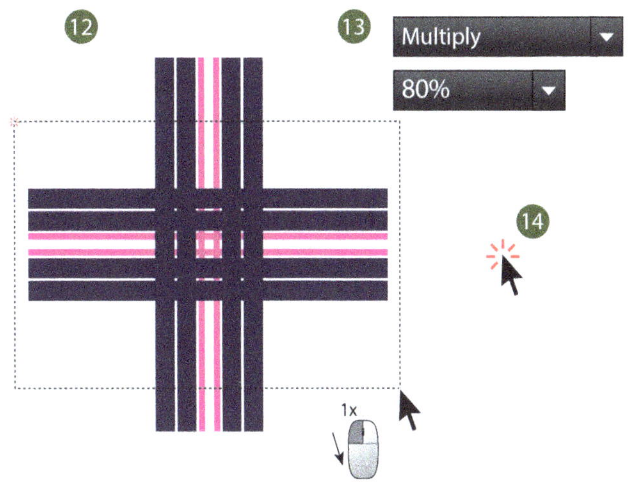

Step 14. Click on V key (Selection Tool) and click on a empty drawing area to deselect the object. Alternatively you can activate the shortcut command+Shift+A / Ctrl+Shift+A.

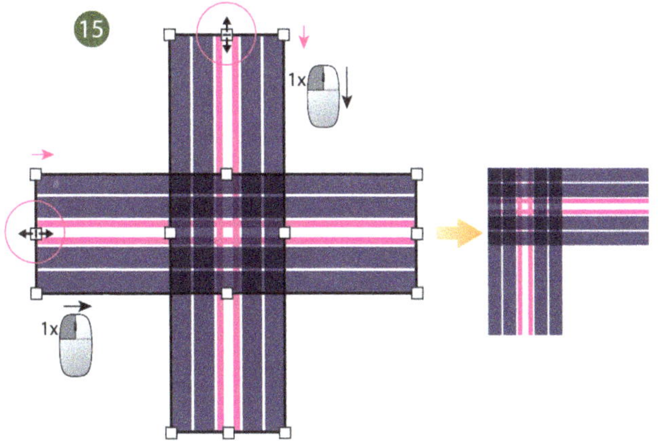

Step 15. Transform the objects (see figure).

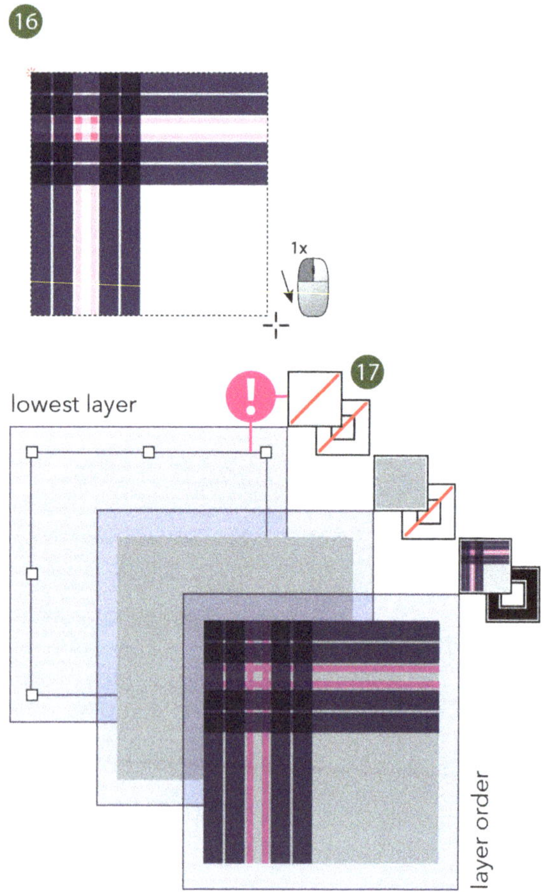

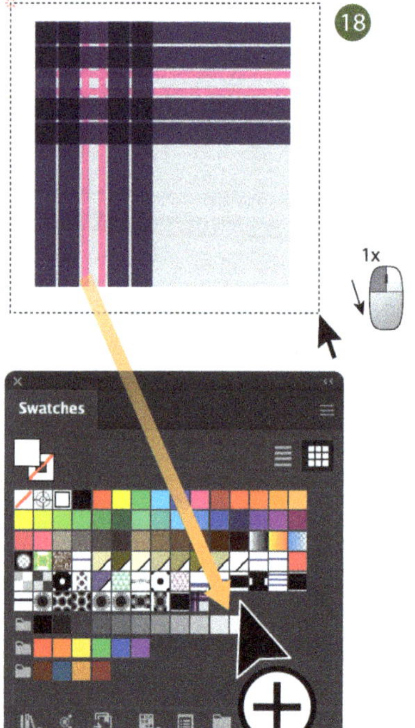

Step 16. Select the **Rectangle Tool** (M) and create an rectangle without Stroke colour and with grey fill colour, then place the rectangle in the background (**Object>Arrange>Send to Back**).

Step 17. Create an further rectangle without stroke colour and without grey fill colour, then place the rectangle in the background (**Object>Arrange>Send to Back**).

The lowermost object without stroke and fill color in the layer order is always the rapport.

Step 18. Hold down the left mouse button and drag with the **Selection Tool** (V) around the objects. And then drag the objects into the dialog box "**Swatches**" (drag&drop method) **Window>Swatches**.

Step 19. For the fill colour activate now the "check pattern" (Swatches panel), the square of the "fill" in the tools panel should be in the foreground. Now fill the objects with the "check pattern".

Step 20. Click the object with the **Direct Selection Tool** (A).

Hold down the **less/greater than symbol** key (only Mac) or doubleclick on the **Selection Tool** (V) and deactivate „Trannsform objects" and move horizontal the pattern to position it better.

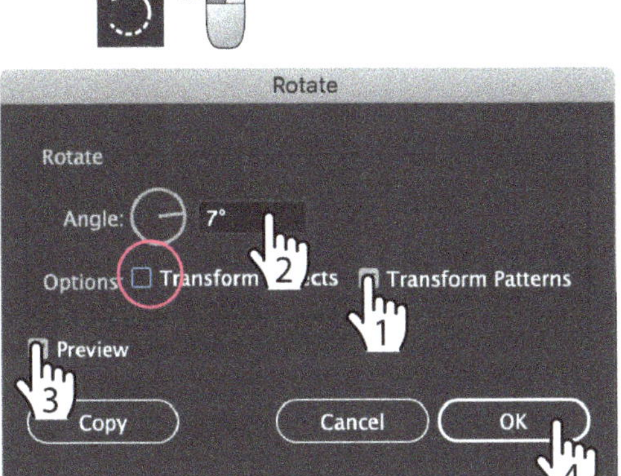

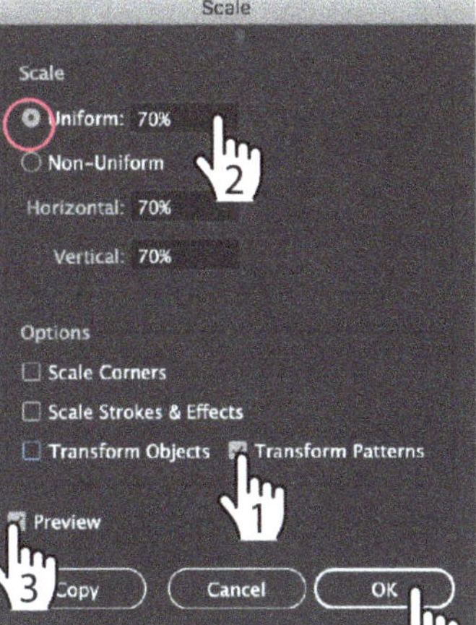

Step 21. Click with the **Direct Selection Tool** (A) on the object and double-click on the **Rotate Tool** (R). In the dialog box deactivate the option „Transform Objects", we want only to rotate the pattern, then activate the „Preview", for „Angle" type **38°** and confirm with "OK".

Step 22 -24. Repeat the step 21. angle indication see figure.

Step 25. Hold down the left mouse button and drag with the vv**Selection Tool** (V) around the object (blouse).

Step 26. Double-click in the tools panel on the **Scale Tool** (S).

In the scale tools dialog box activate only the option „Transform Pattern" (deactivate "Transform Objects"), then activate the option „Uniform" and type 70%, then activate „Preview". The size of the pattern will be reduced to 30% and confirm the settings with "OK".

8.12 TUTORIAL: ZIP DRESS

REQUIREMENTS

-Choose in the tools panel the stroke color „black" and the fill color „None".

-Set in the stroke panel (**Window > Stroke**) the stroke weight to **1pt** or **2pt**.
-Choose: **View > Rules >Show Rules, View > Guides > Lock Guides, View > Guides > Show Guides, View > Smart Guides, View > Snap to Point** and place a vertical guide.

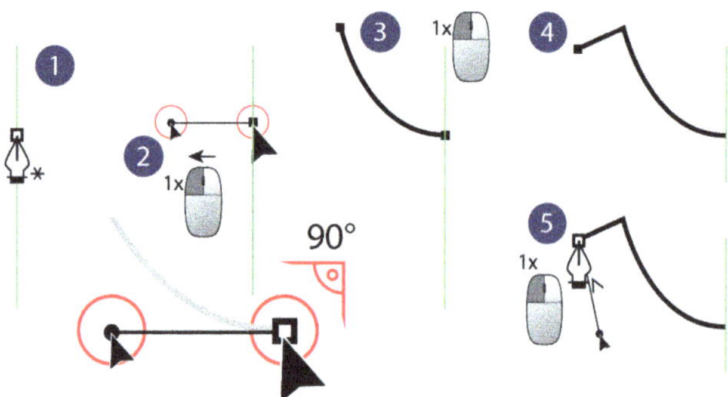

Step 1. Select the **Pen Tool** (P) and position it on the vertical guide, now hold down the left mouse button (do not release) to create the first anchor-point.
Step 2. Additionally hold down the **Shift** key (90° angle), also do not release, now drag the direction point to the left, then release first the mouse button and then the **Shift** key.
Step 3. Create a further anchor point (press and release the left mouse button, do not drag).
Step 4. Create a further anchor point (press and release the left mouse button, do not drag).

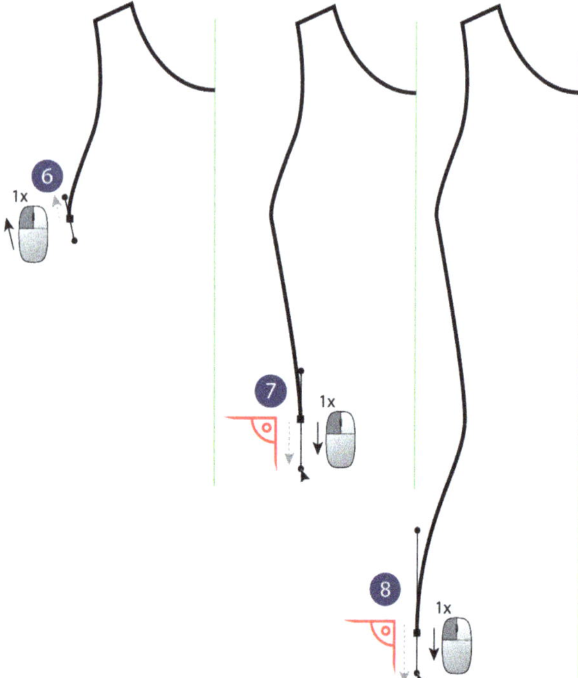

Step 5. Drag from the last anchor point an new direction line and direction point (see figure).
Step 6. Create a further anchor point (drag the direction point diagonally to the left up).
Step 7. Create a further anchor point (do not release the left mouse button), additionally hold down the **Shift** key and drag the direction point to the bottom.
Step 8. Create a further anchor point (do not release the left mouse button), additionally hold down the **Shift** key and drag the direction point to the bottom.

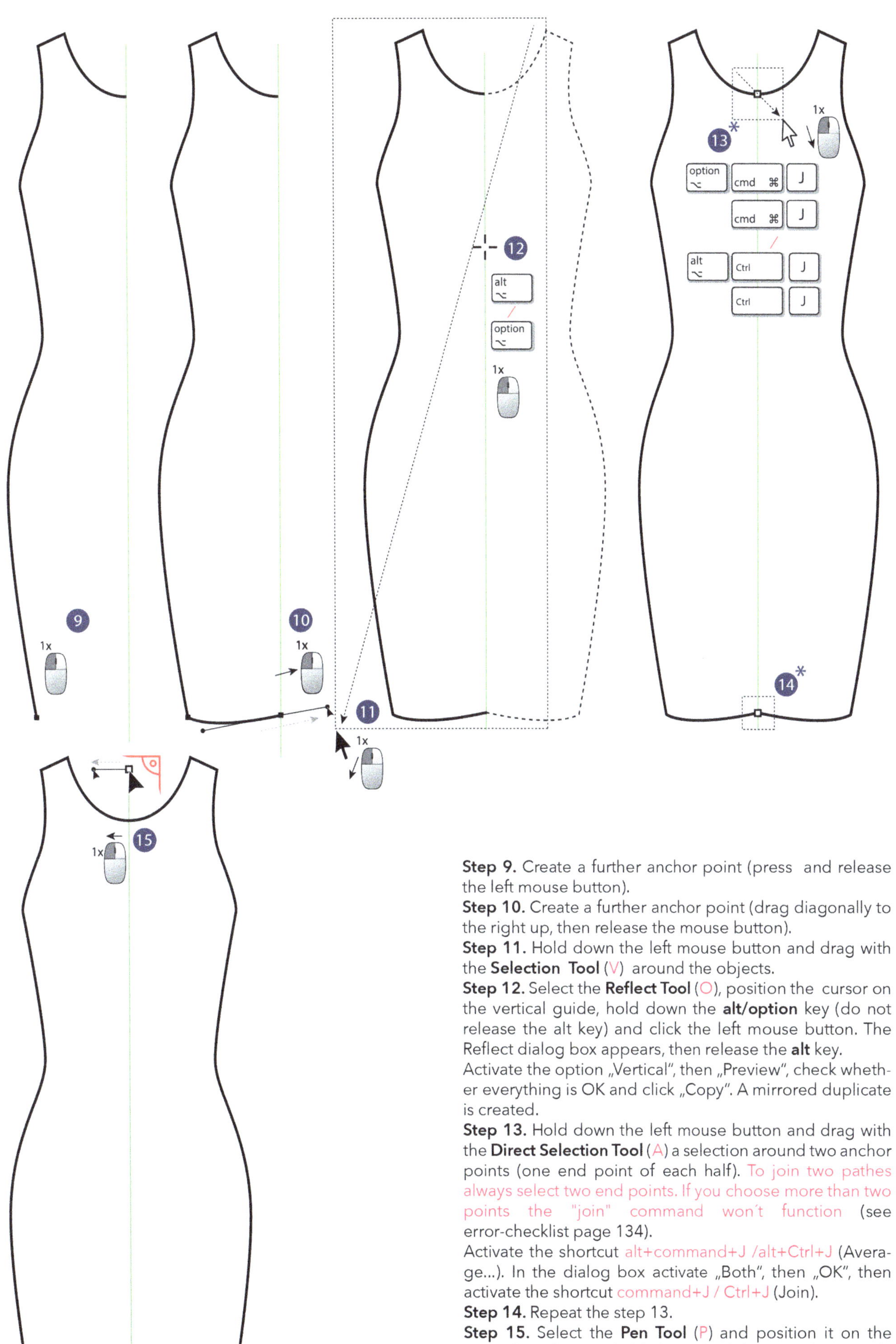

Step 9. Create a further anchor point (press and release the left mouse button).

Step 10. Create a further anchor point (drag diagonally to the right up, then release the mouse button).

Step 11. Hold down the left mouse button and drag with the **Selection Tool** (V) around the objects.

Step 12. Select the **Reflect Tool** (O), position the cursor on the vertical guide, hold down the **alt/option** key (do not release the alt key) and click the left mouse button. The Reflect dialog box appears, then release the **alt** key.
Activate the option „Vertical", then „Preview", check whether everything is OK and click „Copy". A mirrored duplicate is created.

Step 13. Hold down the left mouse button and drag with the **Direct Selection Tool** (A) a selection around two anchor points (one end point of each half). To join two pathes always select two end points. If you choose more than two points the "join" command won´t function (see error-checklist page 134).
Activate the shortcut alt+command+J /alt+Ctrl+J (Average...). In the dialog box activate „Both", then „OK", then activate the shortcut command+J / Ctrl+J (Join).

Step 14. Repeat the step 13.

Step 15. Select the **Pen Tool** (P) and position it on the vertical guide, now hold down the left mouse button (do not release) additionally hold down the **Shift** key (90° angle), also do not release, now drag the direction point to the left, then release first the mouse button and then the **Shift** key.

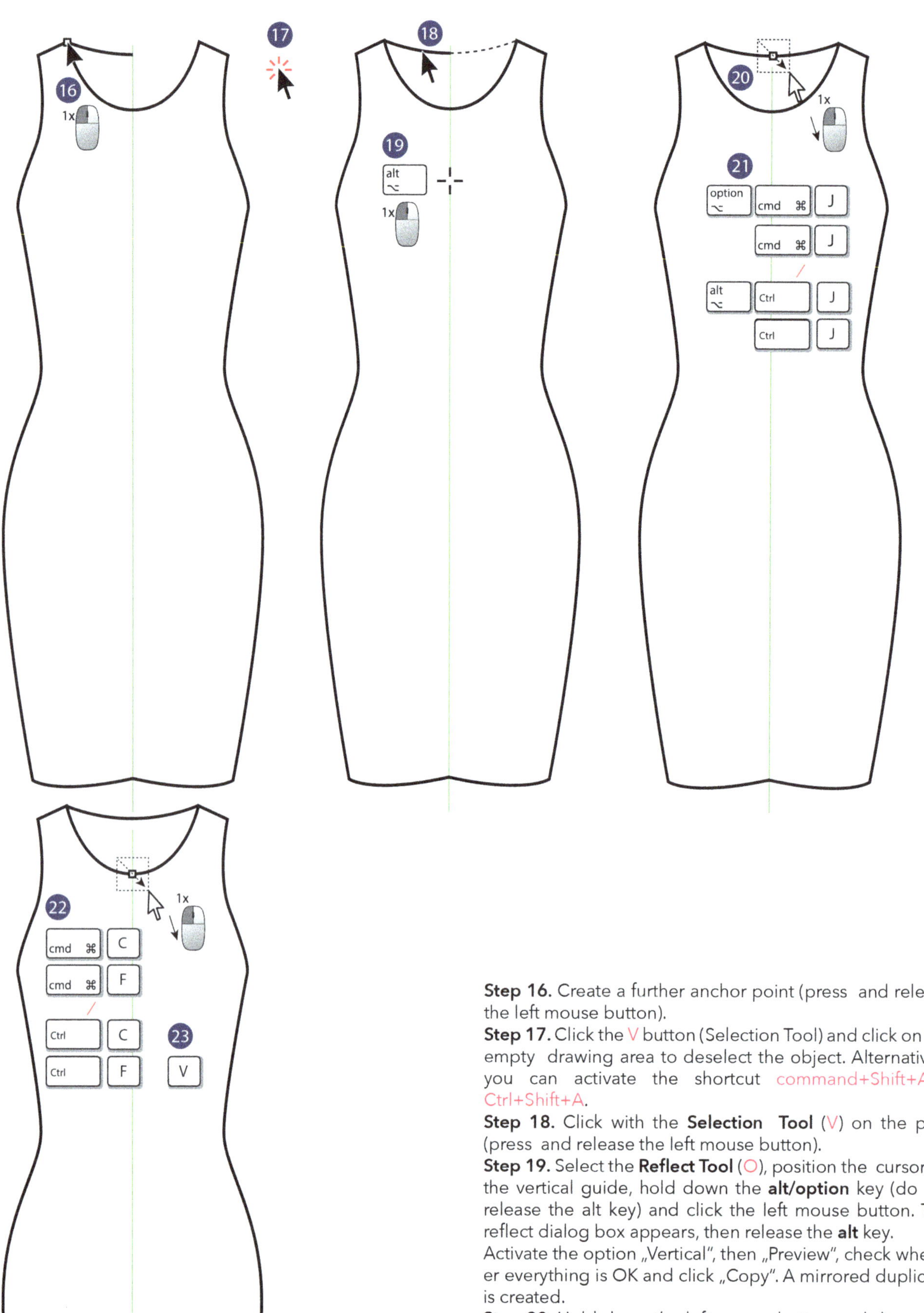

Step 16. Create a further anchor point (press and release the left mouse button).

Step 17. Click the V button (Selection Tool) and click on the empty drawing area to deselect the object. Alternatively you can activate the shortcut command+Shift+A / Ctrl+Shift+A.

Step 18. Click with the **Selection Tool** (V) on the path (press and release the left mouse button).

Step 19. Select the **Reflect Tool** (O), position the cursor on the vertical guide, hold down the **alt/option** key (do not release the alt key) and click the left mouse button. The reflect dialog box appears, then release the **alt** key.
Activate the option „Vertical", then „Preview", check whether everything is OK and click „Copy". A mirrored duplicate is created.

Step 20. Hold down the left mouse button and drag with the **Direct Selection Tool** (A) a selection.

Step 21. Activate the shortcut option+command+J /alt+Ctrl+J (Average...). In the dialog box activate „Both" and „OK", then activate the shortcut command+J / Ctrl+J (Join).

Step 22. Hold down the left mouse button, drag with the **Direct Selection Tool** (A) a selection (see figure). Activate the shortcut command+C / Ctrl+C (Copy) and the shortcut command+F / Ctrl+F (Paste in Front).

Step 23. Click on V key (Selection Tool).

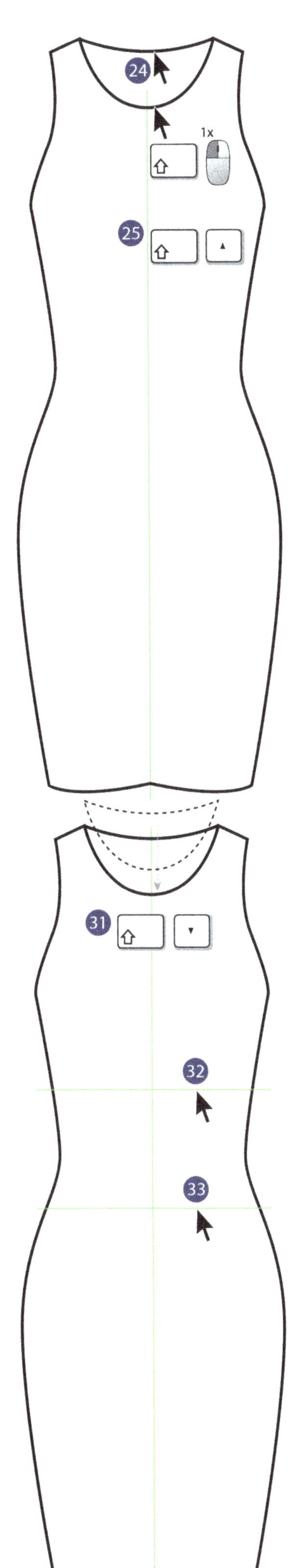

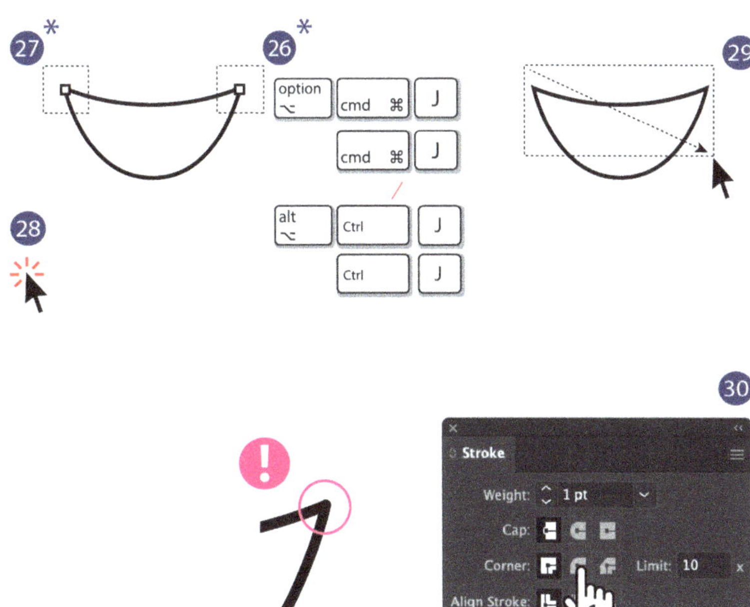

Step 24. Click on the line with the **Selection Tool** (V), then press **Shift** key (do not release Shift) and click the second line (to the existing selection further object are added).

Step 25. Hold down the **Shift** key, double click on the up arrow key. The lines are displaced to the top.

Step 26. Hold down the left mouse button and drag with the **Direct Selection Tool** (A) a selection around two anchor points (one end point of each half). To join two pathes always select two end points. If you choose more than two points the "join" command won´t function (see error-checklist page 134).

Activate the shortcut option+command+J /alt+Ctrl+J (Average...). In the dialog box activate „Both", then „OK", then activate the shortcut command+J / Ctrl+J (Join).

Step 27. Repeat the step 26.

Step 28. Click on V key (Selection Tool) and click on a empty drawing area to deselect the object.

Step 29. Hold down the left mouse button and drag with the **Selection Tool** (V) around the object.

Step 30. Open the „Stroke" panel **Window > Stroke** and set the „Corner" to „Round Join".

Step 31. Hold down the **Shift** key double click on the down arrow key. The object is displaced to the original position.

Step 32 and 33. Place two another guides.

Step 34 and 35. Click on the anchor point with the **Scissors Tool** (C) to separate the shape at that point.

Step 36. Hold down the left mouse button and drag with the **Selection Tool** (V) around the object.

Activate the effect: **Distort & Transform> Roughen...** Change the „Size" to 0,3% ("Relative"), „Detail" to 20 Zoll and „Point" to „Smooth". Confirm the input with „OK", then activate the command **Object> Expand Appearance** (or **Object> Expand...**).

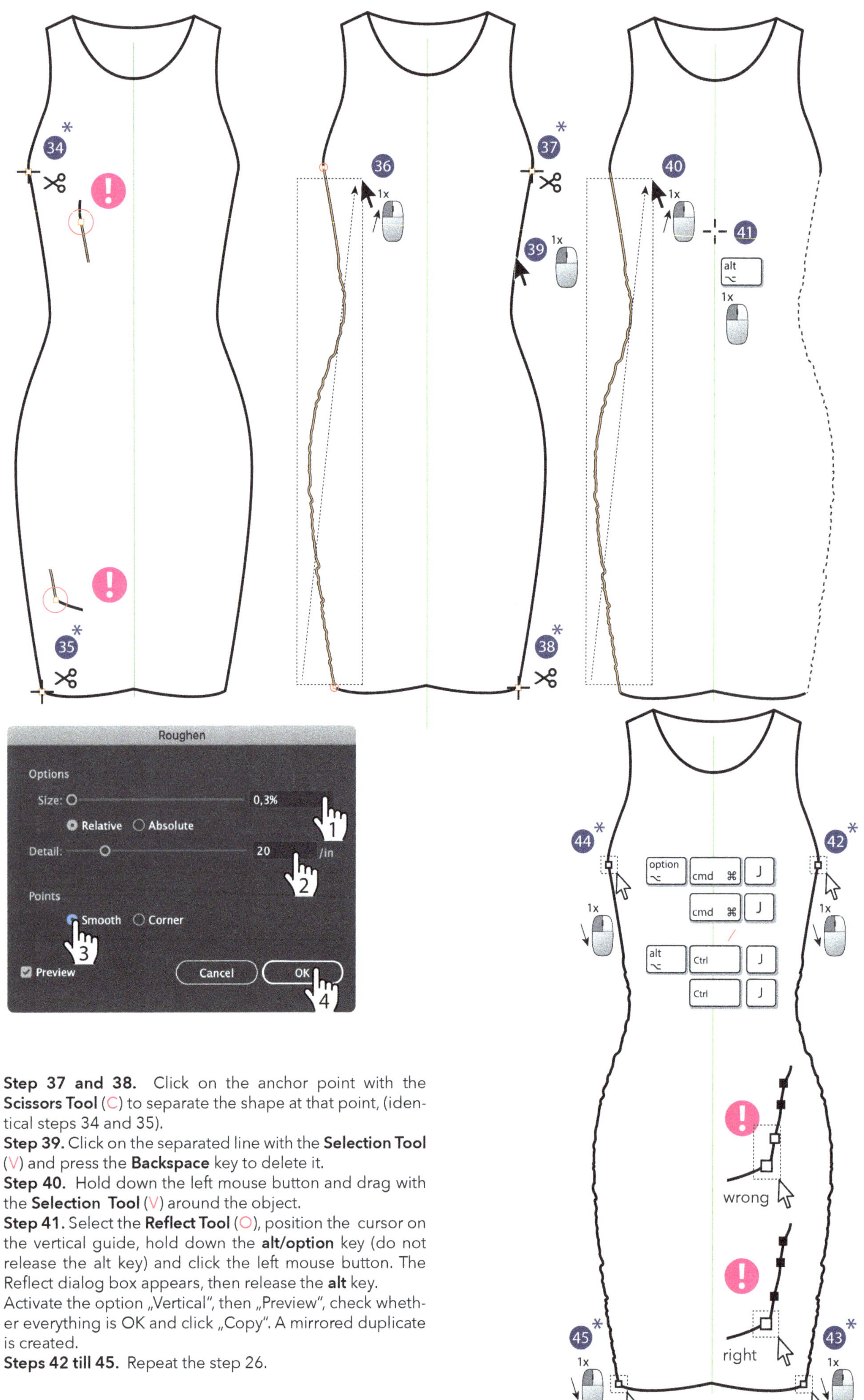

Step 37 and 38. Click on the anchor point with the **Scissors Tool** (C) to separate the shape at that point, (identical steps 34 and 35).

Step 39. Click on the separated line with the **Selection Tool** (V) and press the **Backspace** key to delete it.

Step 40. Hold down the left mouse button and drag with the **Selection Tool** (V) around the object.

Step 41. Select the **Reflect Tool** (O), position the cursor on the vertical guide, hold down the **alt/option** key (do not release the alt key) and click the left mouse button. The Reflect dialog box appears, then release the **alt** key.

Activate the option „Vertical", then „Preview", check whether everything is OK and click „Copy". A mirrored duplicate is created.

Steps 42 till 45. Repeat the step 26.

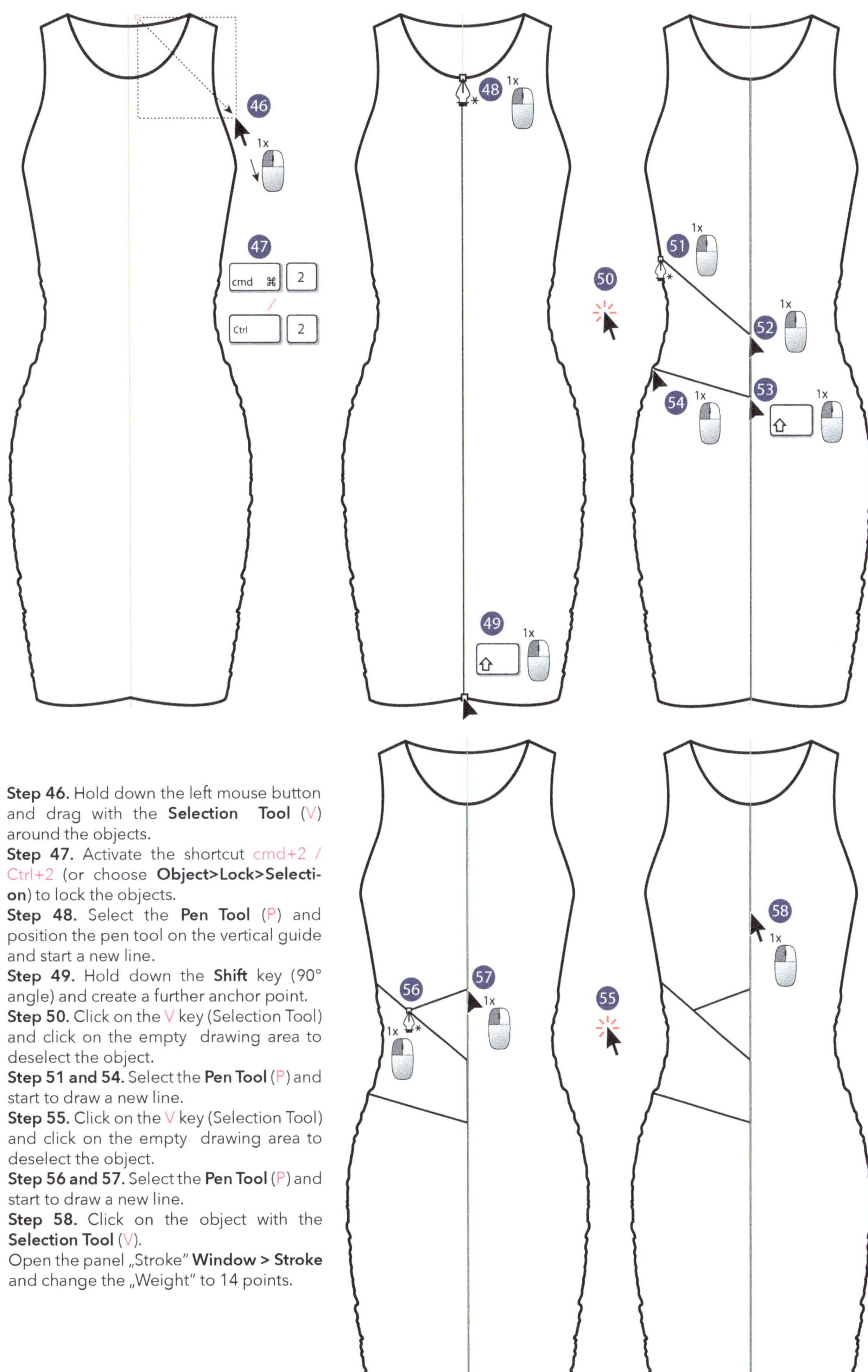

Step 46. Hold down the left mouse button and drag with the **Selection Tool** (V) around the objects.

Step 47. Activate the shortcut cmd+2 / Ctrl+2 (or choose **Object>Lock>Selection**) to lock the objects.

Step 48. Select the **Pen Tool** (P) and position the pen tool on the vertical guide and start a new line.

Step 49. Hold down the **Shift** key (90° angle) and create a further anchor point.

Step 50. Click on the V key (Selection Tool) and click on the empty drawing area to deselect the object.

Step 51 and 54. Select the **Pen Tool** (P) and start to draw a new line.

Step 55. Click on the V key (Selection Tool) and click on the empty drawing area to deselect the object.

Step 56 and 57. Select the **Pen Tool** (P) and start to draw a new line.

Step 58. Click on the object with the **Selection Tool** (V).

Open the panel „Stroke" **Window > Stroke** and change the „Weight" to 14 points.

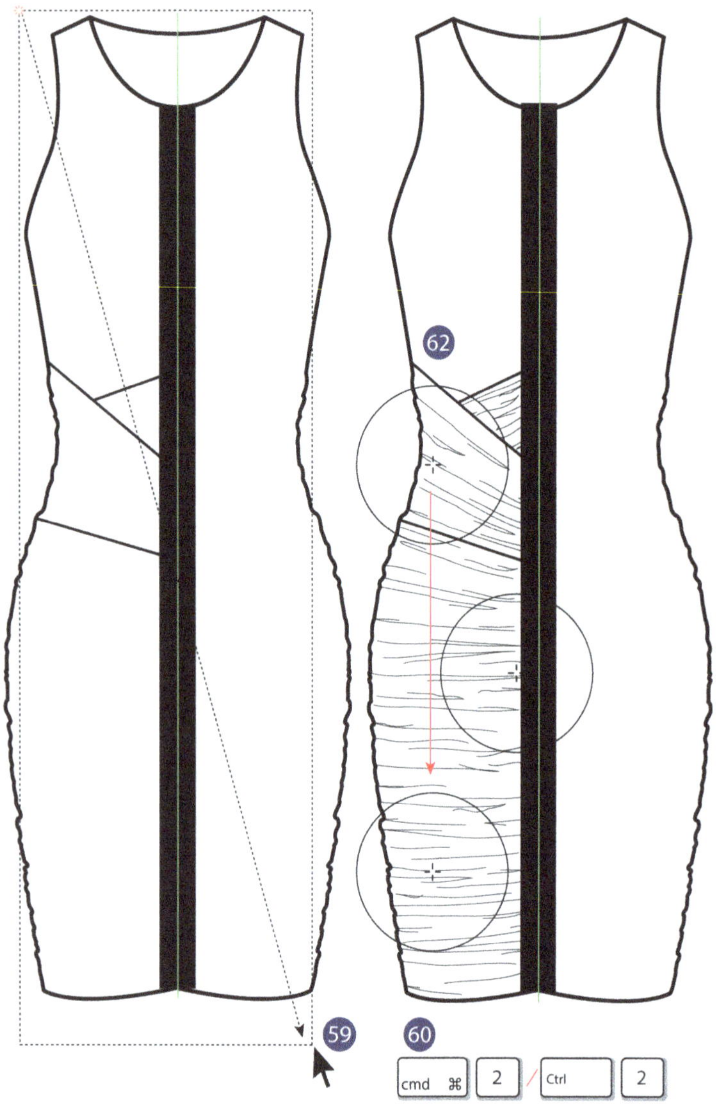

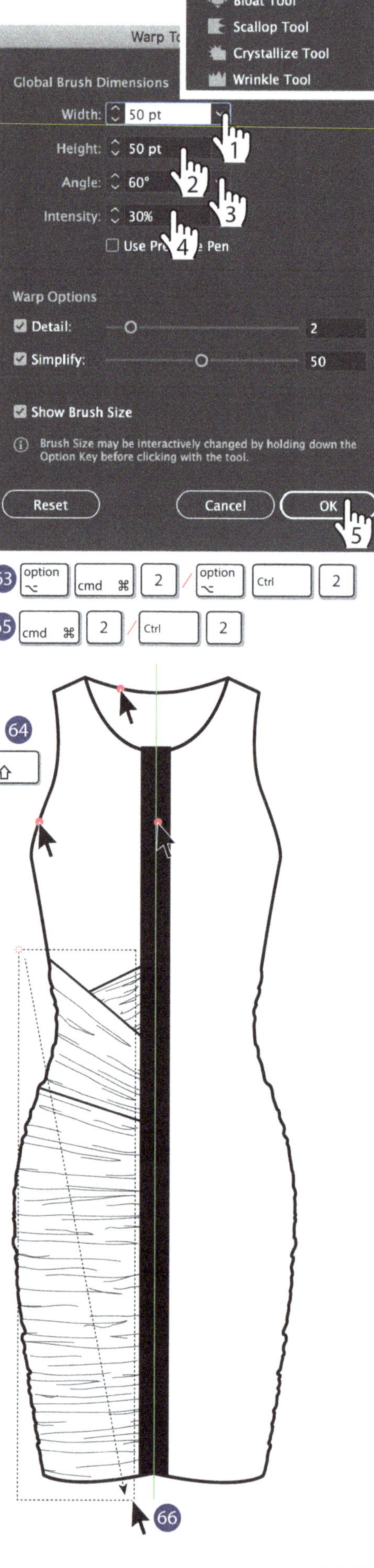

Step 59. Hold down the left mouse button and drag with the **Selection Tool** (V) around the objects.
Step 60. Activate the shortcut cmd+2 / Ctrl+2 (or choose **Object>Lock>Selection**) to lock the objects.
And draw further lines for pleats. See figure below.

Try to create the line with max. 3 anchor points.
Step 61. Double-click on the **Wrap Tool** (Shift+R) to open the dialog box. Change the options (see figure) (this is only an example, the settings can vary depending on the size of the drawing).
Step 62. Hold down the left mouse button and drag the cursor several times down to loosen up the pleats.
Step 63. Activate the shortcut option+cmd+2 / alt+Ctrl+2 (or choose **Object>Unlock All**) to unlock the object in the document.
Step 64. Hold down the **Shift** key and select the followings objects (see figure).
Step 65. Activate the shortcut cmd+2 / Ctrl+2 (or choose **Object>Lock>Selection**) to lock the objects.
Step 66. Hold down the left mouse button and drag with the **Selection Tool** (V) around the objects.

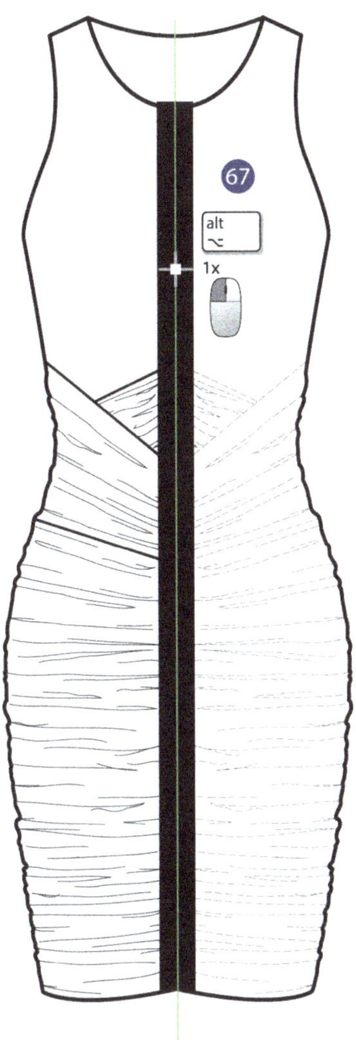

Step 67. Select the **Reflect Tool** (O), position the cursor on the vertical guide, hold down the **alt/option** key (do not release the alt key) and click the left mouse button. The reflect dialog box appears, then release the **alt** key.
Activate the option „Vertical", then „Preview", check whether everything is OK and click „Copy". A mirrored duplicate is created.

8.13 TUTORIAL: ZIP DRESS ZIPPER
REQUIREMENTS

-Change in the tools panel the stroke color to „None" and the fill color to „grey".

-Activate: **View > Rules >Show Rules, View > Guides > Lock Guides, View > Guides > Show Guides, View > Smart Guides, View > Snap to Point**

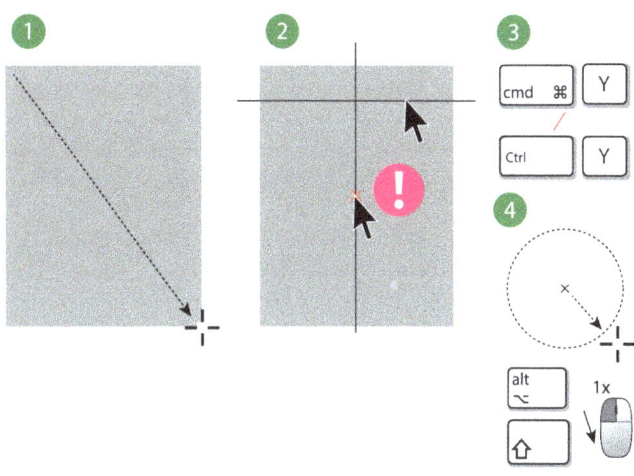

Step 1. Select the **Rectangle Tool** (M) and create an rectangle.
Step 2. Drag a vertical guide. While dragging, place the cursor over the middle square below (object center-point). The guide is magnetically fixed to the point.
Step 3. Activate the outline preview (cmd+Y / Ctrl+Y). After step 4 deactivate the outline preview (cmd+Y / Ctrl+Y).
Step 4. Activate **Ellipse Tool** (L), hold down **alt/option** and **Shift** key, then create a circle. First release the mouse button and then the alt & Shift keys.

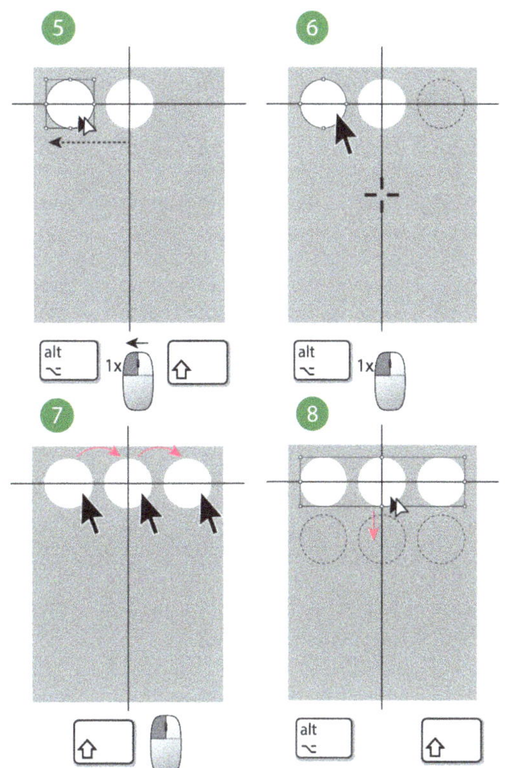

Step 5. Activate the **Selection Tool** (V), click on the circle to select it, then hold down **alt/option** key (do not release), drag the circle with the cursor to the left and activate additionally the **Shift** key. Then first release the mouse button and then the alt & Shift keys.

Step 6. Select the **Reflect Tool** (O) and reflect the circle to the right (Copy) hold down the **alt/option** key (do not release the alt key) and click the left mouse button. The reflect dialog box appears, then release the **alt/option** key. Activate the option „Vertical", then „Preview", check whether everything is OK and click „Copy". A mirrored duplicate is created.

Step 7. Activate the **Selection Tool** (V), hold down **Shift** key and select the three circles.

Step 8. Hold down **alt/option** key (do not release), drag the objects with the cursor down and activate additionally **Shift** key. Then first release the mouse button and then the alt & Shift keys.

Step 9. Activate the shortcut cmd+D / Ctrl+D (Transform Again), this will lead to several duplicates created with the same distance.

Step 10. Click the V button (Selection Tool) and click on the empty drawing area to deselect the object.

Step 11. Activate the **Selection Tool** (V) and transform the object on the middle white square to the red mark (see figure).

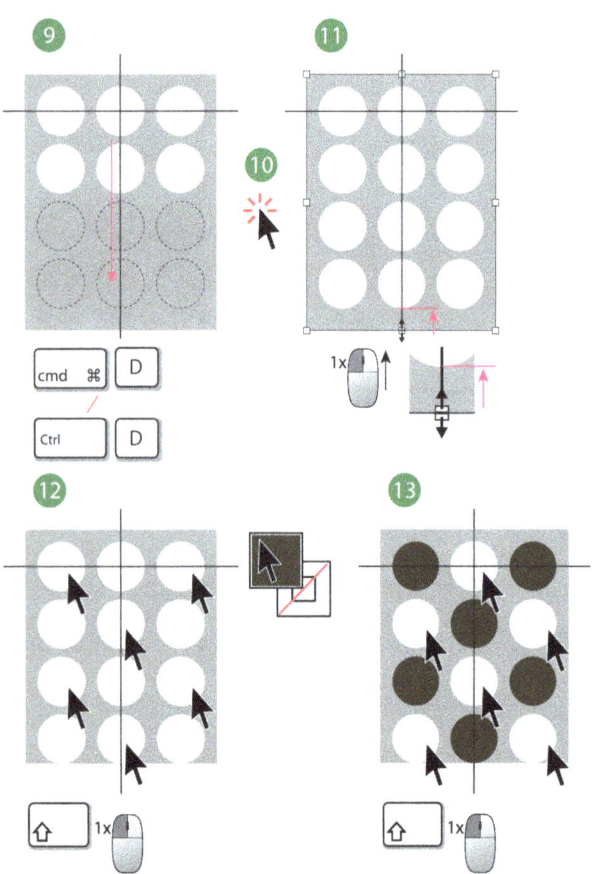

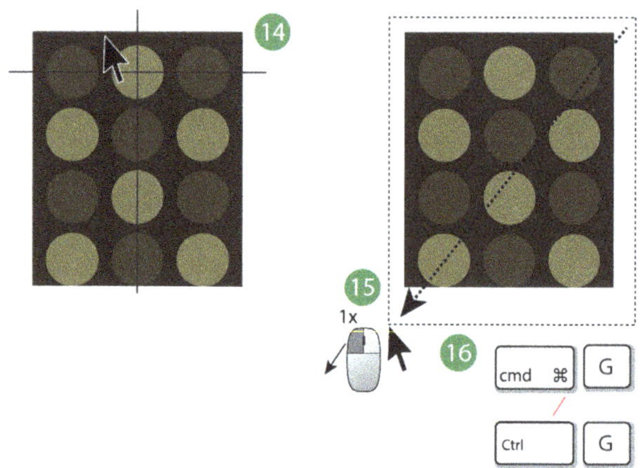

Step 18. Select the **Reflect Tool** (O) and reflect the objects to the right to create a copy.

Step 19 and 20. Place additional two vertical guides (see figure).

Step 21. Select the **Rectangle Tool** (M) and create an rectangle. (fill colour same as the rectangle in the background).

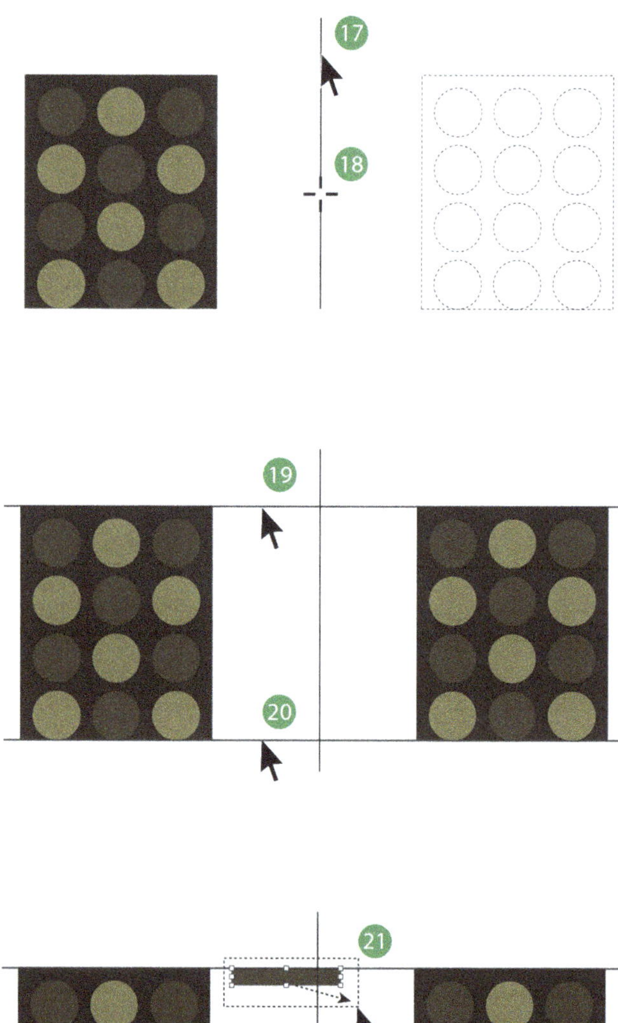

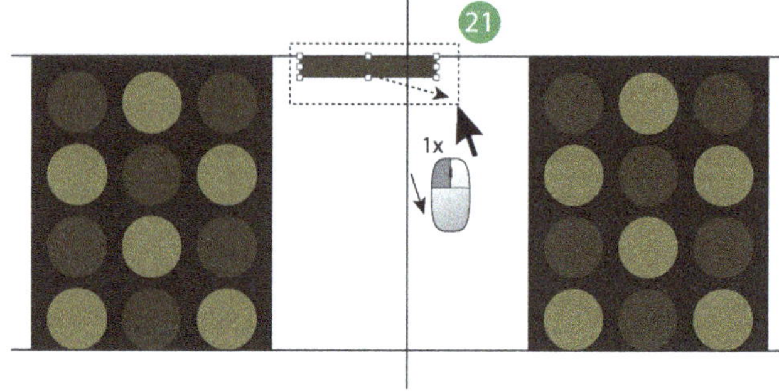

Step 12. Hold down the **Shift** key and click on the following objects with the **Selection Tool** (V) (see figure), then change fill colour (e.g. #5B5436).

Step 13. Repeat the last step for other objects (e.g. #998B4F).

Step 14. Change the colour for the background rectangle to #3F3A25.

Step 15. Hold down the left mouse button and drag with the **Selection Tool** (V) around the objects.

Step 16. Activate the shortcut cmd+G / Ctrl+G to group the objects.

Step 17. Place a vertical guide (see figure).

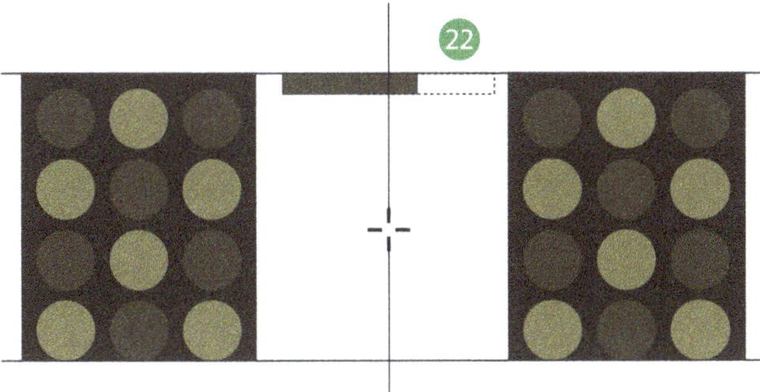

Step 22. Select the **Reflect Tool** (O) and reflect the rectangle to the right to create a copy.

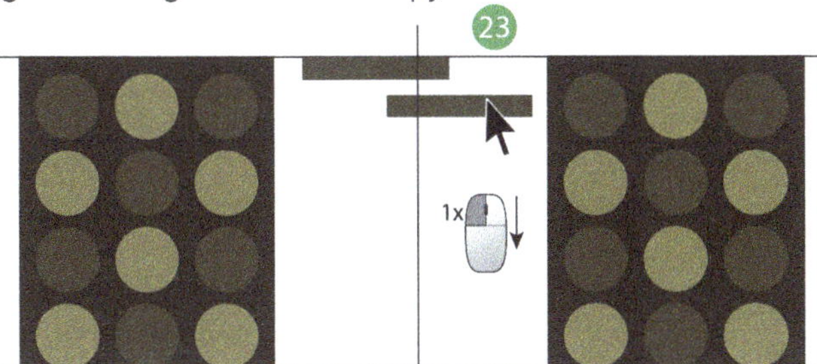

Step 23. Move the duplicate either with the **Selection Tool** (V) or with the keyboard arrow keys to the bottom.
Step 24. Hold down the **Shift** key and select both objects with the **Selection Tool** (V), then release **Shift** key.
Step 25. Hold down **alt/option** key (do not release), drag the both objects with the cursor down and hold down additionally **Shift** key. Then first release the mouse button and then the alt & Shift keys.

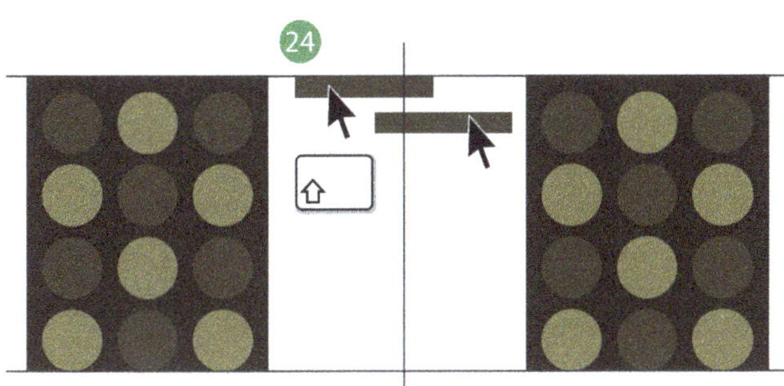

Step 26. Activate the shortcut cmd+D / Ctrl+D (Transform Again), this will lead to several duplicates created with the same distance.
Step 27. Click the V button (Selection Tool) and click on the empty drawing area to deselect the object.
Step 28. Hold down **Shift** key and select the objects with the **Selection Tool** (V) (see figure).
Step 29. Transform the objects on the middle square below, so that on the bottom after the last rectangle a distance will be created. This distance should be the same (visual judgment is sufficient) as the distance between the other rectangles.

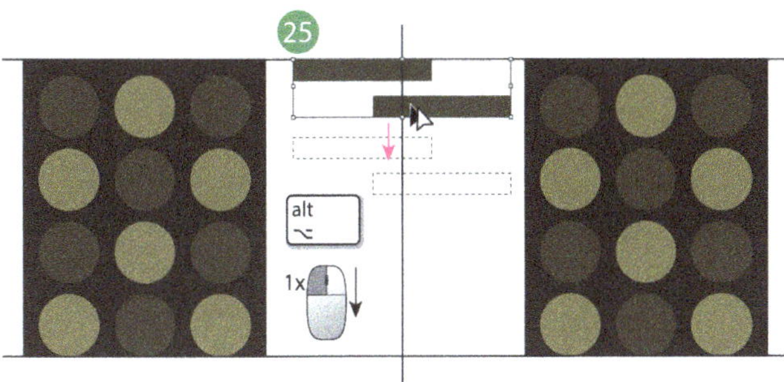

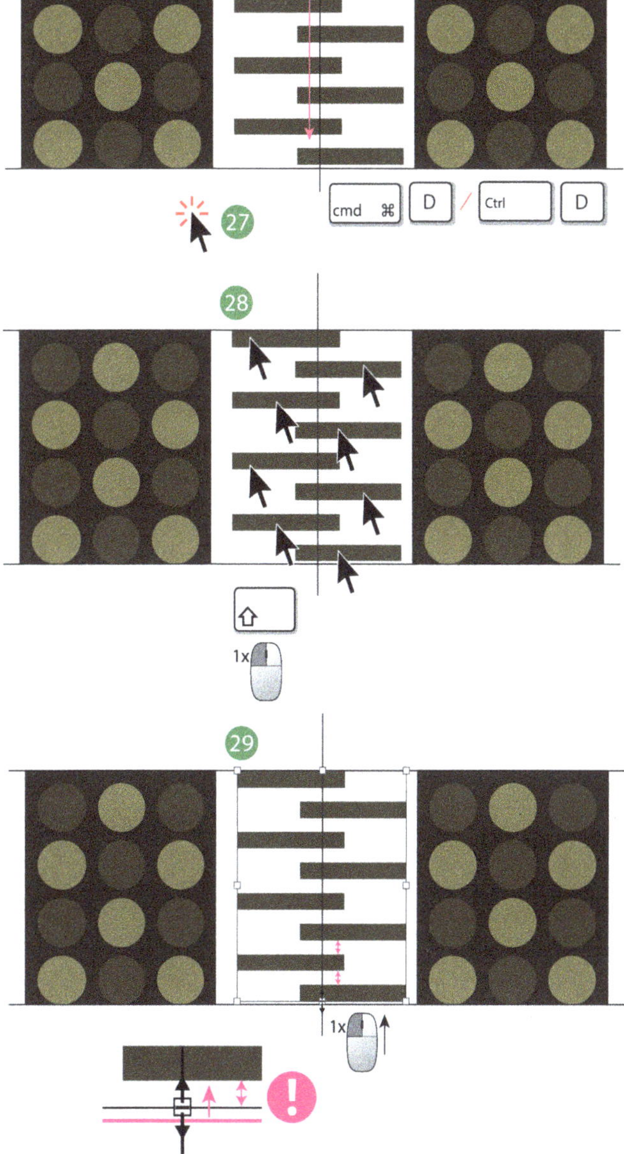

Step 30. Select the **Rectangle Tool** (M) and create an rectangle (without stroke colour, only with fill colour).
Important: The option **View > Smart Guides**, **View > Snap to Point** should be activated to create the rectangle precisely.

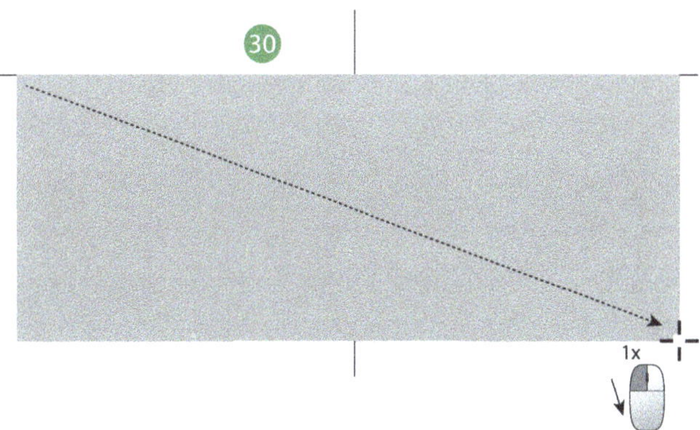

Step 31. Change the fill colour for the rectangle (e.g. #BCB289). And place the rectangle in the background (**Object>Arrange>Send to Back**)

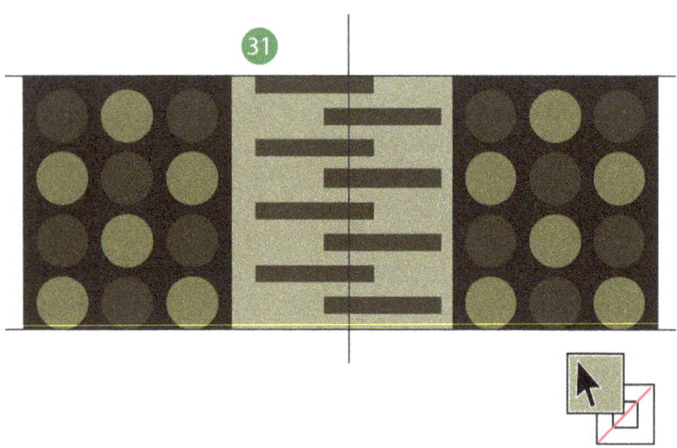

Step 32. So that the rapport works, check whether the first and last rectangle appears as shown in the figure.

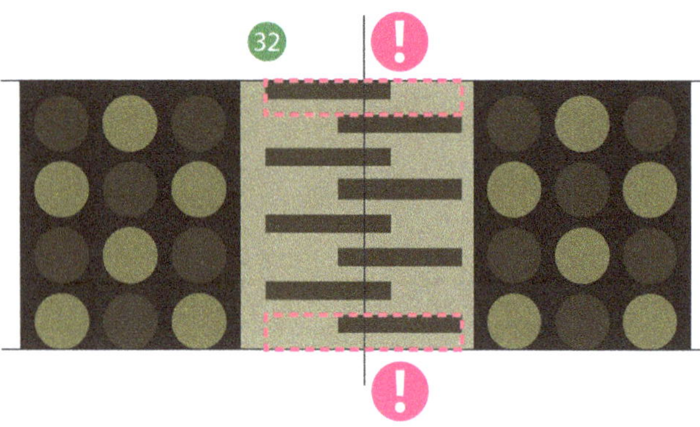

Step 33. Hold down the left mouse button and drag with **Selection Tool** (V) around the objects.

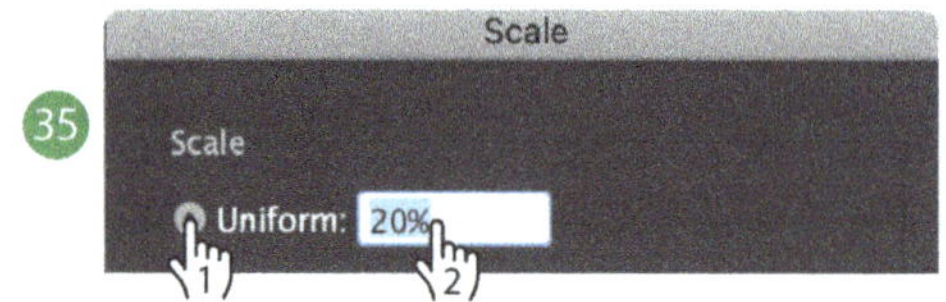

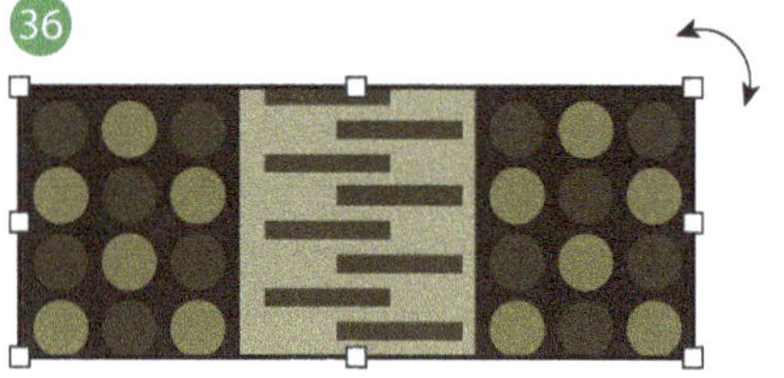

Step 34. Activate the shortcut cmd+G / Ctrl+G to group the objects.

Step 35. Double-click on the **Scale Tool** (S) and reduce the size of the object to e.g. 80% (change the value „Uniform" to 20%, then confirm with „OK"), the rapport for the zipper shouldn´t be to big.

Step 36. Hold down the **Shift** key and rotate now the object with the **Selection Tool** (V) about 90%. (To rotate an object, place the cursor near an object corner until a double arrow is visible (see figure).

Then release first the mouse button and then the **Shift** key.

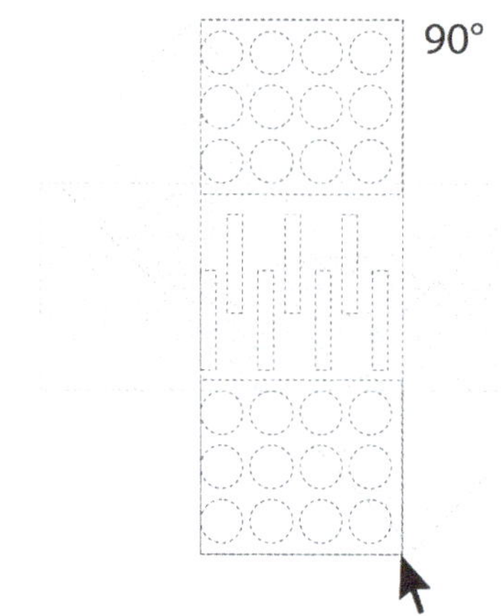

Step 37. Drag with the **Selection Tool** (V) a selection around the objects. Then open the panel **Brushes (Window>Brushes)** and drag the object to the panel „Stroke" (Drag&Drop method) or alternatively click on the symbol „New"

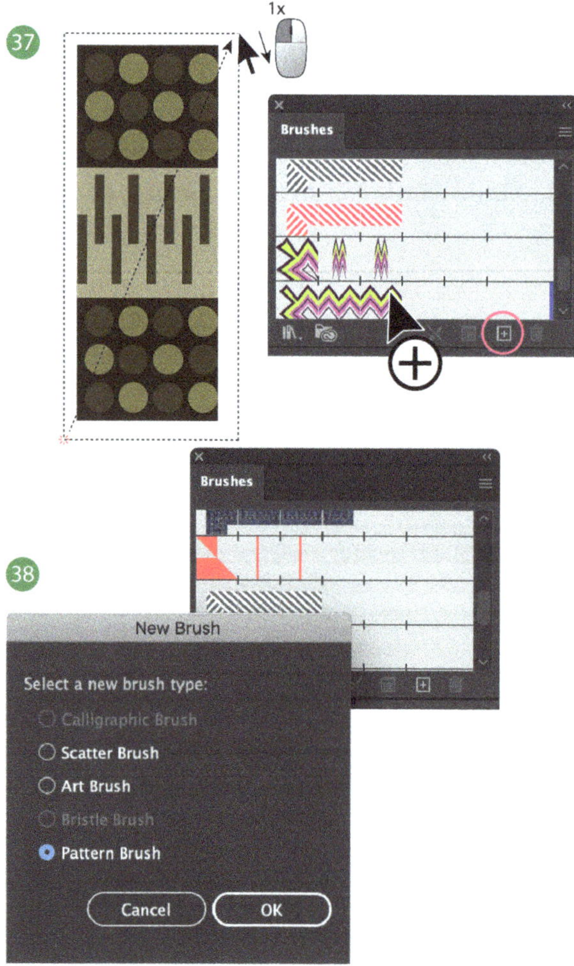

Step 38. Activate in the dialog box „Pattern Brush" and confirm the settings with „OK".

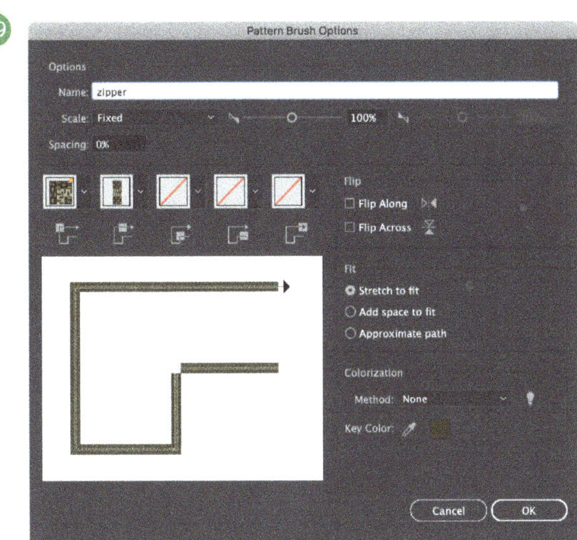

Step 39. In the second dialog box type a name for the „Pattern Brush" and confirm the settings with „OK", (further informations about „Pattern Brush" see page 122).

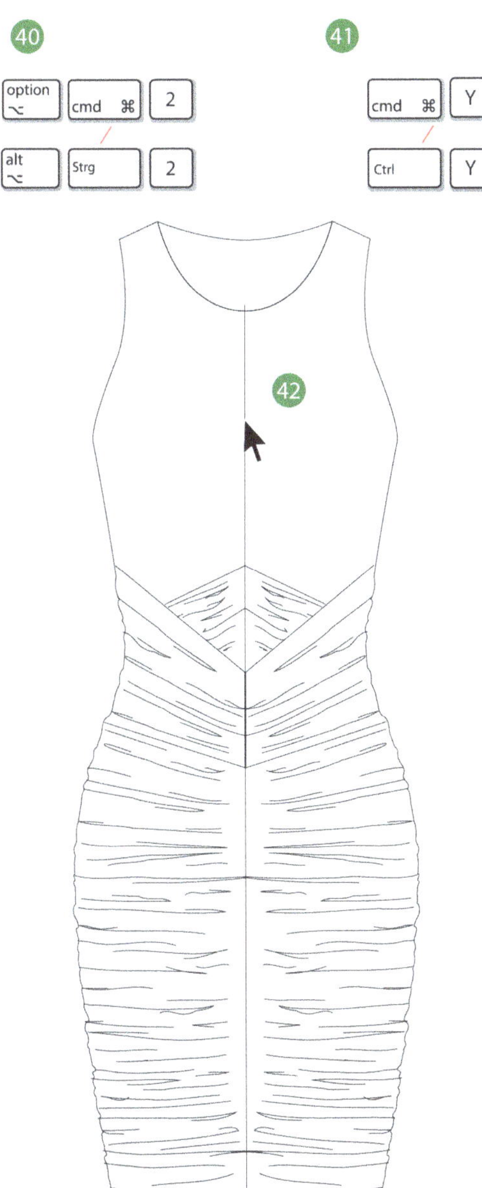

Step 40.
Open the dress from the last tutorial.
Activate the shortcut option+cmd+2 / alt+Ctrl+2 (or choose **Object>Unlock All**) to unlock the object in the document.

Step 41. Activate the „Outline" preview (cmd+Y / Ctrl+Y). After step 42 deactivate again the „Outline" preview (cmd+Y / Ctrl+Y).

Step 42. With the **Selection Tool** (V) click on the line (see figure).

Step 43. Open the panel „Stroke" **Window > Stroke** and change the „Weight" e.g. to **1pt** or smaller, this will change the size of the zipper rapport.

Schritt 44. Open the panel „Brush" **Window > Brush** and activate the „Pattern Brush" you have just created. Then activate the command **Object>Arrange>Bring to Front** („Zipper puller" see next tutorial).

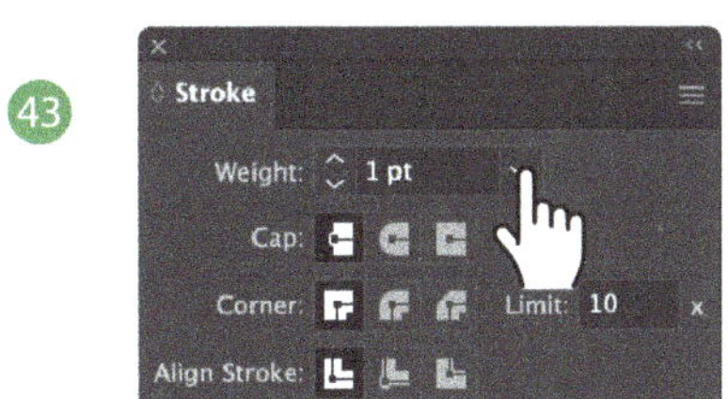

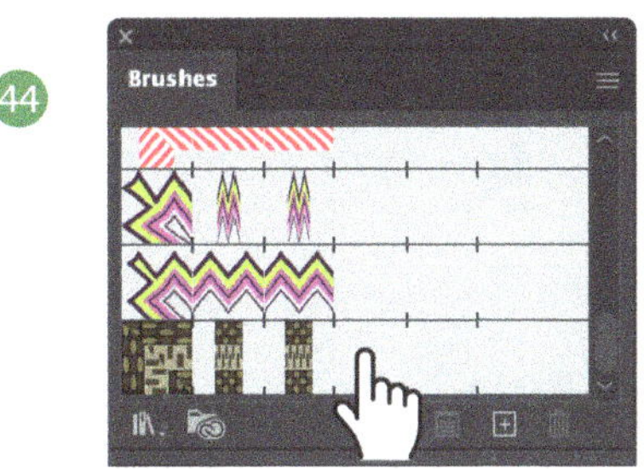

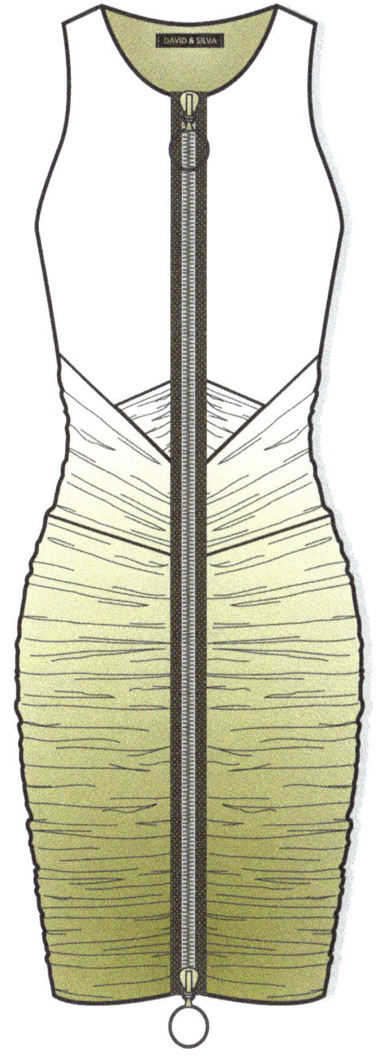

8.14 TUTORIAL: ZIPPERPULLER

REQUIREMENTS

-Choose in the tools panel the stroke color „black" and the fill color „None".

-Set in the stroke panel (**Window > Stroke**) the stroke weight to **1pt** or **2pt**.

-Choose: **View > Rules >Show Rules**, **View > Guides > Lock Guides**, **View > Guides > Show Guides**, **View > Smart Guides**, **View > Snap to Point** and place a vertical guide.

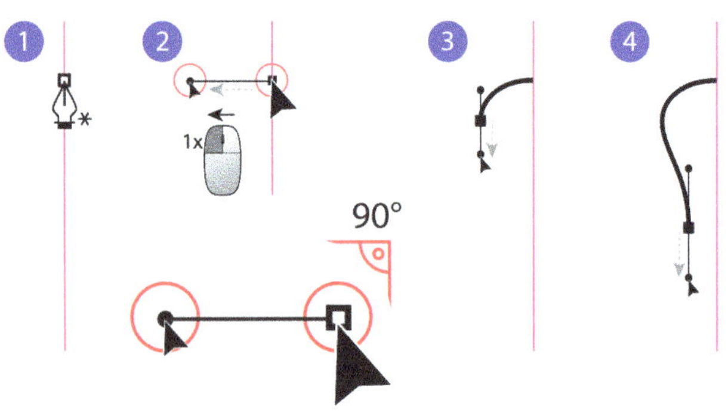

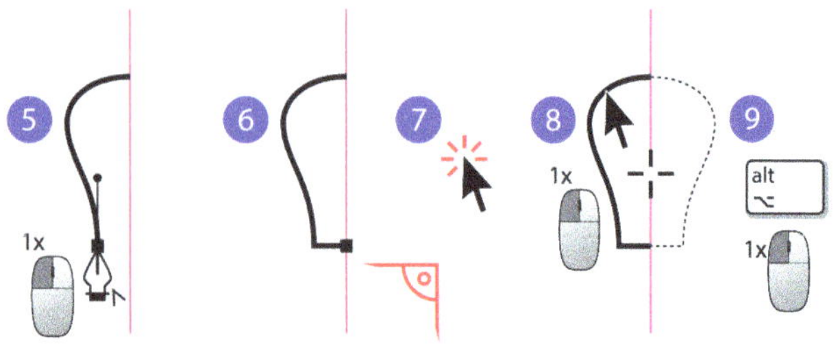

Step 1. Select the **Pen Tool** (P) and position it on the vertical guide, now hold down the left mouse button (do not release) to create the first anchor-point.
Step 2. Additionally hold down the **Shift** key (90° angle), also do not release, now drag the direction point to the left, then release first the mouse button and then the **Shift** key.
Step 3. Create with the **Pen Tool** (P) a further anchor point, hold down additionally **Shift** key and drag the direction point down, then release first the mouse button and then **Shift** key.

Step 4. Create with the **Pen Tool** (P) a further anchor point, hold down additionally **Shift** key and drag the direction point down, then release first the mouse button and then **Shift** key.
Step 5. Click the last anchor point (press and release the left mouse button) to create a corner. In this case the „pen tool" will be changed to „anchor point tool".
Step 6. Hold down the **Shift** key and create a further anchor point.
Step 7. Click on V key (Selection Tool) and click on a empty drawing area to deselect the object.
Step 8. Click with the **Selection Tool** (V) on the path.
Step 9. Select the **Reflect Tool** (O), position the cursor on the vertical guide, hold down the **alt/option** key (do not release the alt key) and click the left mouse button. The reflect dialog box appears, then release the **alt/option** key. Activate the option „Vertical", then „Preview", check whether everything is OK and click „Copy". A mirrored duplicate is created.

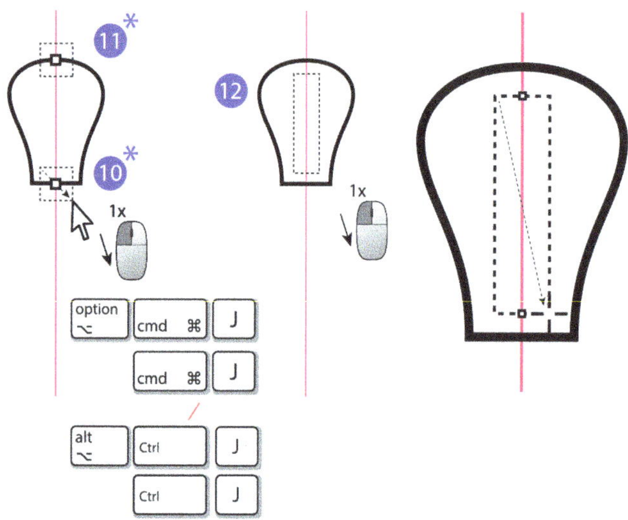

Step 10 and 11. Hold down the left mouse button and drag with the **Direct Selection Tool** (A) a selection around two anchor points (one end point of each half). Activate the shortcut option+command+J /alt+Ctrl+J (Average...). In the dialog box activate „Both", then „OK", then activate the shortcut command+J / Ctrl+J (Join).

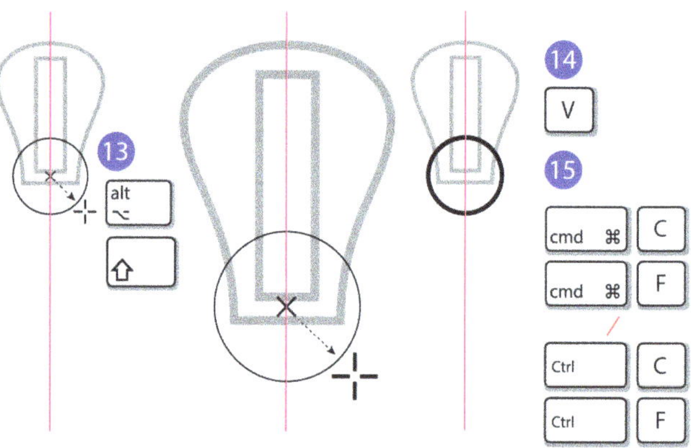

Step 12. Select the **Rectangle Tool** (M) and create an rectangle.
Step 13. Activate **Ellipse Tool** (L), hold down **alt/option** and **Shift** key, then create a circle.
Step 14. Click V key (Selection Tool).
Step 15. Activate the shortcut command+C / Ctrl+C (Copy) and the shortcut command+F / Ctrl+F (Paste in Front).

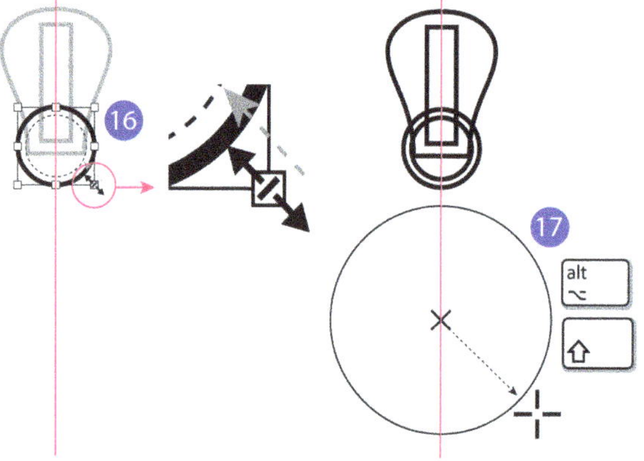

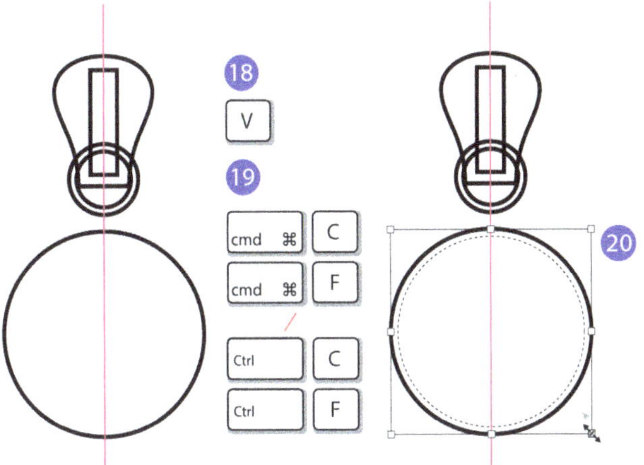

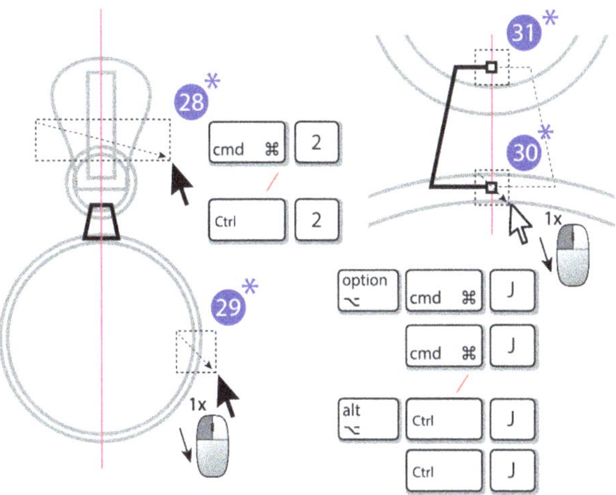

Step 16. Click V key (Selection Tool), hold down **alt/option** and **Shift** key and drag on the corner to reduce the size of the copy.
Step 17. Activate **Ellipse Tool** (L), hold down **alt/option** and **Shift** key, then create a circle.
Step 18. Click V key (Selection Tool).
Step 19. Activate the shortcut command+C / Ctrl+C (Copy) and the shortcut command+F / Ctrl+F (Paste in Front).
Step 20. Click V key (Selection Tool), hold down **alt/option** and **Shift** key and drag on the corner to reduce the size of the copy.

Step 30. Hold down the left mouse button and drag with the **Direct Selection Tool** (A) a selection around two anchor points (one end point of each half).
To join two pathes always select two end points. If you choose more than two points the "join" command won´t function. Activate the shortcut option+command+J /alt+Ctrl+J (Average…). In the dialog box activate „Both", then „OK", then activate the shortcut command+J / Ctrl+J (Join).
Step 31. Repeat step 30.

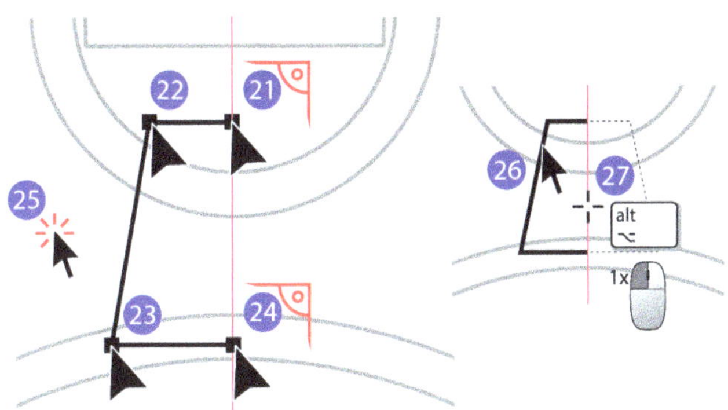

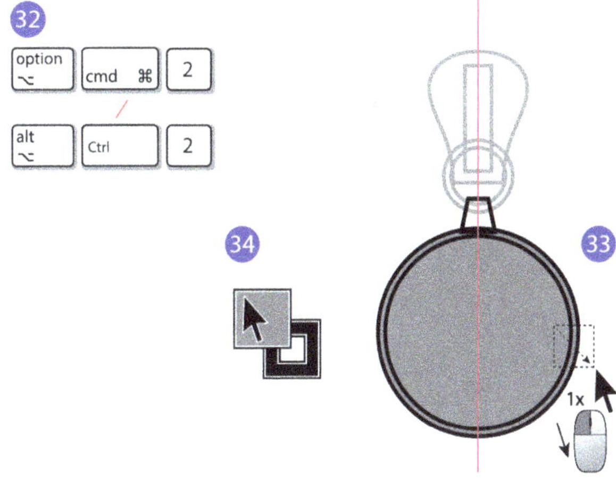

Step 21 - 24. Draw with the **Pen Tool** (P) a new line (click, do not drag!). At step 21, 22 and 24 hold down **Shift** key to create a straight lign (90°).
Step 25. Click on the V key (Selection Tool) and click on the empty drawing area to deselect the object. Alternatively you can activate the shortcut command+Shift+A / Ctrl+Shift+A.
Step 26. Click with the **Selection Tool** (V) on the path (press and release the left mouse button).
Step 27. Select the **Reflect Tool** (O), position the cursor on the vertical guide, hold down the **alt/option** key (do not release the alt key) and click the left mouse button. The reflect dialog box appears, then release the **alt/option** key. Activate the option „Vertical", then „Preview", check whether everything is OK and click „Copy". A mirrored duplicate is created.
Step 28 and 29. Drag with the **Selection Tool** (V) a selection around the objects.
Activate the shortcut cmd+2 / Ctrl+2 (or choose **Object>Lock>Selection**) to lock the objects.

Step 32. Activate the shortcut option+cmd+2 / alt+Ctrl+2 (or choose **Object>Unlock All**) to unlock the object in the document.
Step 33. Hold down the left mouse button and drag with the **Selection Tool** (V) around the both objects to select them.
Step 34. Change the fill colour for both objects to „grey".

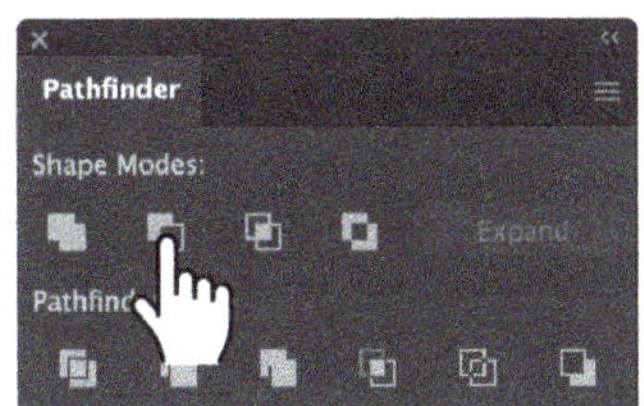

Step 35. Open the panel „Pathfinder" (**Window>Pathfinder**) and click on „Minus Front". The front object will be cut out from the lower object.

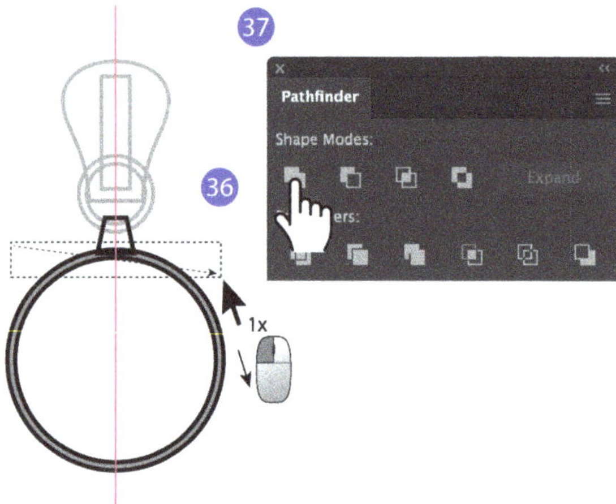

Step 36. Drag with **Selection Tool** (V) a selection around the objects.
Step 37. Click in the panel „Pathfinder" on „Unite". From several objects a single object is created.

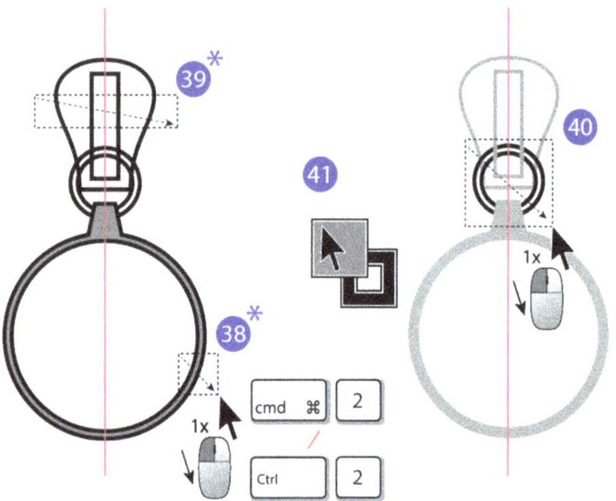

Step 38 and 39. Drag with **Selection Tool** (V) a selection around the objects.
Activate the shortcut cmd+2 / Ctrl+2 (or choose **Object>Lock>Selection**) to lock the objects.
Step 40. Drag with the **Selection Tool** (V) a selection around both circles.
Step 41. Change the fill colour for both objects to „grey".

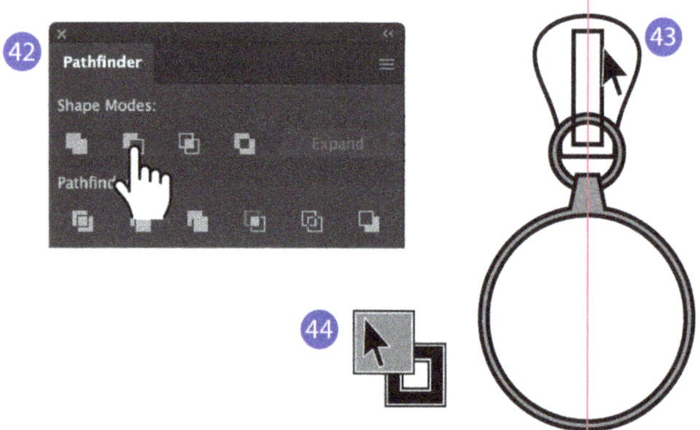

Step 42. Open the panel „Pathfinder" (**Window>Pathfinder**) and click on „Minus Front". The front object will be cut out from the lower object. Activate the shortcut option+cmd+2 / alt+Ctrl+2 (or choose **Object>Unlock All**) to unlock the object in the document.
Step 43. Click with the **Selection Tool** (V) on the path.
Step 44. Change the fill colour to „grey".

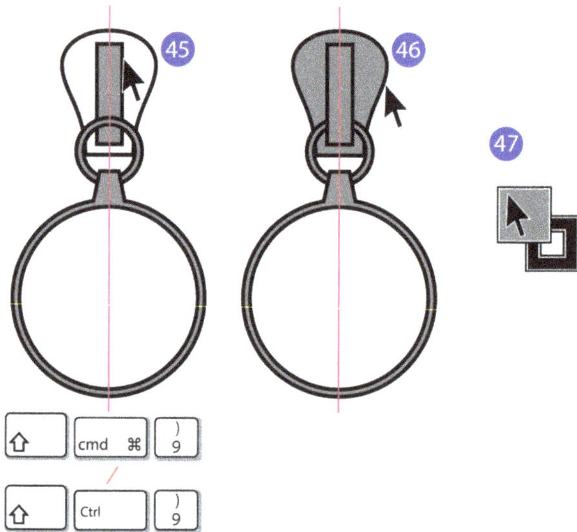

Step 45. Activate **Object>Arrange>Bring to Front** (alternativelly activate the shortcut Shift+cmd+9/ Shift+Ctrl+9. The object is displaced to the front.
Step 46. Click with the **Selection Tool** (V) on the path.
Step 47. Change the fill colour to „grey".

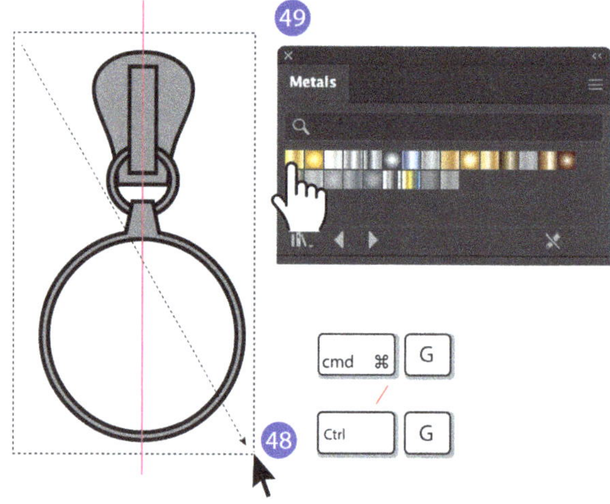

Step 48. Drag with the **Selection Tool** (V) a selection around the objects and activate the shortcut cmd+G/ Ctrl+G (Group).
Step 49. Open the „Swatch Libraries" with metal gradients **Window>SwatchLibraries>Gradients>Metals.** Click on one of the gradient, the gradient will be applied to the selected objects and will be automatically adjusted to the swatches of the document.

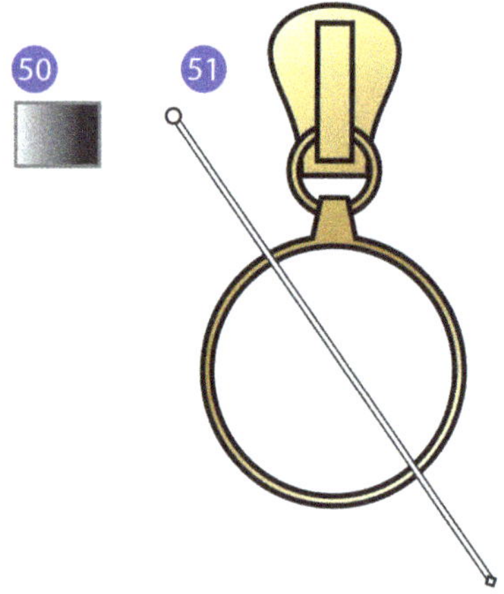

Step 50. Activate the **Gradient Tool** (G)
Step 51. Drag diagonally with the cursor along the objects to change the direction of the gradient.

8.15 TUTORIAL: EVENING DRESS

REQUIREMENTS

-Choose in the tools panel the stroke color „black" and the fill color „None".

-Set in the stroke panel (**Window > Stroke**) the stroke weight to **1pt** or **2pt**.

-Choose: **View > Rules >Show Rules, View > Guides > Lock Guides, View > Guides > Show Guides, View > Smart Guides, View > Snap to Point** and place a vertical guide.

-Work in this exercise with a figure template that you can download using the following link:
www.dimitridesign.org/templates

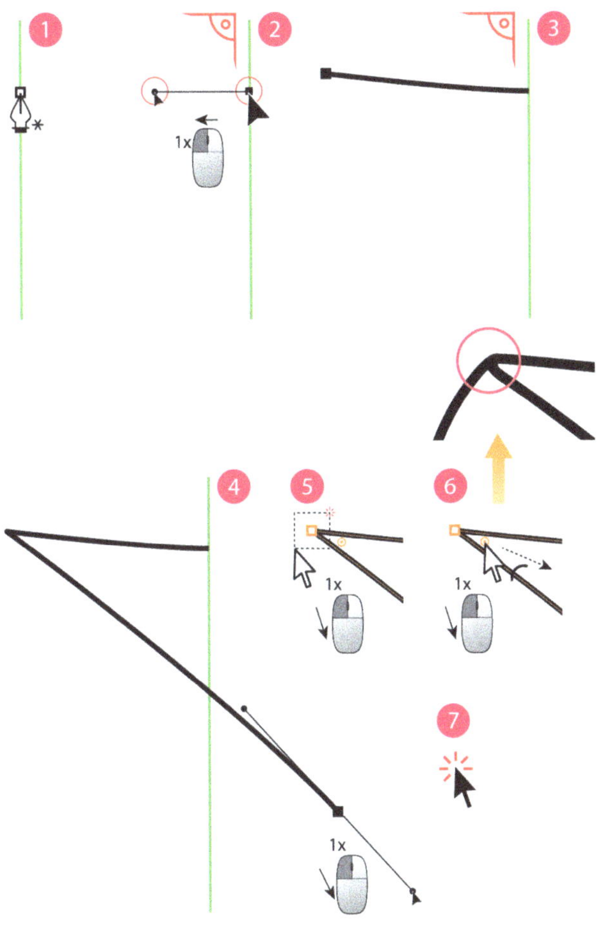

Step 1. Select the **Pen Tool** (P) and position it on the vertical guide, now hold down the left mouse button (do not release) to create the first anchor-point.
Step 2. Additionally hold down the **Shift** key (90° angle), also do not release, now drag the direction point to the left, then release first the mouse button and then the **Shift** key.
Step 3. Create a further anchor point (press and release the left mouse button, do not drag).
Step 4. Create a further anchor point (drag the direction point diagonally to the left down).
Step 5. Hold down the left mouse button and drag with the **Direct Selection Tool** (A) a selection.
Step 6. Hold down the left mouse button and drag the cursor diagonally on the circle-symbol to the center point of the rectangle. The corner is rounded.

Step 7. Click on the V key (Selection Tool) and click on the empty drawing area to deselect the object. Alternatively you can activate the shortcut command+Shift+A / Ctrl+Shift+A.

Step 8. Hold down the left mouse button and drag with the **Selection Tool** (V) around the object.

Step 9. Select the **Reflect Tool** (O), position the cursor on the vertical guide, hold down the **alt/option** key (do not release the alt key) and click the left mouse button. The reflect dialog box appears, then release the **alt** key.

Activate the option „Vertical", then „Preview", check whether everything is OK and click „Copy". A mirrored duplicate is created.

Step 16. Create a further anchor point (do not release the mouse button), drag the direction point diagonally to the left down, then release the mouse button.

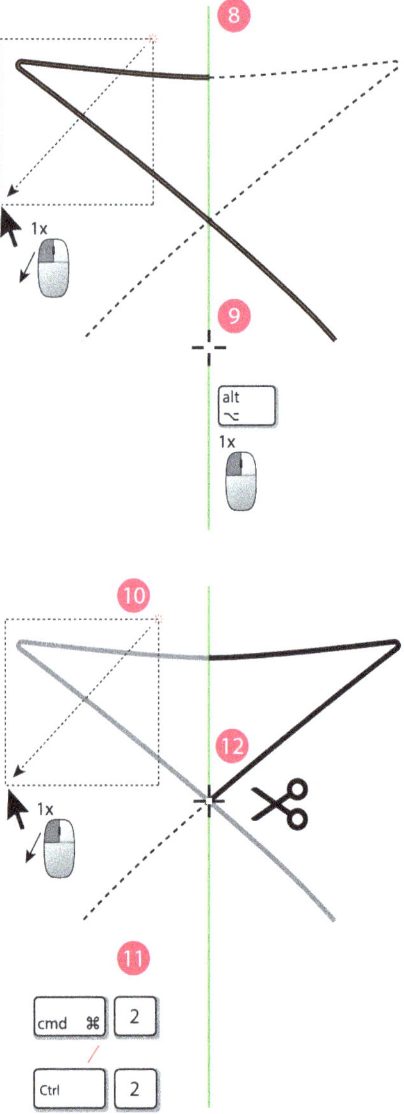

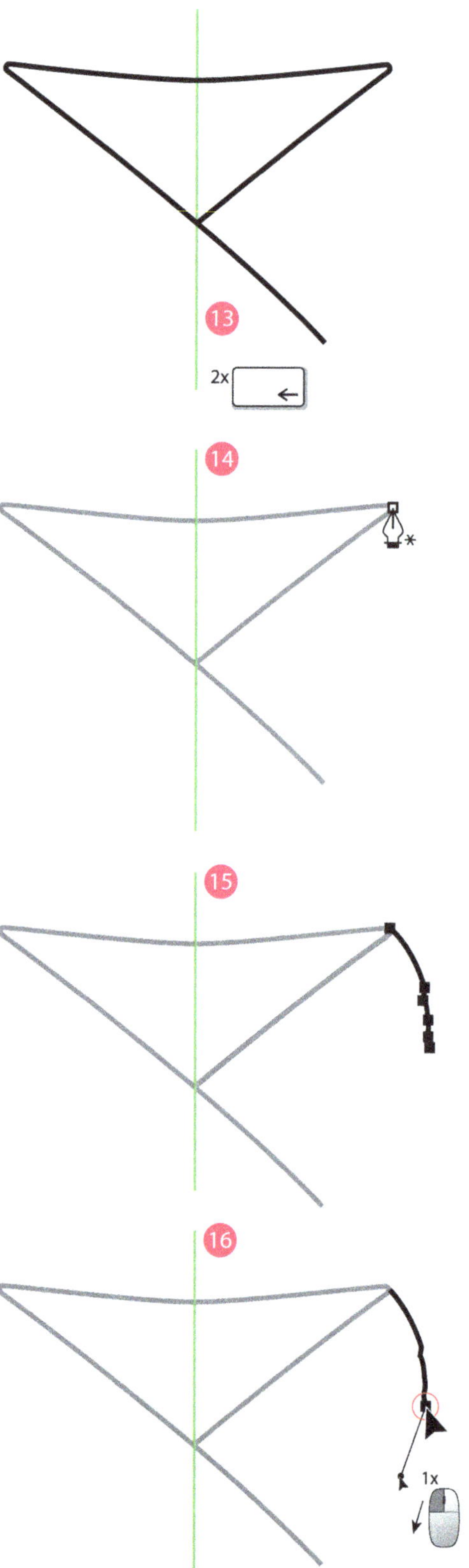

Step 10. Hold down the left mouse button and drag with the **Selection Tool** (V) around the object.

Step 11. Activate the shortcut cmd+2 / Ctrl+2 (or choose **Object>Lock>Selection**) to lock the objects.

Step 12. Click on the path with **Scissors Tool** (C) to separate the line at that point (see figure).

Step 13. Click on the **Backspace** key to delete the unnecessary line.

Step 14. Start to draw with the **Pen Tool** (P) a new line.

Step 15. Create a further anchor points.

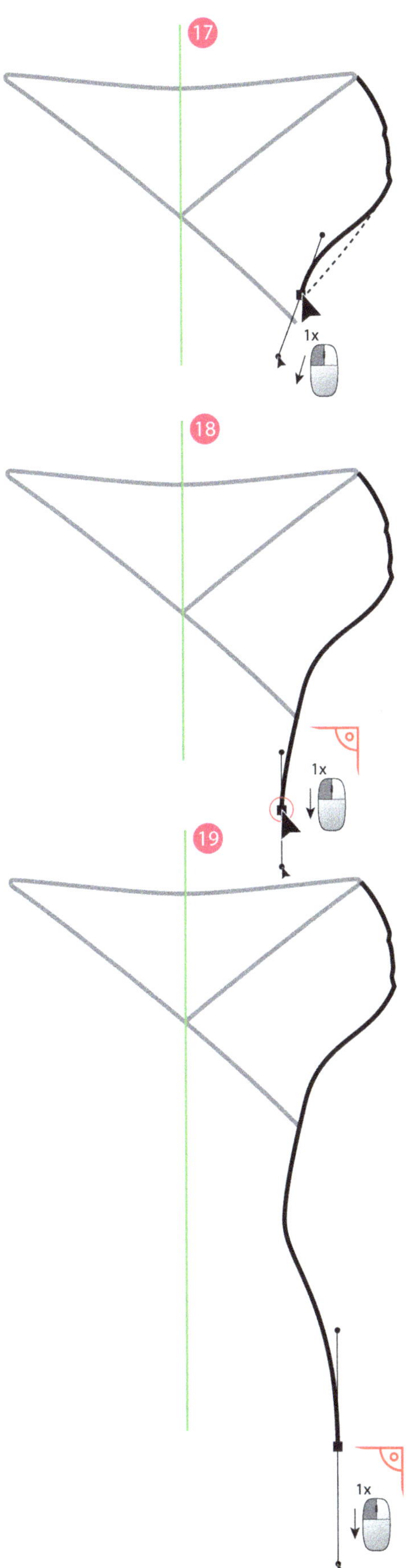

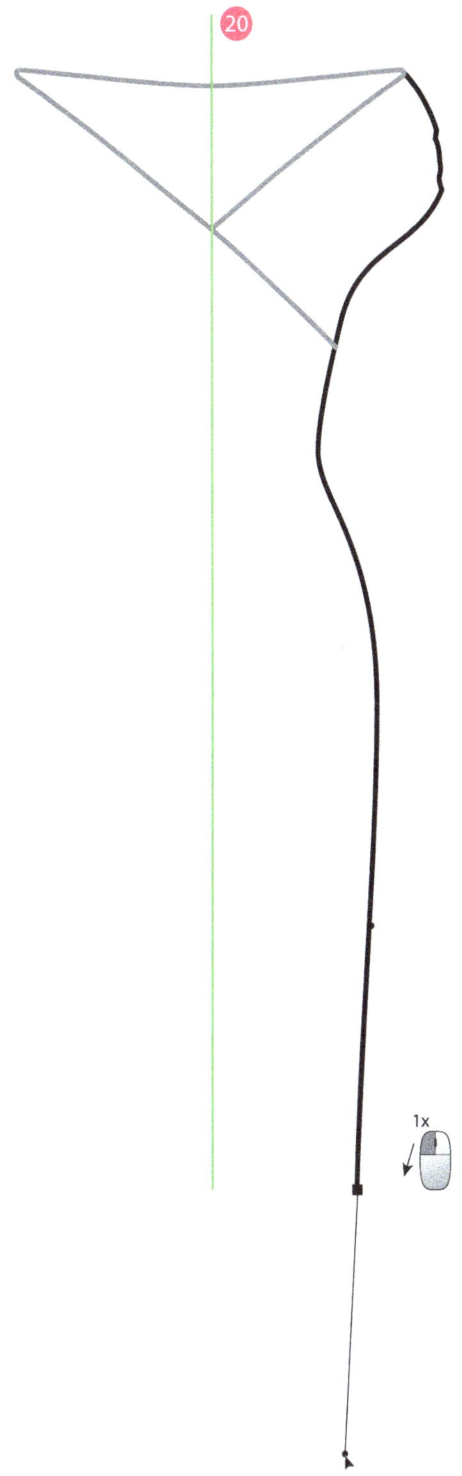

Step 17. Create a further anchor point (do not release the mouse button), drag the direction point diagonally to the left down, then release the mouse button.

Step 18. Create a further anchor point (do not release the left mouse button), additionally hold down the **Shift** key (90° angle), also do not release the **Shift** key and drag the direction point down, then release first the mouse button and then the **Shift** key.

Step 19. Create a further anchor point (do not release the left mouse button), additionally hold down the **Shift** key (90° angle), also do not release the **Shift** key and drag the direction point down, then release first the mouse button and then the **Shift** key.

Step 20. Create a further anchor point, drag the direction point down, then release the mouse button.

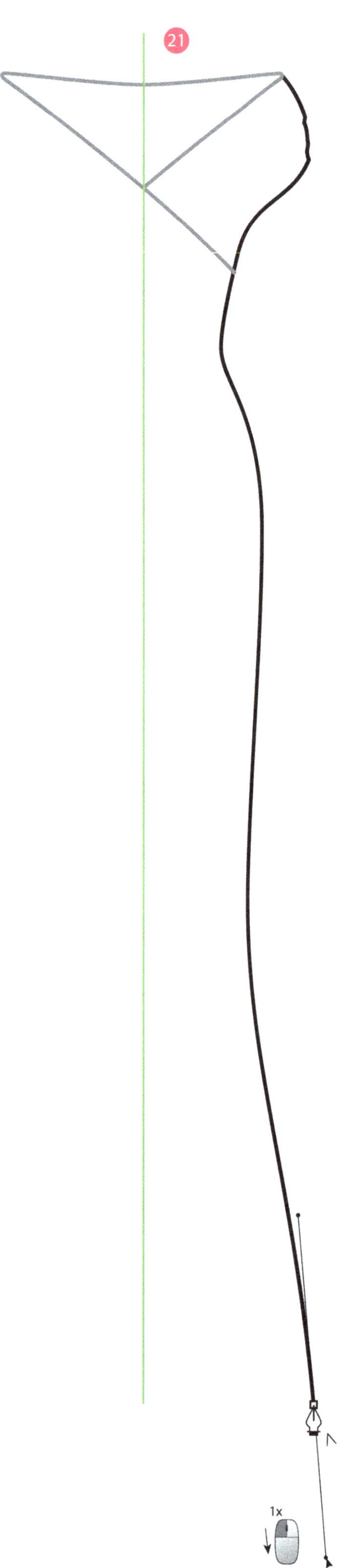

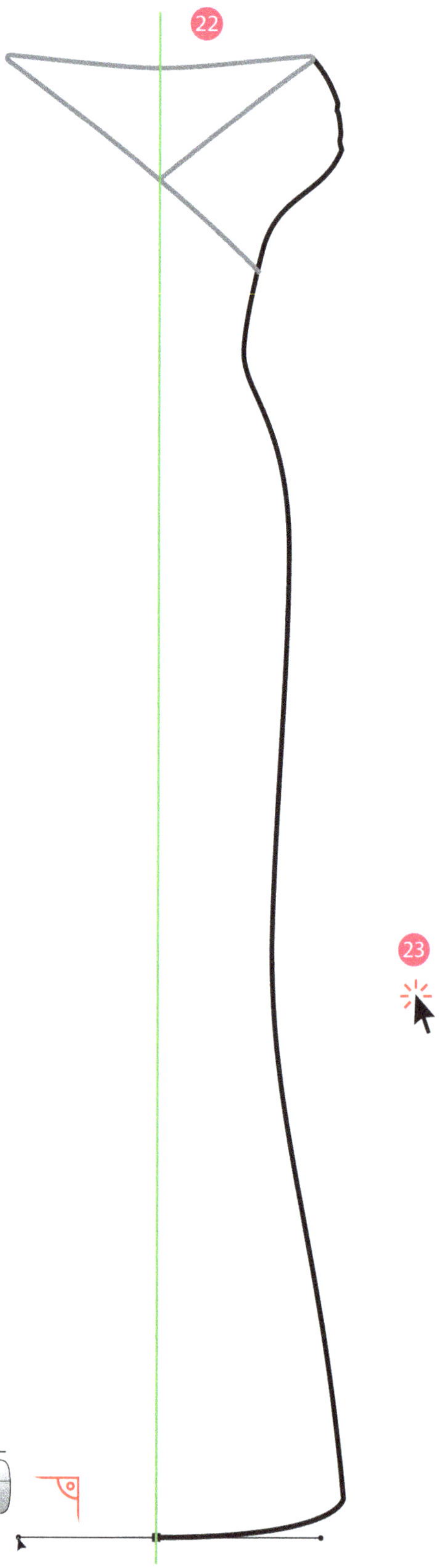

Step 21. Create a further anchor point and drag the direction point down then release the mouse button.
Click the last anchor point (press and release the left mouse button) to create a corner.

Step 22. Create a further anchor point (do not release the left mouse button), additionally hold down the **Shift** key (90° angle), also do not release the **Shift** key and drag the direction point to the left, then release first the mouse button and then the **Shift** key.

Step 23. Click on the V key (Selection Tool) and click on the empty drawing area to deselect the object. Alternatively you can activate the shortcut command+Shift+A / Ctrl+Shift+A.

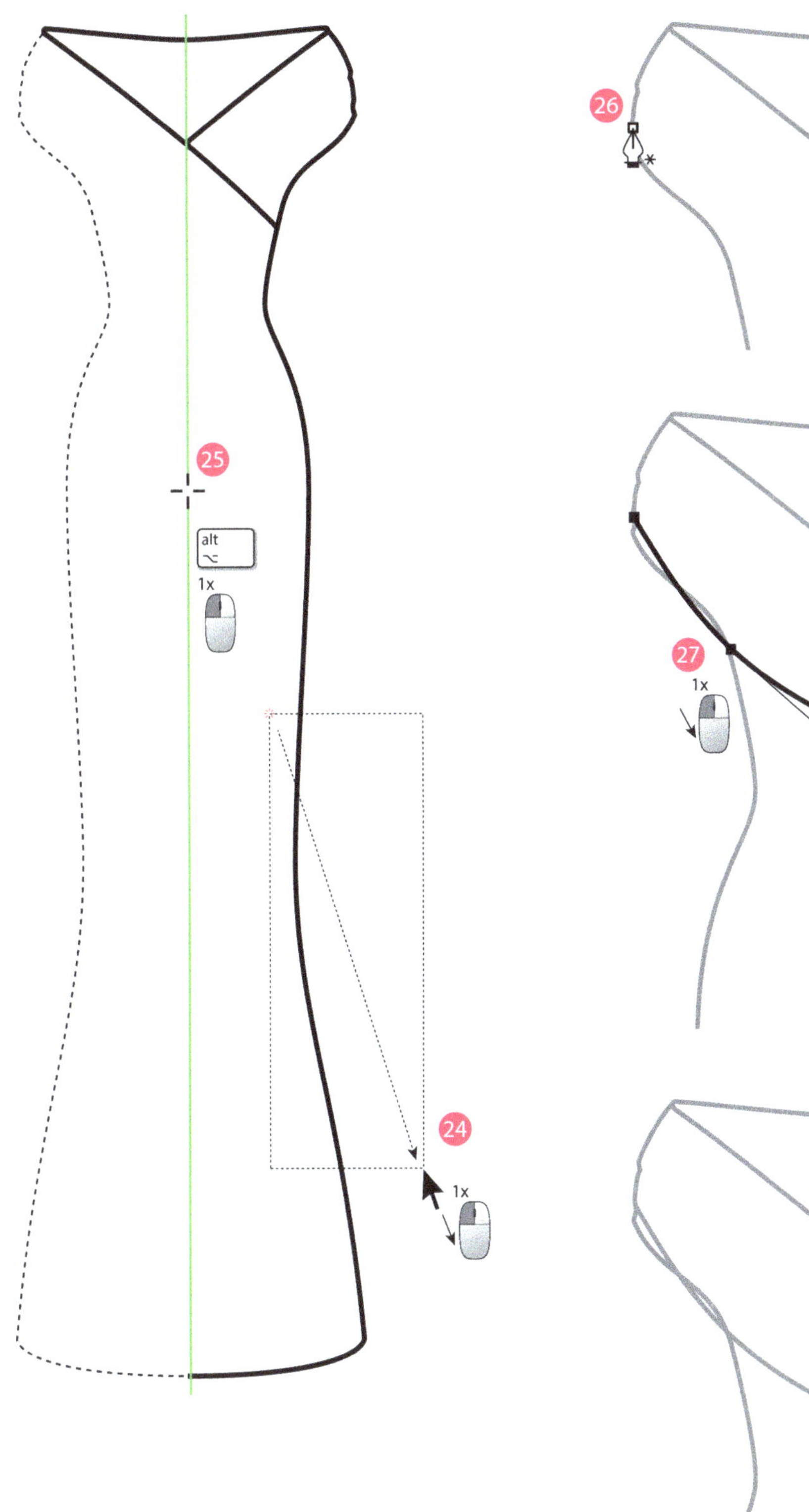

Step 24. Hold down the left mouse button and drag with the **Selection Tool** (V) around the object.

Step 25. Select the **Reflect Tool** (O), position the cursor on the vertical guide, hold down the **alt/option** key (do not release the alt key) and click the left mouse button. The reflect dialog box appears, then release the **alt** key.

Activate the option „Vertical", then „Preview", check whether everything is OK and click „Copy". A mirrored duplicate is created.

Step 26. Start to draw with the **Pen Tool** (P) a new line.

Step 27. Create a further anchor point and drag the direction point down right then release the mouse button.

Step 28. Create a further anchor point and drag the direction point down right then release the mouse button.

Click on the V key (Selection Tool) and click on the empty drawing area.

Step 29. Create with the **Pen Tool** (P) a new line (two points).

Step 30. Click on the V key (Selection Tool) and click on the empty drawing area to deselect the object. Alternatively you can activate the shortcut command+Shift+A / Ctrl+Shift+A.

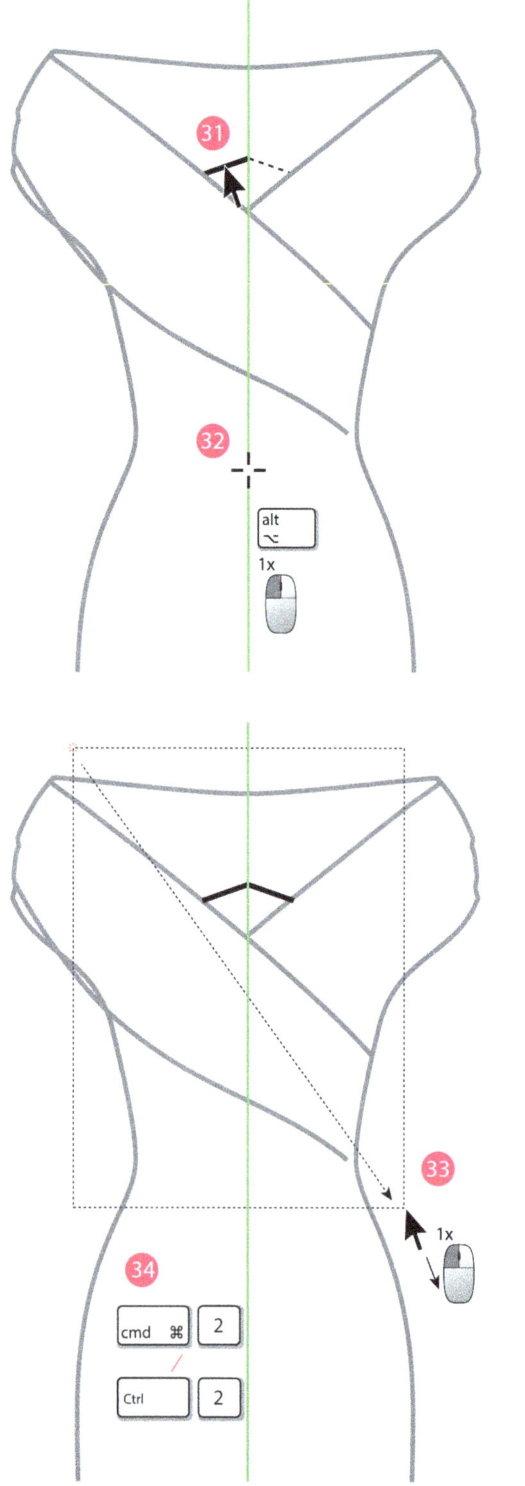

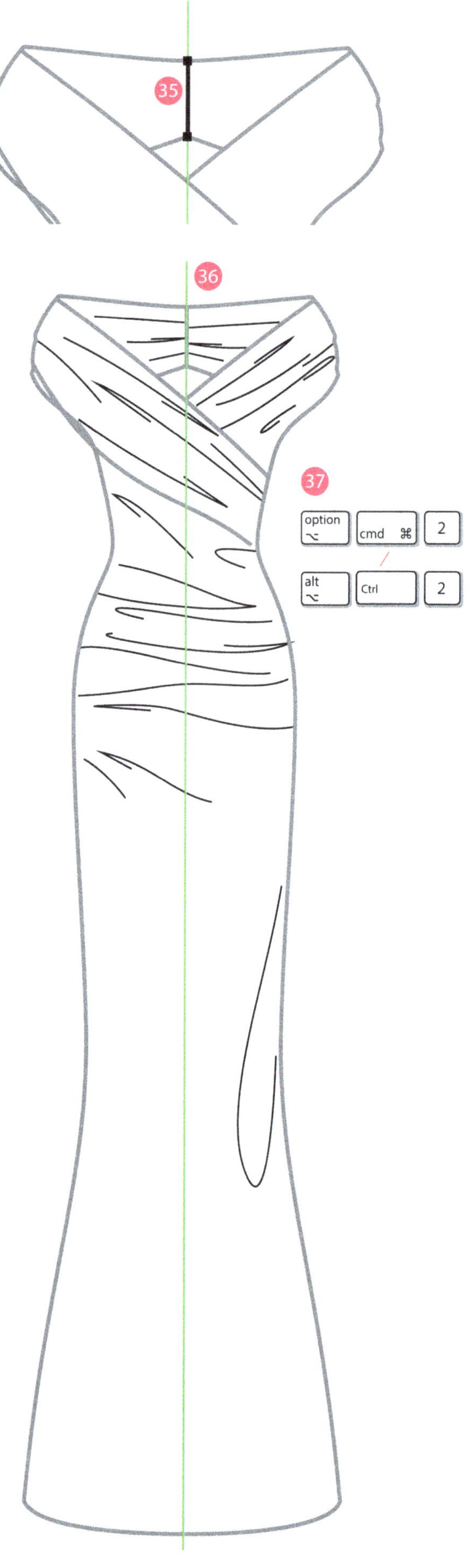

Step 31. Click on the line with the **Selection Tool** (V).
Step 32. Select the **Reflect Tool** (O), position the cursor on the vertical guide, hold down the **alt/option** key (do not release the alt key) and click the left mouse button. The reflect dialog box appears, then release the **alt** key.
Activate the option „Vertical", then „Preview", check whether everything is OK and click „Copy". A mirrored duplicate is created.
Step 33. Hold down the left mouse button and drag with the **Selection Tool** (V) around the objects.
Step 34. Activate the shortcut cmd+2 / Ctrl+2 (or choose **Object>Lock>Selection**) to lock the objects.
Step 35. Create with the **Pen Tool** (P) a new line.

Step 36. Create with the **Pen Tool** (P) further lines (pleats).
Step 37. Activate the shortcut option+cmd+2 / alt+Ctrl+2 (or choose **Object>Unlock All**) to unlock all objects.

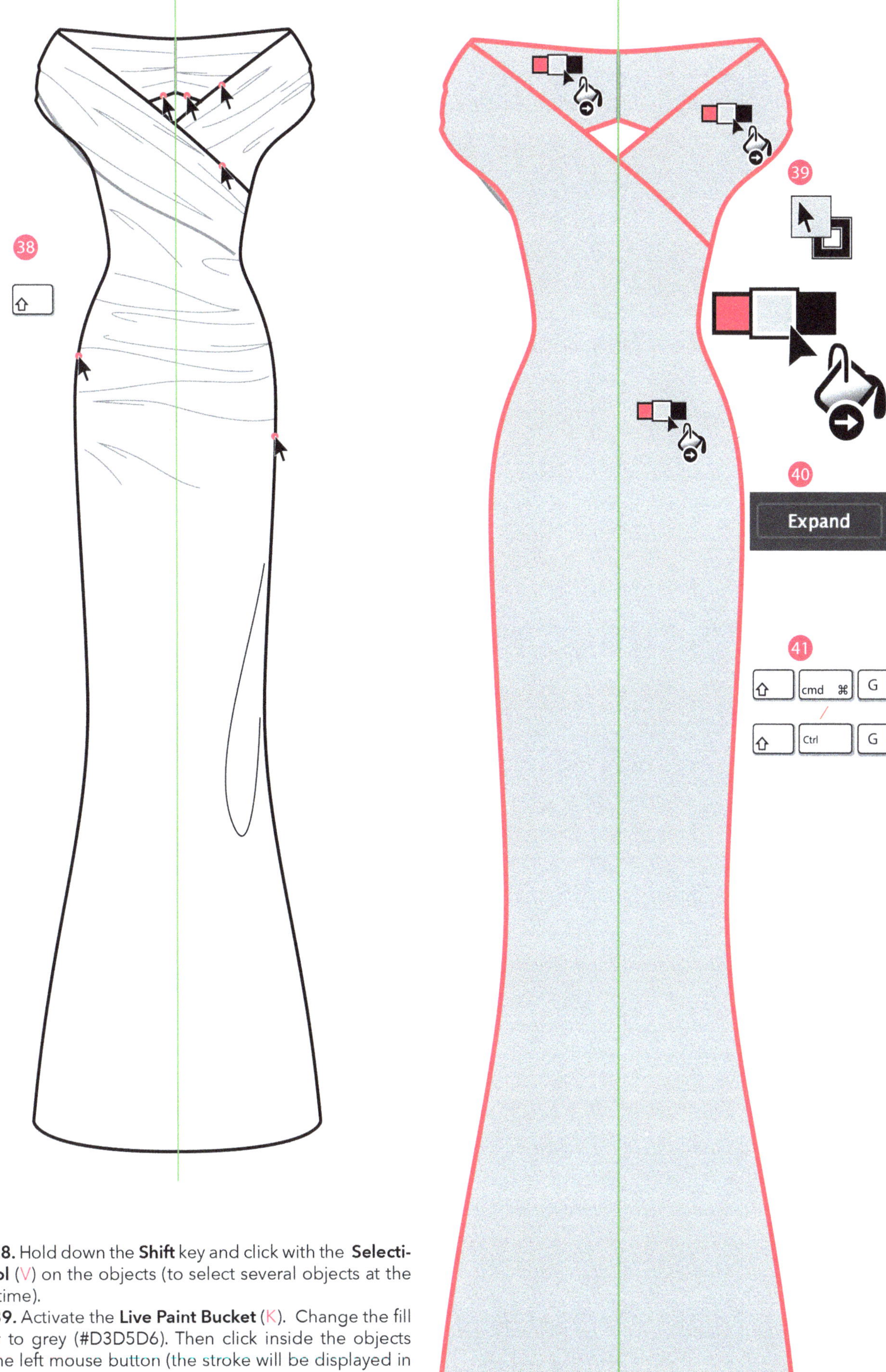

Step 38. Hold down the **Shift** key and click with the **Selection Tool** (V) on the objects (to select several objects at the same time).

Step 39. Activate the **Live Paint Bucket** (K). Change the fill colour to grey (#D3D5D6). Then click inside the objects with the left mouse button (the stroke will be displayed in red).

Step 40. Then activate the command **Expand** in the control panel or the command **Object>Expand..** After that command the objects are grouped together.

Step 41. Activate **two times** the shortcut Shift+cmd+G / Shift+Ctrl+G (or choose **Object>Ungroup**, also two times).

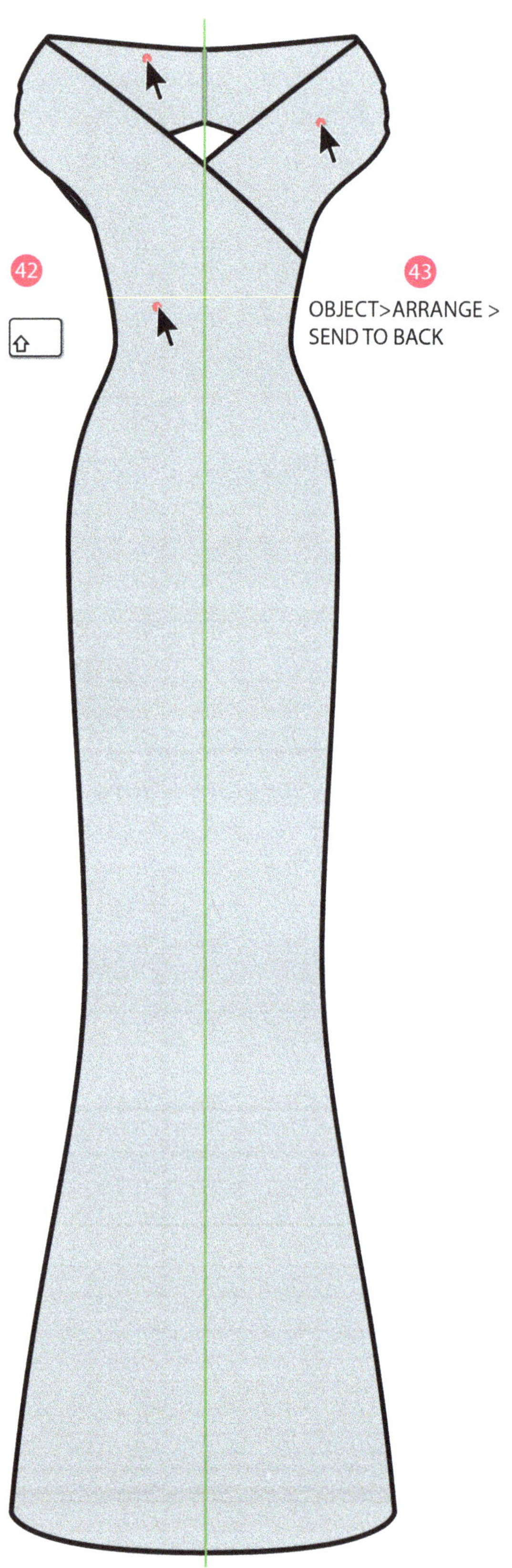

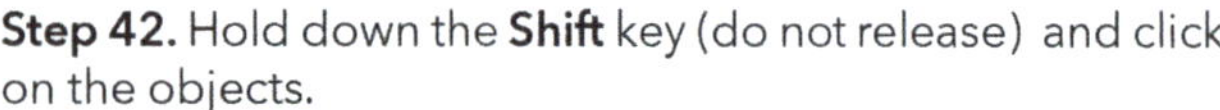

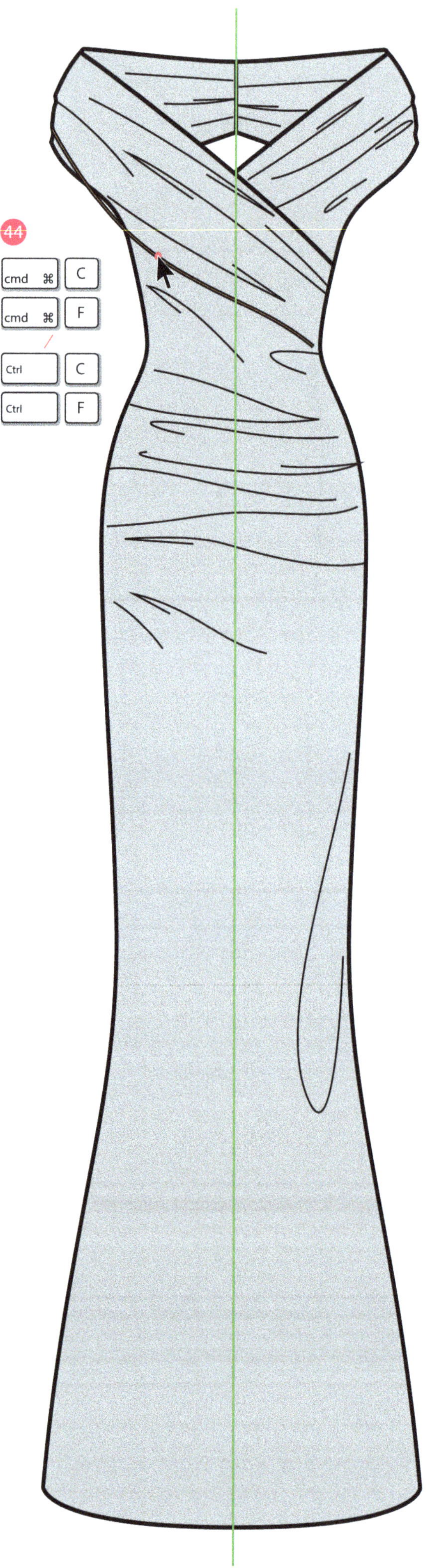

Step 42. Hold down the **Shift** key (do not release) and click on the objects.

Step 43. Choose **Object>Arrange>Send to Back** to place the objects in the background.

Step 44. Select the line with the **Selection Tool** (V) (see figure) and activate the shortcut command+C / Ctrl+C (Copy) and the shortcut command+F / Ctrl+F (Paste in Front).

Step 45. Click with the **Pen Tool** (P) on the initial point to continue to draw on the line.

Step 46. Click on the end point to finish the shape.

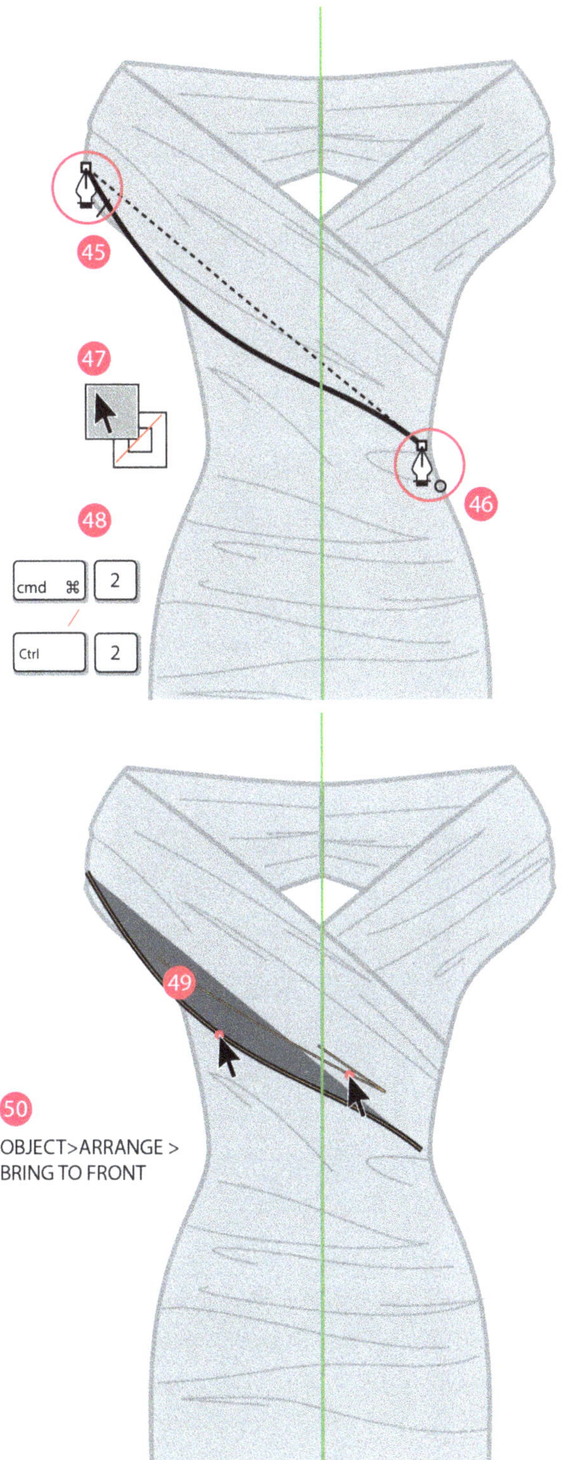

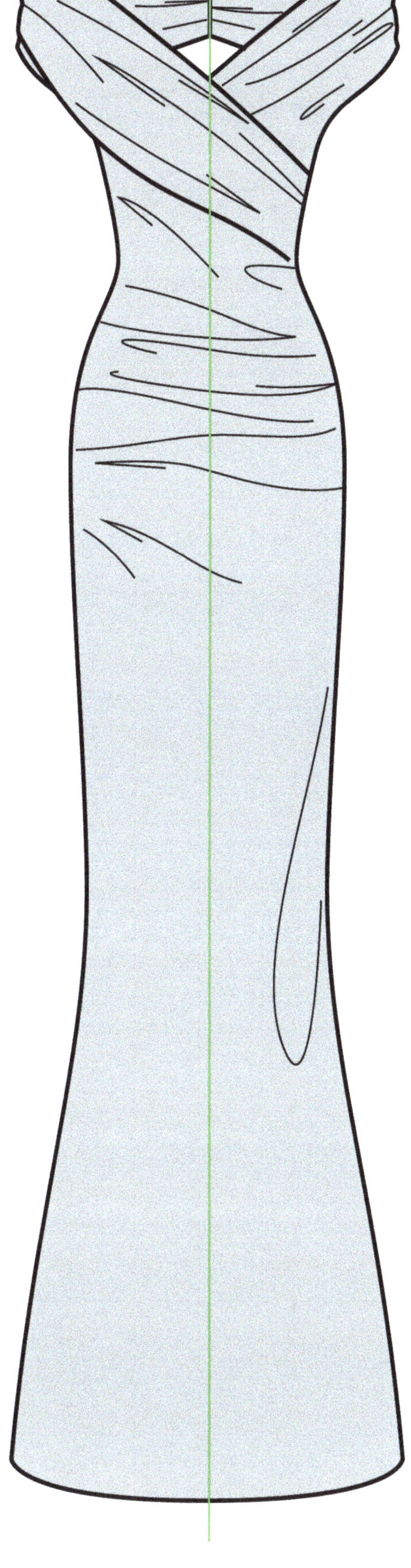

Step 47. Change the fill colour to grey (#D3D5D6) and set the stroke colour to „None".
Step 48. Activate the shortcut cmd+2 / Ctrl+2 (or choose **Object>Lock>Selection**) to lock the objects.
Step 49. Hold down the **Shift** key an click on both lines.
Step 50. Choose **Object>Arrange>Bring to Front** to bring both lines to the front.

8.16 TRANSPARENCY PANEL

Use the Transparency panel (Window > Transparency) to specify the opacity and blending mode of objects. Also to knock out a portion of one object with the overlying portion of a transparent object or create opacity masks.
To show all options in the transparency panel choose „show options" from the menu panel.

Opacity
You can change the opacity of a single object, the opacity of all objects in a group or layer, or the opacity of an object's fill or stroke.

Blending modes
Blending modes let you vary the ways that the colors of objects blend with the colors of underlying objects.
The effect of the blending mode is seen on any objects that lie beneath the object's layer or group.

Multiply
Multiplies the base color by the blend color. The resulting color is always a darker color.

Color Burn
Darkens the base color to reflect the blend color.

Lighten
Selects the base or blend color, whichever is lighter, as the resulting color.

Overlay
Multiplies or screens the colors, depending on the base color.

Difference
Subtracts either the blend color from the base color or the base color from the blend color, depending on which has the greater brightness value.

Hue
Creates a resulting color with the luminance and saturation of the base color and the hue of the blend color.

Saturation
Creates a resulting color with the luminance and hue of the base color and the saturation of the blend color.

Luminosity
You can create a resulting color with the hue and saturation of the base color and the luminance of the blend color. Luminosity creates an inverse effect from that of the color mode.

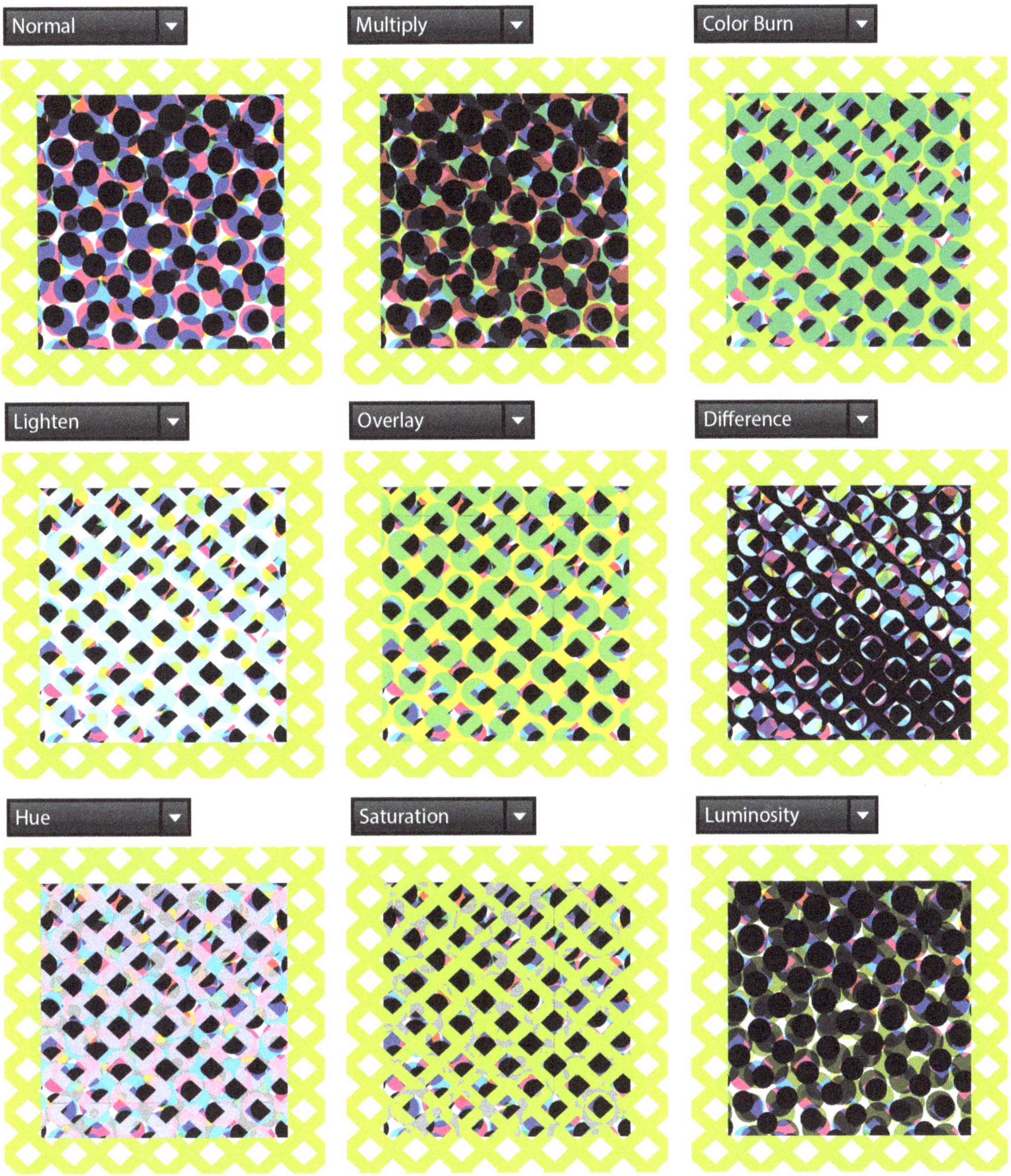

Select a single object or group (or target a layer in the Layers panel).

To change only the transparency of the fill or stroke select first the object, then choose in the „Appearance" panel (Window > Appearance) the fill or the stroke.

Select in the transparency panel a fill method (pop-up menu) (**1**).
With the opacity (**2**) you can change the opacity of a single object, the opacity of all objects in a group or layer, or the opacity of an object's fill or stroke.
It is also possible to create a mask for some other interesting effects (**3**).

To do this, select two overlapping objects and activate in the "Transparency" panel the option "Make Mask" (**4**).

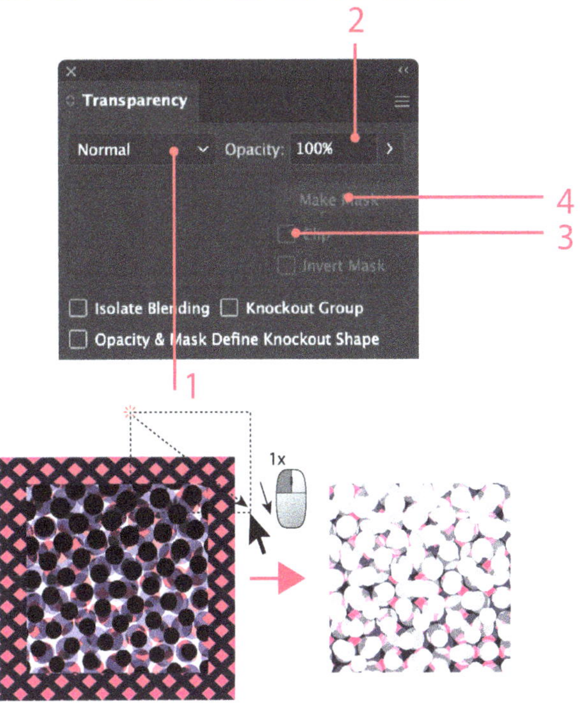

8.17 EFFECTS (COLOR HALFTON)

REQUIREMENTS

-In the tool panel, set "stroke color" to black and "fill Color to "without".

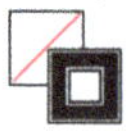

-In the stroke panel (**Window > Stroke**) set the stroke weight to **1pt** to **2pt**.

Illustrator offers you a variety of effects that can be applied to objects, groups, or layers to change properties of those objects.
Once an effect is applied to an object, it appears in the Appearance panel (**Window > Appearance**). Use this panel to edit, duplicate, move, and delete the effects. After you apply an effect, you should first convert the object to edit each anchor point.
The effects menu is split into two sections (Illustrator effects and Photoshop effects). Many of these effects can be applied to both vector objects and bitmap objects.

EFFECT>PIXELATE>COLOR HALFTON

Step 1. Activate the **Rectangle tool** (M) and create a rectangle, the object should be slightly larger than DIN A4 page (see example).

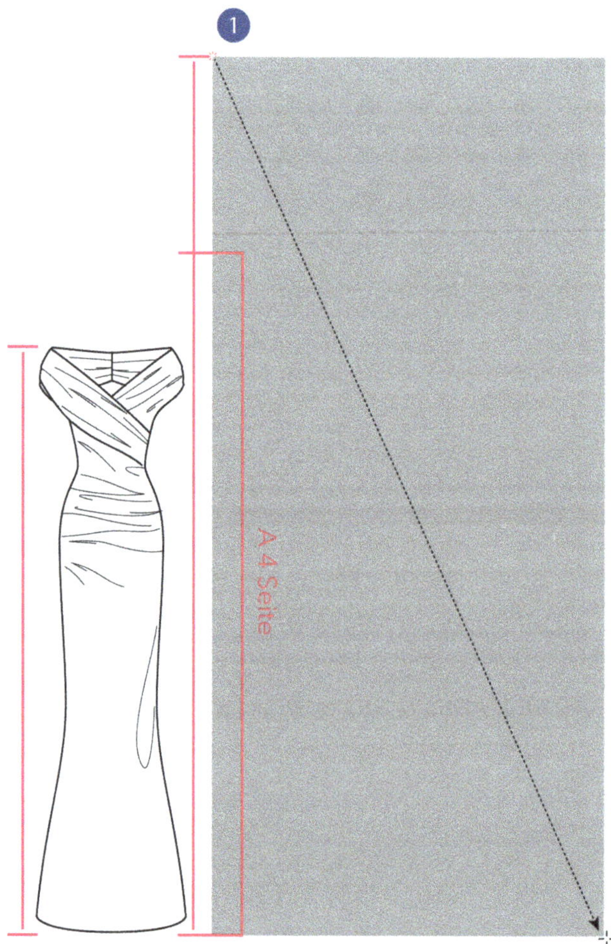

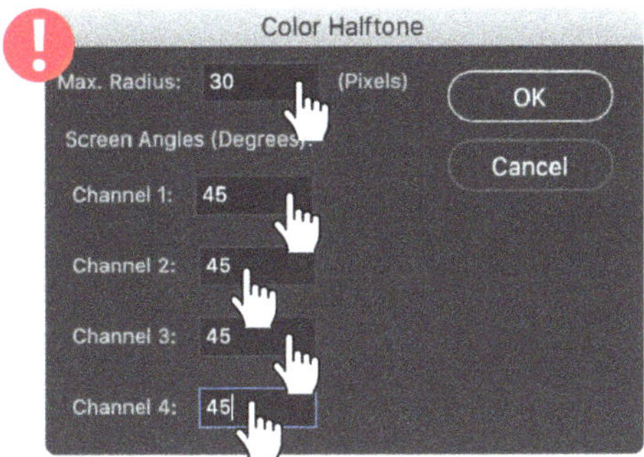

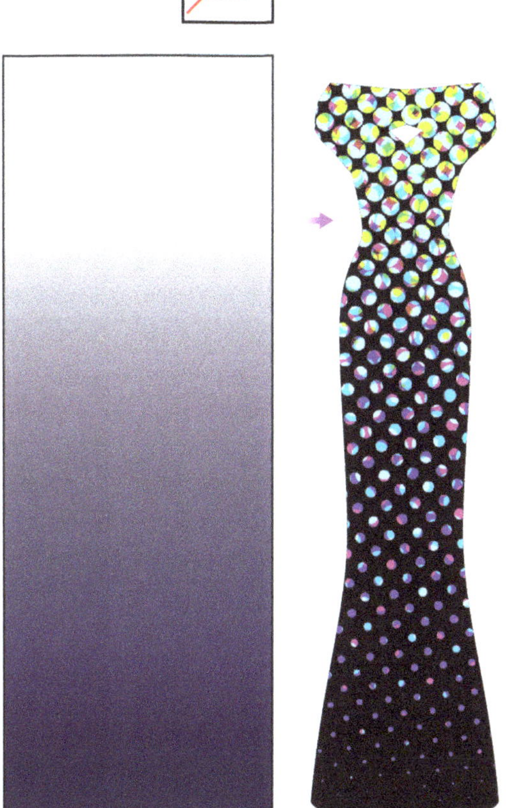

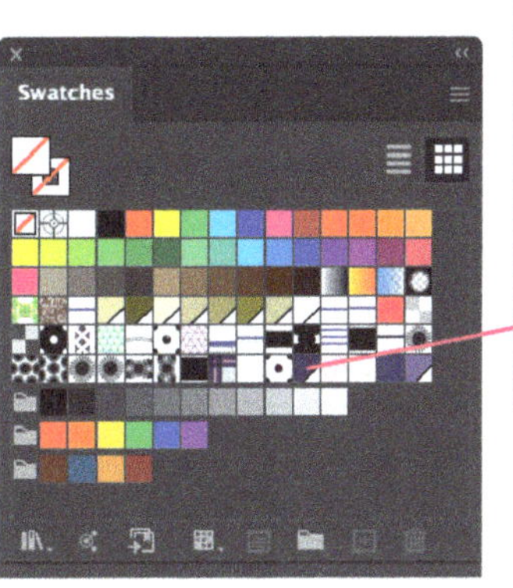

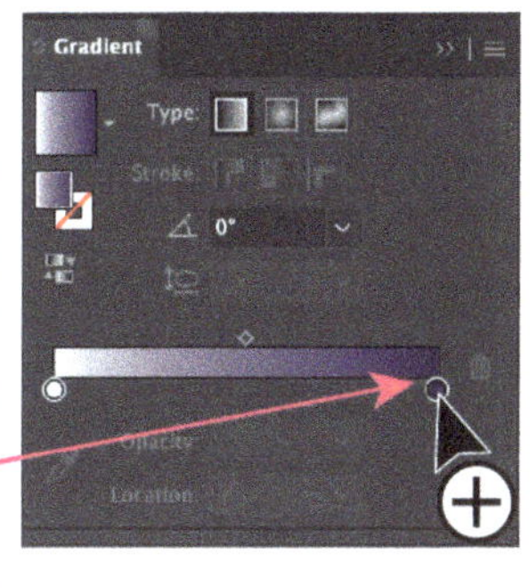

Step 2. Activate the "black/white" gradient.
Step 3. Activate the **Gradient Tool** (G).
Step 4. Hold down the **Shift**- key (do not release) and change the direction of the gradient.
Step 5. From the effects menu, select **Effect > Pixelate>Color Halfton** or click in the appearance panel „Add New Effect" _fx_ and select: **Effect > Pixelate>Color Halfton**.

Enter different values in the options field (see figure).
Step 6. If the gradient is colored, you can create other interesting colored effects (**Effect > Pixelate>Color Halften**).

From the effects menu, select **Effect > Pixelate>Color Halften** or click in the appearance panel „Add New Effect" _fx_ and select: **Effect > Pixelate>Color Halften**.

Enter different values in the dialog box (see screenshot), then confirm the inputs with "OK."

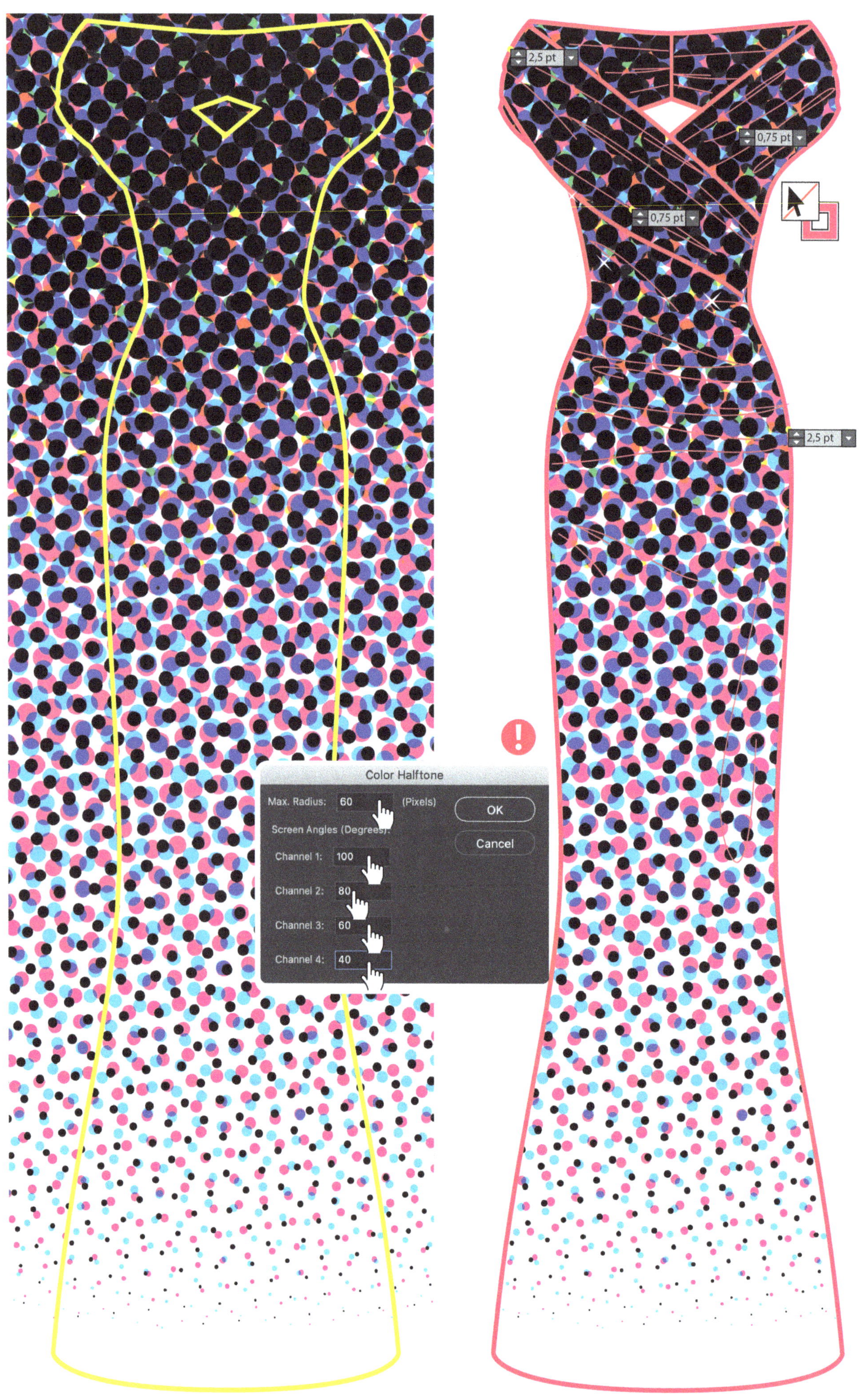

2,5 pt
0,75 pt
0,75 pt
2,5 pt
Color Halftone
Max. Radius: 60 (Pixels)
OK
Screen Angles (Degrees):
Cancel
Channel 1: 100
Channel 2: 80
Channel 3: 60
Channel 4: 40

8.18 GRADIENT TOOL

REQUIREMENTS

-For "Gradient" and "Gradient Tool," see page 20-21.
- Create the dress from exercise 8.15.

Step 1. Use the **Selection tool** (V) to click on the three "grey" fills (hold down the **Shift** key).
Step 2. Activate the command **Object > Arrange > Bring to Front**.
Step 3. And in the Pathfinder panel (**Window > Pathfinder**) click Unite at the top left. This creates a single object from multiple objects.
Step 4. Open a gradient **Window > Swatch Libraries > Gradients > Color Harmonies**. Apply a gradient to the fill. For "Type", enable "Radial Gradient". Activate the **Gradient Tool** (G) and change the direction of the gradient. You can also change individual colors in the "Gradient" panel, double-click the gradient slider to open swatches.

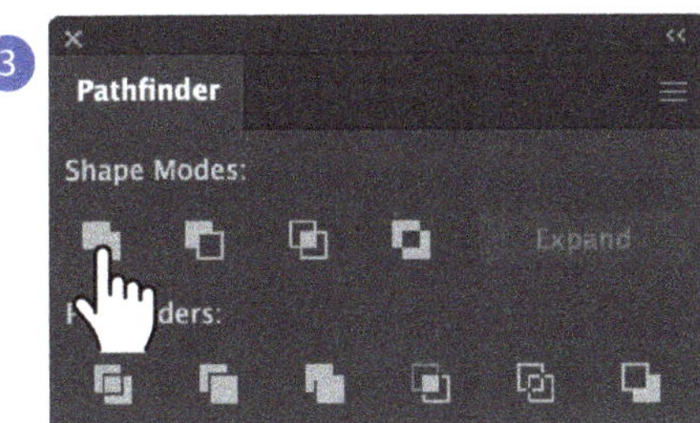

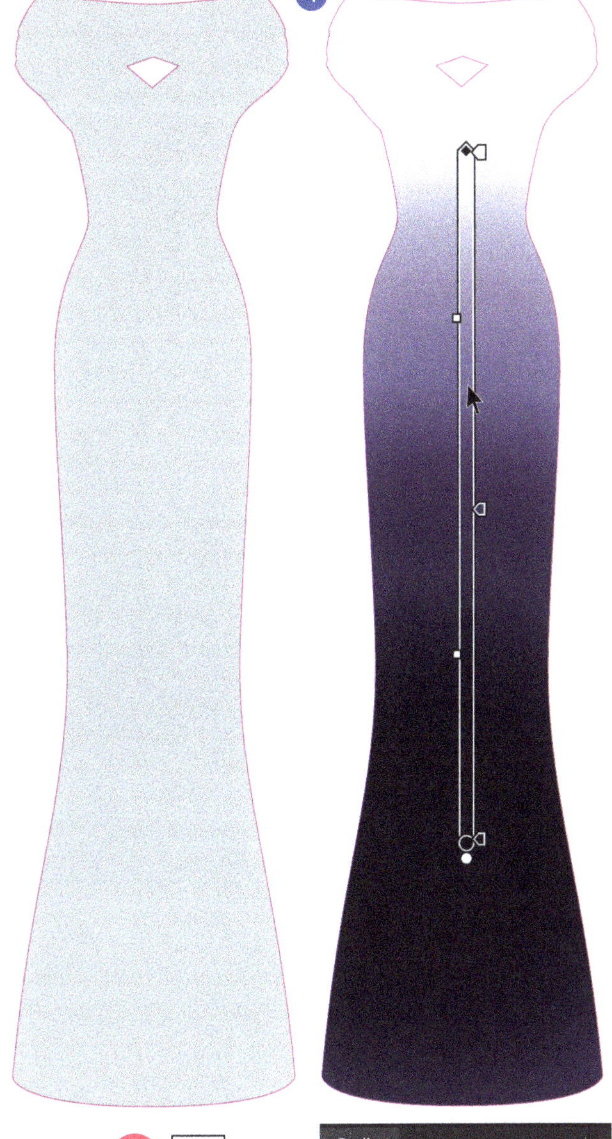

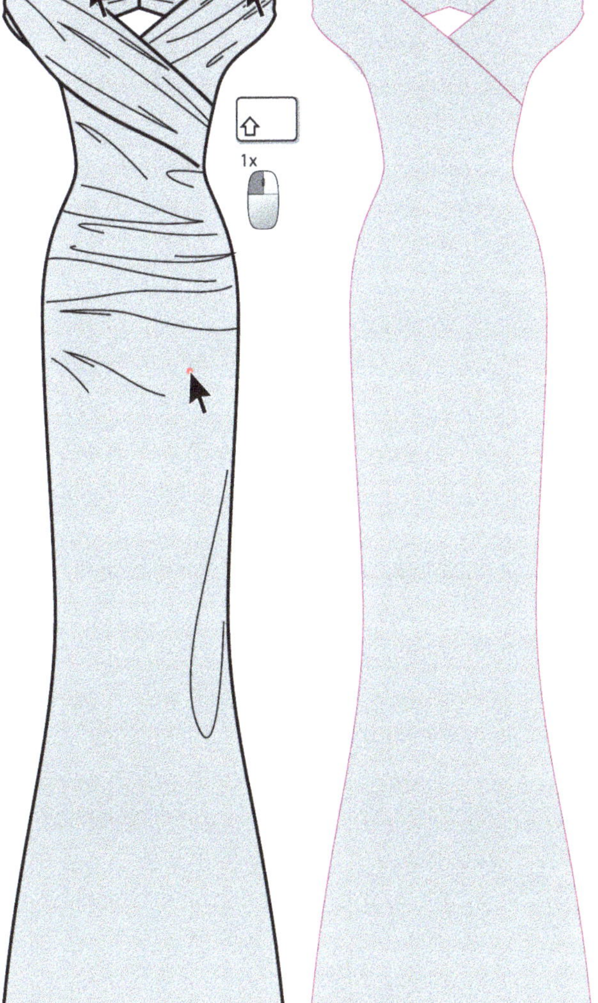

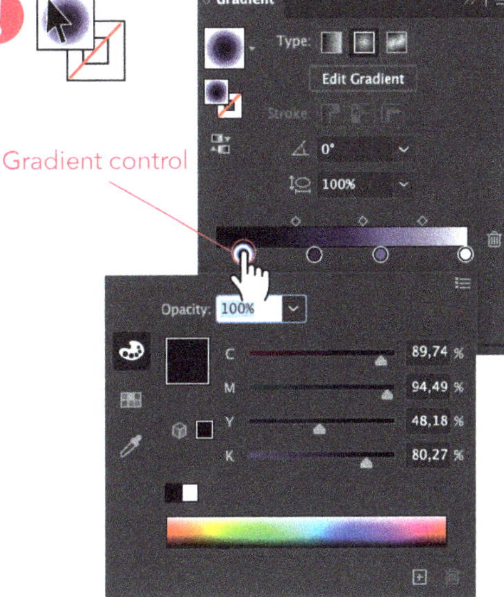

8.19 MASKING

Place the object (color halfton) from the tutorial 8.17 and place it in the foreground (**Object > Arrange > Bring to Front**).

Step 1. Use the **Selection Tool** (V) to select the object (Dress).

Step 2. Activate the short key command cmd+C / Ctrl+C (Copy) and the short key command cmd+F / Ctrl+F (Paste in Front), a copy of the dress has been created, this copy is used for the mask.

Step 3. Activate the **Shift**- key and select **both** objects (see figure).

Step 4. Activate the shortcut command cmd+7 / Ctrl+7 (**Object > Clipping Mask >Make**).

Step 5. Click on the object with the **Selection Tool** (V) and activate the command **Object > Arrange > Bring to Front.**

Step 6. Click on the object with the **Selection Tool** (V) and activate the command **Object > Arrange > Send to Back.**

The gradient and color halfton are now on the lowest sublayers, so that the stroke and fold lines of the dress become visible.

lowest layer
Layer order
?

8.20 TRACE IMAGE

You can create a drawing (vector graphic) based on existing artwork (pixel image), for which you can trace the artwork. For example, you can use this method to create different repeats based on pixel images (e.g. scanned jeans fabric) for alloverprints.

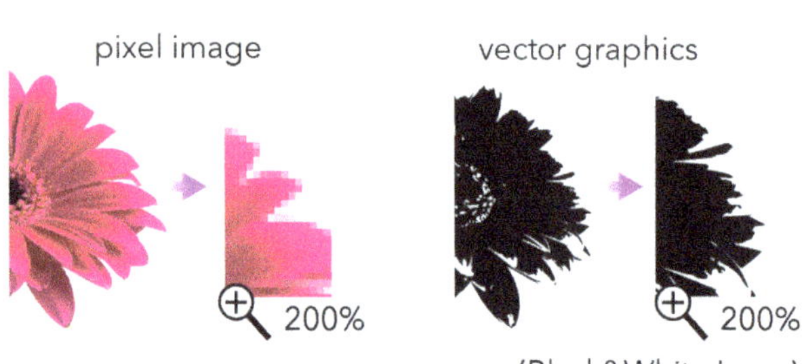

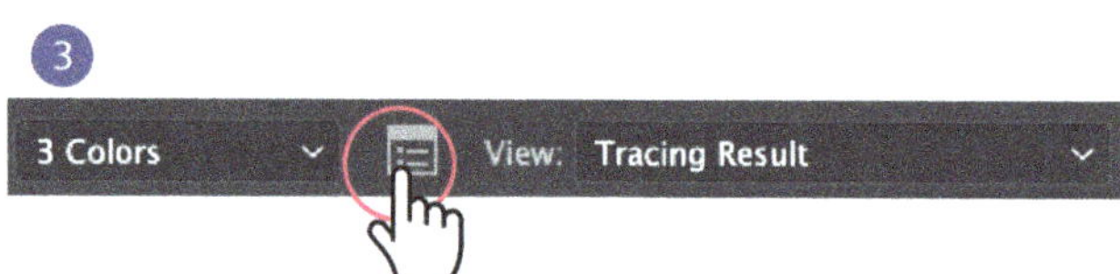

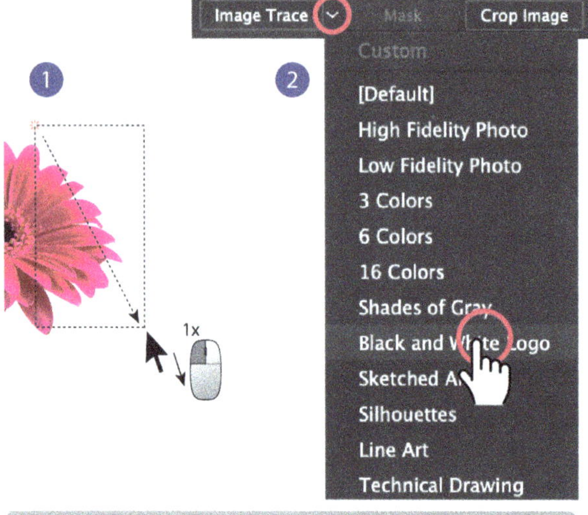

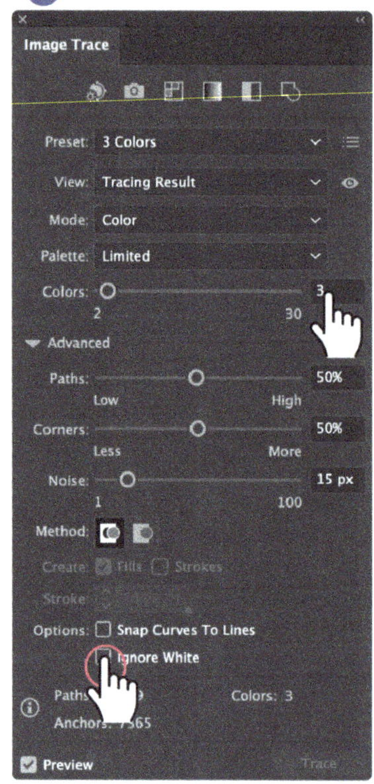

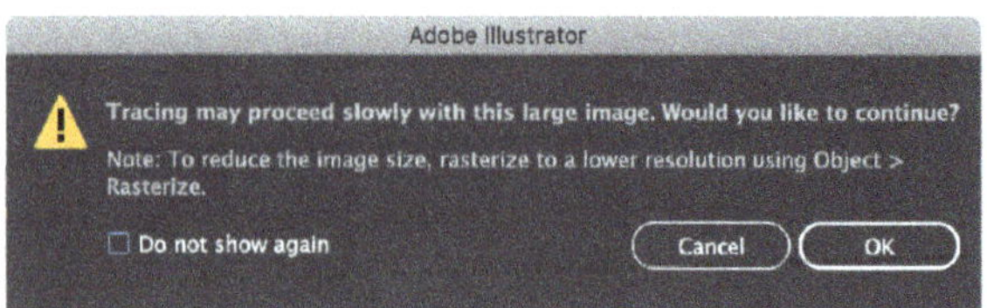

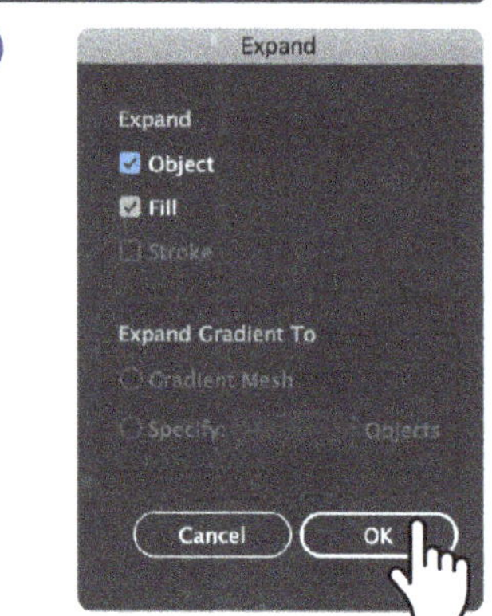

Step 1. Click a pixel image using the **Selection Tool** (V) or **Direct Selection Tool** (A).

Step 2. In the control panel, for example, select the "black and white logo" preset.

If the pixel image is too large, a warning appears, confirm with "OK." Then the pixel image is converted into a vector graphic.

Step 3. Click the icon at the top of the control panel. The image trace panel opens.

Step 4. You can make various settings in the image trace panel:

Preset: Select the tracing preset.

View: Viewing options.

Mode: Color mode used for tracing.

Palette: Palette used for tracing.

Threshold: Threhold specifies the number of colors to use in a color tracer result.

Advanced

Paths: Sets the distance between the traced shape and the original pixel shape.

Corners: This option specifies the highlighting of corners. The higher the value, the more corners.

Noise: Specifies a range in pixels that is ignored when tracing. The higher the value, the less noise.

Method: Sets a method for tracing.

Fills/Strokes: Create filled regions or stroked paths.

Stroke: Creates stroked paths in the tracer result.

Options: Snap curves to lines determines whether slightly curved lines are replaced by straight lines.

Ignore White: Determines whether white-filled areas are replaced by areas without a fill.

8.21 TUTORIAL: ZICKZACK PATTERN

REQUIREMENTS

- Choose in the tools panel the stroke color „black" and the fill color „None".

-Choose: **View > Rules >Show Rules, View > Guides > Lock Guides, View > Guides > Show Guides, View > Smart Guides, View > Snap to Point** and place a vertical guide.

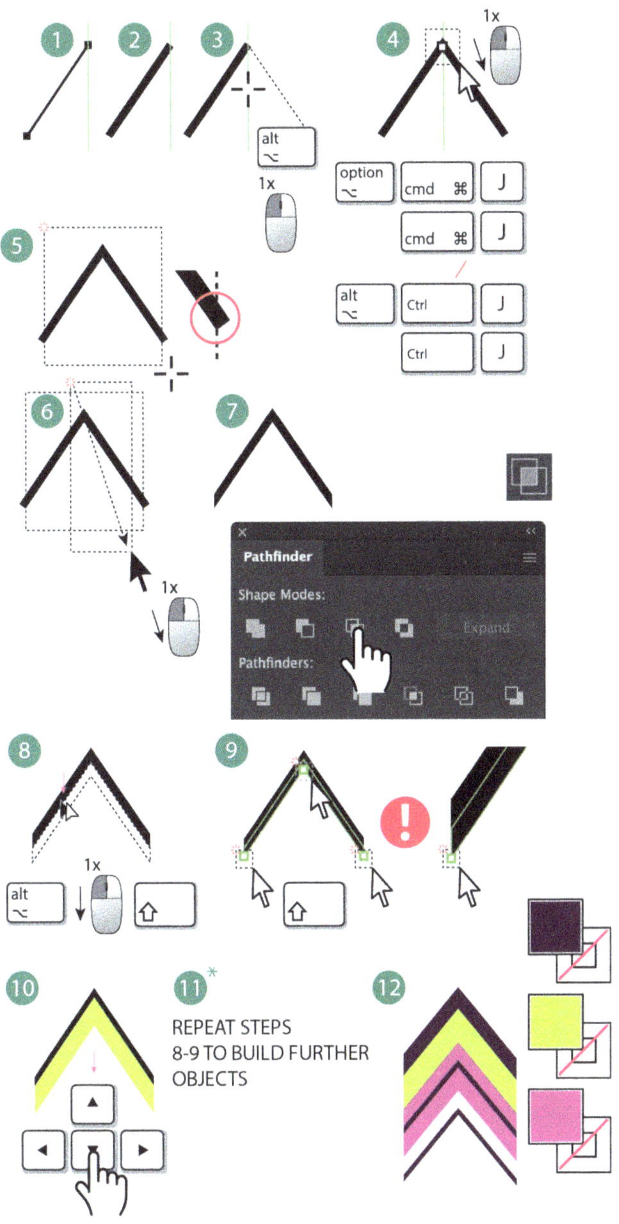

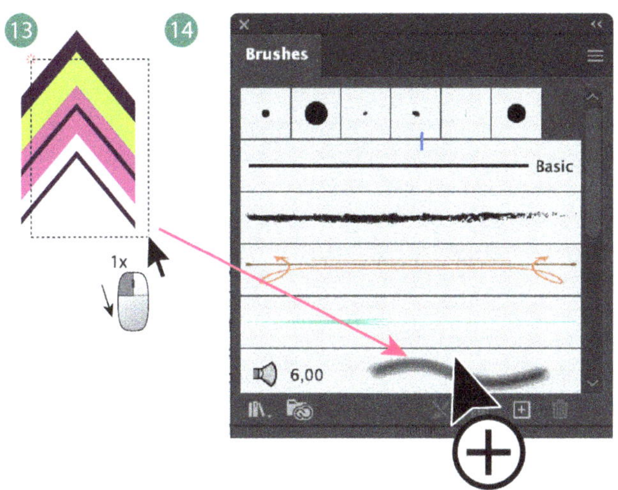

Step 4. Hold down the left mouse button and drag with **Direct Selection Tool** (A) a selection.
Activate the shortcut option+command+J /alt+Ctrl+J (Average...). In the dialog box activate „Both", then „OK", then activate the shortcut command+J / Ctrl+J (Join). Two paths have been joined together.
Step 5. Create with **Rectangle Tool** (M) an rectangle without stroke and fill colour (see figure).
Step 6. Hold down the left mouse button and drag with **Selection Tool** (V) around the objects to select them. Activate then the shortcut command+7 / Ctrl+7 (**Object>Clipping Mask>Make**).
Step 7. Activate the command **Object>Expand...** (activate „Fill", „Stroke" and confirm with OK), then open the „Pathfinder" panel and activate „Merge".
Step 8. Click the object with the **Selection Tool** (V), hold down **alt/option-** key, move the object with mouse cursor down, in addition hold down **Shift-** key, then release first the mouse button and then the keyboard keys. A copy of the object is created.
Step 9. Choose with **Direct Selection Tool** (A) three lower anchor points (work with **Zoom Tool** Z).
Step 10. Transform the object with down arrow key (see figure).
Step 11. Repeat the steps 8 to 9 to create further objects.
Step 12. Change the object fill colours.
Step 13. Hold down the left mouse button and drag with **Selection Tool** (V) around the objects to select them.
Step 14. Then open the **Brushes (Window>Brushes)** panel and drag the object to the panel „Brushes", then drop them (drag&drop method) or alternatively click on the "New" symbol.
In the dialog box activate the „Pattern Brush" and confirm with „OK". Pattern Brush „Start" is finished.
Step 15. Hold down the left mouse button and drag again with **Selection Tool** (V) around the objects to select them.
Step 16. Transform the objects with the mouse (see figure), then repeat the steps 13 and 14. Pattern Brush „End" is created.
Step 17. Activate the **Pen Tool** (P), in addition hold down **Shift** key and create the line with two anchor points (stroke weight 1pt).

Step 1. Activate the **Pen Tool** (P) and create a line consisting of two anchor points.
Step 2. Change the stroke to **3pt** (**Window > Stroke**).
Step 3. Select the **Reflect Tool** (O), position the mouse cursor on the vertical guide, hold down the **alt/option** key (do not release the alt key) and click the left mouse button. The reflect dialog box appears ,then release the **alt** key.
Activate the option „Vertical", then „Preview", check whether everything is OK and click „Copy". A mirrored duplicate is created.

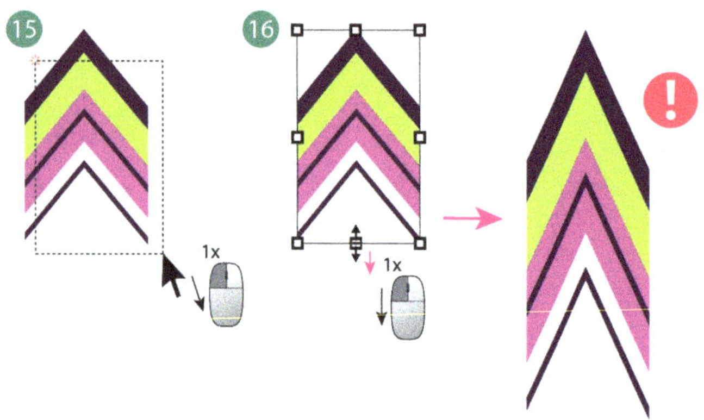

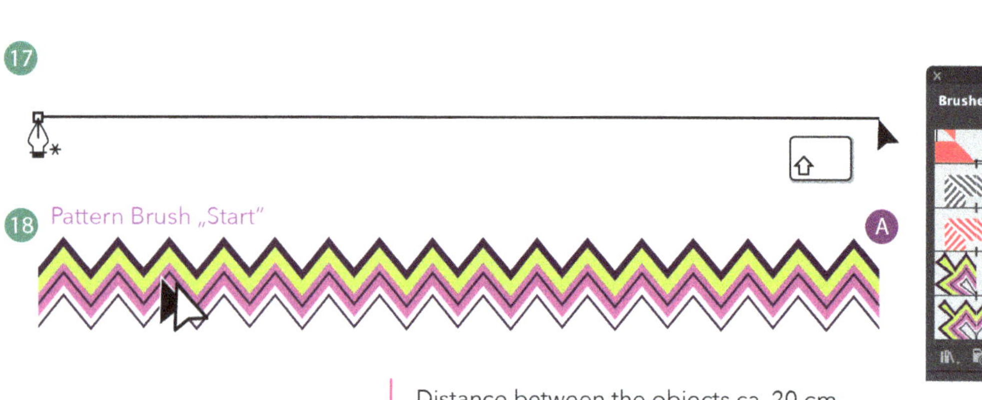

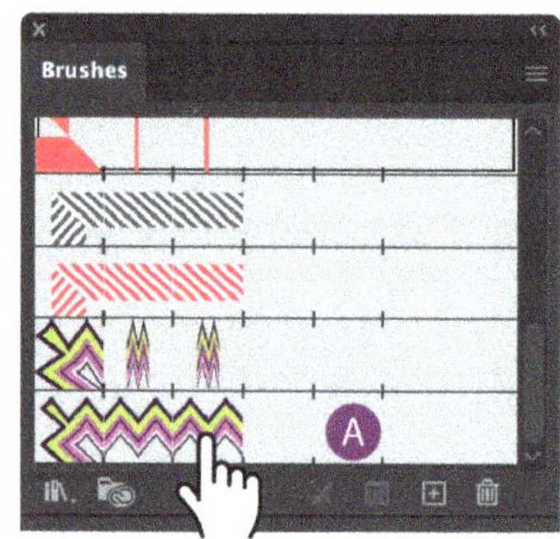

Distance between the objects ca. 20 cm
(ca. 3/4 of the DIN A4 page)

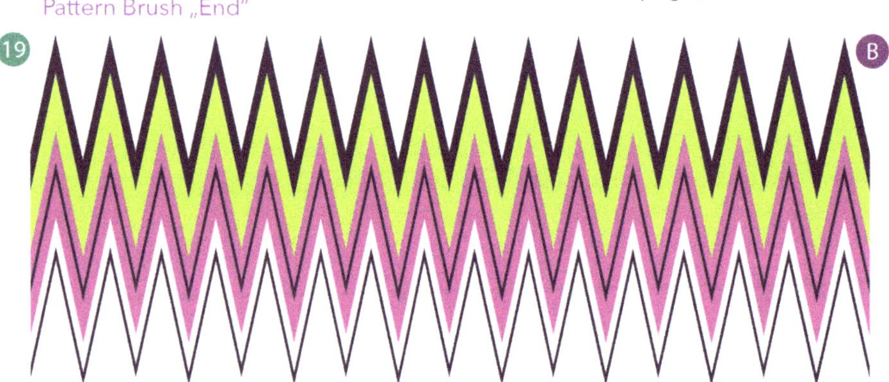

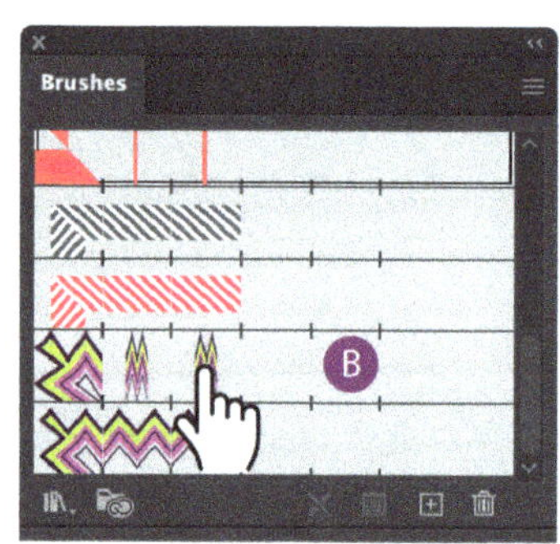

Step 18 and 19.
Apply to the line first pattern brush „Start"
A , then copy the line, displace the line down and apply to
the copy the pattern brush „End" B .

Step 20. Activate the **Blend Tool** (W) and click the both
objects (first the „start" and then the „end" object).
You can use the Blend Tool to create a set of objects to
match colors and shapes of multiple objects.

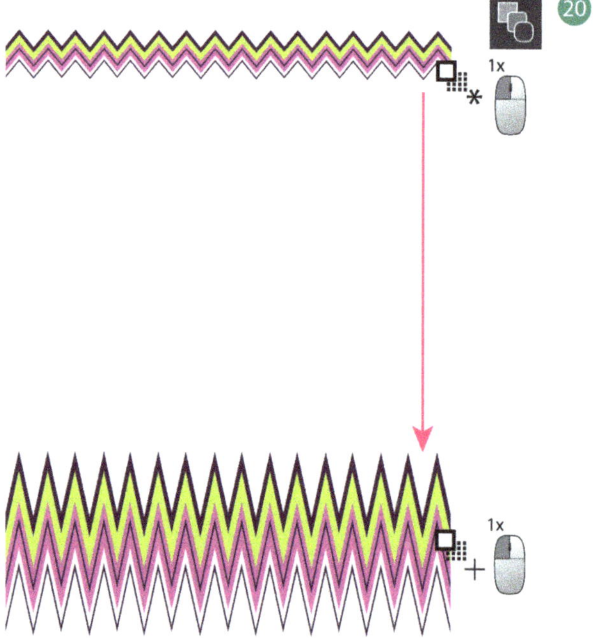

Step 21. Double-click on the **Blend Tool** (W).
Step 22. Change the settings in the dialog box (see figure), then confirm with „OK". Activate finally the command **Object>Expand Appearance**.

Result

©dimitridesign.org

8.22 TUTORIAL:
CREATE COLOR VARIATIONS

OPTION 1

Step 1. Select the pattern with **Selection Tool** (V) (from the previous exercise), then activate the command **Object>Expand**.

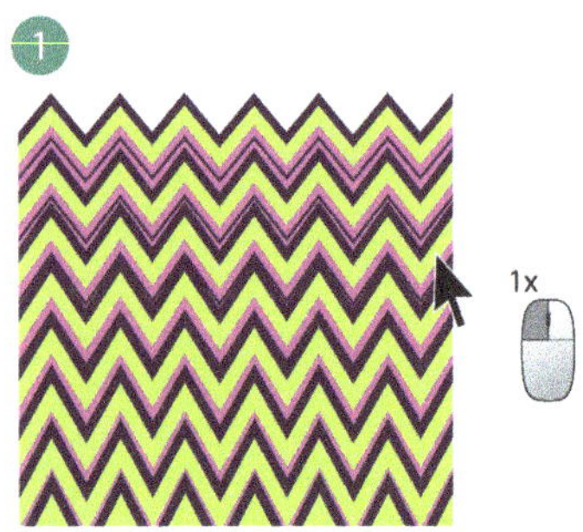

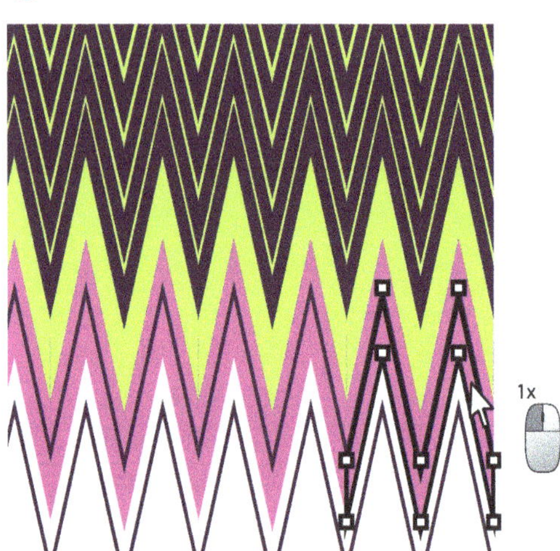

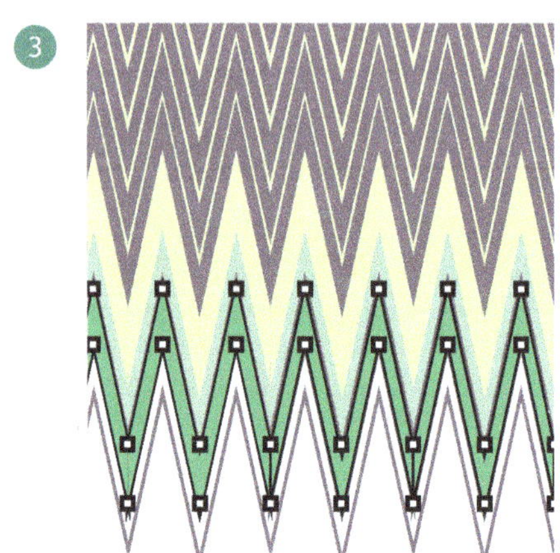

Step 2. Click with **Direct Slection Tool** (A) on a part of the pattern with a specific color to select it and to change the color of this object. Then activate the command **Select>Same>Fill Color** to select all objects with this color in the document.

Step 3. Change the fill colour.

Step 4. Place the pattern (object) beneath e.g. a dress (**Object >Arrange> In the Back**).

Step 5. Hold down the left mouse button and drag with **Selection Tool** (V) around the objects to select them. Activate then the shortcut command+7 / Ctrl+7 (**Object>Clipping Mask>Make**). For more information about the clipping mask see tutorial 8.19.

Important: You can use for the clipping mask only **one object.** You can create this object with the pen tool or other tools. The position of the object (for clipping mask) must be always be on top in the layers order.

OPTION 2

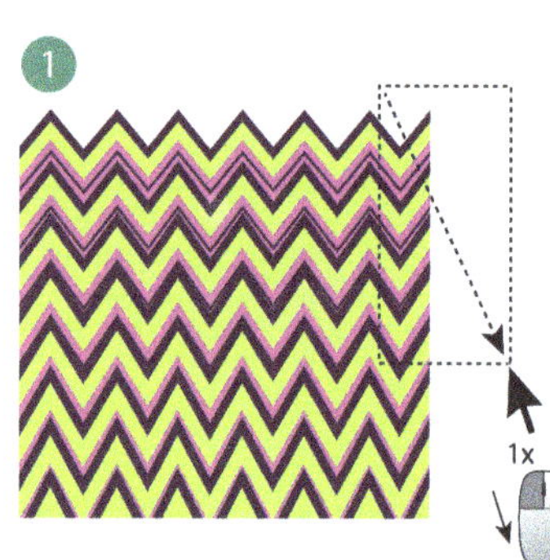

Step 1. Select the pattern with **Selection Tool** (V) (from the previous exercise) 8.21, then activate the command **Object>Expand**.

Step 2. Activate the command **Edit>Edit Colors>Recolor Artwork** or click on the button

Step 3. Click on **Advanced Options...**

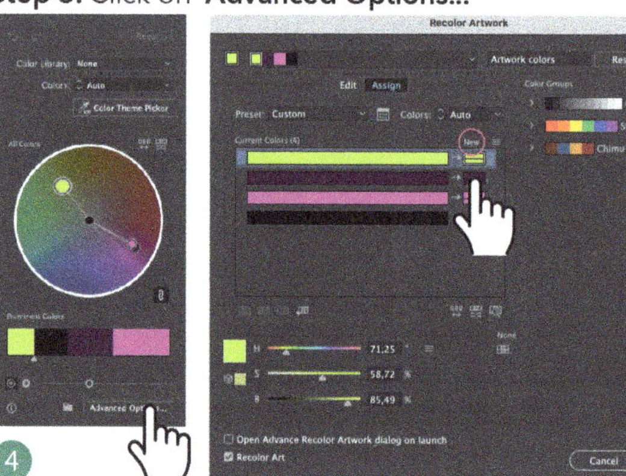

Step 4. In the **Recolor Artwork** window you can select a specific color and double click on the **New** entry to open and change the colors in the **Color Picker** window.

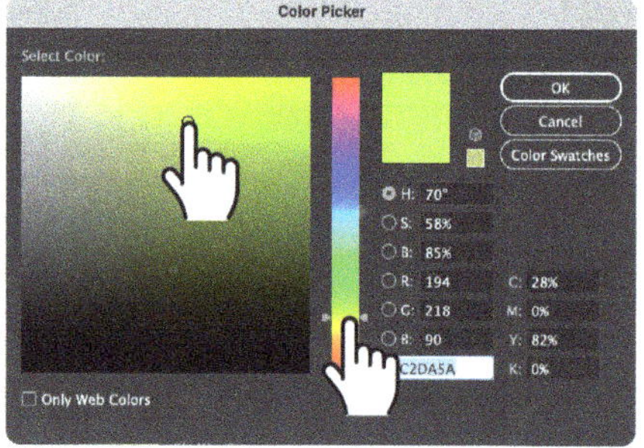

8.23 TUTORIAL: PLEATED DRESS

REQUIREMENTS

-Choose in the tools panel the stroke color „black" and the fill color „None".

-Change the stroke weight (**Window > Stroke**) to **1pt** or **2pt**.

-Choose: **View > Rules >Show Rules, View > Guides > Lock Guides, View > Guides > Show Guides, View > Smart Guides, View > Snap to Point** and place a vertical guide.

-Work in this exercise with a figure template that you can download using the following link:

www.dimitridesign.org/templates

Step 1. Select the **Pen Tool** (P) and click on the vertical guide (press and release the left mouse button, do not drag) to create the first anchor-point.

Step 2. Create a further anchor point (press and release the left mouse button, do not drag).

Step 3. Create a further anchor point (press and release the left mouse button, do not drag).

Step 4. Create a further anchor point (drag the direction point diagonally to the left down), then release the mouse button.

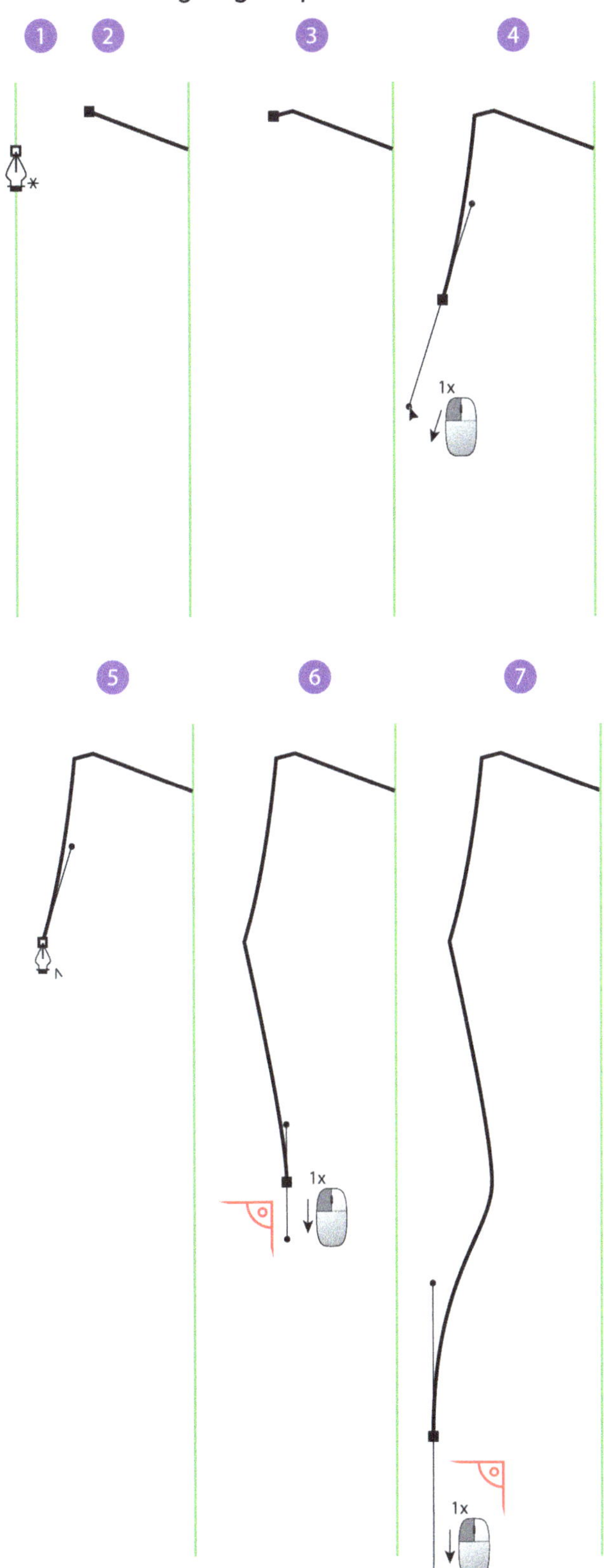

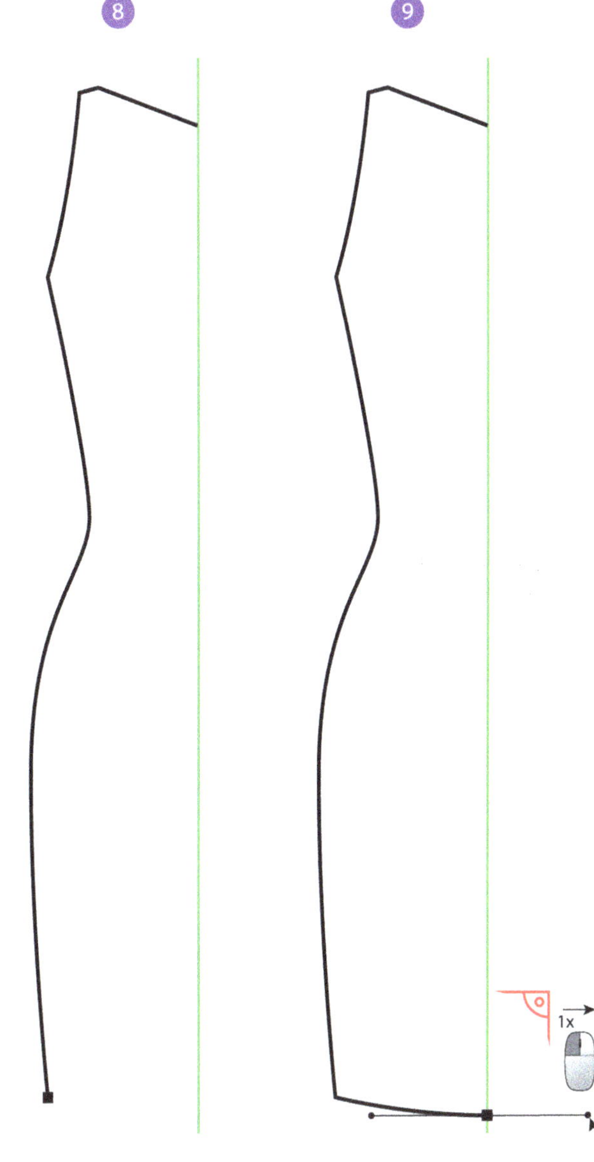

Step 5. Click the last anchor point (press and release the left mouse button) to create a corner.

Step 6. Create a further anchor point (do not release the left mouse button), additionally hold down the **Shift** key (90° angle), also do not release the **Shift** key and drag the direction point down, then release first the mouse button and then the **Shift** key.

Step 7. Repeat step 6.

Step 8. Create a further anchor point (without **Shift** key).

Step 9. Create a further anchor point (do not release the left mouse button), additionally hold down the **Shift** key (90° angle), also do not release the **Shift** key and drag the direction point to the right, then release first the mouse button and then the **Shift** key.

Step 10. Hold down left mouse button and drag with the **Selection Tool** (V) around the object to select it.

Step 11. Select the **Reflect Tool** (O), position the mouse cursor on the vertical guide, hold down the **alt/option** key (do not release the alt key) and click the left mouse button. The Reflect dialog box appears ,then release the **alt** key. Activate the option „Vertical", then „Preview", check whether everything is OK and click „Copy". A mirrored duplicate is created.

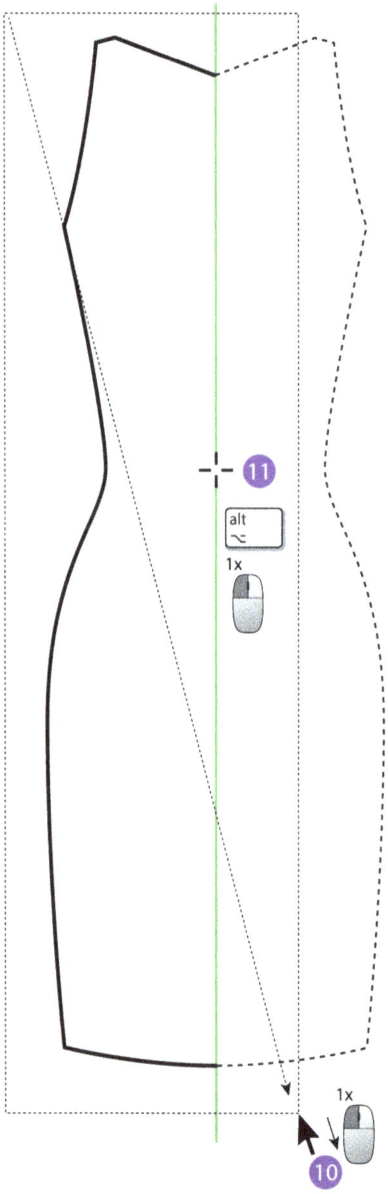

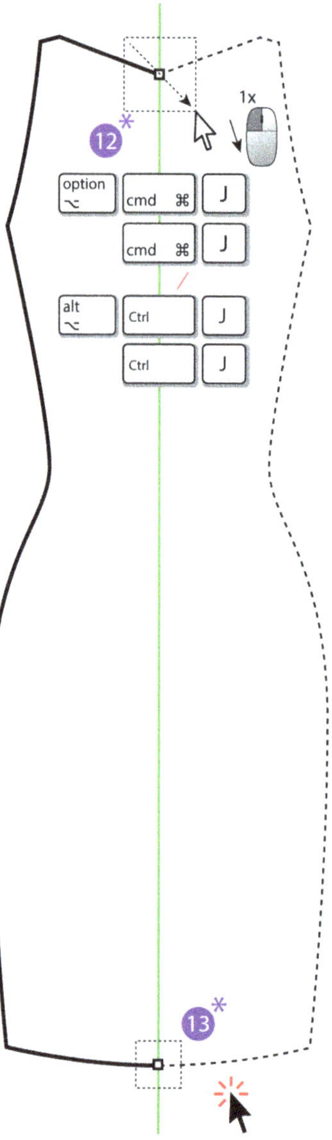

Step 14. Select the **Pen Tool** (P) and start to draw a new line (press and release the left mouse button, do not drag) to create the first anchor-point.

Step 15. Create a further anchor point (drag the direction point diagonally to the left down), then release the mouse button.

Step 16. Create a further anchor point,additionally hold down **Shift** key and drag the direction point down, then release first the mouse button and the the **Shift** key.

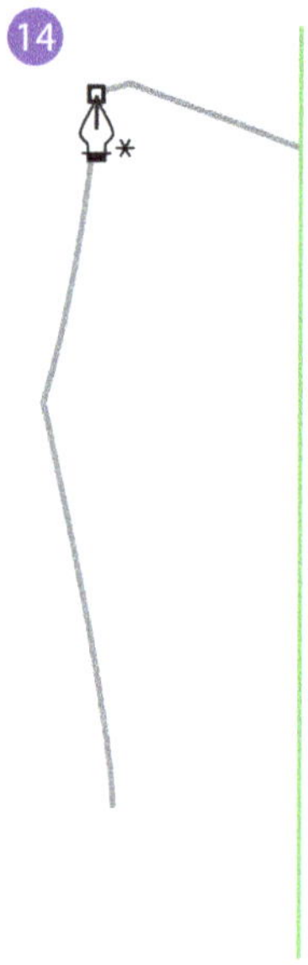

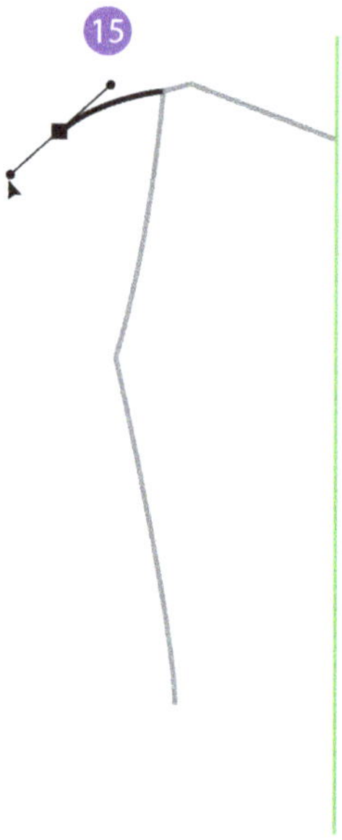

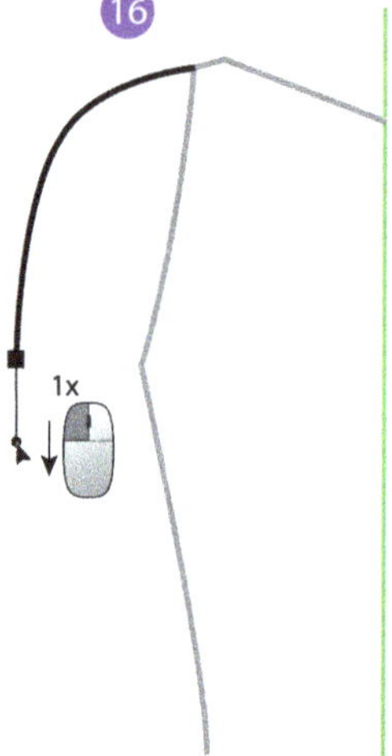

Step 12. Hold down the left mouse button and drag with the **Direct Selection Tool** (A) a selection around two anchor points (one end point of each half).
To join two paths always select two end points. If you choose more than two points the "join" command won´t function (see error-checklist on page 134, or video tutorial on the website).
Activate the shortcut option+command+J/alt+Ctrl+J (Average...). In the dialog box activate „Both", then „OK", then activate the shortcut command+J / Ctrl+J (Join).

Step 13. Repeat step 12. Then click on V key (Selection Tool) and click on a empty drawing area to deselect the object. Alternatively you can activate the shortcut command+Shift+A / Ctrl+Shift+A.

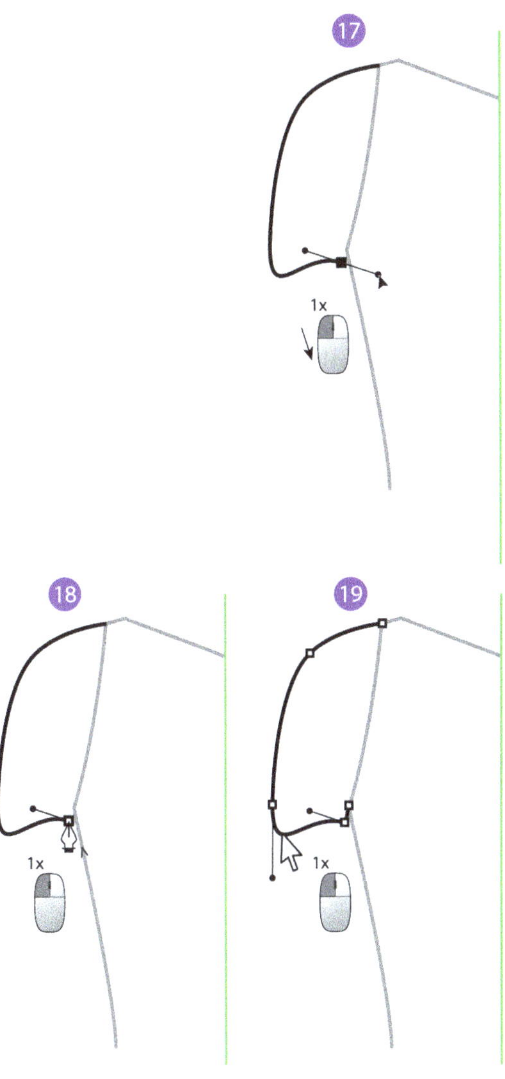
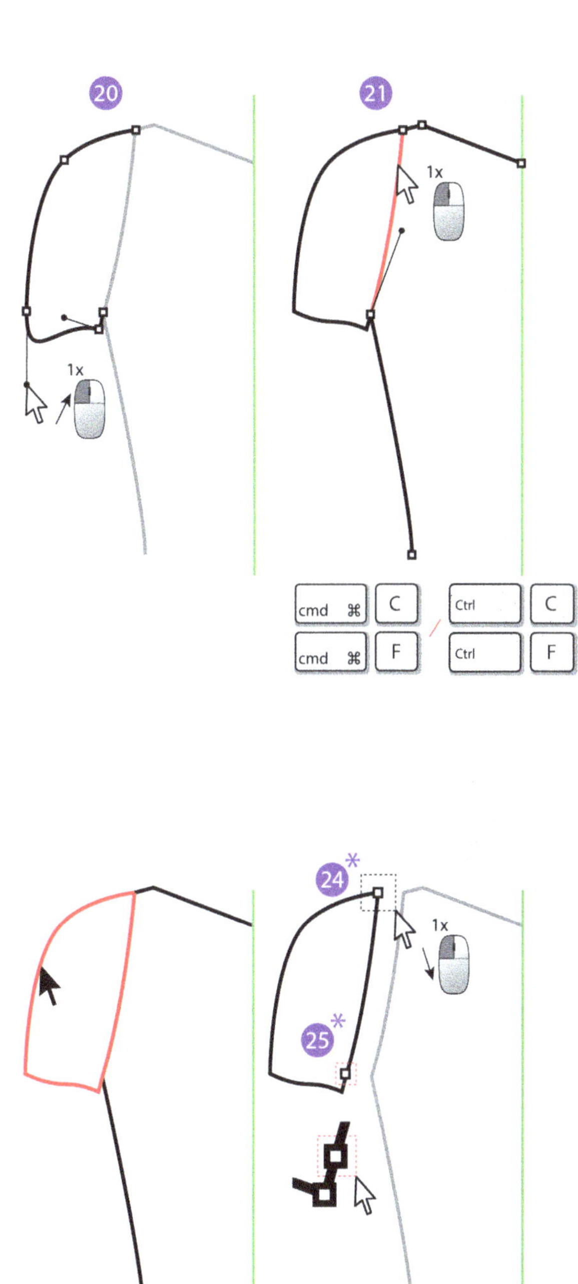

Step 17. Create a further anchor point (drag the direction point diagonally to the right), then release the mouse button.

Step 18. Click the last anchor point (press and release the left mouse button) to create a corner.

Step 19. Create a further anchor point. Activate the **Direct Selection Tool** (A), click on the path to activate the direction points and lines.

Step 20. Now drag on the both directions points until the line becomes the right shape (see figure).

Step 26. Click the V key (Selection Tool) and click on the empty drawing area to deselect the object. Alternatively you can activate the shortcut command+Shift+A / Ctrl+Shift+A.

Step 21. Click with the **Direct Selection Tool** (A) on the path (only a fragment of the line between the nearest anchor points is selected), then activate the shortcut command+C / Ctrl+C (Copy) and the shortcut command+F / Ctrl+F (Paste in Front).

Step 22. Activate V key (Selection Tool) (press and release).

Step 23. Activate **Shift** key and click several times on the left arrow key to displace the object.

Step 24 and 25. Hold down the left mouse button and drag with the **Direct Selection Tool** (A) a selection around two anchor points (one end point of each half).

Activate the shortcut option+command+J /alt+Ctrl+J (Average...). In the dialog box activate „Both", then „OK", then activate the shortcut command+J / Ctrl+J (Join).

Step 27. Hold down the left mouse button and drag with the **Selection Tool** (V) around the object to select it.
Step 28. Hold down the **Shift** key and click several times on the right arrow key to displace the object.
Step 29 and 30. Create with the **Pen Tool** (P) a new line.

Step 31. Hold down the left mouse button and drag with the **Selection Tool** (V) around the object to select it.
Step 32. Select the **Reflect Tool** (O), position the mouse cursor on the vertical guide, hold down the **alt/option** key (do not release the alt key) and click the left mouse button. The Reflect dialog box appears, then release the **alt** key. Activate the option „Vertical", then „Preview", check whether everything is OK and click „Copy". A mirrored duplicate is created.

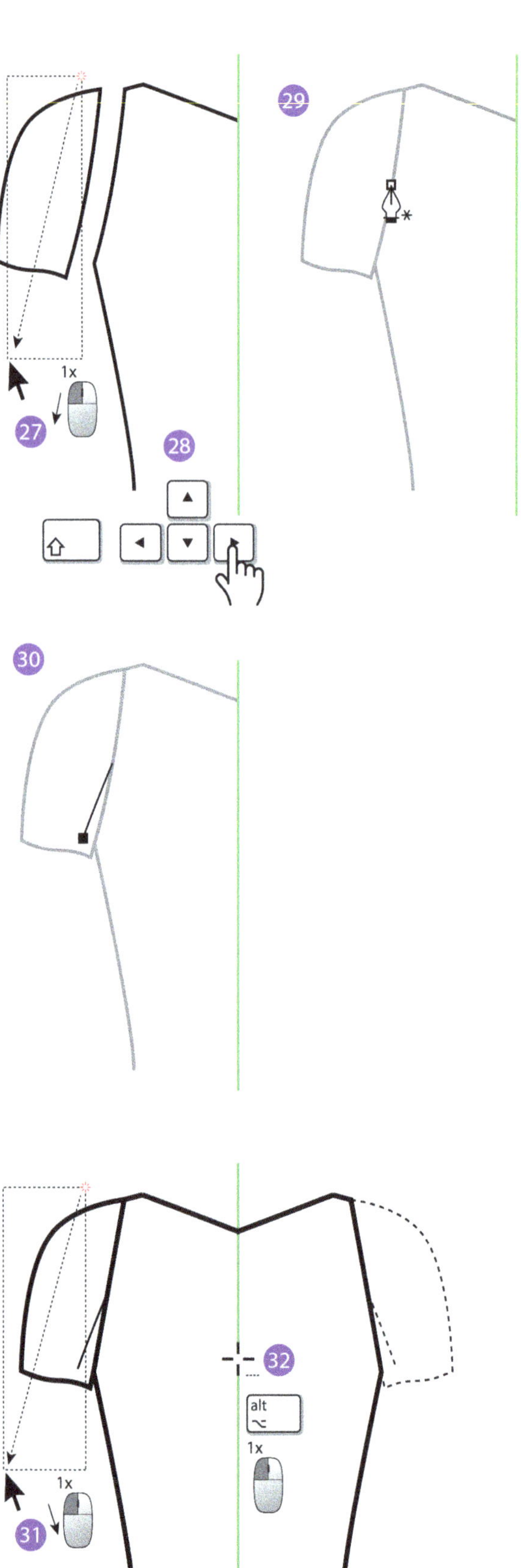

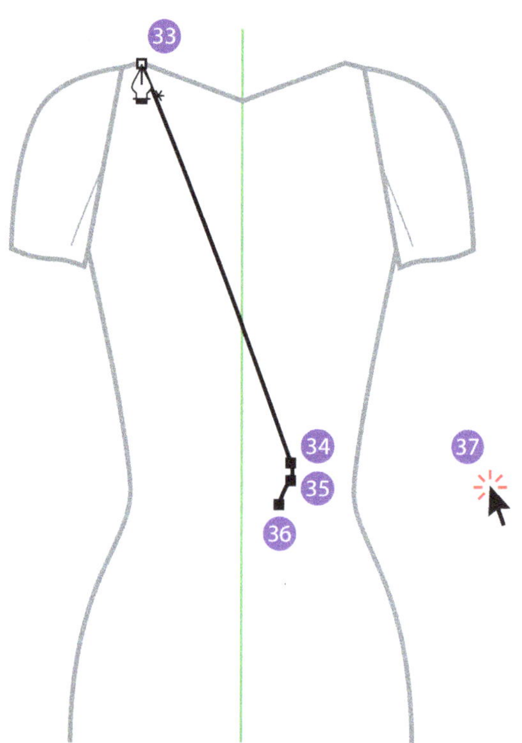

Step 33 - 36. Create with the **Pen Tool** (P) a new line.
Step 37. Click the V key (Selection Tool) and click on the empty drawing area to deselect the object.
Step 38 - 39. Create with the **Pen Tool** (P) a new line.

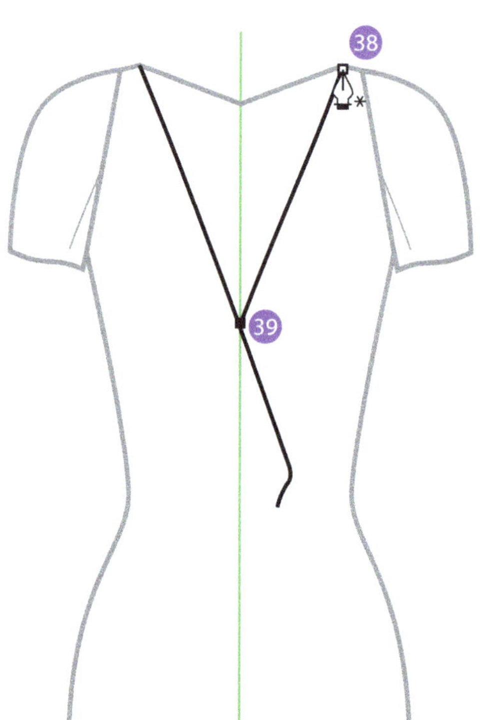

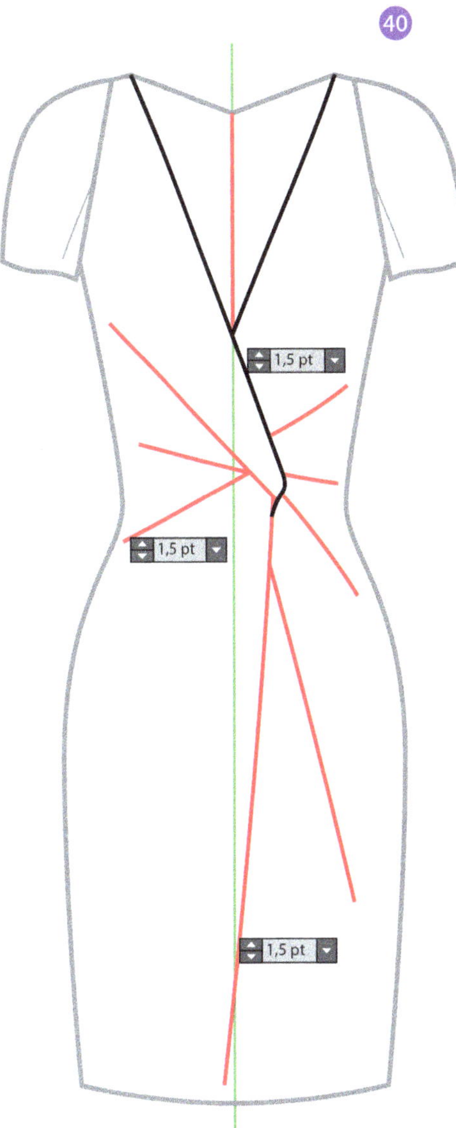

Step 40. Create with the **Pen Tool** (P) a further line (pleats). In case of internal elements such as pleats, stitchings etc. it makes sense to reduce the stroke weight to e.g. 0.75 or 0.5 pt. so that the illustration looks graphically better.

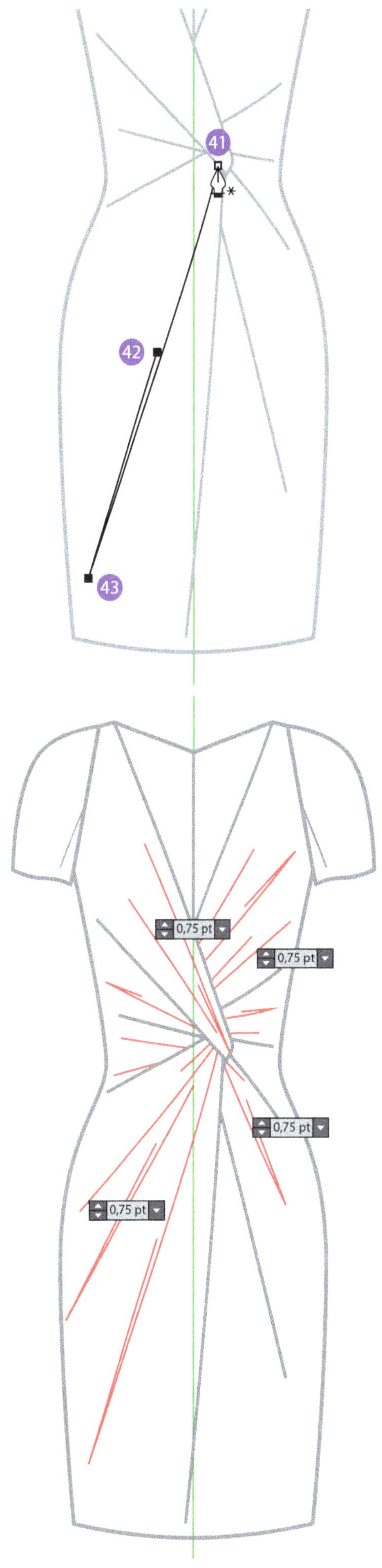

Step 41 - 43. Create with the **Pen Tool** (P) new lines (pleats) consisting of three points.

Step 44 - 46. Click with the **Selection Tool** (V) on the object and change the fill colour (e.g. #ED2458).
Step 47. Hold down the **Shift** key and click on the following line (see figure).
Step 48. Activate in the Tools panel the **Live Paint Bucket** (K).

Step 49. Change the fill colour (e.g. #550021).
Step 50. And click with the **Live Paint Bucket** (K) on the shape (see figure), the bold red mark shows which area will be filled.

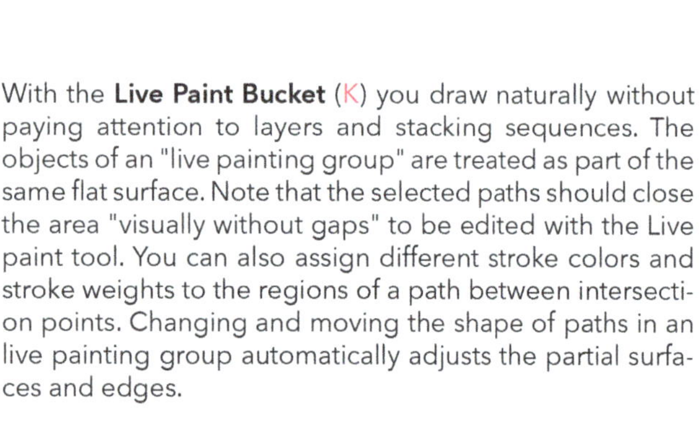

With the **Live Paint Bucket** (K) you draw naturally without paying attention to layers and stacking sequences. The objects of an "live painting group" are treated as part of the same flat surface. Note that the selected paths should close the area "visually without gaps" to be edited with the Live paint tool. You can also assign different stroke colors and stroke weights to the regions of a path between intersection points. Changing and moving the shape of paths in an live painting group automatically adjusts the partial surfaces and edges.

Step 51. To finish the process and to expand the „Live Paint Group" to normal objects, activate the command **Object> Expand...**
After that the objects are automatically grouped together. In order to be able to edit these objects, this group should be ungrouped.
Step 52. Therefor activate two times the shortcut Shift+command+G / Shift+Ctrl+G (because mostly it contains two groups).
Step 53. Then click on V key (Selection Tool) and click on a empty drawing area to deselect the object.
Step 54. Activate the „Outline" view cmd+Y/ Ctrl+Y (**View > Outline**). After step 55 deactivate again the „Outline" view (cmd+Y / Ctrl+Y).
Step 55. Click with the **Selection Tool** (V) on the line (see figure) and activate the command **Object> Arrange> Bring to Front** to displace the line to the front.

50
51
Expand
52
⇧ cmd ⌘ G
⇧ Ctrl G
53
54
cmd ⌘ Y
Ctrl Y
55

9.0 TUTORIAL: PATTERN BRUSHES

Pattern brushes are very often used in technical drawings for representation of e.g. overlock seam, double quilt seam, zigzag stitch, blind stitch, smock folds, etc. The pattern brush consists of different tiles. Different tiles can be set for the sides, inner corner, outer corner, beginning and end of the pattern brush. To create a pattern brush, first define the image to use as a tile. When you drag the edge into the **Brushes panel** (F5), the pattern brush options dialog box opens where you can generate the remaining four tiles. The Pattern Brush Options dialog box uses a sample path to preview the brush. You can also change the tiles (drop-down menu) and preview the effect.

CREATE PATTERN BRUSHES

1. Drag the object (Rapport) into the **Brushes panel** (F5) or click the new icon ⊞
2. Select „Pattern Brush".
3. In the pattern brush options dialog box, you can select a tile for each corner.

Auto Generated Corners:
Dialogbox „Auto Generated Corners"

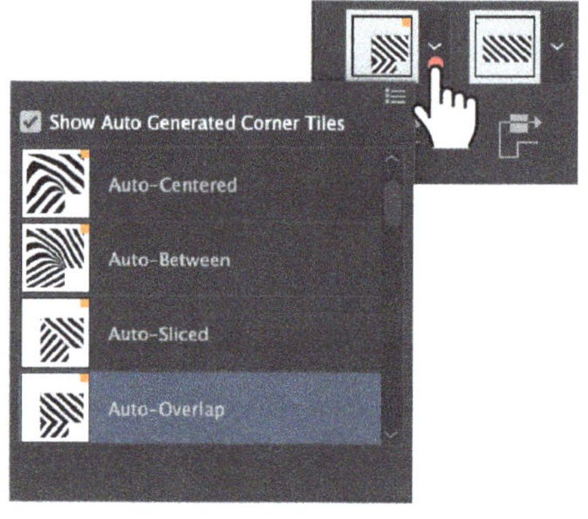

Auto-Centered

Auto-Between

Auto-Sliced

Auto-Overlap

Digital drawing with Adobe Illustrator

9.1 TUTORIAL: DOUBLE QUILTING SEAM

REQUIREMENTS

-Choose in the tools panel the stroke color „None" and the fill color „black".

-Choose: **View > Rules >Show Rules, View > Guides > Lock Guides, View > Guides > Show Guides, View > Smart Guides, View > Snap to Point**.

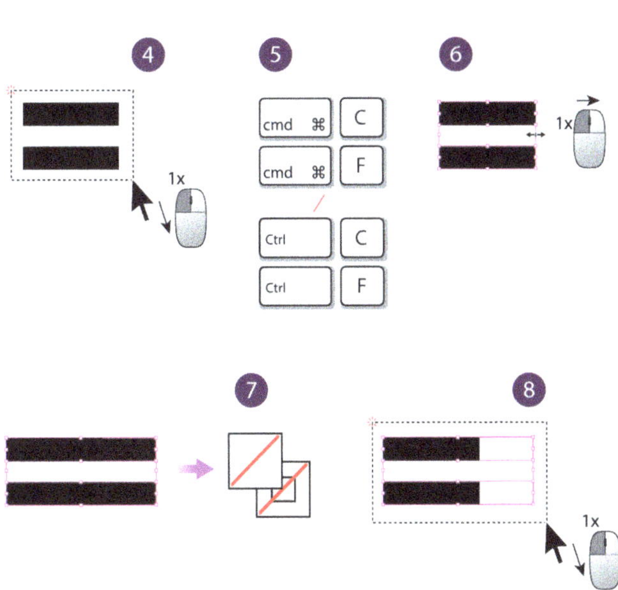

Step 1. Create with **Rectangle Tool** (M) an rectangle (stroke colour „None" and fill colour „black").
Step 2. Click the V key (Selection Tool**).
Step 3. Click the object with the **Selection Tool** (V), hold down **alt/option-** key, move the object with the mouse cursor down, in addition hold down **Shift-** key, then release first the mouse button and then the keyboard keys. A copy of the object is created.
Step 4. Hold down the left mouse button and drag with the **Selection Tool** (V) around the objects to select them.
Step 5. Activate the shortcut command+C / Ctrl+C (Copy) and the shortcut command+F / Ctrl+F (Paste in Front).
Step 6. Activate the **Selection Tool** (V) and transform both object-copies (hold down left mouse button and drag on the middle rectangle, see figure).

Step 7. Turn off the „stroke" and „fill" colour for both object-copies.
Step 8. Hold down the left mouse button and drag with the **Selection Tool** (V) around all objects to select them.
Step 9. Then open the panel **Brushes (Window>Brushes)** and drag the objects to the „Brushes" panel, then drop them (drag&drop method) or alternatively click on the "New" symbol , then activate in the dialog box „Pattern brush" and confirm the settings with „OK".

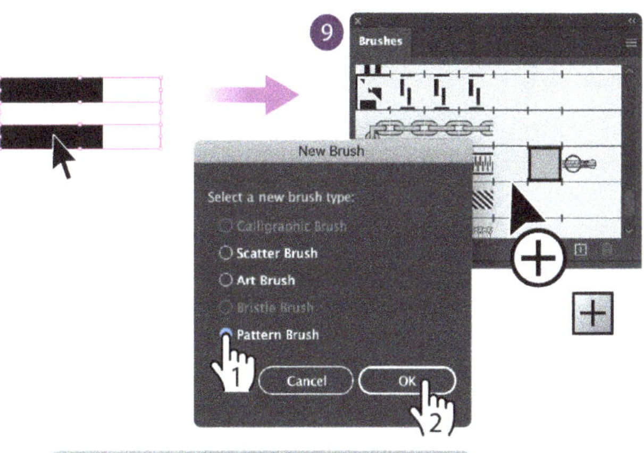

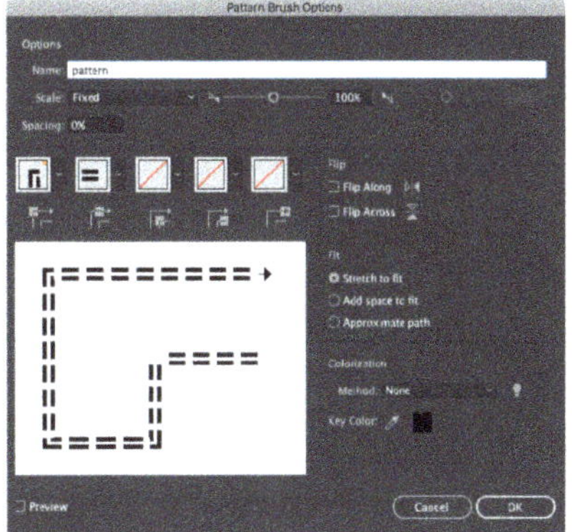

Step 10. Activate the **Pen Tool** (P) and create a line with two anchor points.
Step 11. Apply to the line the new pattern brush.
(in the „Brushes" panel **Window>Brushes** click on the new „double quilting seam" brush).

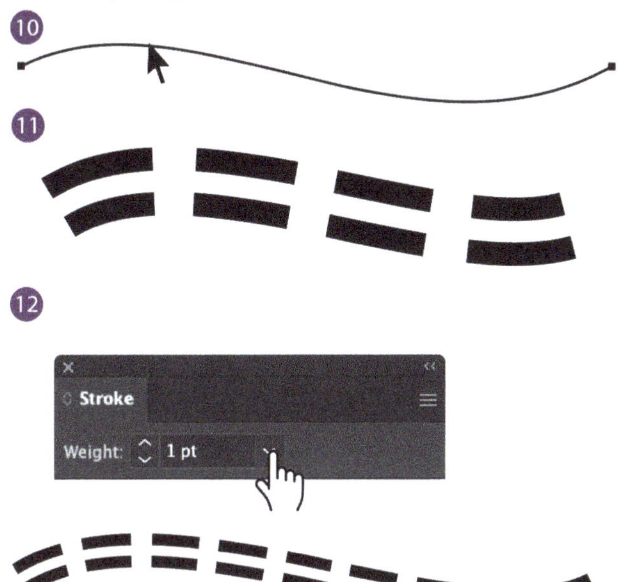

Step 12. Open the **Stroke** panel **(Window>Stroke)** and change the stroke weight of the line (e.g. 0,5 pt), this will reduce the size of the rapport
Step 13. Then in the **Brushes** panel **(Window>Brushes)** activate the „Stroke Options" (see figure).
Here you can change the „Spacing" between the rapport elements or flip them (see figure).

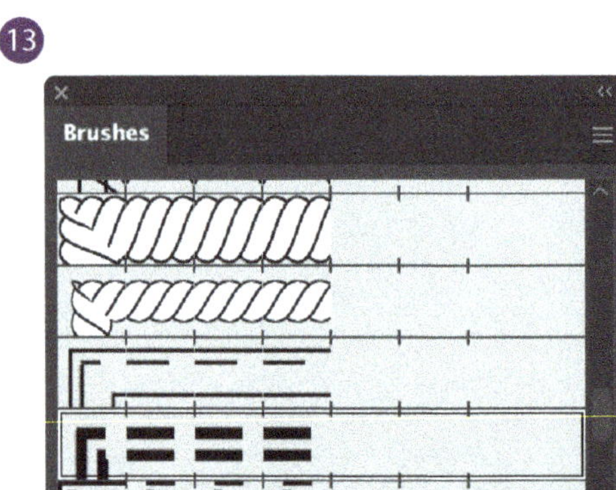

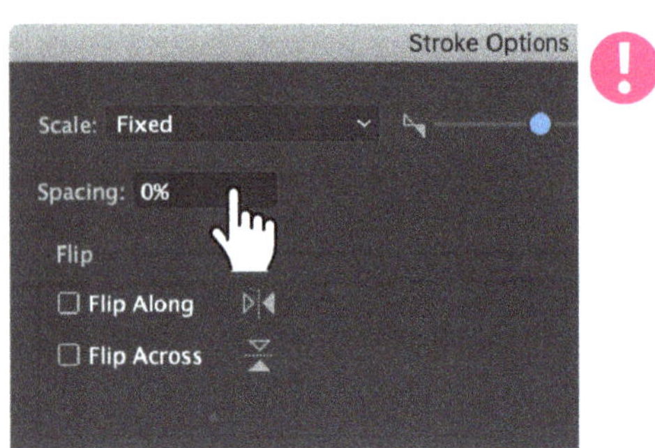

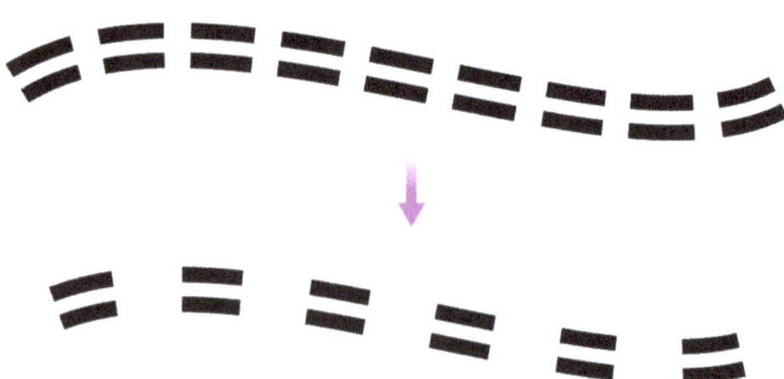

9.2 TUTORIAL: ZIP FASTENER 1

REQUIREMENTS

-Choose in the tools panel the stroke color „None" and the fill color „black".

-Choose: **View > Rules >Show Rules, View > Guides > Lock Guides, View > Guides > Show Guides, View > Smart Guides, View > Snap to Point.**

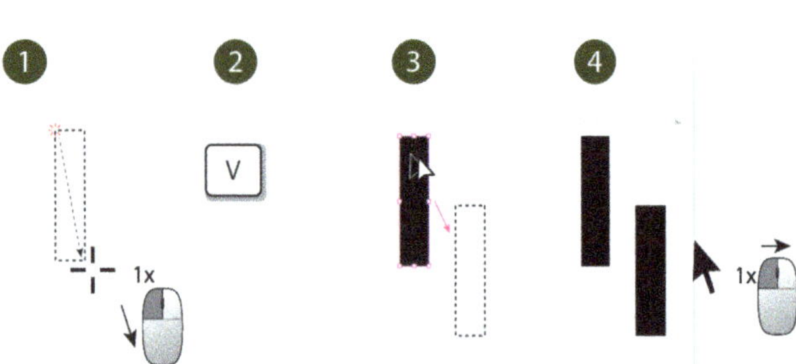

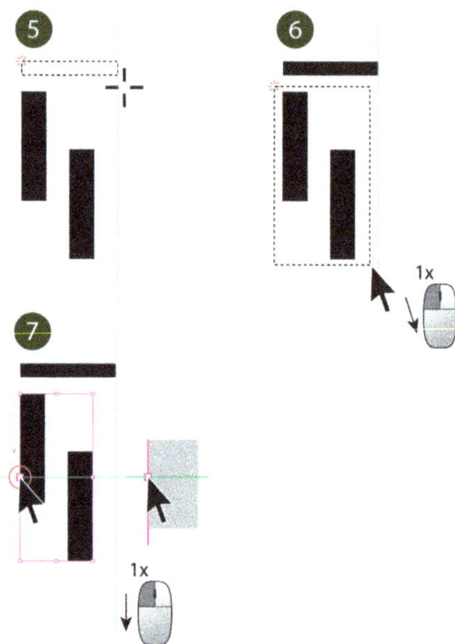

Step 1. Create with the **Rectangle Tool** (M) an rectangle (stroke colour „None" and fill colour „black").
Step 2. Click the V key (Selection Tool**).**
Step 3. Click the object with **Selection Tool** (V), hold down **alt/option-** key, move the object with the mouse cursor diagonally to the right down, in addition hold down **Shift-**key, then release first the mouse button and then the keyboard keys. A copy of the object is created.
Step 4. Place a vertical guide.
Step 5. Create a further rectangle.
Step 6. Hold down the left mouse button and drag with the **Selection Tool** (V) around the objects to select them.
Step 7. Place a horizontal guide (see figure).
Step 8. Click the object with the **Selection Tool** (V).
Step 9. Select the **Reflect Tool** (O), position the mouse cursor on the horizontal guide, hold down the **alt/option** key (do not release the alt key) and click the left mouse button. The Reflect dialog box appears ,then release the **alt/option** key.
Activate the option „Horizontal", then „Preview", check whether everything is OK and click „Copy". A mirrored duplicate is created.

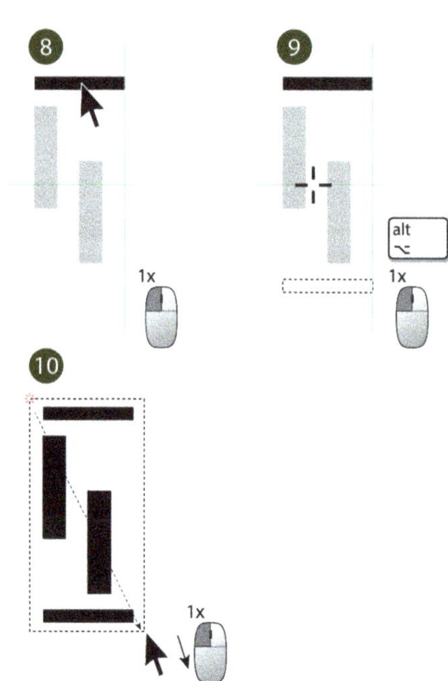

Step 10. Hold down the left mouse button and drag with the **Selection Tool** (V) around the objects to select them.

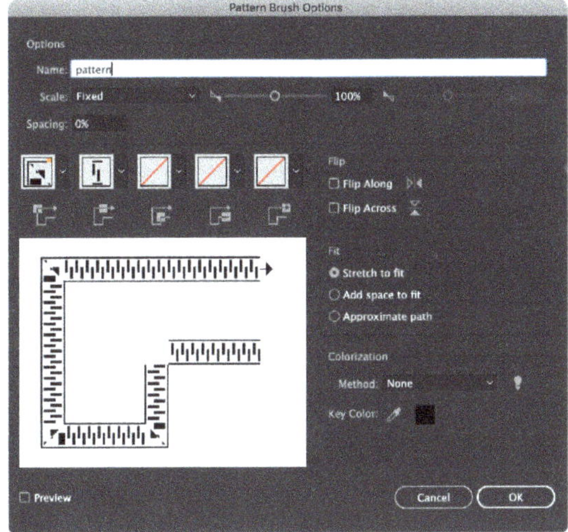

9.3 TUTORIAL: BINDING

REQUIREMENTS

-Choose in the tools panel the stroke color „None" and the fill color „black".

-Choose: **View > Rules >Show Rules, View > Guides > Lock Guides, View > Guides > Show Guides, View > Smart Guides, View > Snap to Point**.

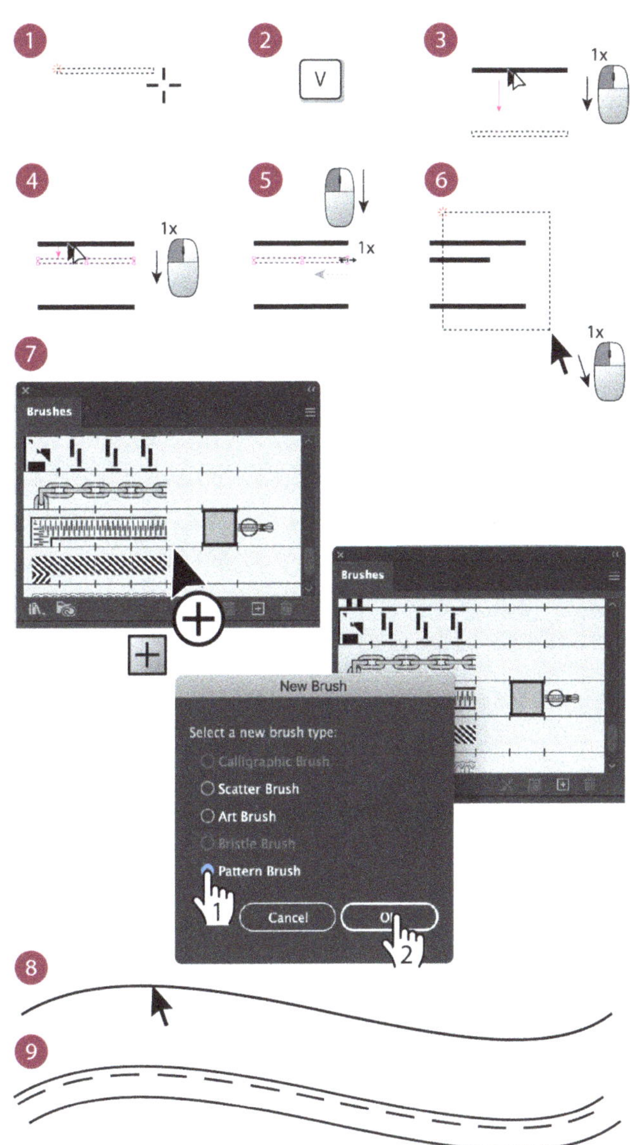

Step 11. Then open the panel **Brushes (Window>Brushes)** and drag the objects to the „Brushes" panel, then drop them (drag&drop method) or alternatively click on the "New" symbol ⊞ , then activate in the dialog box „Pattern brush" and confirm the settings with „OK".
Step 12. Activate the **Pen Tool** (P) and create a line with two anchor points.
Step 13. Apply to the line the new pattern brush.
(in the „Brushes" panel **Window>Brushes** click on the new „zip fastener" brush).

Step 1. Create with the **Rectangle Tool** (M) an rectangle (stroke colour „None" and fill colour „black").
Step 2. Activate the V key (Selection Tool**).**
Step 3. Click the object with the **Selection Tool** (V), hold down **alt/option-** key, move the object with the mouse cursor down, in addition hold down **Shift-** key, then release first the mouse button and then the keyboard keys. A copy of the object is created.
Step 4. Repeat the step 3 (see figure).
Step 5. Transform the object (see figure). Work precisely, use the **Zoom Tool** (Z) to zoom in and out.
Step 6. Hold down the left mouse button and drag with the **Selection Tool** (V) around all objects to select them.

Step 7. Then open the panel **Brushes (Window>Brushes)** and drag the objects to the „Brushes" panel, then drop them (drag&drop method) or alternatively click on the "New" symbol ⊞ , then activate in the dialog box „Pattern brush" and confirm the settings with „OK".
Step 8. Activate the **Pen Tool** (P) and create a line with two anchor points.
Step 9. Apply to the line the new pattern brush.
(in the „Brushes" panel **Window>Brushes** click on the new „binding" brush).

9.4 TUTORIAL: ZIP FASTENER 2
REQUIREMENTS

-Choose in the tools panel the stroke color „black" and the fill color „None".

-Change the stroke weight (**Window > Stroke**) to **1pt** or **2pt**.

-Choose: **View > Rules >Show Rules, View > Guides > Lock Guides, View > Guides > Show Guides, View > Smart Guides, View > Snap to Point.**

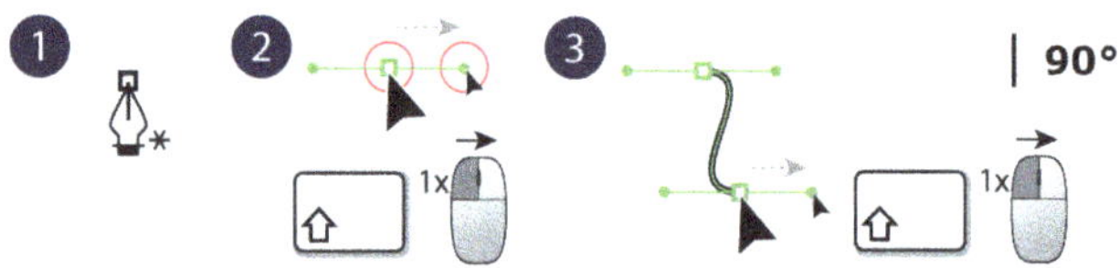

Step 1. Select the **Pen Tool** (P) and create the first anchor-point (press and release the left mouse button, do not drag).
Step 2. In addition hold down the **Shift** key (90° angle), also do not release the **Shift** key and drag the direction point to the right, then release first the mouse button and then the **Shift** key.
Step 3. Create with the **Pen Tool** (P) a further anchor-point, in addition hold down the **Shift** key (90° angle), also do not release the **Shift** key and drag the direction point to the right, then release first the mouse button and then the **Shift** key.

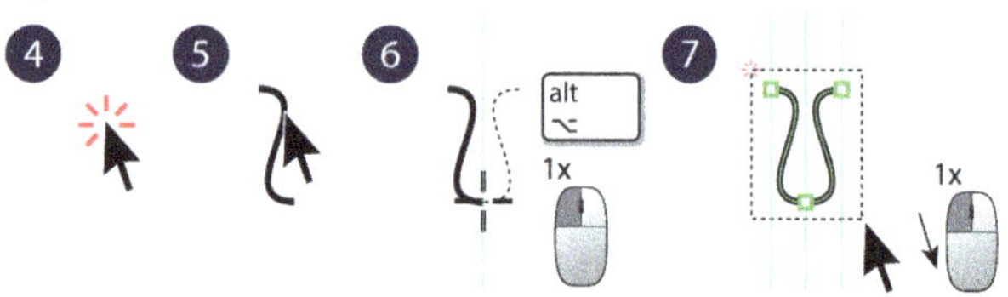

Step 4. Click the V key (Selection Tool) and click on the empty drawing area to deselect the object. Alternatively you can activate the shortcut command+Shift+A / Ctrl+Shift+A.
Step 5. Select the line with the **Selection Tool** (V).
Step 6. Place a vertical guide. Select the **Reflect Tool** (O), position the mouse cursor on the vertical guide, hold down the **alt/option** key (do not release the alt key) and click the left mouse button. The Reflect dialog box appears ,then release the **alt/option** key.
Activate the option „Vertical", then „Preview", check whether everything is OK and click „Copy". A mirrored duplicate is created.
Step 7. Hold down the left mouse button and drag with **Selection Tool** (V) around all objects to select them.

Step 8. Then open the panel **Brushes (Window>Brushes)** and drag the objects to the „Brushes" panel, then drop them (drag&drop method) or alternatively click on the "New" symbol ⊞ , then activate in the dialog box „Pattern brush" and confirm the settings with „OK".

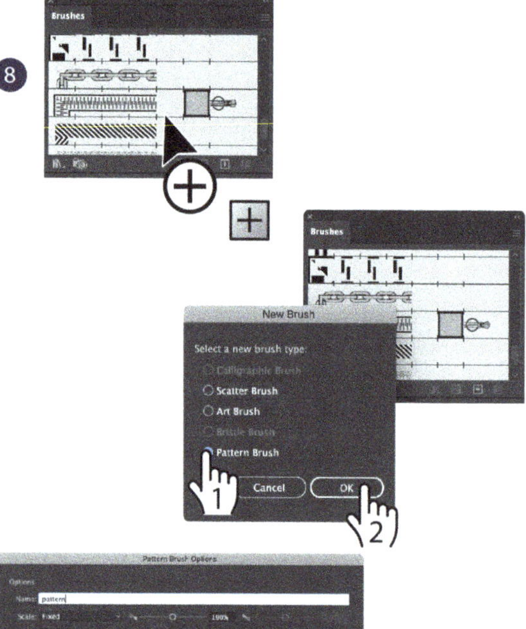

Step 9. Activate the **Pen Tool** (P) and create a line with two anchor points.
Step 10. Apply to the line the new pattern brush.
(in the „Brushes" panel **Window>Brushes** click on the new „zip fastener 2" brush).

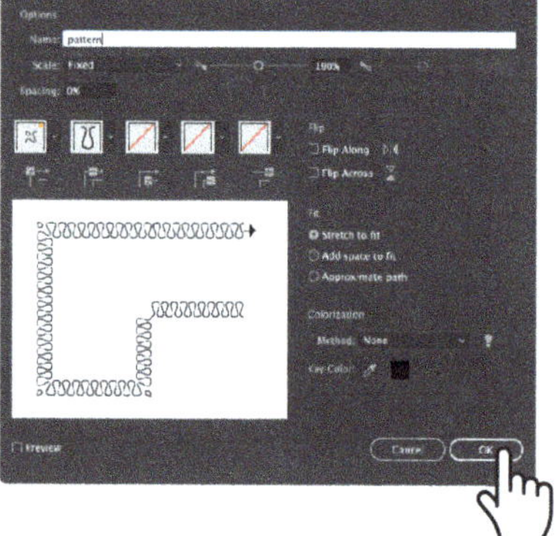

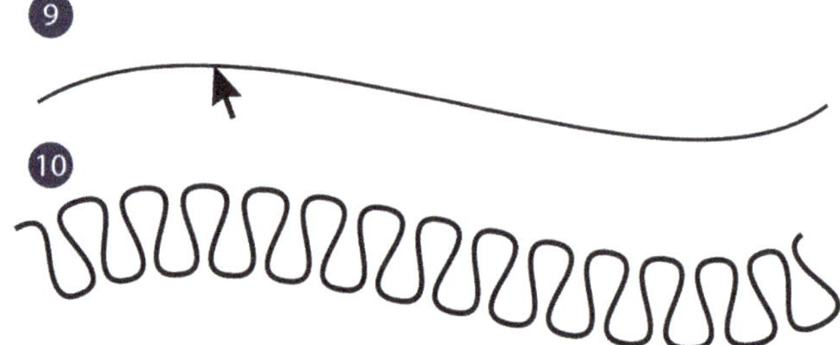

9.5 TUTORIAL: KNIT GOODS

REQUIREMENTS

-Choose in the tools panel the stroke color „Black" and the fill color „white".

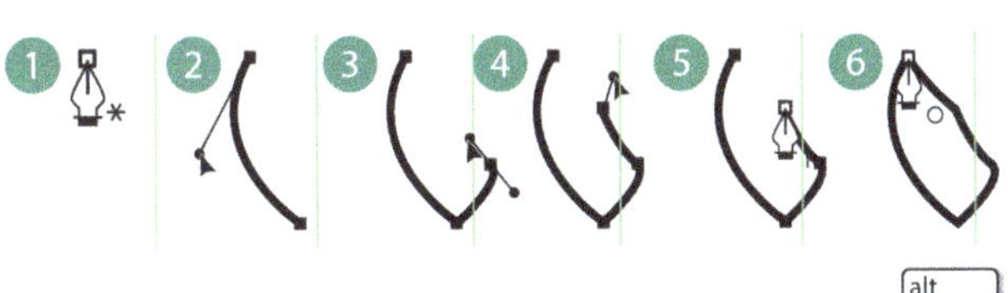

-Choose: **View > Rules >Show Rules, View > Guides > Lock Guides, View > Guides > Show Guides, View > Smart Guides, View > Snap to Point** and place a vertical guide.

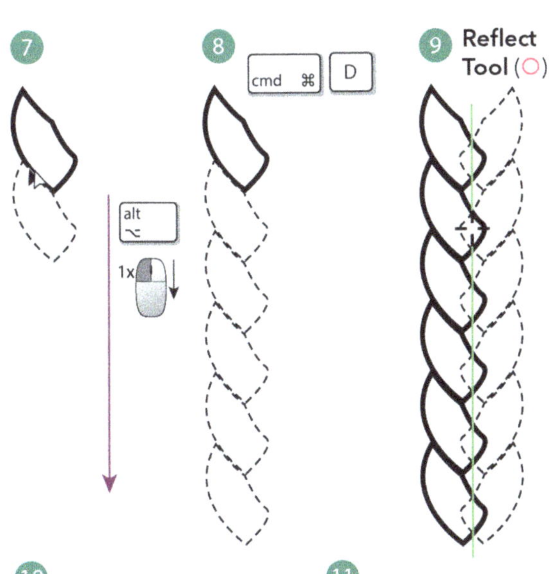

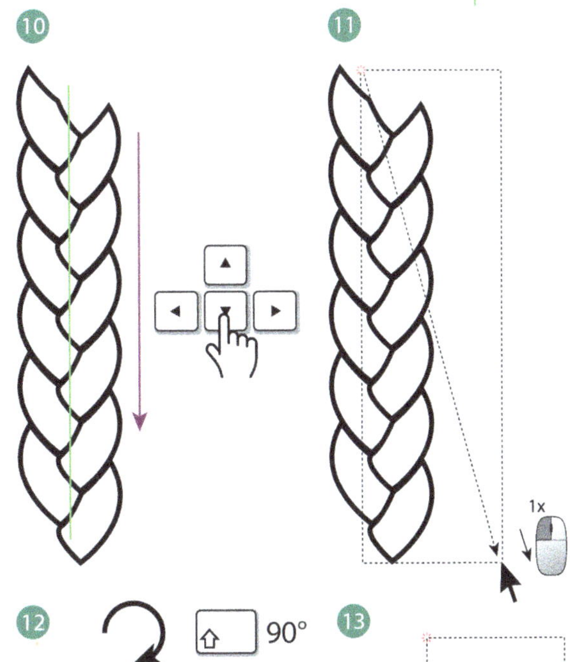

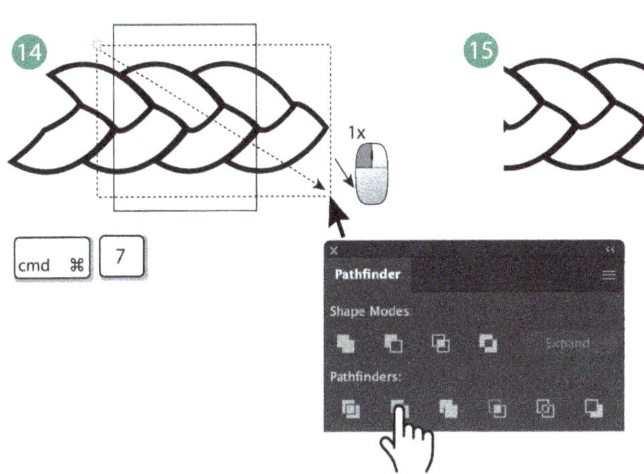

Step 1. Hold down the **Pen Tool** (P) and drag the anchor-point diagonally to the left down, then release the mouse button.

Step 2. Create a further anchor-point (press and release the mouse button).

Step 3. Create a further anchor-point (do not release the mouse button) and drag the anchor-point diagonally to left up, then release the mouse button.

Step 4. Create a further anchor-point (do not release the mouse button) and drag the anchor-point diagonally to right up, then release the mouse button.

Step 5. Click the last anchor point (press and release the left mouse button) to create a corner. In this case the „pen tool" will be changed to **Anchor Point Tool** (Shift+C).

Step 6. Activate the **Shift** key and close the shape with a click on the first anchor-point.

Step 7. Click the object with the **Selection Tool** (V), hold down **alt/option-** key, move the object with the mouse cursor down, in addition hold down **Shift-** key, then release first the mouse button and then the keyboard keys. A copy of the object is created.

Step 8. Activate the shortcut command+D / Ctrl+D (Transform Again), this will lead to several duplicates with the same distance.

Step 9. Select the **Reflect Tool** (O), position the mouse cursor on the vertical guide, hold down the **alt/option** key (do not release the alt key) and click the left mouse button. The reflect dialog box appears ,then release the **alt** key.
Activate the option „Vertical", then „Preview", check whether everything is OK and click „Copy". A mirrored duplicate is created.

Step 10. Displace the objects with arrow keys down (see figure).

Step 11. Hold down the left mouse button and drag with the **Selection Tool** (V) around all objects to select them.

Step 12. Activate the **Shift** key and rotate the objects (90°).

Step 13. Create with the **Rectangle Tool** (M) an rectangle without stroke and fill colour (see figure). This frame shows the rapport.

Step 14. Hold down the left mouse button and drag with the **Selection Tool** (V) around the objects to select them. Activate then the shortcut command+7 / Ctrl+7 (**Object>Clipping Mask>Make**).

Step 15. Activate the command **Object>Expand...** (activate „Fill", „Stroke" and confirm with OK), then open the „Pathfinder" (**Window>Pathfinder**) panel and activate „Trim".

Rectangle Tool (M)

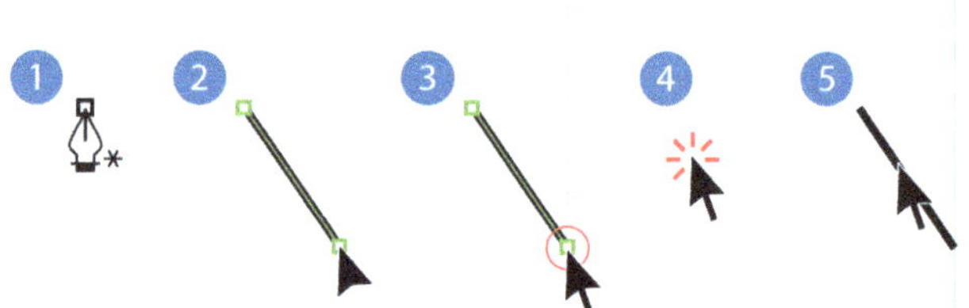

9.6 TUTORIAL: ZIGZAG RAPPORT

REQUIREMENTS

-Choose in the tools panel the stroke color „black" and the fill color „None".

-Change the stroke weight (**Window > Stroke**) to **1pt** or **2pt**.
-Choose: **View > Rules >Show Rules, View > Guides > Lock Guides, View > Guides > Show Guides, View > Smart Guides, View > Snap to Point**.

Step 1. Select the **Pen Tool** (P).
Step2. And create a line with two anchor points.
Step 3. Place a vertical guide (see figure).
Step 4. Click the V key (Selection Tool) and click on the empty drawing area to deselect the object.
Step 5. Select the line with the **Selection Tool** (V).
Step 6. Select the **Reflect Tool** (O), position the mouse cursor on the vertical guide, hold down the **alt/option** key (do not release the alt key) and click the left mouse button. The Reflect dialog box appears ,then release the **alt** key.
Activate the option „Vertical", then „Preview", check whether everything is OK and click „Copy". A mirrored duplicate is created.

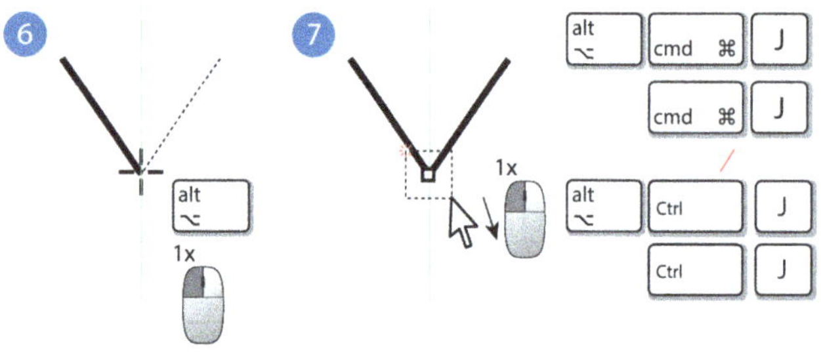

Step 7. Hold down the left mouse button and drag with the **Direct Selection Tool** (A) a selection around two anchor points (one end point of each half).
Activate the shortcut option+command+J /alt+Ctrl+J (Average...). In the dialog box activate „Both", then „OK", then activate the shortcut command+J / Ctrl+J (Join).

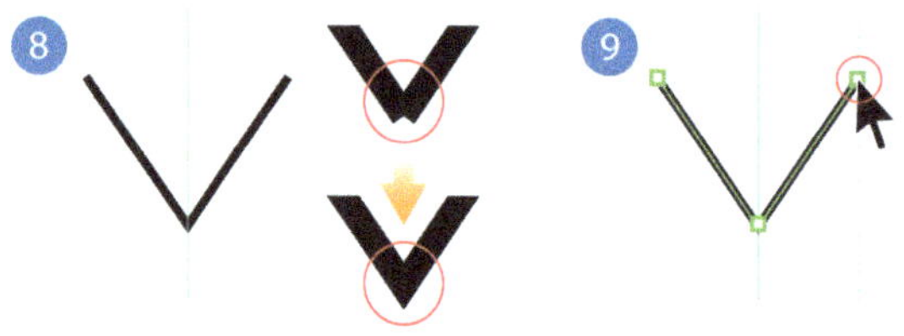

Step 8. In the panel „Stroke" (**Window>Stroke**) activate the **Miter Join** „Corner".
Step 9. Place a further vertical guide (see figure).

Step 16. Hold down the left mouse button and drag with **Selection Tool** (V) around the objects to select them.
Now open the panel **Brushes (Window>Brushes)** and drag the objects to the „Brushes" panel, then drop them (drag&drop method) or alternatively click on the "New" symbol ⊞ , then activate in the dialog box „Pattern brush" and confirm the settings with „OK".
Step 17. Activate the **Pen Tool** (P) and create a line with two anchor points.
Step 18. Apply to the line the new pattern brush.
(open the „Brushes" panel **Window>Brushes** click on the new „knit goods" brush).

❗ Remember: You can always change the size of the brush by changing the „stroke weight" in the „stoke" panel (e.g. 0,5pt, 0,2pt etc.) **Window>Stroke**.

Now activate the command **Object>Expand Appearance**.
Step 19. Activate the **Direct Selection Tool** (A) and click on the white fill, then activate the command **Selection>Same>Fill Color** to select all white fills and change in the „Tools panel" the fill color of the objects to „grey".

Step 10. Hold down left mouse button and drag with the **Selection Tool** (V) around the object to select it.

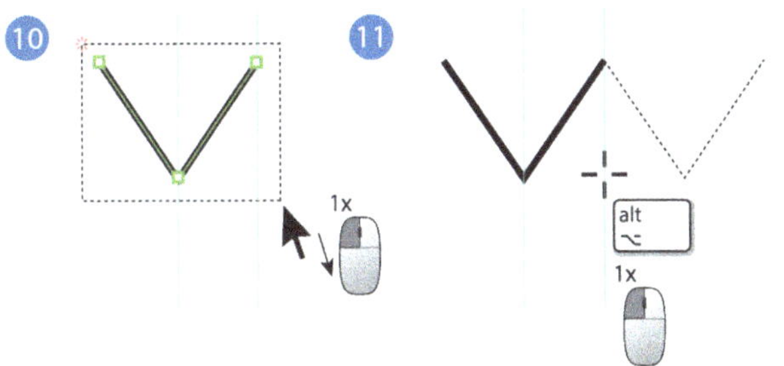

Step 11. Select the **Reflect Tool** (O), position the mouse cursor on the vertical guide, hold down the **alt/option** key (do not release the alt key) and click the left mouse button. The reflect dialog box appears ,then release the **alt** key. Activate the option „Vertical", then „Preview", check whether everything is OK and click „Copy". A mirrored duplicate is created.

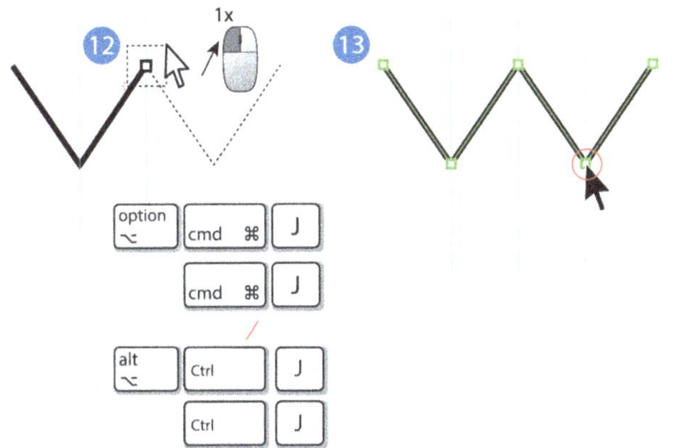

Step 12. Hold down the left mouse button and drag with the **Direct Selection Tool** (A) a selection around two anchor points (one end point of each half).
Activate the shortcut option+command+J /alt+Ctrl+J (Average...). In the dialog box activate „Both", then click „OK", then activate the shortcut command+J / Ctrl+J (Join).
Step 13. Place a further vertical guide (see figure).

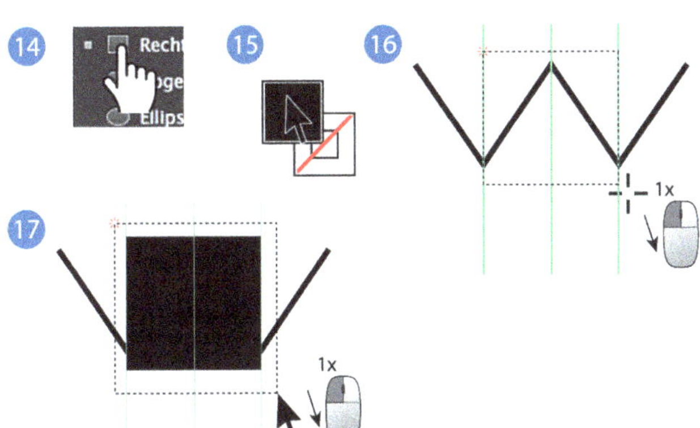

Step 14. Activate the **Rectangle Tool** (M).
Step 15. Change in the tools panel the fill colour to „black" and the stroke colour to „none".
Step 16. Now create with the **Rectangle Tool** (M) an rectangle, this frame shows the rapport (see figure).
Step 17. Hold down left mouse button and drag with the **Selection Tool** (V) around the objects to select them.

Step 18. Activate now the shortcut command+7 / Ctrl+7 (**Object>Clipping Mask>Make**).

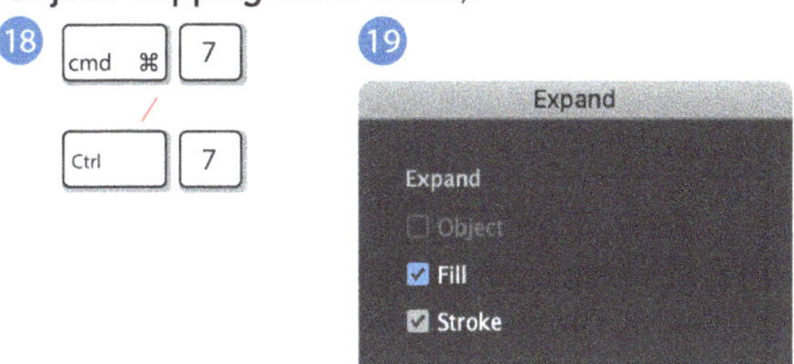

Step 19. Activate the command **Object>Expand...** (activate „Fill", „Stroke" and confirm with OK).
Step 20. Now open the „Pathfinder" (**Window>Pathfinder**) panel and activate „Trim".

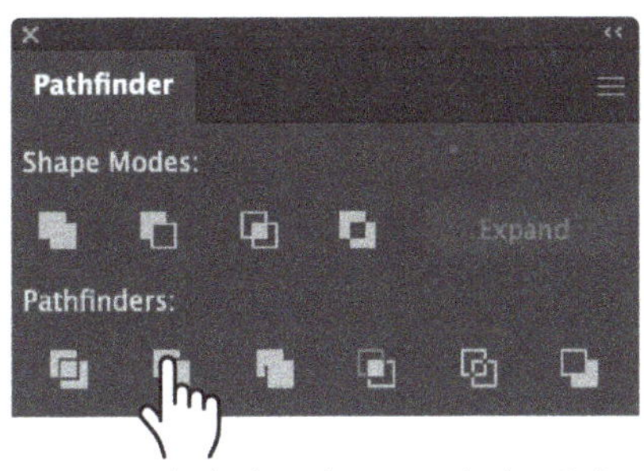

Step 21. Click the object with the **Selection Tool** (V).
Step 22. Now open the panel **Brushes (Window>Brushes)** and drag the objects to the „Brushes" panel, then drop them (drag&drop method) or alternatively click on the "New" symbol ⊞ , then activate in the dialog box „Pattern brush" and confirm the settings with „OK".

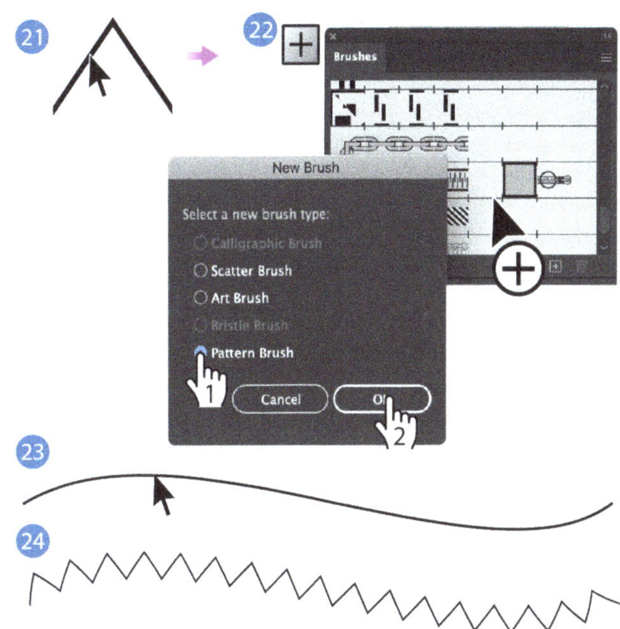

Step 23. Activate the **Pen Tool** (P) and create a line with two anchor points.
Step 24. Apply to the line the new pattern brush (open the „Brushes" panel **Window>Brushes** and click on the new „zigzag" brush).

9.7 TUTORIAL: OVERLOCK SEAM

REQUIREMENTS

-Choose in the tools panel the stroke color „black" and the fill color „None".

-Change the stroke weight (**Window > Stroke**) to **1pt** or **2pt**.
-Choose: **View > Rules >Show Rules, View > Guides > Lock Guides, View > Guides > Show Guides, View > Smart Guides, View > Snap to Point**.
Create the object from the tutorial 9.6 (zigzag rapport).

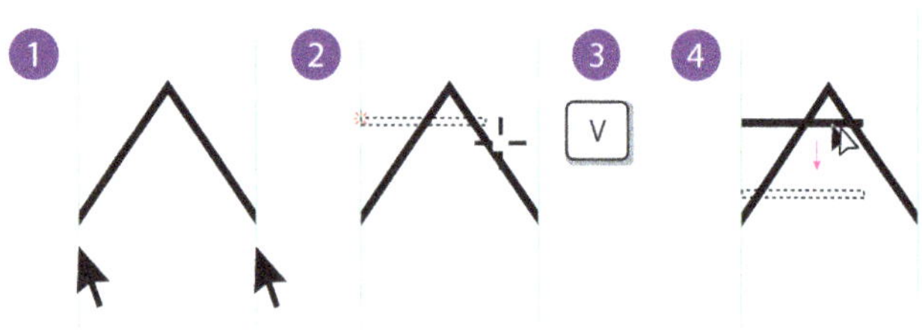

Step 1. Place two vertical guides (see figure).
Step 2. Now create with the **Rectangle Tool** (M) an rectangle.
Step 3. Click the V key (Selection Tool).
Step 4. Click the object with the **Selection Tool** (V), hold down **alt/option-** key, move the object with the mouse cursor down, in addition hold down **Shift-** key, then release first the mouse button and then the keyboard keys. A copy of the object is created.

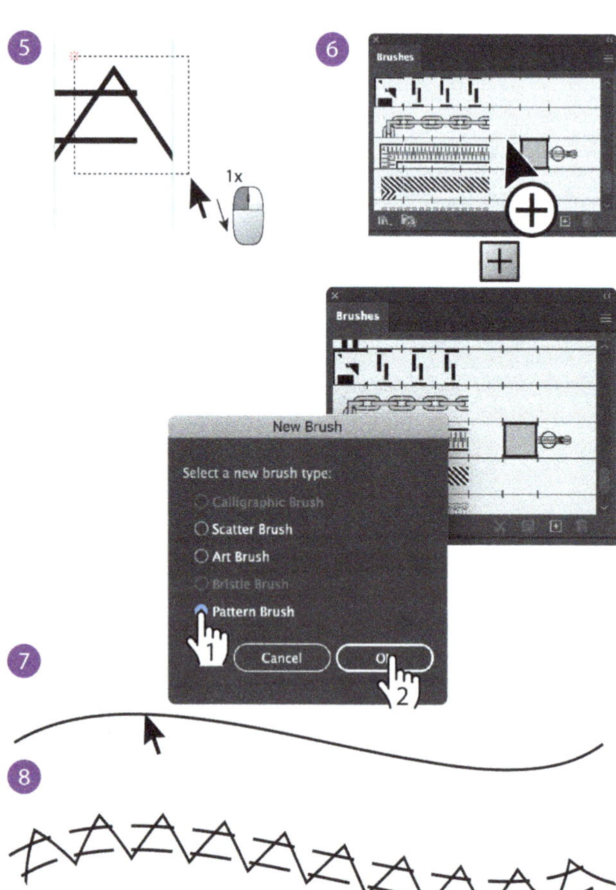

Step 5. Hold down the left mouse button and drag with the **Selection Tool** (V) around the objects to select them.

Step 6. Now open the panel **Brushes (Window>Brushes)** and drag the objects to the „Brushes" panel, then drop them (drag&drop method) or alternatively click on the "New" symbol , then activate in the dialog box „Pattern brush" and confirm the settings with „OK".
Step 7. Activate the **Pen Tool** (P) and create a line with two anchor points.
Step 8. Apply to the line the new pattern brush (open the „Brushes" panel **Window>Brushes** and click on the new „overlock seam" brush).

9.8 TUTORIAL: ROPE

REQUIREMENTS

--Choose in the tools panel the stroke color „black" and the fill color „None".

-Change the stroke weight (**Window > Stroke**) to **1pt** or **2pt**.
-Choose: **View > Rules >Show Rules, View > Guides > Lock Guides, View > Guides > Show Guides, View > Smart Guides, View > Snap to Point**.

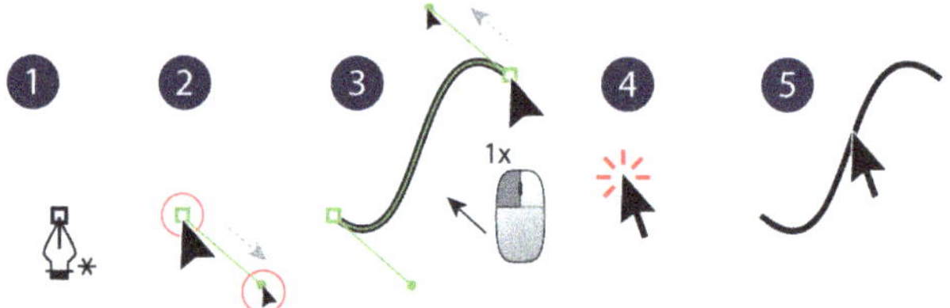

Step 1. Select the **Pen Tool** (P) and create the first anchor-point (do not release left mouse button).
Step 2. Now drag the direction point to the right down, then release the mouse button.
Step 3. Create now a further anchor point (do not release the left mouse button) and drag the direction point to the left up, then release the mouse button.
Step 4. Click the V key (Selection Tool) and click on the empty drawing area to deselect the object.
Step 5. Select the line with the **Selection Tool** (V).

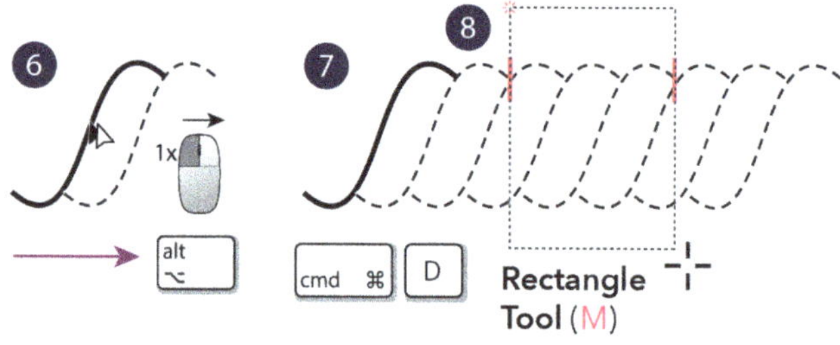

Step 6. Now hold down **alt/option-** key, move the object with the mouse cursor to the right, in addition hold down the **Shift-** key, then release first the mouse button and then the keyboard keys. A copy of the object is created.
Step 7. Activate the shortcut command+D / Ctrl+D (Transform Again), this will lead to several duplicates with the same distance.
Step 8. Create with the **Rectangle Tool** (M) an rectangle without stroke and fill colour (see figure). This frame shows the rapport.

©dimitridesign.org

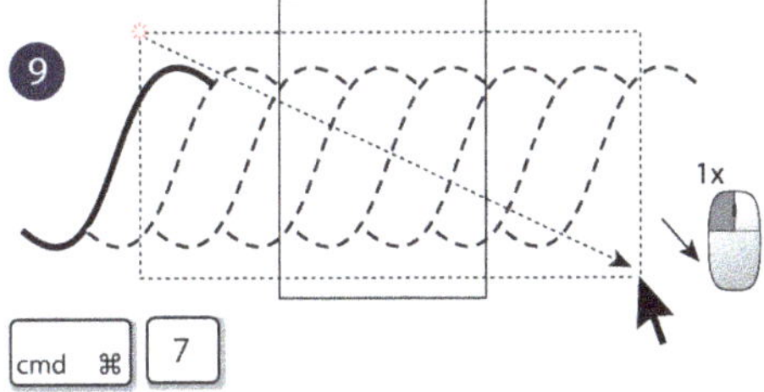

Step 9. Hold down the left mouse button and drag with the **Selection Tool** (V) around the objects to select them. Activate now the shortcut command+7 / Ctrl+7 or (**Object>Clipping Mask>Make**).

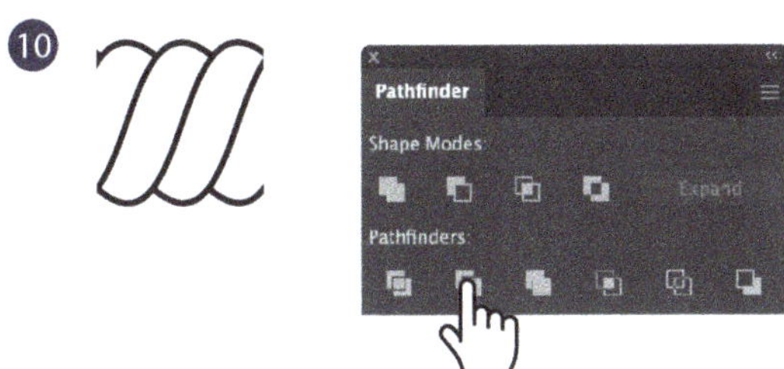

Step 10. Activate the command **Object>Expand...** (activate „Fill", „Stroke" and confirm with OK). Now open the „Pathfinder" (**Window>Pathfinder**) panel and activate „Trim".

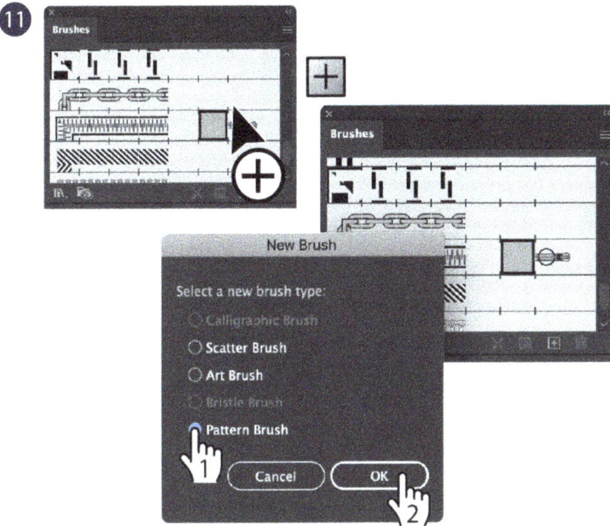

Step 11. Now open the panel **Brushes (Window>Brushes)** and drag the objects to the „Brushes" panel, then drop them (drag&drop method) or alternatively click on the "New" symbol ⊞, then activate in the dialog box „Pattern brush" and confirm the settings with „OK".

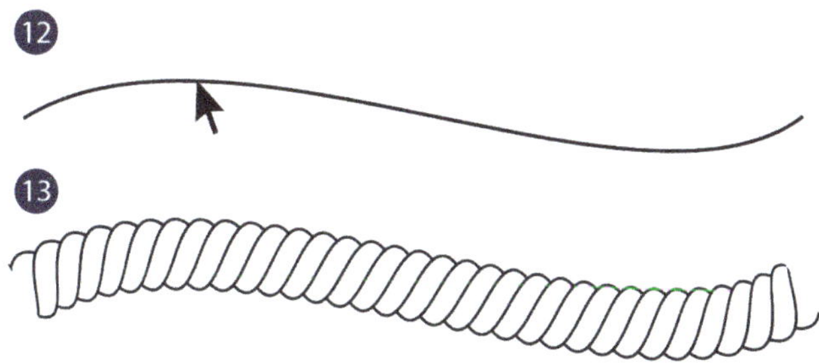

Step 12. Activate the **Pen Tool** (P) and create a line with two anchor points.
Step 13. Apply to the line the new pattern brush (open the „Brushes" panel **Window>Brushes** and click on the new „rope" brush).

9.9 TUTORIAL: CHAIN

REQUIREMENTS

- Choose in the tools panel the stroke color „black" and the fill color „None".

-Change the stroke weight (**Window > Stroke**) to **1pt** or **2pt**.
-Choose: **View > Rules >Show Rules, View > Guides > Lock Guides, View > Guides > Show Guides, View > Smart Guides, View > Snap to Point.**

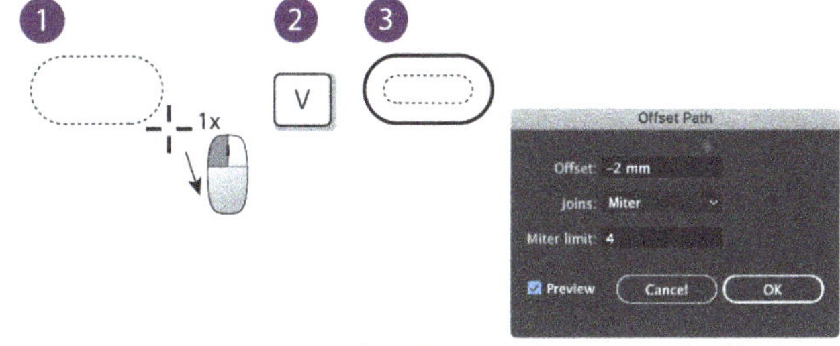

Step 1. Create with the **Rounded Rectangle Tool** an rounded rectangle.
Step 2. Click the V key (Selection Tool).
Step 3. Activate the command **Object>Path>Offset Path...** and confirm with „OK". (the size of the „Offset" depends on the size of the object).
Step 4. Create with the **Rounded Rectangle Tool** a further rounded rectangle.
Step 5. Hold down left mouse button and drag with the **Selection Tool** (V) around the objects to select them, now set the fill colour to "grey".

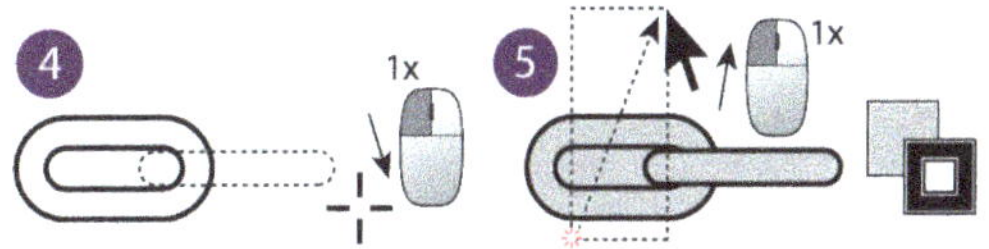

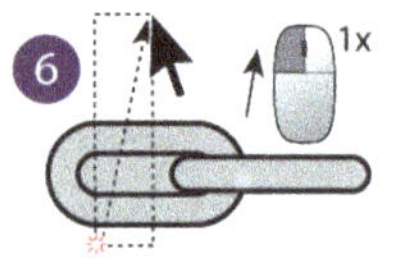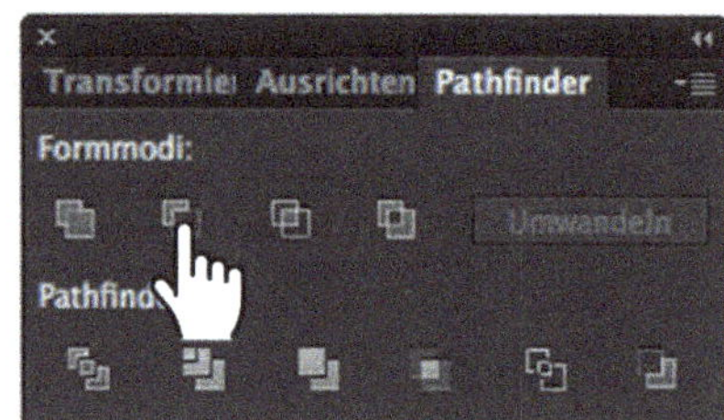

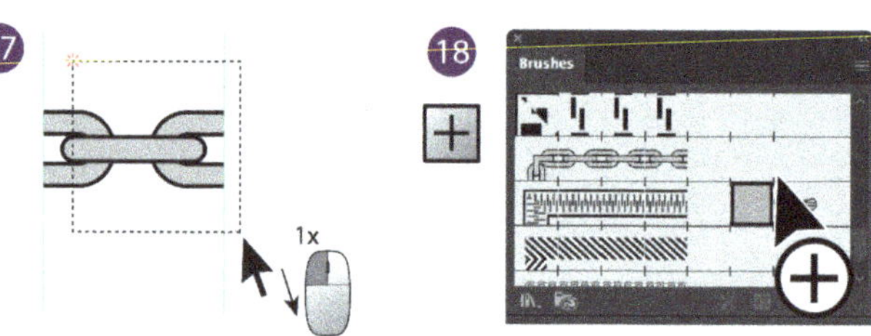

Step 6. Hold down the left mouse button and drag with the **Selection Tool** (V) around two objects (see figure), now open the panel „Pathfinder" (**Window>Pathfinder**) and click on „Minus Front".

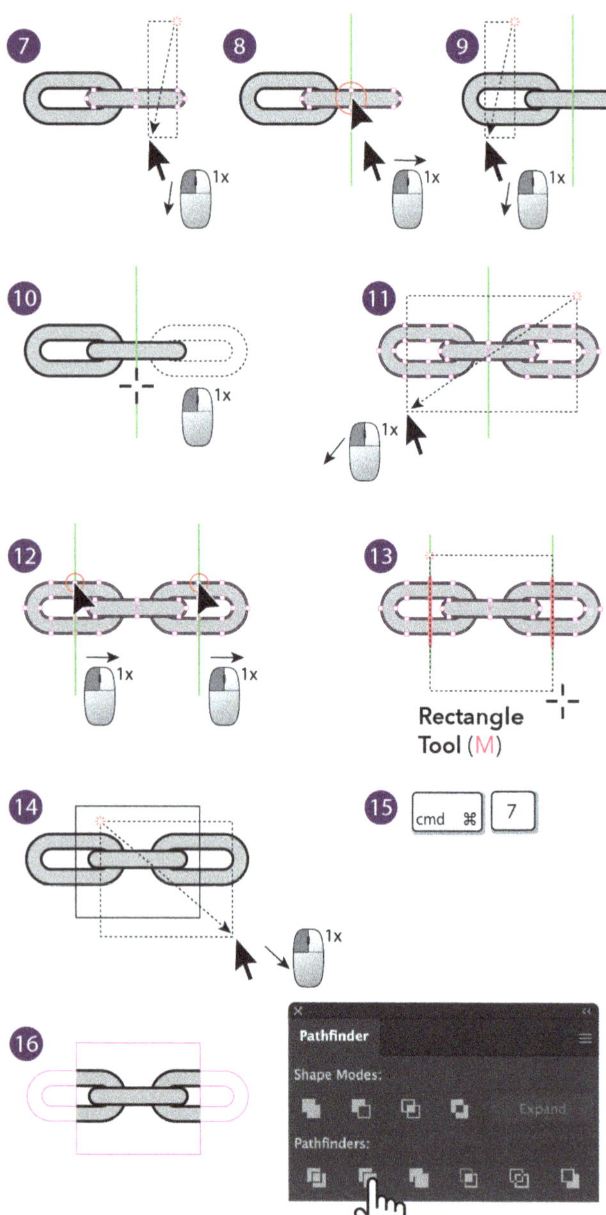

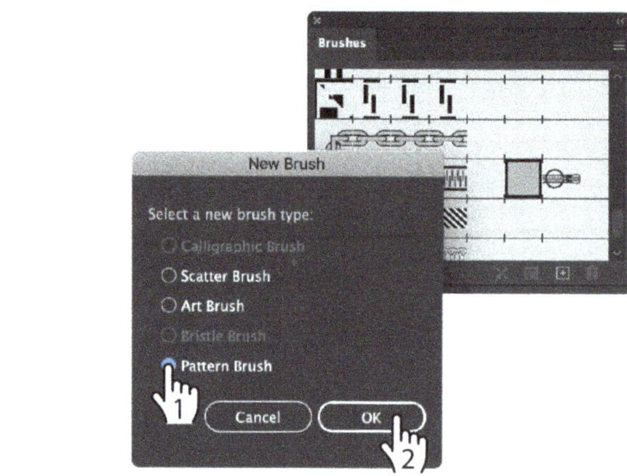

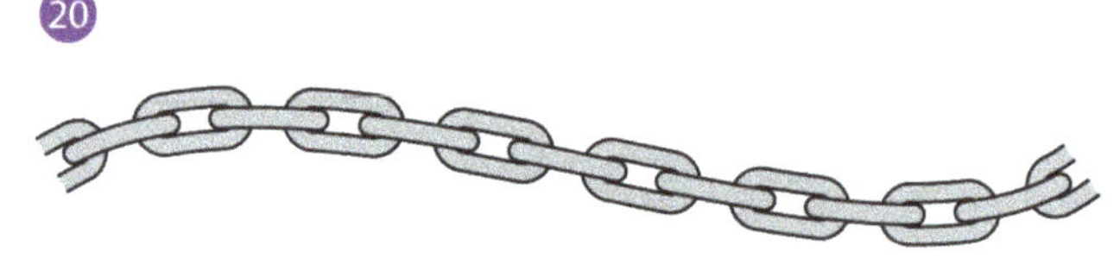

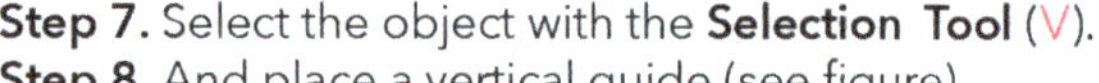

Step 11. Select all objects with the **Selection Tool** (V).
Step 12. And place a further vertical guide (see figure).
Step 13. Create with the **Rectangle Tool** (M) an rectangle (see figure). This frame shows the rapport.
Step 14. Select all objects with the **Selection Tool** (V).
Step 15. Activate now the shortcut command+7 / Ctrl+7 or (**Object>Clipping Mask>Make**).
Step 16. Activate the command **Object>Expand...** (activate „Fill", „Stroke" and confirm with OK). Now open the „Pathfinder" (**Window>Pathfinder**) panel and activate „Trim".
Step 17. Select the object with the **Selection Tool** (V).
Step 18. Now open the panel **Brushes (Window>Brushes)** and drag the objects to the „Brushes" panel, then drop them (drag&drop method) or alternatively click on the "New" symbol, then activate in the dialog box „Pattern brush" and confirm the settings with „OK".
Step 19. Activate the **Pen Tool** (P) and create a line with two anchor points.
Step 20. Apply to the line the new pattern brush (open the „Brushes" panel **Window>Brushes** and click on the new „chain" brush).

Step 7. Select the object with the **Selection Tool** (V).
Step 8. And place a vertical guide (see figure).
Step 9. Select the object with the **Selection Tool** (V).
Step 10. Select the **Reflect Tool** (O), position the mouse cursor on the vertical guide, hold down the **alt/option** key (do not release the alt key) and click the left mouse button. The reflect dialog box appears ,then release the **alt** key. Activate the option „Vertical", then „Preview", check whether everything is OK and click „Copy". A mirrored duplicate is created.

9.10 TUTORIAL: ZIP FASTENER 3

-Choose: **View > Rules >Show Rules, View > Guides > Lock Guides, View > Guides > Show Guides, View > Smart Guides, View > Snap to Point.**

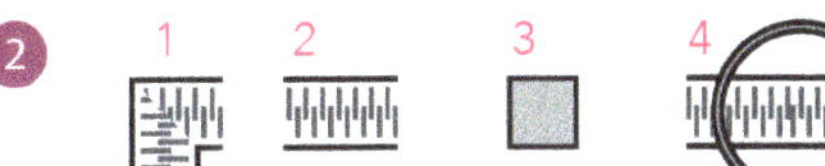

1. Outer Corner Tile
2. Side Tile
3. Start Tile
4. End Tile

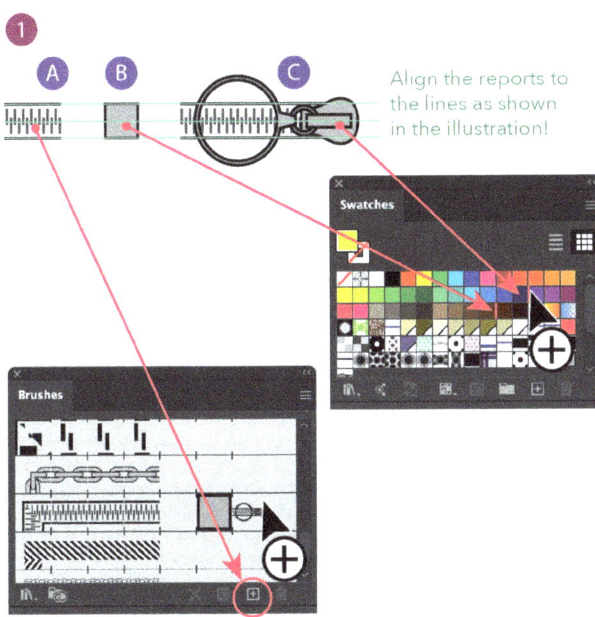

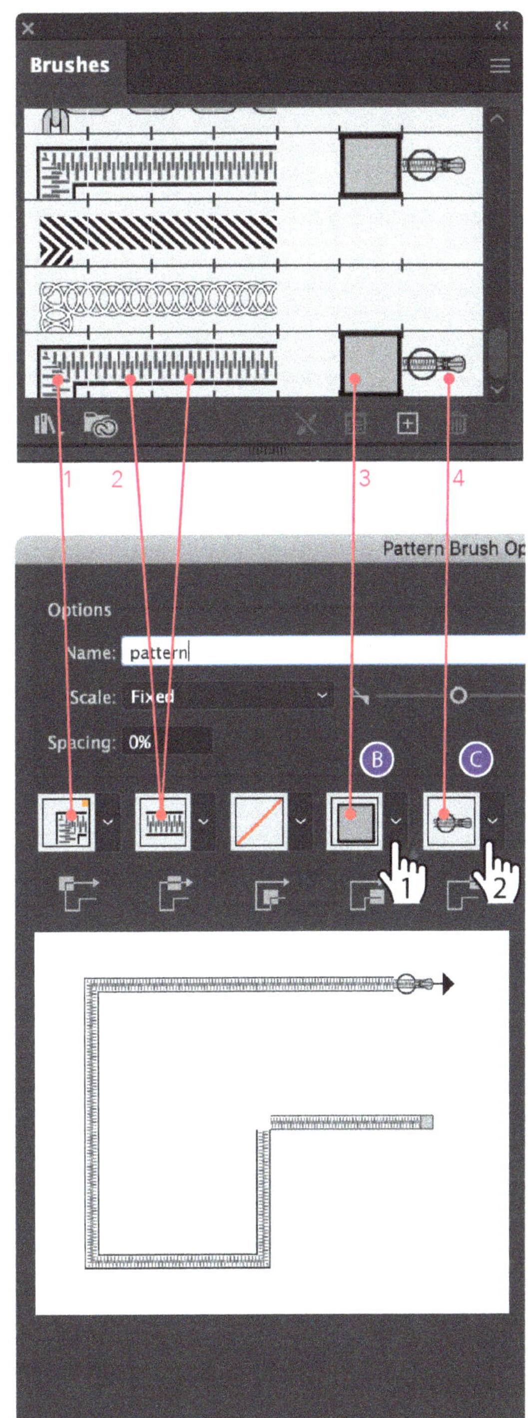

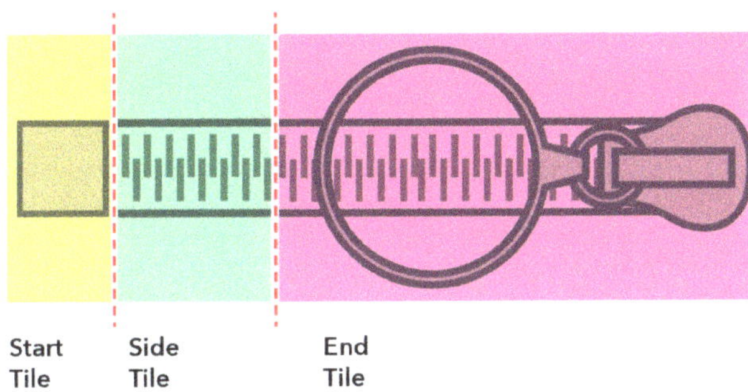

Step 1. Create three rapports (A,B,C).

Open the panel **Swatches (Window>Swatches)** and drag the first **B** rapport, then **C** rapport to the „Swatches" panel (drag&drop method) and type a name for each rapport (e.g. Z1 and Z2).
Now open the panel **Brushes (Window>Brushes)** and drag the rapport **A** to the „Brushes" panel (drag&drop method) or alternatively click on the "New" symbol , then activate in the dialog box „Pattern brush".

Step 2. In the „Pattern Brush Options" dialog box choose following settings from the „drop-down" menus (see figure), then confirm with „OK".

Step 3. Activate the **Pen Tool** (P) and create a line with two anchor points.

Step 4. Apply to the line the new pattern brush (open the „Brushes" panel **Window>Brushes** and click on the new „zipper fastener" brush).

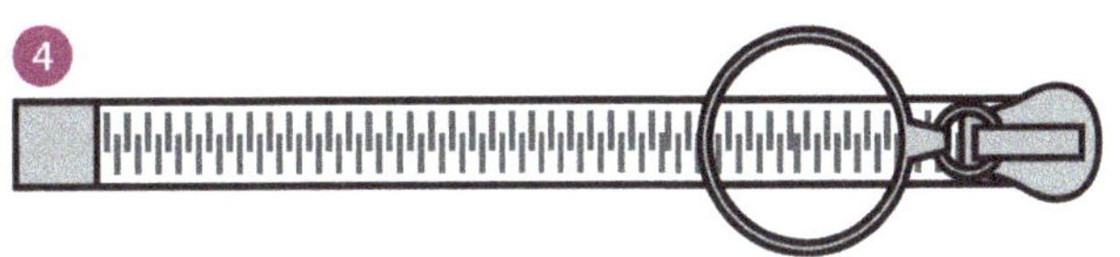

10. ERROR-CHECKLIST

10.1 JOIN THE ANCHOR POINTS
A warning message appears when joining anchor points (see screenshot below). There are two main reasons for this.

Problem:

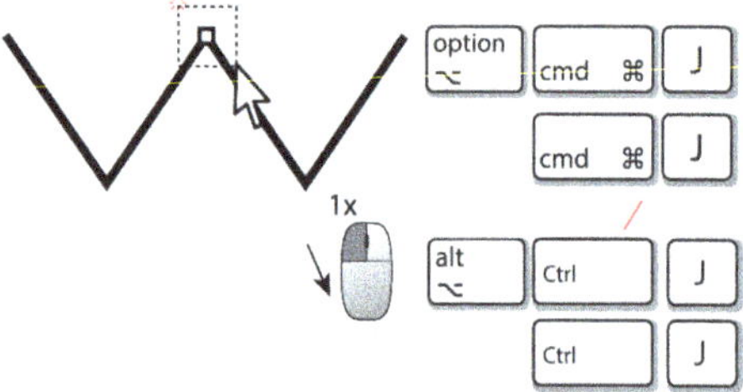

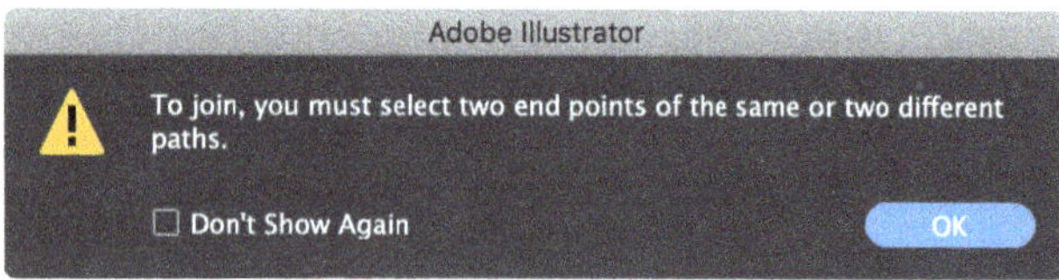

Reason 1:

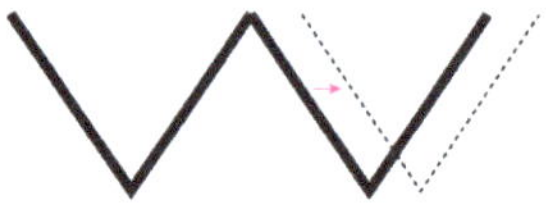

The reason for this could be that several objects are matched. Note that only two end or start points (anchor points) can be merged. If multiple objects are superimposed, more than two points are selected.

Solution:
Delete all unnecessary objects.
(Click with the Selection tool (V) the unnecessary object and press the **Backspace key**)

Reason 2:

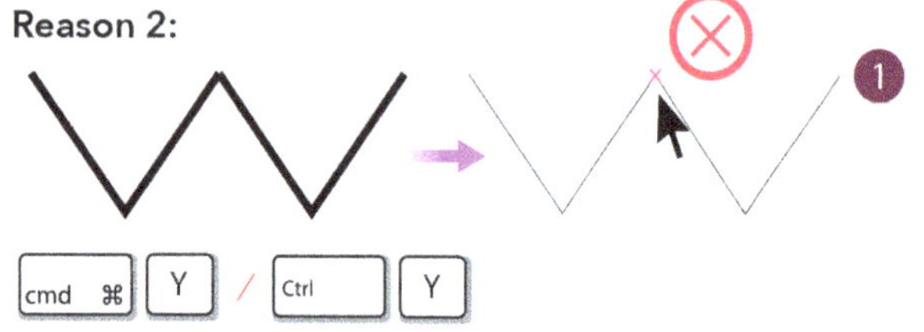

The reason for this could also be that there are unnecessary anchor points on the work surface. These anchorpoints are marked by a cross in the path view (cmd+Y / Strg+Y).

Solution:
- Choose **Object> Path> Clean up...**, activate in the dialogue field „Stray points".
- Or activate the outline view (cmd+Y / Strg+Y), lock all objects at this point (2), select the anchor points (Stray points) and activate the backspace key (3).

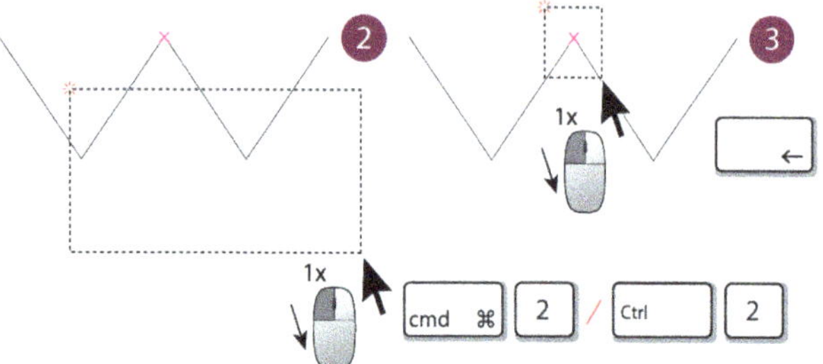

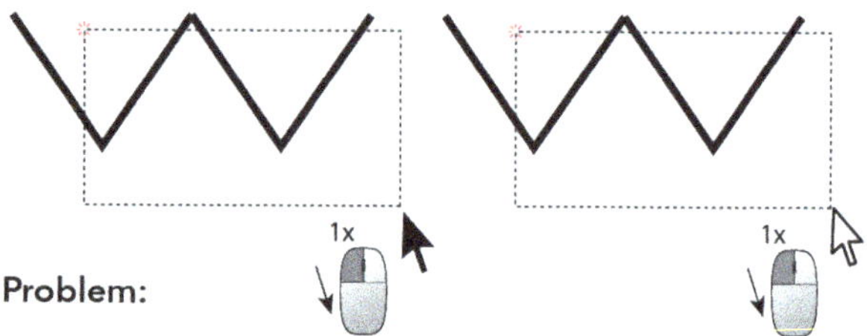

Problem:
The object cannot be selected.
Reason and Solution:
The object is locked. Activate alt/option+cmd+2 / alt/option+Strg+2 (**Object>Unlock All**).
Problem:
Some objects (paths) are no longer visible.

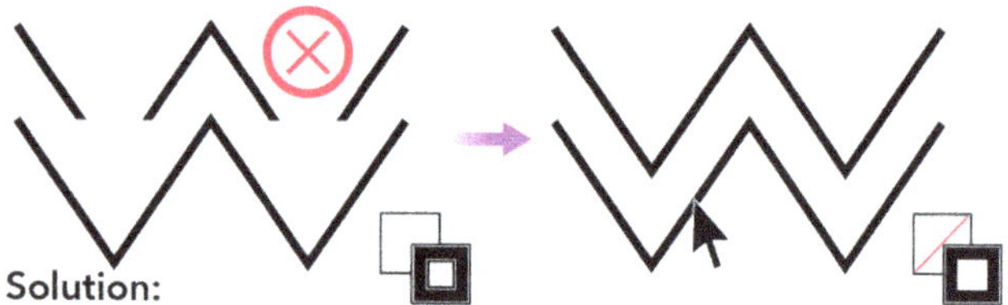

Solution:
Select the object and deactivate „white" fill color in the Tools panel.

10.3 CLIPPING MASK

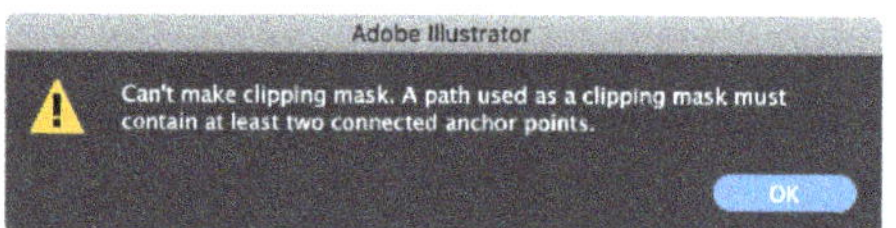

(Do not forget that at least two objects must be selected to create a clipping mask).

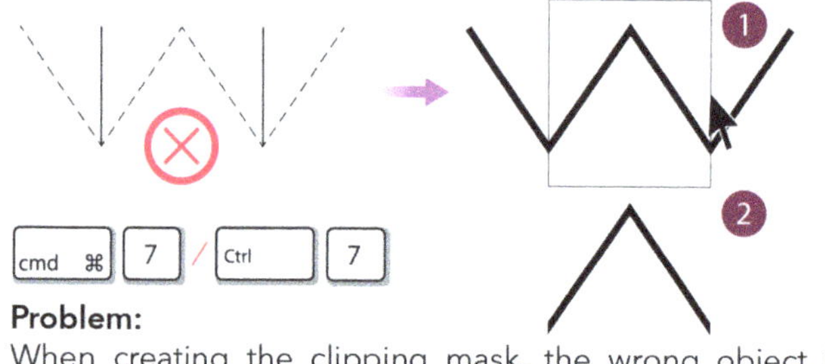

Problem:
When creating the clipping mask, the wrong object is masked.
Reason and Solution:
The shape (rectangle) of the "mask" is in the background. Place the rectangle in the foreground (**Object > Arrange > Bring to Front**), because the shape of the boundary must always be above the object to be clipped. Then select both objects and activate the shortcut command cmd+7 / Strg+7.

10.4 LIFE PAINT GROUP

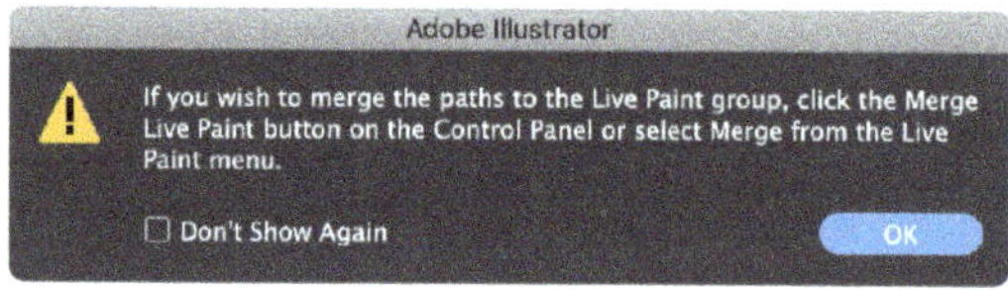

Problem: With the **Life Paint Bucket** (K) it is not possible to create a life paint group.
Reason and Solution 1: When creating a „live paint group", do not forget to convert the live paint group: **Object > Expand**. To allow you to edit individual objects. In the Expand dialog box, always activate Object, Fill and Stroke and confirm with OK. Than activate twice the command **Object > Ungroup** (because the objects are mostly grouped twice).

Reason and Solution 2: If individual areas of the drawing have already been convected into an life paint group and new objects are added to these areas, all of these objects must first be merged: Select all objects with the **Selection Tool** (V) and select **Object > Life Paint > Merge**.

Reason and Solution 3: Patterns and pattern brushes must be converted first (**Object> Expand**) before an life paint group is applied. Otherwise the paths lose their properties (pattern and pattern brushes).

Reason and Solution 4: Life paint groups can not contain clipping masks. Before selecting objects, lock all clipping masks first.

10.5 GUIDES

If the following errors occur: e.g. clipping mask, pattern brushes cannot be created, first check if guides are locked (**View > Guides > Lock Guides**), because this is often the reason.

10.6 BLEND OBJECTS

Problem:
The blend seems distorted or shows disturbances.

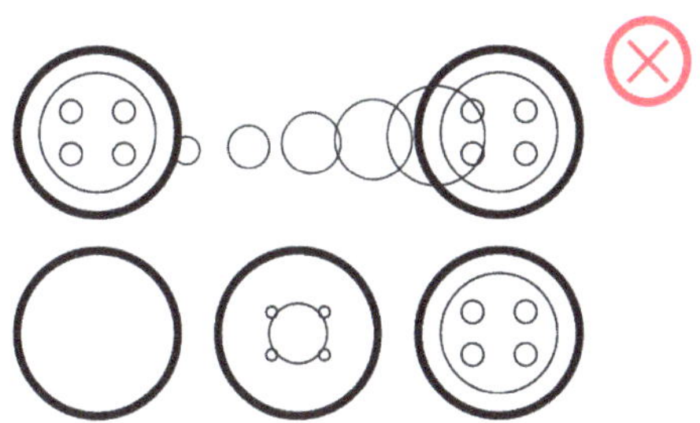

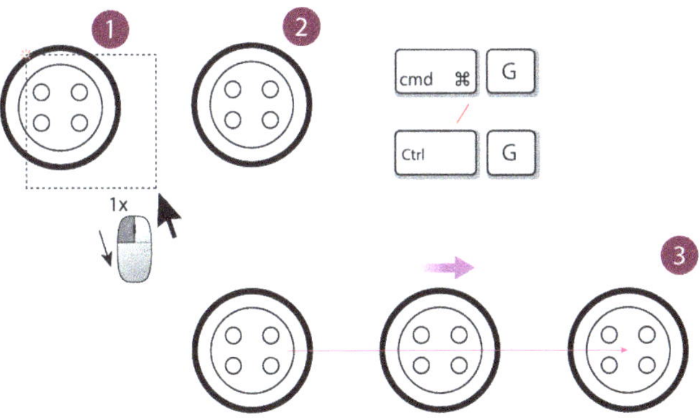

Solution 1:
First, undo the blending using the short key command cmd+Z / Strg+Z or **Object>Blend>Release**.

Step 1. Then use the **Selection Tool** (V) to drag a selection box around all objects that belong together.

Step 2. And activate the short key command cmd+G / Strg+G (Group).

Step 3. Than activate the **Blend Tool** (W) and create a new blending.

Problem and Solution 2:
If an blending appears twisted, first undo the blending with cmd+Z / Strg+Z. Then create a new blending and click on the anchor points with the same alignment.

10.7 PATTERN BRUSHES

Problem:
Pattern brush shows gaps and fractures.

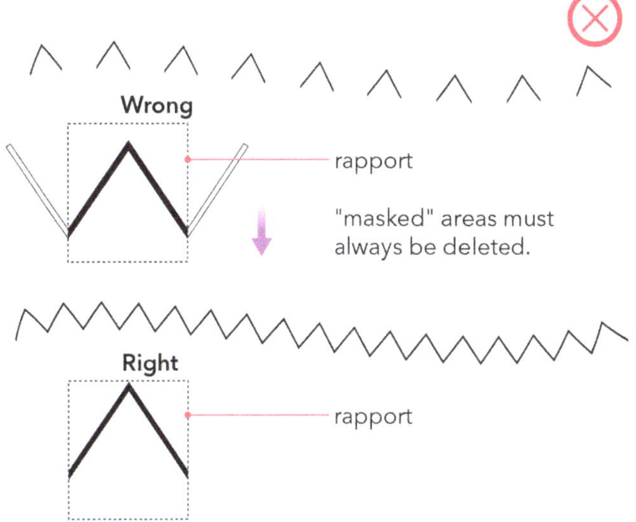

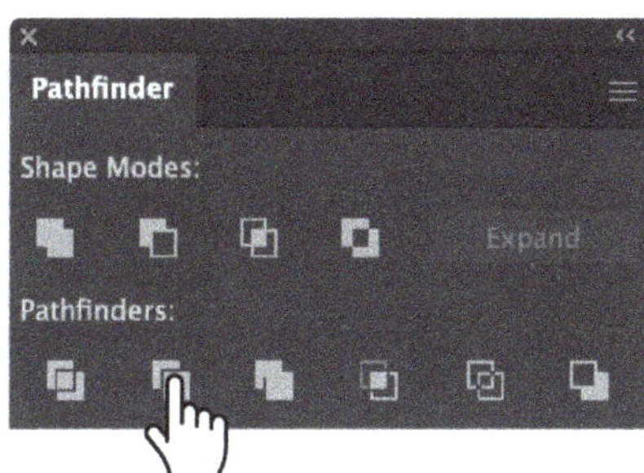

Reason and Solution:
Pattern details must always be drawn flush, otherwise gaps arise in the offset.

After applying the clipping mask cmd+7 / Strg+7 (the rectangle serves as the rapport limit), you probably forgot to activate the command **Object > Expand** and activate the option "**Trim**" in the "Pathfinder" panel (**Window > Pathfinder**).

If corner tiles are absent in the pattern brush, it leads to gaps on the corner points in the path.

Pattern elements are extremely compressed when the path is drawn too short.

If the curve points are too strong, the shape of the pattern brush is distorted.

THE SELECTED ARTWORK CONTAINS AN ELEMENT THAT CANNOT BE USED IN A PATTERN BRUSH

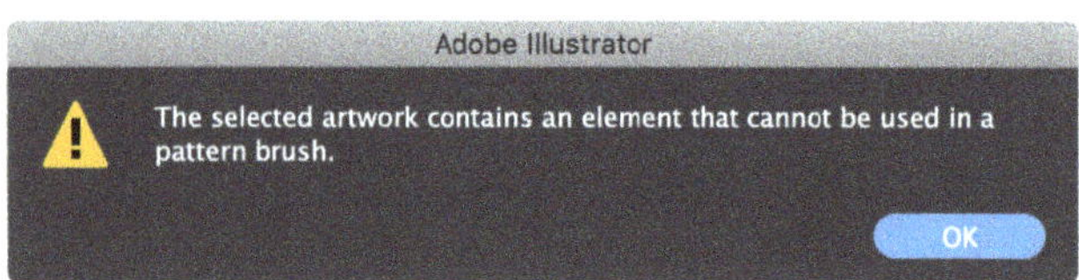

Reason and Solution 1:
The guides are not locked. Select **View > Guides > Lock Guides** to Lock Guides.

Reason and Solution 2:
Gradients cannot be recorded in pattern brushes. Replace the gradient with a color.

Reason and Solution 3:
If the rapport is not correct, there may be unnecessary anchor points, therefore select **Object > Path > Clean Up > Stray points**, then confirm with OK.

Reason and Solution 4:
A pattern fill has been assigned to an object belonging to a pattern brush. The pattern fill must first be expanded **Object > Expand** before it can be included to the pattern brush.

Reason and Solution 5:
The rapport of the pattern elements was created in the vertical direction. Align the rapport horizontally.

Reason and Solution 6:
Verify that all elements belonging to the pattern brush are unlocked (**Object>Unlock All**).

Reason and Solution 7:
Objects and paths do not end flush at the edge of the repport. Rapport should start and end always vertically (90° angle).

Reason and Solution 8:
A „base rectangle" exists in the wrong place. Use the **Selection tool** (V) to drag a selection box around all objects and determine where the wrong rectangle is located, then delete it.

10.8 CANNOT ENABLE PROGRAM FUNCTIONS
If you cannot enable certain program functions, click the esc button, probably an option window was opened by a tool or command.

10.9 SURFACE PATTERN

Rapport became wrong construction

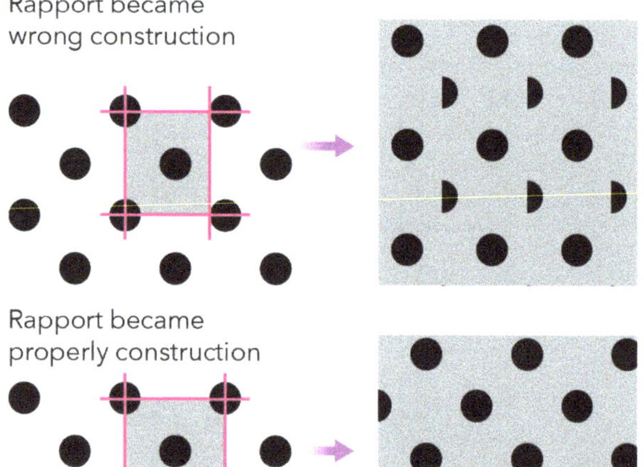

Rapport became properly construction

Rapport should always start and end vertically and horizontally in the same place.

Rapport enclosing rectangle should contain no fill color and no stroke color , otherwise the rectangle will not be recognized as a repeat.

Rapport enclosing rectangle should always be in the background (**Object>Arrange>Send to Back**).

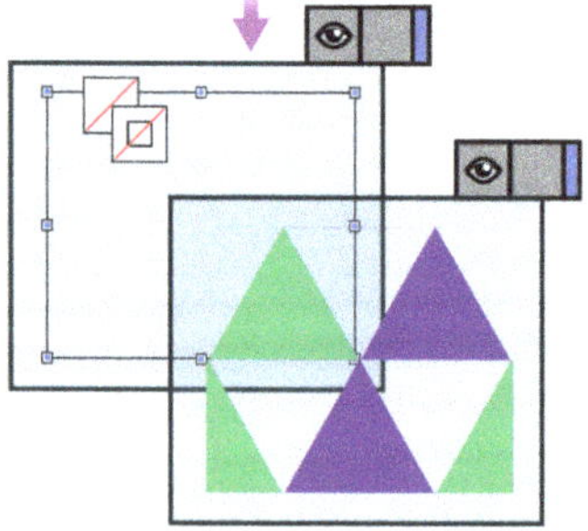

10.10 ISOLATION MODE
You can isolate objects in isolation mode, making it easier to select and edit specific objects. Isolation mode is activated by double-clicking with the selection tool on an object. **Therefore, sometimes the isolation mode is accidentally switched on.** To turn isolation mode off, double-click a blank area in the document or click the esc button.

Isolation mode

11. TECHNICAL DRAWING
DIFFERENT REPRESENTATION FORMS

DIFFERENT TYPES:

-- FLAT TECHNICAL DRAWING (USED IN MOST CASES)
-- PRODUCTION-READY TECHNICAL DRAWING (FLAT TECHNICAL DRAWING + DIMENSION INPUTS)
- COLOURED TECHNICAL DRAWING (E.G. WITH A PATTERN OR WITH COLOUR VARIATIONS)
- TECHNICAL SKETCH (USED AS A TEMPLATE FOR COMPUTER-GENERATED TECHNICAL DRAWINGS)
- ILLUSTRATIVE TECHNICAL DRAWING (USUALLY A FLAT TECHNICAL DRAWING SHOULD BE CREATED ADDITIONAL)

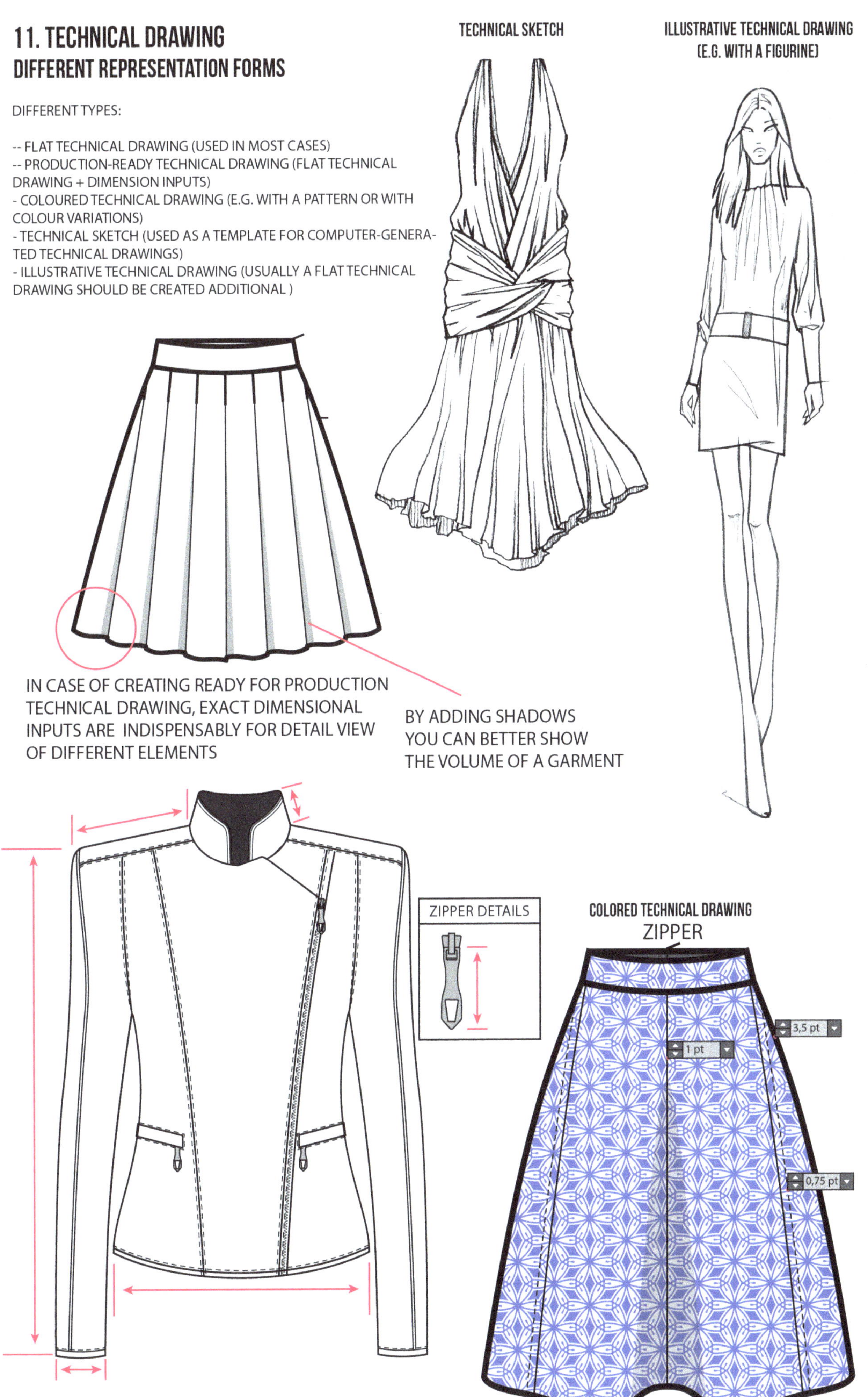

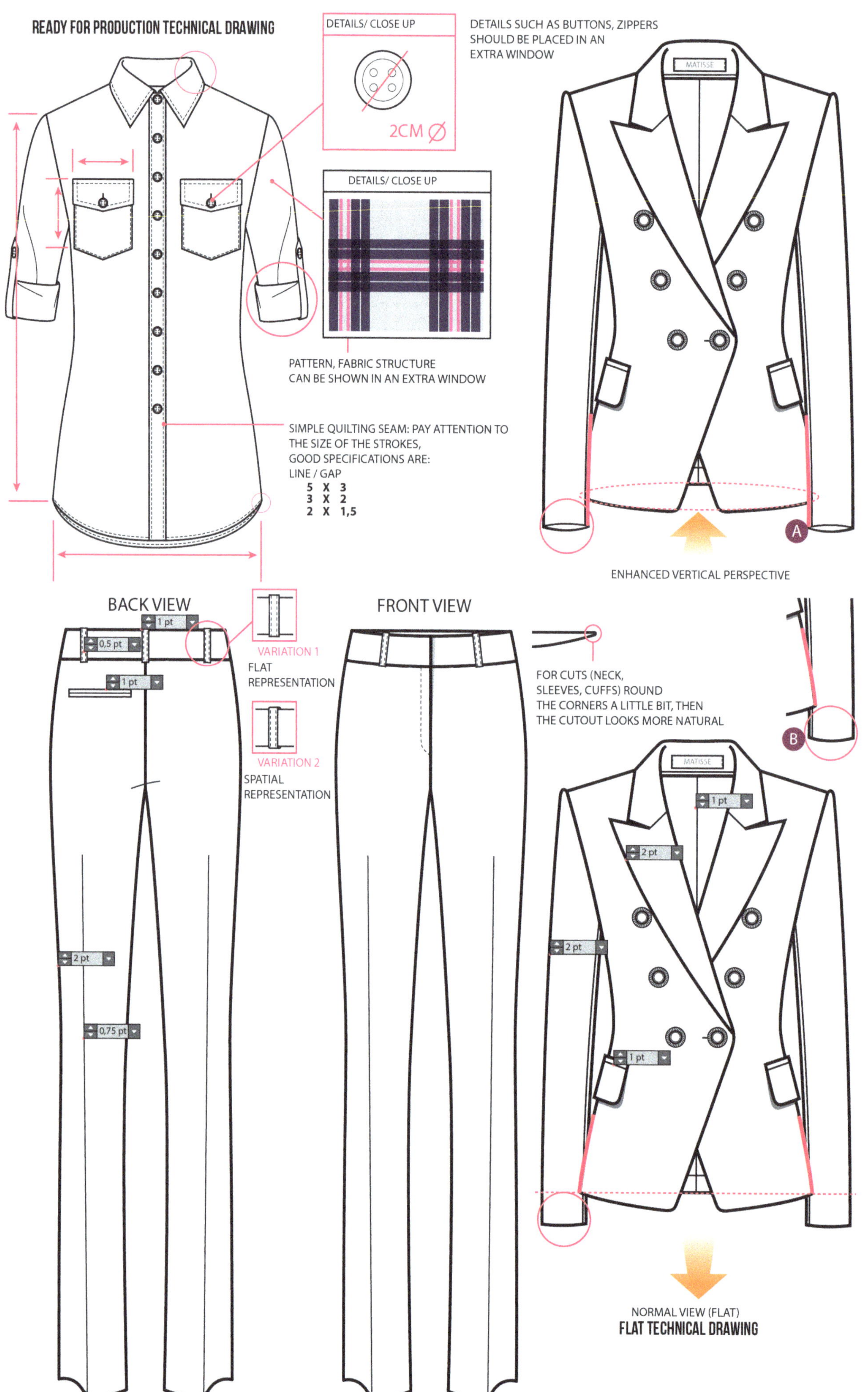

READY FOR PRODUCTION TECHNICAL DRAWING
DETAILS/ CLOSE UP
2CM Ø
DETAILS SUCH AS BUTTONS, ZIPPERS SHOULD BE PLACED IN AN EXTRA WINDOW
MATISSE
DETAILS/ CLOSE UP
PATTERN, FABRIC STRUCTURE CAN BE SHOWN IN AN EXTRA WINDOW
SIMPLE QUILTING SEAM: PAY ATTENTION TO THE SIZE OF THE STROKES, GOOD SPECIFICATIONS ARE:
LINE / GAP
5 X 3
3 X 2
2 X 1,5
A
ENHANCED VERTICAL PERSPECTIVE
BACK VIEW
1 pt
0,5 pt
1 pt
VARIATION 1
FLAT REPRESENTATION
VARIATION 2
SPATIAL REPRESENTATION
2 pt
0,75 pt
FRONT VIEW
FOR CUTS (NECK, SLEEVES, CUFFS) ROUND THE CORNERS A LITTLE BIT, THEN THE CUTOUT LOOKS MORE NATURAL
B
MATISSE
1 pt
2 pt
2 pt
1 pt
NORMAL VIEW (FLAT)
FLAT TECHNICAL DRAWING